Sherry **BISHOP**

Australia • Brazil • Mexico • Singapore • United Kingdom • United States

Adobe Dreamweaver Creative Cloud Revealed
Sherry Bishop

Product Director: Kathleen McMahon

Senior Product Manager: Jim Gish

Content Developer: Megan Chrisman

Senior Marketing Manager: Eric La Scola

Senior Content Project Manager: Jennifer Feltri-George

Developmental Editor: Barbara Clemens

Technical Editor: John Shanley

Managing Art Director: Jack Pendleton

Manufacturing Planner: Julio Esperas

IP Analyst: Sara Crane

Senior IP Project Manager: Kathy Kucharek

Production Service: Integra Software Services Pvt. Ltd

Text Designer: Liz Kingslein

Proofreader: Harold Johnson

Indexer: Alexandra Nickerson

Cover Image: Cengage Learning

For product information and technology assistance, contact us at **Cengage Learning Customer & Sales Support, 1-800-354-9706**

For permission to use material from this text or product, submit all requests online at **www.cengage.com/permissions.**

Further permissions questions can be emailed to **permissionrequest@cengage.com.**

Library of Congress Control Number: 2014944161

ISBN-13: 978-1-305-11871-3
ISBN-10: 1-305-11871-5

Cengage Learning
20 Channel Center Street
Boston, MA 02210
USA

Cengage Learning is a leading provider of customized learning solutions with office locations around the globe, including Singapore, the United Kingdom, Australia, Mexico, Brazil, and Japan. Locate your local office at **www.cengage.com/global**

Cengage Learning products are represented in Canada by Nelson Education, Ltd.

To learn more about Cengage Learning Solutions, visit **www.cengage.com**.

Purchase any of our products at your local college store or at our preferred online store **www.cengagebrain.com**.

Printed in the United States of America

Print Number: 01   Print Year: 2014

Revealed Series Vision

The Revealed Series is your guide to today's hottest digital media applications. For years, the Revealed Series has kept pace with the dynamic demands of the digital media community, and continues to do so with the publication of six exciting titles covering the latest Adobe Creative Cloud products. Each comprehensive book teaches not only the technical skills required for success in today's competitive digital media market, but the design skills as well. From animation, to web design, to digital image-editing and interactive media skills, the Revealed Series has you covered.

We recognize the unique learning environment of the digital media classroom, and we deliver text books that include:

■ Comprehensive step-by-step instructions
■ In-depth explanantions of the "why" behind a skill
■ Creative projects for additional practice
■ Full-color visuals for a clear explanation of concepts
■ Comprehensive online material offering additional instruction and skills practice

With the Revealed Series, we've created books that speak directly to the digital media and design community—one of the most rapidly growing computer fields today.

—The Revealed Series

New to This Edition

The latest edition of Adobe Dreamweaver Creative Cloud Revealed includes many exciting new features, some of which are listed below:

■ Guide to Using Creative Cloud
■ New Fluid Grid Layouts
■ CSS Designer
■ New HTML5 video and sound integration
■ Adobe Edge Web Fonts
■ Element Quick View
■ Editable Live View
■ Inspect Mode
■ CSS Transitions
■ Canvas

CourseMate

A CourseMate is available with *Adobe Dreamweaver Creative Cloud Revealed*, which helps you make the grade!

The CourseMate includes:

■ An interactive eBook, with highlighting, note-taking, read-aloud, and search capabilities
■ Interactive learning tools including:
  ■ Chapter quizzes
  ■ Flash cards
  ■ Crossword puzzles
  ■ And more!

Go to login.cengagebrain.com to access these resources.

AUTHOR'S VISION

This book introduces you to Dreamweaver, a fascinating tool to create rich and exciting websites. Although the world of technology moves more quickly than we sometimes like, we are in a particularly exciting time with the Adobe Creative Cloud. With HTML5 and CSS3, we are challenged to learn more efficient, sleeker methods for designing sites.

Many talented and creative individuals created this text for you. Our Content Developer, Megan Chrisman, guided and directed the team from start to finish. She listens to others, correctly assesses each situation, and makes timely and appropriate decisions. We appreciated these talents as we worked through an aggressive schedule.

Barbara Clemens, my Development Editor, is an example of so many things I value: joy, kindness, patience, and determination. We have worked together on the Dreamweaver book for many years and I appreciate her more with each new edition. She can pull deep inside me to bring out my best. Thank you for all these years of dedication, Barbara.

The legal information about copyright in Chapter 7 was based on content from the book *Internet Surf and Turf Revealed: The Essential Guide to Copyright, Fair Use, and Finding Media* by my good friend, Barbara Waxer, author of the Can I Use It blog, www.barbarawaxer.com.

John Shanley is our Dreamweaver Technical Editor for both Mac and PC. He had a daunting job, juggling two sets of files as he carefully tested each step to make sure that the end product was as error-free as possible. He gave exceptional feedback as he reviewed each chapter.

Suwathiga Velayutham, Senior Project Manager, Jennifer Feltri-George, Senior Content Project Manager, and Jack Pendleton, Managing Art Director, managed the layout and kept the production schedule on track. We thank them for keeping up with the many details and deadlines. The work is beautiful.

Harold Johnson quietly worked behind the scenes to ensure that all grammatical and punctuation errors were corrected. He also provided valuable insight on the accuracy of content specifics. Harold has been on our team for many editions and I always feel good knowing he will be reviewing my work.

Thanks also to Jim Gish, Senior Product Manager. He embraced the Revealed books with enthusiasm and provided us with excellent resources to produce books that make us all proud. I would also like to express my gratitude to others who have worked on this book during the last 13 years: Jane Hosie-Bounar, Nicole Pinard, Rebecca Berardy, Ann Fisher, Barbara Waxer, Marjorie Hunt, Karen Stevens, Jeff Schwartz, Ashlee Wetz, and Joe Villanova.

I would also like to extend my appreciation to the Adobe Dreamweaver beta team. My participation in the beta process is always a positive, energizing experience. The Dreamweaver engineers clearly dedicate themselves to meeting and exceeding designer and developer needs and expectations. Kirsti Aho was the first Adobe visionary with whom I had the pleasure to work, beginning in the Macromedia Dreamweaver days.

Thanks to the Beach Club in Gulf Shores, Alabama, beachclubal.com, for being such a delightful place to visit. Several photographs of their stunning property appear in The Striped Umbrella website. They also generously provided several new photographs for this edition that added beauty to the page designs. Thank you, also, to each of you that allowed us to use images of your websites and to Pleasure Island Parasail LLC for a small video clip.

Typically, your family is the last to be thanked. My husband, Don, supports and encourages me every day. Our travels with our children and grandchildren provide happy memories for us and content for the websites.

Thank you to each student and instructor using this book as you travel along your educational path, and for making this book a part of your journey.

—Sherry Bishop

Introduction to Adobe Dreamweaver Creative Cloud—Revealed

Welcome to *Adobe Dreamweaver Creative Cloud—Revealed*. This book offers complete coverage of basic to intermediate Dreamweaver skills, helping you to create polished, professional-looking websites. Use this book both in the classroom and as your own reference guide.

This text is organized into ten chapters, as well as a special introductory section covering Adobe's Creative Cloud features. In these chapters, you will explore the many options Dreamweaver provides for creating dynamic Dreamweaver websites. You'll also work with many of the exciting features new to this release of the software. This edition is written for the Dreamweaver CC 2014 release. The commands/steps/figures may change slightly as new updates are made available through the Creative Cloud. When updates are made available, follow the "What's New?" link in the Creative Cloud app to read the new feature notes.

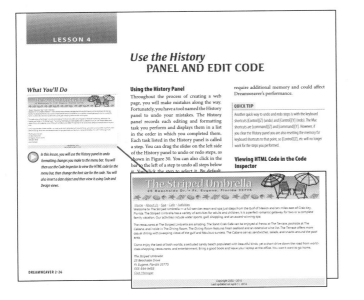

What You'll Do

A What You'll Do figure begins every lesson. This figure gives you an at-a-glance look at what you'll do in the chapter, either by showing you a file from the current project or a tool you'll be using.

Comprehensive Conceptual Lessons

Before jumping into instructions, in-depth conceptual information tells you "why" skills are applied. This book provides the "how" and "why" through the use of professional examples. Also included in the text are tips and sidebars to help you work more efficiently and creatively, or to teach you a bit about the history or design philosophy behind the skill you are using.

Step-by-Step Instructions

This book combines in-depth conceptual information with concise steps to help you learn Dreamweaver Creative Cloud. Each set of steps guides you through a lesson where you will create, modify, or enhance a Dreamweaver Creative Cloud file. Step references to large colorful images and quick step summaries round out the lessons. The Data Files for the steps are provided on Cengage Brain. For information on how to access Cengage Brain, see "Read This Before You Begin."

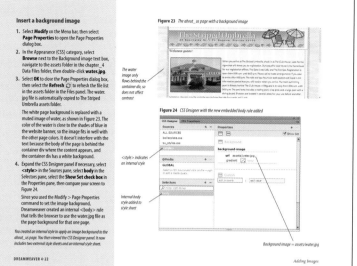

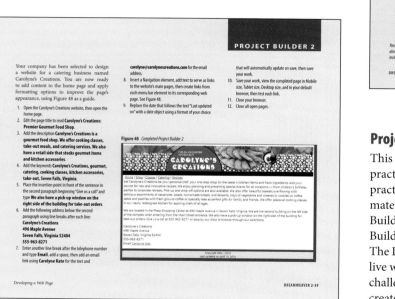

Projects

This book contains a variety of end-of-chapter materials for additional practice and reinforcement. The Skills Review contains hands-on practice exercises that mirror the progressive nature of the lesson material. The chapter concludes with four projects: two Project Builders, one Design Project, and one Portfolio Project. The Project Builders require you to apply the skills you've learned in the chapter. The Design Project incorporates critical thinking skills while evaluating live websites. The Portfolio Project encourages you to address and solve challenges based on the content explored in the chapter in order to create portfolio-quality work.

What Instructor Resources Are Available with This Book?

The Instructor Resources are Cengage's way of putting the resources and information needed to teach and learn effectively into your hands. All the resources are available for both Mac OS and Windows operating systems. These resources can be found online at **http://login.cengage.com**. Once you log in or create an account, search for the title under 'Add a product to your Instructor Resource Center' using the ISBN. Then select the instructor companion site resources and select 'Add Selected to Instructor Resource Center.'

Instructor's Manual

The Instructor's Manual includes chapter overviews and detailed lecture topics for each chapter, with teaching tips.

Sample Syllabus

The Sample Syllabus includes a suggested syllabus for any course that uses this book.

PowerPoint Presentations

Each chapter has a corresponding PowerPoint presentation that you can use in lectures, distribute to your students, or customize to suit your course.

Data Files for Students

To complete most of the chapters in this book, your students will need Data Files, which are available online. Instruct students to use the Data Files List at the end of this book. This list gives instructions on organizing files.

To access the Data Files for this book, take the following steps:

1. Open your browser and go to http://www.cengagebrain.com.
2. Type the author, title, or ISBN of this book in the Search window. (The ISBN is listed on the back cover.)
3. Select the book title in the list of search results.
4. When the book's main page is displayed, select the Access Now button under Free Materials.
5. To download Data Files, select a chapter number and then select the Data Files link on the left navigation bar to download the files.

Solutions to Exercises

Solution Files are Data Files completed with comprehensive sample answers. Use these files to evaluate your students' work. Or distribute them electronically so students can verify their work. Sample solutions to all lessons and end-of-chapter material are provided, with the exception of some Portfolio Projects.

Test Bank and Test Engine

Cengage Learning Testing Powered by Cognero is a flexible, online system that allows you to:

- author, edit, and manage test bank content from multiple Cengage Learning solutions
- create multiple test versions in an instant
- deliver tests from your LMS, your classroom, or wherever you want

Start Right Away!

Cengage Learning Testing Powered by Cognero works on any operating system or browser.

- No special installs or downloads needed.
- Create tests from school, home, the coffee shop—anywhere with Internet access.

What Will You Find?

- Simplicity at every step. A desktop-inspired interface features drop-down menus and familiar, intuitive tools that take you through content creation and management with ease.
- Full-featured test generator. Create ideal assessments with your choice of 15 question types (including true/false, multiple choice, opinion scale/likert, and essay). Multi-language support, an equation editor, and unlimited metadata help ensure your tests are complete and compliant.
- Cross-compatible capability. Import and export content into other systems.

CONTENTS

CHAPTER 2: DEVELOPING A WEB PAGE

CHAPTER 3: WORKING WITH TEXT AND CASCADING STYLE SHEETS

CHAPTER 4: ADDING IMAGES

CHAPTER 5: WORKING WITH LINKS AND NAVIGATION

Intended Audience

This text is designed for the beginner or intermediate user who wants to learn how to use Dreamweaver. The book is designed to provide basic and in-depth material that not only educates, but also encourages you to explore the nuances of this exciting program.

Adobe Updates to Dreamweaver

As new Dreamweaver updates are posted to Creative Cloud, you have the choice of updating or continuing to use your existing version. If you decide to keep your existing version until you finish using this book, your screens and menus should stay consistent with the book figures and instructions. If you decide to update to a newer version, read the What's New? material after you have downloaded the new version to determine what has changed. The changes may not affect the book figures and instructions very much at all, or they could affect them significantly. Visit www.cengage.com to find resources for Adobe Dreamweaver updates.

Approach

The text allows you to work at your own pace through step-by-step tutorials. A concept is presented and the process is explained, followed by the actual steps. To learn the most from the use of the text, you should adopt the following habits:

- Proceed slowly: Accuracy and comprehension are more important than speed.
- Understand what is happening with each step before you continue to the next step.
- After finishing a skill, ask yourself if you could do it on your own, without referring to the steps. If the answer is no, review the steps.

General

Throughout the initial chapters, students are given precise instructions regarding saving their work. Students should feel that they can save their work at any time, not just when instructed to do so. Wherever possible, "select" has been used in place of "click" to accommodate users of both touchscreens and traditional mouse/keyboard setups.

Icons, Buttons, and Pointers

Symbols for icons, buttons, and pointers are shown in the step each time they are used. Icons may look different in the files panel depending on the file association settings on your computer.

Skills Reference

As a bonus, a Power User Shortcuts table is included near the end of chapters. This table contains the quickest method of completing tasks covered in the chapter. It is meant for the more experienced user, or for the user who wants to become more experienced. (Please note: If you are using a mini keyboard, your keyboard shortcuts may differ.)

Fonts

The Data Files contain a variety of commonly used fonts, but there is no guarantee that these fonts will be available on your computer. In a few cases, fonts other than those common to a PC or a Macintosh are used. If any of the fonts in use is not available on your computer, you can make a substitution, realizing that the results may vary from those in the book.

Windows and Mac OS

Adobe Dreamweaver CC works virtually the same on Windows and Mac OS operating systems. In those cases where there is a significant difference, the abbreviations (Win) and (Mac) are used.

Data Files

To complete the lessons in this book, you need the Data Files. To access the Data Files for this book, take the following steps:

1. Open your browser and go to http://www.cengagebrain.com.
2. Type the author, title, or ISBN of this book in the Search window. (The ISBN is listed on the back cover.)
3. Select the book title in the list of search results.
4. When the book's main page is displayed, select the Access Now button under Free Materials.
5. To download Data Files, select a chapter number and then select the Data Files link on the left navigation bar to download the files.

Your instructor will tell you where to store the files as you work, such as the hard drive, a network server, or a USB drive. The instructions in the lessons will refer to "the drive and folder where you store your Data Files" when referring to the Data Files for the book.

When you copy the Data Files to your computer, you may see lock icons that indicate that the files are read-only when you view them in the Dreamweaver Files panel. To unlock the files, right-click on the locked file name in the Files panel, then select Turn off Read Only.

Images vs. Graphics

Many times these terms seem to be used interchangeably. For the purposes of this book, the term images is used when referring to pictures on a web page. The term graphics is used as a more encompassing term that refers to non-text items on a web page such as photographs, logos, navigation bars, Flash animations, graphs, background images, and drawings. You may define these terms in a slightly different way, depending on your professional background or business environment.

System Preference Settings

The learning process will be much easier if you can see the file extensions for the files you will use in the lessons. To do this in Windows 7, open Windows Explorer, select Organize, Folder and Search Options, select the View tab, then uncheck the box Hide Extensions for Known File Types. In Windows 8, open Windows Explorer, select the View tab, and then select the File name extensions check box in the Show/Hide group. To do this for a Mac, go to Finder, select the Finder menu, and then select Preferences. Select the Advanced tab, then select the Show all file extensions check box.

The figures in the book were taken using the Windows setting of Smaller. If you want to match the figures exactly, change your system to match this setting. It is located in the Control Panel, Appearance and Personalization, Display dialog box.

Creating a Portfolio

The Portfolio Project and Project Builders allow you to use your creativity to come up with original Dreamweaver designs. It is a good idea to create a portfolio in which you can store your original work.

Dreamweaver CC system requirements

Windows

- Intel® Pentium® 4 or AMD Athlon® 64 processor
- Windows 7 with Service Pack 1, Windows 8, or Windows 8.1
- 1 GB of RAM
- 1 GB of available hard-disk space for installation; additional free space required during installation (cannot install on removable flash storage devices)
- 1280 × 800 display with 16-bit video card
- Java™ Runtime Environment 1.6 (included)
- Internet connection and registration are necessary for required software activation, membership validation, and access to online services.*

Mac OS

- Multicore Intel processor
- Mac OS X v10.7, v10.8, v10.9
- 1 GB of RAM
- 1 GB of available hard-disk space for installation; additional free space required during installation (cannot install on a volume that uses a case-sensitive file system or on removable flash storage devices)
- 1280 × 1024 display with 16-bit video card
- Java Runtime Environment 1.6
- QuickTime 7.6.6 software required for HTML5 media playback
- Internet connection and registration are necessary for required software activation, membership validation, and access to online services.*

*This product may integrate with or allow access to certain Adobe or third-party hosted online services ("Online Services"). Online Services are available only to users 13 and older and require agreement to additional terms and Adobe's online privacy policy. Online Services are not available in all countries or languages, may require user registration, and may be discontinued or modified in whole or in part without notice. Additional fees or subscription charges may apply.

Building a Website

You will create and develop several websites named The Striped Umbrella, Blooms & Bulbs, TripSmart, and Carolyne's Creations in the lesson material and end of unit exercises in this book. Because each chapter builds from the previous chapter, it is recommended that you work through the chapters in consecutive order. Your screens should match the figures in The Striped Umbrella and Blooms & Bulbs sites, as these sites are built with specific instructions. The TripSmart and Carolyne's Creations sites are built with less specific instructions to encourage individual creativity. Your screens will probably not match the figures for those sites.

Websites Used in Figures

Each time a website is used for illustration purposes in a lesson, where necessary, a statement acknowledging the source of the website is included. Sites whose content is in the public domain, such as federal government websites, are acknowledged as a courtesy.

GUIDE TO USING
CREATIVE CLOUD

GETTING STARTED WITH
CREATIVE CLOUD

Introduction

With the introduction of **Adobe Creative Cloud** in 2012, Adobe introduced a new way to purchase, use, and upgrade its products. All Adobe applications and tools are now available under an online **Creative Cloud account**. Instead of purchasing a group of related products, you purchase a monthly or yearly subscription that gives you instant access to all Adobe applications, tools, and services, including Creative Cloud services such as file sharing and file storage. The applications remain active and available as long as the subscription is kept current. In May 2013 Adobe announced that they would no longer offer new versions of the Creative Suite except by subscription through Creative Cloud.

Creative Cloud lets you work from anywhere on any device, and share your work with others. When product updates are available, they can be automatically downloaded and installed seamlessly at no additional cost, giving Creative Cloud users unlimited access to the latest versions of all Adobe applications. From this point forward, we will refer to Adobe applications as **Adobe apps**.

Creative Cloud: Apps and Services

In addition to serving as the hub that gives you access to all Adobe apps, Creative Cloud accounts include other services. For instance, you can use Creative Cloud to store your files, share files to collaborate with others, host up to five websites, post an online portfolio of your creative work, and view inspiring videos showcasing creative work by other professionals using Adobe products.

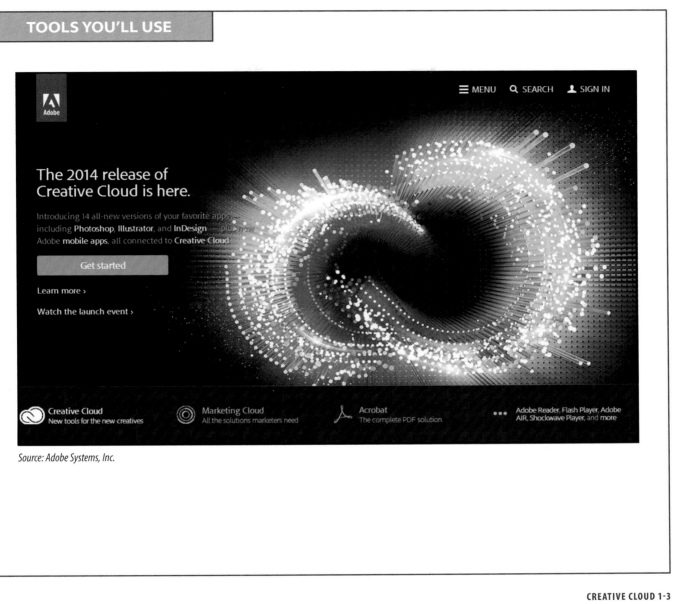

Source: Adobe Systems, Inc.

Explore
CREATIVE CLOUD

What You'll Do

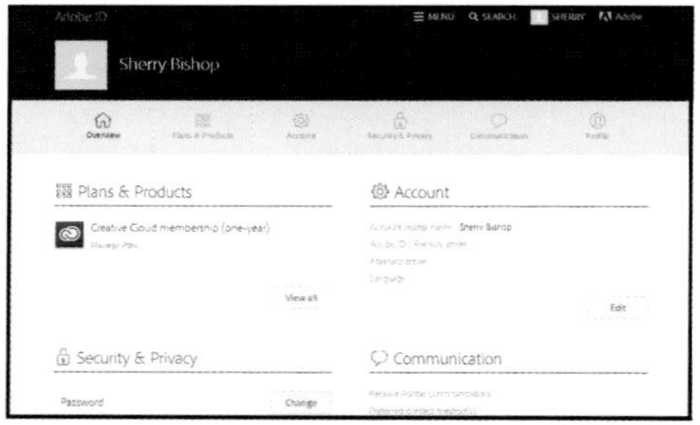

Source: Adobe Systems, Inc.

In this lesson, you will view the Creative Cloud desktop app and the Creative Cloud website Files panel.

Signing up for a Creative Cloud Account

To use Creative Cloud apps and services, you must have an Adobe ID. An **Adobe ID** is an email address and password you use to download free trials, purchase Adobe products, and access Creative Cloud. There is no charge for creating an Adobe ID. If you don't have one, you can create one on the Adobe website at www.adobe.com. Select Sign In on the opening screen, then select

Get an Adobe ID under the Sign in button, as shown in Figure 1.

Signing in to Creative Cloud

Once you have an Adobe ID, you use it to sign in each time you use a Creative Cloud app. Signing in to one app, such as Dreamweaver, automatically signs you in to all other tools you have downloaded when you open them. You can stay signed in when you exit apps, but

Figure 1 *Adobe ID sign-in page*

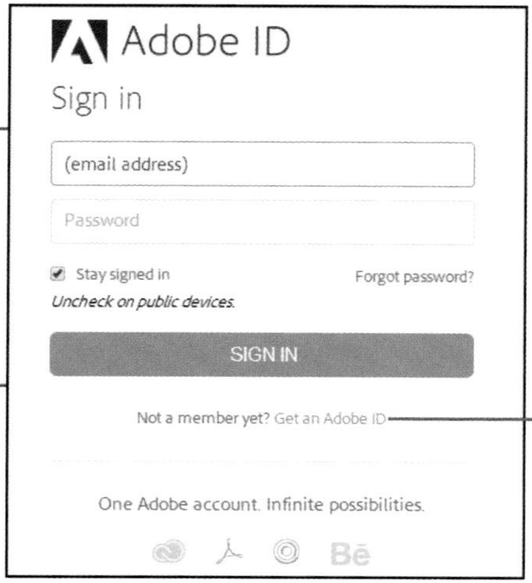

Sign in with Adobe ID and Password

Select to create an Adobe ID

Source: Adobe Systems, Inc.

you will only be able to access Creative Cloud on two active devices. To access Creative Cloud on a third device, you must sign out of Creative Cloud on one of the active devices.

Using the Creative Cloud Desktop App

To use Creative Cloud apps and services, you can begin by downloading the Creative Cloud desktop app from one of these Adobe websites: www.adobe.com/downloads.html or creative.adobe.com/products/creative-cloud. (Remember that websites, by their nature, are easily and frequently updated. If a specific link does not work, you can always search the site to find the current location for the content.) The **Creative Cloud desktop app** is a small dashboard that runs in the background as you use the Adobe apps. Figure 2 shows the Home panel in the Creative Cloud desktop app. The panels take you to the various parts of Creative Cloud: Home, Apps, Assets, and Community. The area below the panels lists your recent Creative Cloud installations and updates. Figure 2 shows four fonts added, updates to Creative Cloud, Photoshop CC, Bridge CC, InDesign CC (2014), and Photoshop CC (2014), and the installation of Flash Professional CC and Mobile Device Packaging (2014) (your list will differ). The links next to each activity can help you learn more: The View tutorials link next to the Flash Professional CC and Mobile Device Packaging (2014) notice provides tutorials that introduce you to those apps. When you select the name of an updated app, such as Photoshop CC (2014), you will be directed to the Adobe website with information about what is new in this release of the app.

The desktop app has three other panels: Apps, Assets, and Community, which let you download and install new apps, share files, add fonts, and share creative works with other members of the Creative Cloud community.

Figure 3 shows the Apps panel, which is divided into two sections. The upper section

Figure 2 *Creative Cloud desktop app Home panel*

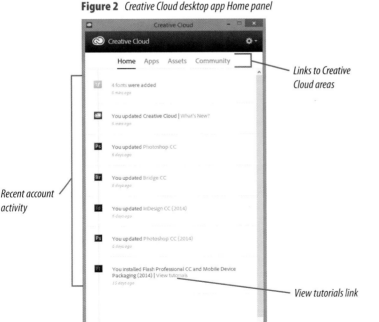

Links to Creative Cloud areas

Recent account activity

View tutorials link

Figure 3 *Creative Cloud desktop Apps panel*

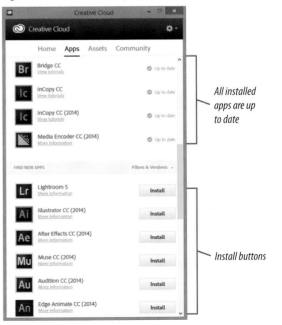

All installed apps are up to date

Install buttons

lists your currently-installed apps. It also tells you if your apps are up to date and provides a link that lets you update any apps that are not current. Each app name includes a link that lets you view tutorials or more information for that app. The lower Find New Apps section lists all available apps, with an Install button next to each one. Select the Install button to download and install any apps you would like to use.

The Assets panel lets you work with your Creative Cloud files, in conjunction with the Creative Cloud website: As you create files, save them to the Creative Cloud Files folder on your local computer, and create a copy on the Creative Cloud website. Then when you save a file on your computer, it will be automatically synced (updated) to the copy on the website. You will be able to either view your files in the Creative Cloud Files folder on your computer, or view the online versions on the Adobe website, using any other computer or device. When you sync your files to the website, your Creative Cloud files will be available to you anywhere.

The Assets panel also has an Open Folder button that lets you view the files on your computer, as well as a View on Web button that lets you view your online files (also known as your **remote files**). The Creative Cloud website provides learning resources, including tutorials on Creative Cloud products.

You might want to keep both the Creative Cloud website and the Creative Cloud desktop app open when you are downloading files and folders or working with online services. When you are simply working within an app, such as Dreamweaver, it is not necessary to keep either open, as an Internet connection is not required for the Creative Cloud apps to run.

Navigating the Creative Cloud Website

After you go to the Creative Cloud website by logging in at creative.adobe.com, you see the **central dashboard**, a navigation bar at the side of the screen, shown in Figure 4. The central dashboard has three main sections: Apps, Assets, and Community. The bottom of the dashboard displays a Sign out button. At the

Figure 4 *Creative Cloud dashboard*

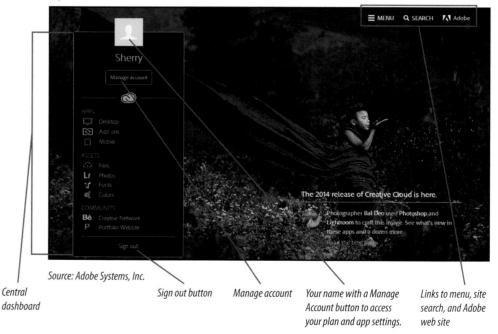

Source: Adobe Systems, Inc.

Central dashboard   Sign out button   Manage account   Your name with a Manage Account button to access your plan and app settings.   Links to menu, site search, and Adobe web site top right corner of the page are links that let you access a main product menu, search the site, and go to the Adobe website, also shown in Figure 4. The next three lessons discuss some of the resources in these sections.

The central dashboard also displays a Manage account button under your name, which gives you access to your plan, profile, and application settings, as shown in Figure 5. You can check your account status, your subscription renewal date, billing information, and transaction history. You can also edit your profile settings such as your password and address.

Figure 5 *Account settings*

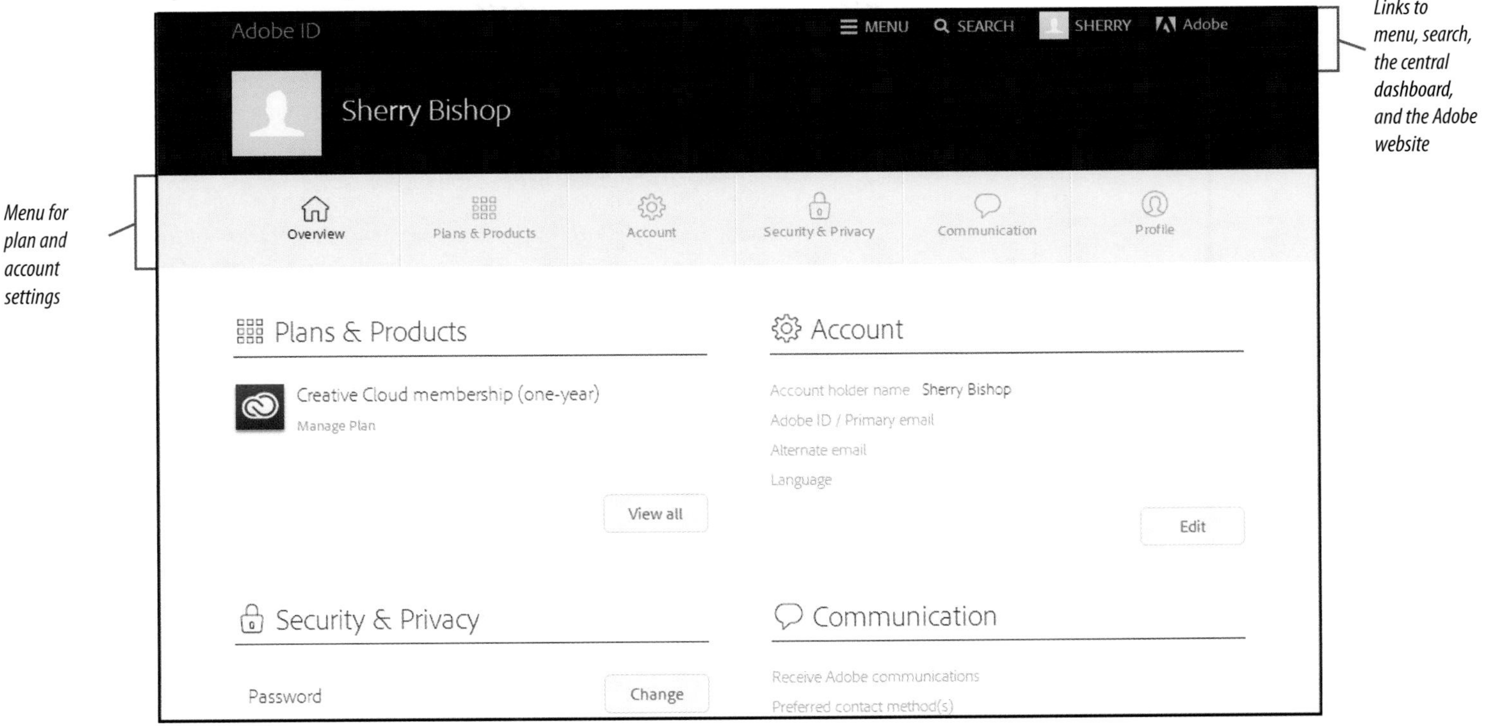

Links to menu, search, the central dashboard, and the Adobe website

Menu for plan and account settings

Source: Adobe Systems, Inc.

Manage Creative
CLOUD FILES

What You'll Do

Source: Adobe Systems, Inc.

In this lesson, you will explore the menu options available in the Actions menu in the Files window.

Accessing Creative Cloud Files

When you first log into the Creative Cloud website, you access your file storage by selecting the Files link listed under the Assets group on the central dashboard. When you select this link, the Creative Cloud Files window opens, as shown in Figure 6. You can also access your files with the CC desktop app by selecting Files, View on the Assets panel. A Creative Cloud account comes with 20 GB of online storage, and you manage your online files on this page. You can view, share, move, and rename your files and folders; you can also create new folders, upload files, search your files and folders, and archive files.

Uploading Files

It is a good idea to use folders to organize your online files. To create a folder in your Creative Cloud online storage area, select the Actions menu, select Create Folder, enter a folder name, then select Create Folder. To add files from your computer to a Creative Cloud folder, select the folder where you want to store the file, select the Actions menu, then select Upload. In the File Upload dialog box, navigate to the location of the files you want to upload, then select them and select Open. The upload will begin immediately and your uploaded file will be listed in your Creative Cloud Files list, in the location you selected. See Figure 6.

QUICK TIP

If you don't see the right column shown in Figure 6, select the small icon to the right of the Actions menu to show it. Select it again to hide this information if you would rather use that space for your files and folders.

Getting Started with Creative Cloud

Figure 6 *Uploaded folders and files are listed in the Files window*

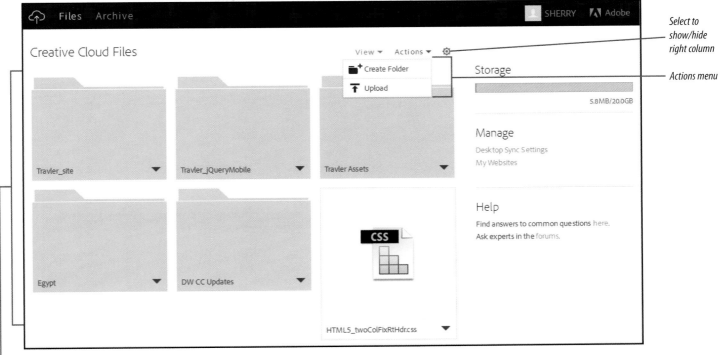

Select to show/hide right column

Actions menu

Source: Adobe Systems, Inc.

Folders and files listed

Working with Files

Once you have uploaded files to your account, you can share them with others by selecting a file and using the Share drop-down menu, as shown in Figure 7. The Post Publicly command lets you post your files to Behance, the Adobe online location where you can share your creative work with other Adobe creative professionals. Behance requires that the files you post be a minimum size of 640 pixels by 320 pixels, but you can share a link to a file of any size. The Send Link command lets you email a link to your documents to others so they can view and download them.

If you want to send someone else a link to your file, first select the file, then select the Send Link command in the Share menu. Next, select the Create Public Link button in the Send Link dialog box. Enter the email address for the person you want to send the link, and select the Send Link button. Your contact will then be sent a public link within the Adobe website to view your file. There is also an Allow File Download button you can select if you want the viewer to have the ability to download your file. Select the Remove Public Link button to delete the link.

You can also download, rename, archive, or replace files using the Actions drop-down menu, as shown in Figure 8. You must select a file before you see these menu options.

If you decide to delete a file, you must move it to the Archives first. To delete a file, select the file you want to delete in the Creative Cloud Files list, select the Actions menu, then select

Figure 7 *Share menu options*

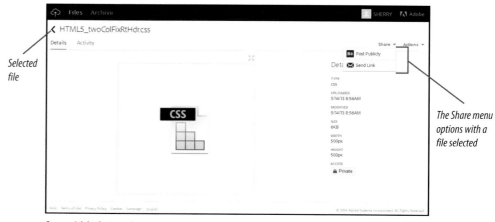

Selected file

The Share menu options with a file selected

Source: Adobe Systems, Inc.

Figure 8 *Archive option in the Actions menu*

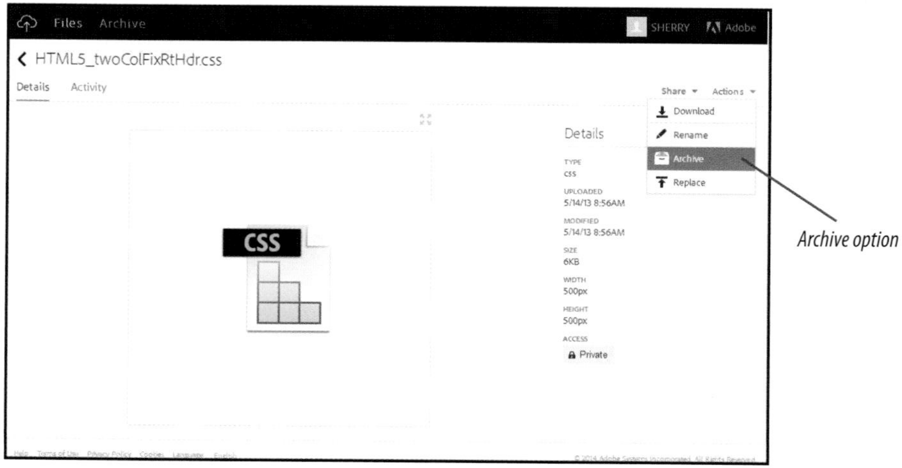

Archive option

Source: Adobe Systems, Inc.

Getting Started with Creative Cloud

Archive, as shown in Figure 8. A dialog box will open to confirm you want to archive the file. Select the Archive button to confirm or the Cancel button to cancel the action.

After you have archived a file, select Archive on the menu bar at the top of the Creative Cloud Files window to view your archived files. Select the check box to the left of the file you want to delete, then select Permanently Delete to delete the file, as shown in Figure 9. A dialog box will open to verify that you want to delete the file. Select Permanently Delete to delete the file. To restore an archived file, select Restore. A dialog box asks you to confirm that you want to restore the file; select the Restore button to restore the file to the active file list. To return to your files list, select Files on the menu bar at the top of the Creative Cloud Files window.

Figure 9 *Archive options*

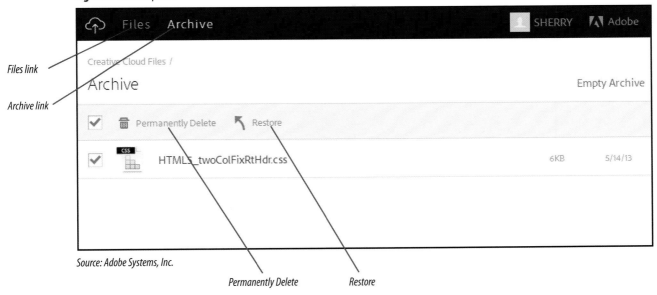

Files link

Archive link

Permanently Delete

Restore

Source: Adobe Systems, Inc.

Download Creative Cloud
APPS AND SERVICES

What You'll Do

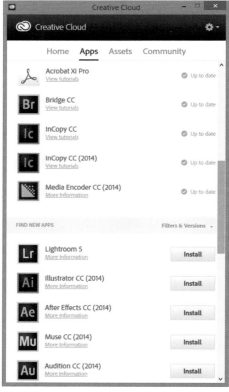

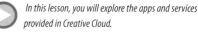

In this lesson, you will explore the apps and services provided in Creative Cloud.

Using the Desktop Apps Window

Your Creative Cloud subscription gives you access to a collection of apps and services. The collection includes familiar products such as Dreamweaver, Flash, Edge, and Photoshop, but also includes additional services and apps such as Adobe Typekit and Behance. Each app clearly documents

Figure 10 *Creative Cloud desktop apps*

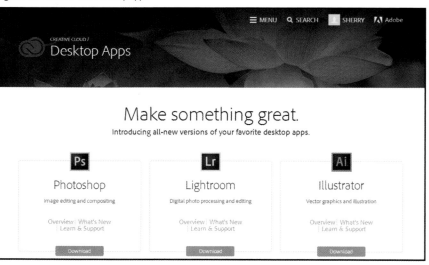

Source: Adobe Systems, Inc.

its new features, so as you upgrade to new versions, you can quickly see what has changed in each app.

To access Adobe apps, select Desktop in the Apps section of the central dashboard, which takes you to the creative.adobe.com website location: www.adobe.com/creativecloud/catalog/desktop.html with the Creative Cloud apps listed, as shown in Figure 10. Each app is listed with Overview, What's New, and Learn & Support links, along with a Download button, shown in Figure 11.

To download a Creative Cloud app, select the Download button below the product name. A window opens, and, depending on the app, may ask you questions about your skill levels before it begins downloading. You can also download apps with the Creative Cloud Desktop with either a Try or Install button.

Figure 11 *Options for exploring and downloading an app*

App resource links

Source: Adobe Systems, Inc.

Download button

Viewing Your Creative Cloud Apps

To view your downloaded apps, open the Creative Cloud desktop app, then select the Apps panel, shown in Figure 12 (Windows). Mac users will see the Apps panel with a slightly different appearance, and it only appears when you select the Creative cloud icon in the Mac menu bar. The Windows Apps panel remains open unless it is minimized or closed. These behaviors can be turned on and off in the Preferences settings. A notification appears to the right of each app name to tell you whether an update is available, or if the app is currently up to date. The Find New Apps section lists apps that are available to download, so you can also download and install apps from the Creative Cloud desktop app in addition to the Creative Cloud download center.

Incorporating Type into Your Project with Typekit

Type is an essential part of any creative project, so Creative Cloud includes Typekit, a type repository that gives you access to over a thousand font families that you can use in your web or print projects. Typekit, founded in 2008 and acquired by Adobe in 2011 to make fonts accessible and universal, is a library of high-quality fonts called Adobe Edge Web Fonts that can be used in any application that uses fonts. Your Adobe subscription provides the license to use these fonts, so you don't have to be concerned about font licensing or compatibility. In Dreamweaver, when you download and apply a font to web page content, JavaScript is added to the page head

Figure 12 *Creative Cloud desktop app with the Apps tab selected (Win)*

Apps panel

List of downloaded apps

All apps are up to date

List of available apps to download

Getting Started with Creative Cloud

section to direct the browser to access the font from the use.edgefonts.net website and apply it to the content.

You can access Typekit through the Typekit website, typekit.com, or through the Creative Cloud desktop app Fonts link in the Assets panel using the Turn Typekit On button the first time you use this feature, then the Add Fonts from Typekit button each subsequent time. The fonts are seamlessly integrated into Creative Cloud apps. Any Typekit font that you download will be available in the Font menus in your apps. For instance, if you are inserting type into a project in Photoshop, your Typekit fonts will be available in the Font-Family menus in the Character and Character Styles panels. When you select the Add Fonts from Typekit button on the Fonts panel, Typekit opens.

The Typekit dashboard makes it easy to browse the font libraries, shown in Figure 13, then save and organize the fonts you select. A search text box helps you locate fonts quickly. On the right side of the screen, filters let you select appropriate fonts, such as by classification (Serif, Script, Decorative), platform (Web or Desktop use), use (Paragraphs or Headings), or properties (such as weight or width). The Typekit dashboard also lets you enter sample text so you can see how a font will look using text from your project. In Figure 13, Dreamweaver has been entered as sample text.

Figure 13 *Browse Fonts tab on the Adobe Typekit site*

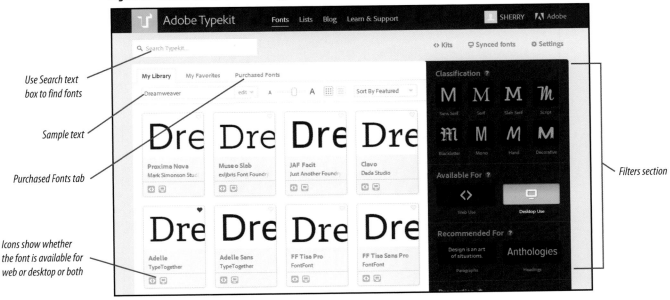

Source: Adobe Systems, Inc.

After filtering and viewing samples, select the font you want to use. You can then view the available weights and styles of that font, such as bold and italic, as well as specimens. You can also test the font by entering text of your choice, and view samples in various browsers. Once you have selected a font you would like to save, point to the font, then select the Use fonts command to sync your selected fonts to your Creative Cloud account. You can store up to 100 fonts for desktop use. Be aware, however, that each font style counts as a separate font. For instance, Adelle Regular, Adelle Bold, and Adelle Italic count as three fonts.

If the font you have selected is your first font, you need to create a new kit, then sync it to your desktop via Creative Cloud. Your new fonts will then be listed in your Creative Cloud account, as shown in Figure 14.

To use a font on a Dreamweaver website, add the font family to an existing one or create a new one. You then publish and embed the website with the JavaScript that is automatically added to the page head content. To use a font for a print project, apply the font to selected text from the application Font menu. For instance, fonts added from Typekit are automatically added to the list of available fonts in both the Edit, Fonts menu and the Fonts list in the Character panel in InDesign.

If you are not a Creative Cloud subscriber, you can still subscribe to Typekit, but you will need to pay a subscription fee.

Using Behance to Share Your Work

Creative Cloud also features Behance, an online service that lets you share and track your creative work with others. An Adobe

Figure 14 *Synced Adelle font listed on the Creative Cloud desktop app*

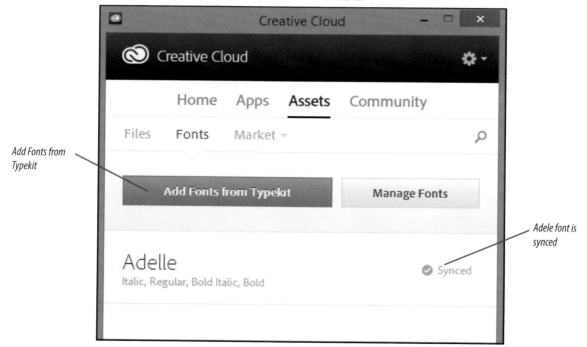

Add Fonts from Typekit

Adele font is synced

subsidiary, Behance offers a professional portfolio site for your work called ProSite, which provides you with a URL to publish your work. Behance is also available as an iPhone and Android app, together with a Creative Portfolio app that can be used without an Internet connection.

To access Behance using the Adobe desktop app, select the Community panel. Or you can open the Behance site at www.behance.net. If you are logged into an Adobe app, you will automatically be logged in to the website. If you are using the Community panel in the desktop app, you'll see the the Behance dashboard tabs, My Activity, My Work, and Discover Work. The My Activity tab shows activites posted for people you are following; My Work and Discover Work let you access your portfolio of creative work, and follow other Behance members' work. (Notice the tab names vary slightly between the desktop app Community panel and the Behance website.) An **Add Work button** lets you upload your work to your portfolio. On the Behance website, you can select **Discover** to explore work posted on Behance, as shown in Figure 15. You may filter by schools, tools used, colors, or galleries.

After selecting a project to view, as shown in Figure 16, you can see the entire project, other projects by the same artist, and see how many users have viewed, appreciated (liked), and commented on the work. You can also message the artist and share the project using social media choices.

Figure 15 *Behance website*

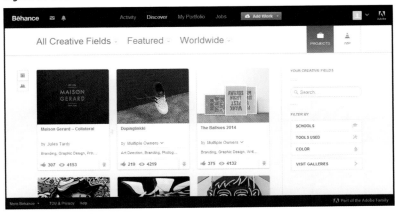

Source: Adobe Systems, Inc.

Figure 16 *Viewing a project posted on Behance*

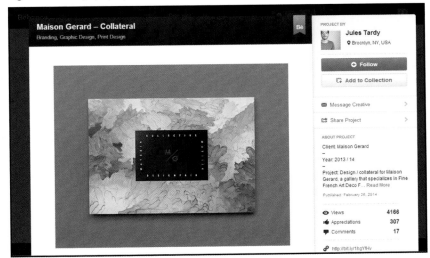

Source: Adobe Systems, Inc.

View Additional
LEARNING TOOLS

What You'll Do

Source: Adobe Systems, Inc.

 In this lesson, you will explore additional Adobe Creative Cloud resources.

Using the Learning Resources

To learn more about Creative Cloud products and services, select the Menu link in the top right corner of the Creative Cloud page, then select the Learn & Support link on the new page that opens, as shown in Figure 17. You can then select Learn at your level to view tutorials, Contact support to contact customer support, or Ask the community to browse postings from Adobe community members. When you select the Learn at your level link, you will see listings for all Adobe apps, with comprehensive video tutorials for each one. You can either watch them or follow along to complete the work as you go. Each tutorial includes data files you can use to work through the tasks. Figure 18 shows the introductory page for an Edge

Figure 17 *The Learn & Support page*

Learn &
Support link

Link for viewing
tutorials

Source: Adobe Systems, Inc.

Getting Started with Creative Cloud

Animate CC video tutorial. The tutorial layout is simple and easy to use. Each lesson begins with a short paragraph; then you can either watch the video lesson or download the data files and work along with the videos.

Viewing Learning Content with Adobe TV

The Learn & Support page also lets you view many of the presentations delivered through Adobe TV. At the bottom of the Learn & Support page, select All learn & support, then select the Adobe TV link in the More learning section to access a library of videos and training materials. The menu at the top of the page has links to Products, Channels, Shows, Translations, and My Library, as shown in Figure 19. Take the time to browse through some of the videos offered and you will find a wealth of information.

Figure 18 *Edge Animate CC video tutorial*

Figure 19 *Adobe TV*

Find and Use
ADOBE ADD-ONS

What You'll Do

Source: Adobe Systems, Inc.

In this lesson, you will view the Adobe Marketplace and explore Adobe Add-ons.

Identifying and Locating Adobe Add-ons

One of the exciting developments in the evolution of Creative Cloud is the introduction of the new Adobe Add-ons website. This website is a marketplace for products and resources developed for Creative Cloud, designed for both producers and end users. **Producers** are people who can use the site to sell, share, and promote products they have developed for an Adobe product, such as an interactive menu bar for Dreamweaver or a new brush tip for Photoshop. They can either distribute their products for a set price, by subscription, or at no charge. **End users** are people looking for new, exciting ways to use Adobe products. They can search, purchase, and install new tools or content for Adobe apps.

The Adobe Add-ons website, shown in Figure 20, has been redesigned to become a richer environment for both producers and end users.

Using Adobe Add-ons for Dreamweaver

To browse through add-ons from Dreamweaver CC, use the Window, Browse Add-ons command. This command opens the Adobe Add-ons website, where you should already be signed in. You can filter add-ons by product, such as Dreamweaver, Photoshop, or Muse, and according to whether they are free or paid. For example, you can show only free add-ons for Photoshop or all add-ons for Dreamweaver. You will notice that some add-ons are compatible with more than one Adobe product. You can also sort available add-ons according to how recently they were created, by title, by price (high to low or low to high), or by rating, and you can search for a specific add-on. Figure 21 shows some Dreamweaver featured add-ons. These listings will change frequently as new add-ons are created and added to the site.

Figure 20 *Adobe Add-ons website*

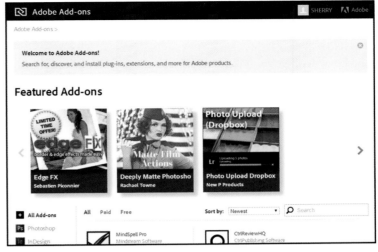

Source: Adobe Systems, Inc.

Figure 21 *Dreamweaver Featured Add-ons*

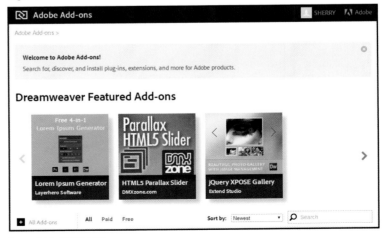

Source: Adobe Systems, Inc.

One free Dreamweaver Add-on, Advanced CSS Menu Light by Ajatix, creates CSS drop-down menus. After selecting the link to Advanced CSS Menu Light, you are directed to a page of product information, ratings and reviews, notes, and where to find it, as shown in Figure 22. The product information includes the platforms that support it and the product versions that it supports.

Select the Free button to download the app, then after the app downloads, you will see a green check mark beside a label "Acquired" as shown in Figure 23.

When you select the Where to find it link, you see instructions on how to locate the Add-on after you have installed it. When you

Figure 22 *Exploring the Advanced CSS Menu Light Add-on*

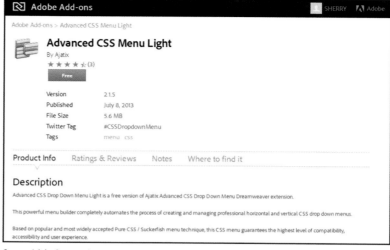

Source: Adobe Systems, Inc.

Figure 23 *An acquired Add-on*

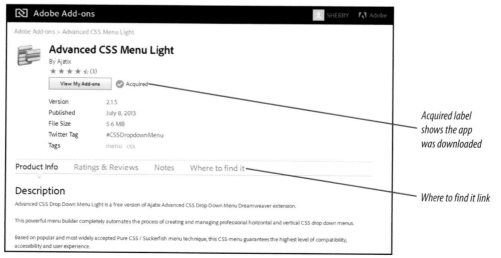

Source: Adobe Systems, Inc.

Getting Started with Creative Cloud

are ready to create your CSS menu bar, follow the instructions, then choose a theme for your menu bar, as shown in Figure 24. After choosing a theme, use the New Menu dialog box to add each menu item, link, and target to build the menu bar.

Other examples of Add-ons for Dreamweaver include shopping carts, image galleries, search pages, form designers, slideshows, and Google analytics tools. Table 1 lists some other possibilities for Add-ons you might find helpful. Take some time browsing the list of Add-ons and explore those that might be useful to you. Each Add-on includes a logo of the Adobe app(s) that it is designed to be used with.

The Adobe Add-ons site is constantly evolving so it can continue to match the talents of producers with the needs of users and the capabilities of Adobe Creative Cloud apps.

Figure 24 *Choosing a menu-bar theme*

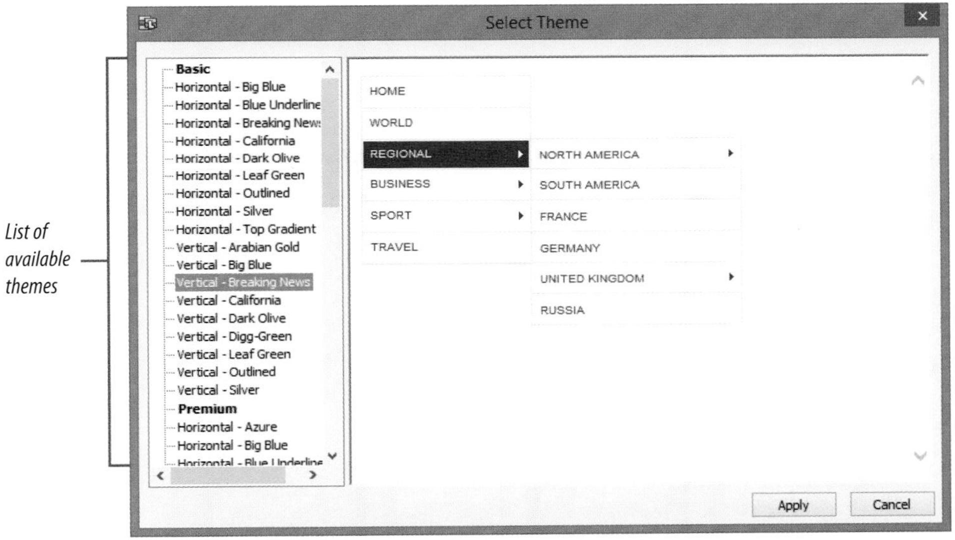

List of available themes

Source: Adobe Systems, Inc.

TABLE 1: ADOBE ADD-ON EXAMPLES AND USES			
Name of Add-on	**Add on to**	**Used To**	**Cost**
HTML5 Data Bindings	Dreamweaver	Connect to your data	Free
DMXzone Bootstrap	Dreamweaver	Create a site layout	Free
Taster	Photoshop InDesign Dreamweaver Illustrator Premier Pro InCopy	Insert 20 web-sized textures for backgrounds	Free
HTML5 Image Gallery	Dreamweaver	Images	Charge
Toolkit for CreateJS	Flash	Create assets for HTML5 projects	Free
Light Date Picker Calendar	Dreamweaver	Insert a calendar into a form	Charge
EAN Barcode Generator	InDesign	Make EAN-8 & EAN-13 barcodes	Free

© 2015 Cengage Learning®

CHAPTER 1 GETTING STARTED WITH DREAMWEAVER

1. Explore the Dreamweaver workspace
2. View a web page and use Help
3. Plan and set up a website
4. Add a folder and pages

CHAPTER 1

GETTING STARTED WITH
DREAMWEAVER

Introduction

Adobe Dreamweaver CC is a web development tool that lets you create dynamic web pages containing text, images, hyperlinks, animation, sounds, video, and interactive elements. You can use Dreamweaver to create individual web pages or complex websites consisting of many web pages. A **website** is a group of related web pages that are linked together and share a common interface and design. Dreamweaver lets you create design elements such as text, forms, rollover images, and interactive buttons, or import elements from other software programs. You can also save Dreamweaver files in many different file formats, including XHTML, HTML, JavaScript, CSS, or XML, to name a few. **XHTML** is the acronym for eXtensible HyperText Markup Language, the current standard language used to create web pages. You can still use **HTML** (HyperText Markup Language) in Dreamweaver; however, it is no longer considered the standard language. You use a web browser to view your web pages on the Internet. A **web browser** is a program, such as Google Chrome, Apple Safari, Mozilla Firefox, or Microsoft Internet Explorer, used to display web pages.

Using Dreamweaver Tools

Creating a robust website is a complex task. Fortunately, Dreamweaver has an impressive number of tools that can help. Using Dreamweaver design tools, you can create dynamic and interactive web pages without writing a word of code. However, if you prefer to write code, Dreamweaver makes it easy to enter and edit the code directly and see the visual results of the code instantly. Dreamweaver also contains organizational tools that help you work with a team of people to create a website. You can also use the Dreamweaver management tools to help you manage a website. For instance, you can use the **Files panel** to create folders to organize and store the various files for your website, and to add pages to your website.

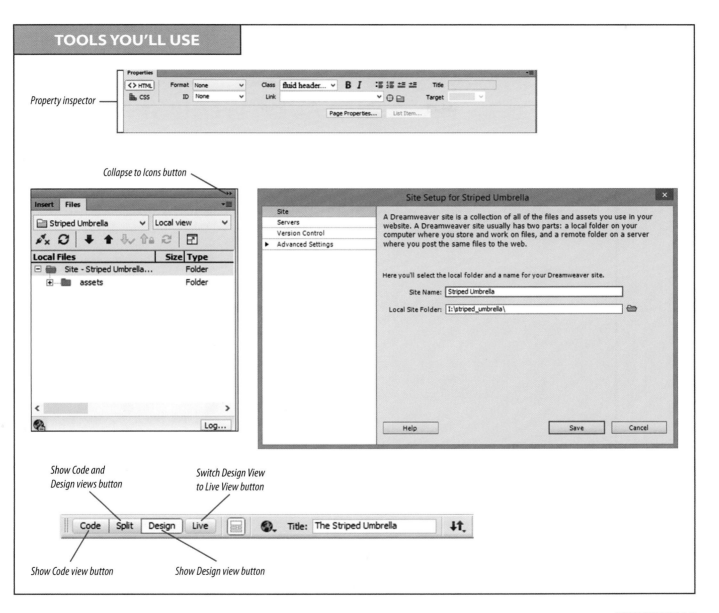

Property inspector

Collapse to Icons button

Show Code and Design views button

Switch Design View to Live View button

Show Code view button

Show Design view button

Explore the DREAMWEAVER WORKSPACE

What You'll Do

In this lesson, you will start Dreamweaver, examine the components that make up the Dreamweaver workspace, and change views.

Examining the Dreamweaver Workspace

The first time you start Dreamweaver, you are offered several video tutorials to help you learn new features. You can watch as many as you like, then select Done to begin using Dreamweaver.

QUICK **TIP**

To return to the list of videos later, select Help on the Menu bar, then select New Feature Videos.

After you start Dreamweaver, you see the **Dreamweaver workspace**, the screen that includes all of the menus, panels, buttons, inspectors, and panes that you use to create and maintain websites. It is designed to give you easy access to all the tools you need to create web pages. Refer to Figure 1 as you locate the components described below.

After you open or create a new file, you see the **Document window**, the large area in the Dreamweaver program window where you create and edit web pages. The **Menu bar** (also called the **Application bar**), located above the Document window, includes menu names, a Workspace switcher, and other application commands. The Menu bar appears on either one bar or two bars, depending on your screen size and resolution. To choose a menu command, select the menu name to open the menu, then select the menu command. The Insert panel appears on the right side of the screen. The **Insert panel**, sometimes called the Insert bar, includes eight categories of buttons displayed through a drop-down menu: Common, Structure, Media, Form, jQuery Mobile, jQuery UI, Templates, and Favorites. Selecting a category in the Insert panel displays the buttons and menus for inserting objects associated with that category. For example, if you select the Structure category, you find buttons for using div tags to create blocks of content on pages; for inserting lists; and for inserting HTML5 elements such as headers and footers.

QUICK **TIP**

The Insert panel drop-down menu also lets you hide or display any panel's button labels. To hide labels and show only icons, select Hide Labels. To display them, select Show Labels.

The **Document toolbar** contains buttons and drop-down menus you can use to change the current work mode, preview web pages, add a title, and use file-management options. One of the buttons on the Document toolbar, the Switch Design View to Live View button, is used to view the current page in Live view.

Live view displays an open document as if you were viewing it in a browser, with interactive elements active. When you switch to Live view, Manage Hidden Elements and Live view

Options buttons are added to the Document toolbar.

One additional toolbar does not appear by default: the Standard toolbar. The **Standard toolbar** contains buttons you can use to execute frequently used commands that are also available on the File and Edit menus such as Cut, Copy, Paste, and Save. To display or hide the Document or Standard toolbars, right-click an empty area of an open toolbar, then select the toolbar name you wish to display or hide. You can also use the View > Toolbars menu.

The **Related Files toolbar** is located below an open document's filename tab and displays the names of any related files. **Related files** are files that are linked to a document and are necessary for the document to display and function correctly. An external style sheet, which contains formatting rules that control the appearance of a document, is a good example of a related file. The **Coding toolbar** contains buttons you can use when working directly in the code and is not visible unless you are in Code view. When visible, it appears on the left side of the Document window.

Figure 1 *Dreamweaver CC workspace*

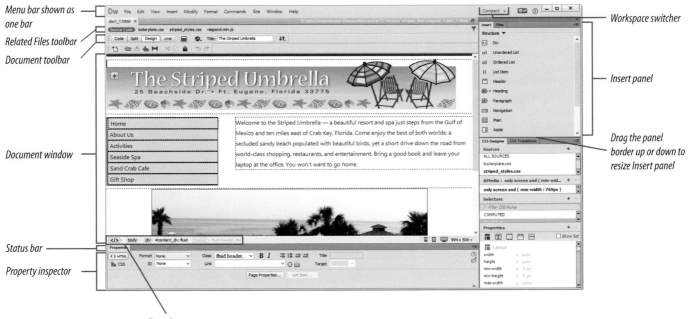

Menu bar shown as one bar

Related Files toolbar

Document toolbar

Document window

Status bar

Property inspector

Tag selector

Workspace switcher

Insert panel

Drag the panel border up or down to resize Insert panel

The **Property inspector**, sometimes referred to as the **Properties pane**, located at the bottom of the Dreamweaver window, lets you view and change the properties (characteristics) of a selected object. The Property inspector is context sensitive, which means it changes according to what is selected in the Document window. The **status bar** is located above the Property inspector. The left side of the status bar displays the **tag selector**, which shows the HTML tags used at the insertion point location. The right side displays icons used for displaying the open page as viewed in a mobile, tablet, or desktop device. The far right side of the status bar shows the Window Size pop-up menu, used to change the page view or edit the default window size settings. You can also change the page orientation to landscape or portrait.

A **panel** is a tabbed window that displays information on a particular topic or contains related commands. **Panel groups** are sets of related panels that are grouped together. A collection of panels or panel groups is called a **dock**. To view the contents of a panel in a panel group, select the panel's tab. Panels are docked on the right side of the screen by default. You can undock or "float" them by dragging the panel tab to another screen location. To collapse or expand a panel group, double-click the panel tab, as shown in Figure 2. When you first start Dreamweaver, the Insert, Files, CSS Designer, and CSS Transitions panels are expanded by default, with the Insert and CSS Designer panels selected. You can open

panels using the Window menu commands or the corresponding shortcut keys.

QUICK TIP

The Collapse to Icons button ▶▶ above the top panel lets you collapse all open panels to icons to enlarge the workspace.

Working with Dreamweaver Views

A **view** is a particular way of displaying page content. Dreamweaver has three working views. **Design view** shows the page similar to how it would appear in a browser and is primarily used for designing and creating a web page. **Code view** shows the underlying HTML code for the page; use this view to read or edit the underlying code.

QUICK TIP

You can also split Code view to enable you to work on two different sections of code at once. To change to Split Code view, select View on the Menu bar, then select Split Code.

Show Code and Design views is a combination of Code view and Design view. Show Code and Design views is the best view for **debugging** or correcting errors because you can immediately see how code modifications change the appearance of the page. The view buttons are located on the Document toolbar. If you want to switch to the same view for all open documents, hold down the Ctrl key (Win) or Command key (Mac) while you select a view button.

Figure 2 *Panels in panel group*

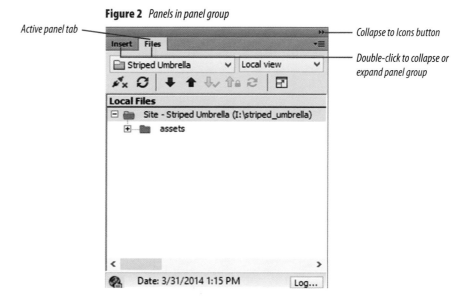

Active panel tab

Collapse to Icons button

Double-click to collapse or expand panel group

Figure 3 *Starting Dreamweaver CC (Windows)*

*Select Adobe
Dreamweaver CC*

Start Dreamweaver (Windows)

1. On the Windows start screen, select the **down arrow** or swipe to your screen that lists all installed programs.

2. Select **Adobe Dreamweaver CC**.

TIP You can right-click a program name, then create a tile by selecting Pin to Start.

or

3. Select the **Adobe Dreamweaver CC tile**, as shown in Figure 3.

You started Dreamweaver CC for Windows.

Viewing and Editing Pages in Live view

When you view your web pages in Dreamweaver, the page elements appear similarly to the way they will appear on the web, but not exactly. To get a better idea of how they will look, you can use the Switch Design View to Live View button on the Document toolbar. This button directs the open document to appear as it would in a browser, with interactive elements active. One recent improvement in Live view is the ability to directly edit page elements in Live view. For instance, you can now use the Insert panel in Live view to either drag and insert or select and insert a new element onto the page. To directly edit text and add or delete page elements such as images in Live view, you must select the Hide Fluid Grid Layout Guides button on the Document toolbar before you can begin editing.

Start Dreamweaver (Macintosh)

1. Select **Finder** in the Dock, then select **Applications**.

2. Select the **Adobe Dreamweaver CC folder**, then double-click the **Adobe Dreamweaver CC application**, as shown in Figure 4.

TIP Once Dreamweaver is running, you can add it to the Dock permanently by [control]-clicking the Dreamweaver icon, selecting Options, then selecting Keep in Dock.

You started Dreamweaver CC for Macintosh.

Figure 4 *Starting Dreamweaver CC (Macintosh)*

Source: Apple Inc.

Using In-App and In-Product Messages

When you start Dreamweaver the first time, you are asked whether you are a new user or a current user. Depending on how you respond, pop-up messages will appear when a "trigger" is activated to guide or suggest tips for boosting productivity. These pop-ups are called In-app and In-product messages. **In-app messages** apply to Dreamweaver workflow content. **In-product messages** apply to Dreamweaver integration with other Creative Cloud apps content. Selecting a pop-up will close it. In-app and In-product messages will only appear once if the you follow the directions given in the pop-ups. If you do not want to use these pop-ups, you can disable them by deselecting the Show In-app help check box in the Preferences dialog box Accessibility category. You can also reset the In-app help to display pop-ups that you have viewed by selecting the Reset button next to the Show In-app help check box.

Getting Started with Dreamweaver

Figure 5 *Code view for new document*

Show Code view button

Show Code and Design views (Split) button

Show Design view button

Switch Design View to Live View button

Menu bar may be displayed as two bars

Select to collapse all panels to icons

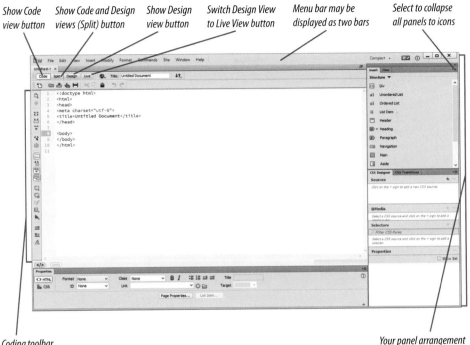

Coding toolbar

Your panel arrangement may differ depending on the last placement

Change views and view panels

1. Select **HTML** in the Create New category on the Dreamweaver Welcome Screen.

   The Dreamweaver Welcome Screen provides shortcuts for opening files and for creating new files or websites.

   TIP If you do not want the Dreamweaver Welcome Screen to appear each time you start Dreamweaver, remove the check mark next to Show Welcome Screen in the General category in the Preferences dialog box.

2. Select the **Show Code view button** `Code` on the Document toolbar.

   The default code for a new document appears in the Document window, as shown in Figure 5.

   TIP The Coding toolbar is available only in Code view and in the Code window in Split view.

3. Select the **Show Code and Design views button** `Split` on the Document toolbar.

4. Select the **Show Design view button** `Design` on the Document toolbar.

   (continued)

5. Select the **Insert panel tab**, then compare your screen to Figure 6.

   Your Insert panel may have a different category selected.

6. Select the **Files panel tab** to display the contents of the Files panel.

7. Double-click **Files** to collapse the panel group.

8. View the contents of the CSS Designer panel.

9. Drag the **blank area** next to the CSS Designer panel tab to the middle of the document window.

   The panel group is now in a floating window. The CSS Designer panel looks like more than one panel because it is divided into four panes: Sources, @Media, Selectors, and Properties.

   (continued)

Figure 6 *Displaying a panel group*

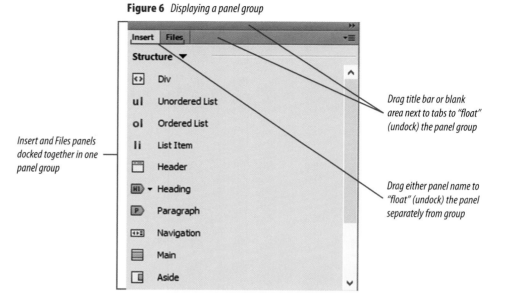

Drag title bar or blank area next to tabs to "float" (undock) the panel group

Insert and Files panels docked together in one panel group

Drag either panel name to "float" (undock) the panel separately from group

Choosing a Workspace Layout

The Dreamweaver interface is an integrated workspace, which means that all of the document windows and panels appear in a single application window. By default, each open document appears as a tab below the document toolbar. To view a tabbed document, select the tab with the document's filename. The **Workspace switcher**, a drop-down menu in the top right corner on the Menu bar, lets you change the workspace layout. The default layout is Compact, where the panels are docked on the right side of the screen. The other workspace layout is Expanded. The Expanded layout increases the width of the panels to allow the CSS Designer panel to flow into two columns. To change the workspace layout, select the Workspace switcher, then select the desired layout. You can also rearrange the workspace using your own choices for panel placement and save the workspace with a unique name using the "New Workspace" and "Manage Workspaces" commands on the Workspace switcher. The Reset 'Current view' option resets the workspace layout to return to the default positions on the screen for the selected view.

Figure 7 *Docking a panel group*

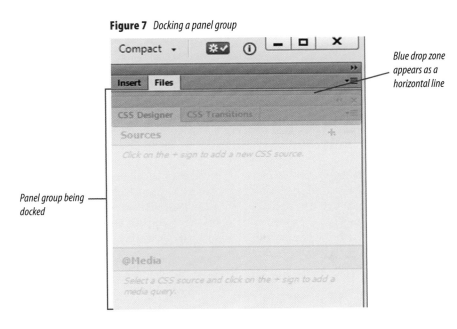

Blue drop zone appears as a horizontal line

Panel group being docked

10. Drag the **panel title bar** back to its original position, then drop it to dock the panel group below the Insert panel.

    Release the mouse only when you see the blue drop zone. The **blue drop zone** is a heavy blue line that appears when the panel is in the correct position to be docked. See Figure 7. If the blue drop zone appears as a box, releasing the button adds the panel to the boxed panel group.

TIP If you have rearranged the panels from their original positions and want to reset them back to their default positions, select the Workspace switcher drop-down menu, then select Reset 'Current view'.

11. Select the **Workspace switcher**, then select **Reset 'Compact'**.

12. Select **File** on the Menu bar, then select **Close** to close the open document.

You viewed a new web page using three views, opened panel groups, viewed their contents, undocked a panel group, then docked a panel group.

Using and Editing Keyboard Shortcuts

Most chapters in this book include a table titled Power User Shortcuts. These tables list keyboard shortcuts that relate to the chapter steps you use in that chapter. To see all of the Dreamweaver keyboard shortcuts, select Edit on the Menu bar (Win) or Dreamweaver on the Menu bar (Mac), then select Keyboard Shortcuts. The Keyboard Shortcuts dialog box opens and displays commands grouped by location; select the Commands list arrow to display a different location. You can add or delete keyboard shortcuts by selecting the Add item or Delete item buttons. You can also change a keyboard shortcut by selecting a current shortcut in the commands list, entering a new key sequence in the Press key dialog box, then selecting the Change button.

View a Web Page
AND USE HELP

What You'll Do

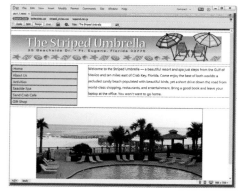

In this lesson, you will open a web page, view several page elements, and access the Help system.

Opening a Web Page

After starting Dreamweaver, you can create a new website, create a new web page, or open an existing website or web page. The first web page that appears when users go to a website is called the **home page**. The home page sets the look and feel of the website and directs users to the rest of the pages in the site.

Viewing Basic Web Page Elements

There are many elements that make up web pages. Web pages can be very simple and designed primarily with text, or they can be media-rich with images, sound, and movies, creating an enhanced interactive web experience. Figure 8 shows a web page with text and graphics that work together to create a simple and attractive page.

Most information on a web page is presented in the form of text. You can type text directly onto a web page in Dreamweaver or import text created in other programs. You can then use the Property inspector to format text so that it is attractive and easy to read. Text should be short and to the point to engage users and prevent them from losing interest and leaving your site.

Hyperlinks, also known as **links**, are images or text elements on a web page that users select to display another location on the page, another web page on the same website, or a web page on a different website.

Images add visual interest to a web page. However, the saying that "less is more" is certainly true with images. Too many images cause the page to load slowly and discourage users from waiting for the page to download. Many pages have **banners**, which are images that appear across the top or down the side of the screen that can incorporate a company's logo, contact information, and links to the other pages in the site.

Menu bars, also called navigation bars, are bars that contain multiple links, usually organized in rows or columns. Sometimes menu bars are used with an image map. An **image map** is an image that has been divided into sections, each of which serves as a link. The way that menu bars and other internal links are used on your pages is referred to as the **navigation structure** of the site.

Rich media content is a comprehensive term that refers to attractive and engaging images, interactive elements, video, or animations. Some of this content can be created in Dreamweaver, but much of it is created with other programs such as Adobe Edge Animate, Fireworks, Photoshop, or Illustrator.

Getting Help

Dreamweaver has many excellent Help features that are comprehensive and easy to use. When questions or problems arise, you can use the commands on the Help menu to find the answers you need. Selecting the Dreamweaver Help menu displays a list of help features including information on what's new in the current version and new feature videos. You also use the Help menu to sign in and out, manage your Creative Cloud account, and check for updates. To access context-specific help, select the Help button on the Property inspector. For example, if you select an image, then select the Help button on the Property inspector, you will be see help about inserting and editing images.

The Help & Support command on the Help menu (and on the Dreamweaver startup screen) opens the Learn & Support / Dreamweaver Help web page. The Search text box at the top of the page lets you enter a keyword to search for a specific topic.

Figure 8 *Common web page elements*

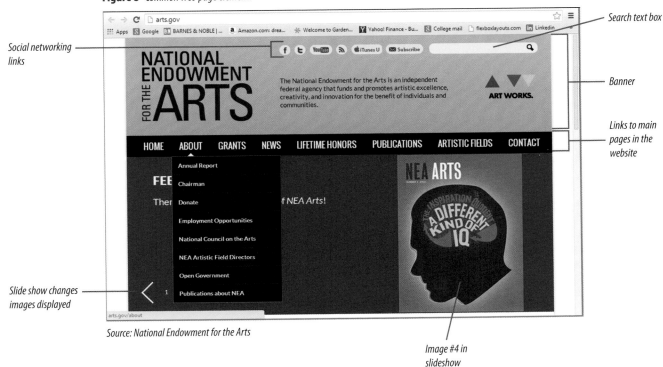

Source: National Endowment for the Arts

Open a web page and view basic page elements

1. Select **File** on the Menu bar, then select **Open**.

2. Navigate to the drive and folder where you store your Data Files, then double-click the **chapter_1 folder** (Win), or select the **chapter_1 folder** (Mac).

3. Select **dw1_1.html**, then select **Open**. You may not see the .html file extension if the option for hiding file extensions for known file types is selected on your operating system.

TIP If you want your screen to match the figures in this book, make sure the Document window is maximized.

4. Select **Window** on the Menu bar, then select **Hide Panels** to temporarily hide the panels and the Property inspector.

If In-app help messages appear, just read and close them. Refer to the sidebar on page 8 for more information.

Hiding the panels gives you a larger viewing area for your web pages. You can also press [F4] to show or hide the panels.

Note to Mac users: On the newest Mac OS, the F-keys are assigned to system functions. (F1=monitor brightness and F4=widgets) You can change this in your system preferences. Newer keyboards have an "FN" or "fn" key that can be used in conjunction with the F-keys so that they function "normally."

5. Locate each of the web page elements shown in Figure 9.

TIP Because you are opening a single page that is not in a website with access to the other pages, the links will not work.

(continued)

Figure 9 *Viewing web page elements (Windows)*

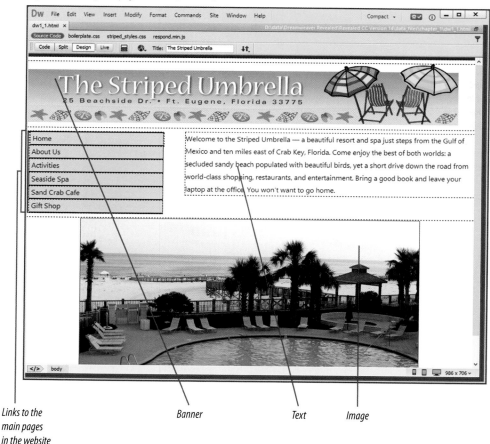

Links to the main pages in the website

Banner

Text

Image

Figure 9 *Viewing web page elements (Macintosh)*

Banner

Links to
the main
pages in the
website

Text

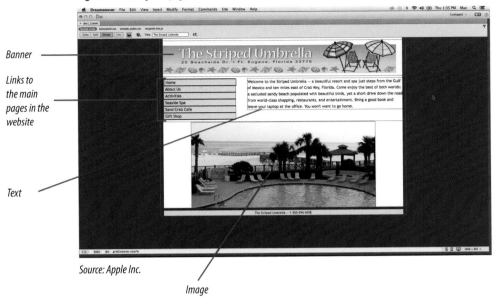

Source: Apple Inc.

Image

6. Press **[F4]** to show the panels.

7. Select the **Show Code view button** `Code` to view the code for the page.

8. Scroll to view all the code, if necessary, then select the **Show Design view button** `Design` to return to Design view.

TIP To show and highlight the code for a particular page element, select the page element in Design view, then select the Show Code view button.

9. Select **File** on the Menu bar, then select **Close** to close the open page without saving it.

TIP You can also select the Close button (the X) on the filename tab to close the page.

You opened a web page, located several page elements, viewed the code for the page, then closed the page without saving it.

Use Dreamweaver Help

1. Close any open files to display the Dreamweaver Welcome Screen.

2. Select **Help** on the menu bar, select **Help and Support**, then select **Dreamweaver Online Help**; or select the **Help & Support link** in the Learn column, as shown in Figure 10.

   The Learn & Support / Dreamweaver Help page opens from the Adobe website.

3. Select the **Dreamweaver CC (June 2014)** link under Help PDFs in the left column.

   The Adobe Dreamweaver CC Help pdf file opens in a new browser window.

4. Scroll down to the Contents page, then select the **Dreamweaver workflow and workspace link** under the Chapter 2: Workspace and workflow heading, as shown in Figure 11.

   The Dreamweaver workflow and workspace content appears.

5. Scroll down to browse through the content, then close the browser tab to return to the Learn & Support / Dreamweaver Help page.

   (continued)

Figure 10 *Learning resources on the Welcome Screen*

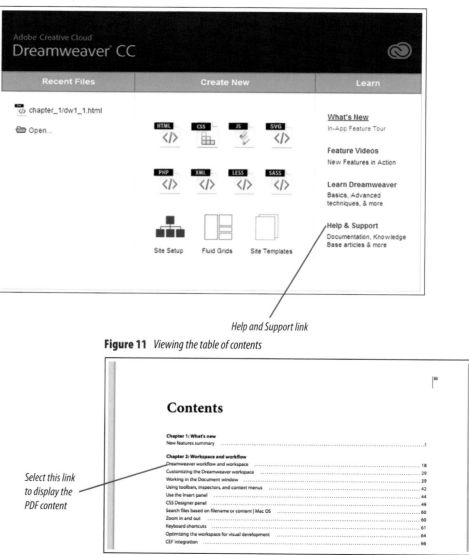

Help and Support link

Figure 11 *Viewing the table of contents*

Select this link to display the PDF content

Source: Adobe Systems, Inc.

Getting Started with Dreamweaver

Figure 12 *The Learn & Support / Dreamweaver Help site*

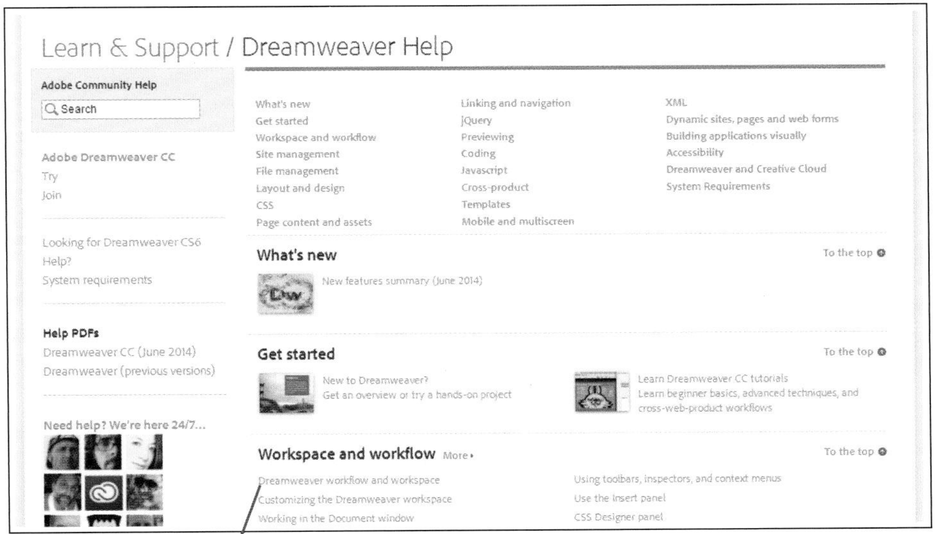

Source: Adobe Systems, Inc.

*Select this link
to display the
HTML content*

6. Scroll down the Learn & Support / Dreamweaver Help page, then select the **Dreamweaver workflow and workspace link** in the first column under Workspace and workflow, as shown in Figure 12.

    This content covers the same topics as the PDF help file, except these topics are organized and presented in live HTML files.

7. Select the **Back button** on your browser toolbar to return to the Learn & Support / Dreamweaver Help screen, then close Dreamweaver Help to return to Dreamweaver.

You used Adobe Help to read information about Dreamweaver.

Learning New Features in Dreamweaver CC

The right column in the Dreamweaver Welcome Screen is divided into four sections: What's New, Feature Videos, Learn Dreamweaver, and Help & Support. This content provides valuable learning materials for both the new Dreamweaver user and the experienced Dreamweaver user who just wants to find out what features have changed in the current version. Take the time to watch the In-App Feature Tour and the New Features in Action videos to help you get up to speed quickly. The Learn Dreamweaver link takes you to a library of Dreamweaver CC tutorials, complete with data files. The Help & Support link takes you to the Learn & Support / Dreamweaver Help page, which includes Dreamweaver CC manuals that are both PDFs and web-based. You can also read about top issues and participate in Dreamweaver forums and blogs.

Plan and Set Up
A WEBSITE

What You'll Do

In this lesson, you will review a website plan for The Striped Umbrella, a beach resort and spa. You will also create a local site folder for The Striped Umbrella website, and then set up the website.

Understanding the Website Development Process

Creating a website is a complex process. It can often involve a large team of people working in various roles to ensure that the website contains accurate information, has an attractive design, and works smoothly.

Figure 13 illustrates the phases in a website development project.

Planning a Website

Planning is probably the most important part of any successful project. Planning is an essential part of creating a website,

Figure 13 *Phases of a website development project*

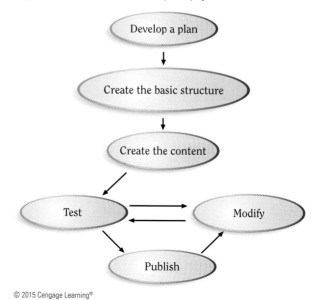

© 2015 Cengage Learning®

and is a continuous process that overlaps the subsequent phases. To start planning your website, you need to create a checklist of questions and answers about the site. For example, what are your goals for the site? Who is the audience you want to target? Teenagers? Children? Sports enthusiasts? Senior citizens? How can you design the site to appeal to the target audience? What content is appropriate for the target audience? What content is relevant to the purpose of the website? The more questions you can answer about the site, the more prepared you will be when you begin the developmental phase. Because of the public demand for up-to-date information, your plan should include not just how to get the site up and running, but how to keep it current. Table 1 lists some of the basic questions you need to answer during the planning phase for almost any type of website. From your checklist, you should create a statement of purpose and scope, a timeline for all due dates, a budget, a task list with work assignments, and a list of resources needed. You should also include a list of deliverables, such as page prototypes and art for approval. The due dates for each deliverable should be included in the timeline.

Planning the Basic Structure

Once you complete the planning phase, you need to determine the structure of the site by creating a wireframe. A **wireframe**, sometimes referred to as a storyboard, is an illustration that represents every page in a website. Like a flowchart, a wireframe shows the relationship of each page in the site to all the other pages. Wireframes also show how each page element is to be placed on each page. Wireframes are helpful when planning a website, because they allow you to visualize how each page in the site links to others. They are also an important tool to help the client see how the pages will look and work together. Make sure that the client and all other interested stakeholders approve the wireframe before the site construction actually begins.

Wireframes range from very simple (known as low-fidelity wireframes) to interactive and multidimensional (known as high-fidelity wireframes). You can create a simple

TABLE 1: WEBSITE PLANNING CHECKLIST	
Question	**Examples**
1. Who is the target audience?	Seniors, teens, children
2. How can I tailor the site to reach that audience?	Specify an appropriate reading level, decide the optimal amount of media content, use formal or casual language
3. What are the goals for the site?	Sell a product, provide information
4. How will I gather the information?	Recruit other employees, write it myself, use content from in-house documents
5. What are my sources for media content?	Internal production department, outside production company, my own photographs
6. What is my budget?	Very limited, well financed
7. What is the timeline?	Two weeks, one month, six months
8. Who is on my project team?	Just me, a complete staff of designers
9. How often should the site be updated?	Every 10 minutes, once a month
10. Who will update the site?	Me, other team members

© 2015 Cengage Learning®

wireframe by using a pencil and paper or by using a graphics program on a computer, such as Adobe Illustrator, Adobe Fireworks, or Microsoft PowerPoint. To create more complex wireframes that simulate the site navigation and user interaction, use a high-fidelity wireframe program such as Adobe InDesign, Adobe Muse, ProtoShare, Microsoft Visio, or Adobe Photoshop.

The basic wireframe shown in Figure 14 shows all the The Striped Umbrella website pages that you will create in this book. The home page appears at the top of the wireframe, and it has four pages linked to it. The home page is called the **parent page**, because it is at a higher level in the web hierarchy and has pages linked to it. The pages linked below it are called **child pages**. The Activities page, which is a child page to the home page, is also a parent page to the Cruises and Fishing pages. You can refer to this wireframe as you create the

actual links in Dreamweaver. More detailed wireframes also include document names, images, text files, and link information. Use your wireframe as your guide as you develop the site to make sure you follow the planned site structure.

In addition to creating a wireframe for your site, you should also create a folder hierarchy on your computer for all of the files that will be used in the site. Start by creating a folder with a descriptive name for the site, such as the company name. This folder, known as the **local site folder**, will store all the pages or HTML files for the site. Traditionally, this folder has been called the **root folder** and many people still use this term; in this book we will call it the local site folder. Then create a subfolder, often called **assets** or **images**, in which you store all of the files that are not pages, such as images and sound files.

After you create the local site folder, you are ready to set up your site. When you **set up** a site, you use the Dreamweaver Site Setup dialog box to assign your site a name and specify the local site folder. After you have set up your site, the site name and any folders and files it contains appear in the **Files panel**, the panel you use to manage your website's files and folders. Using the Files panel to manage your files ensures that the site links work correctly when the website is published. You also use the Files panel to add or delete pages.

Creating the Web Pages and Collecting the Page Content

This is the fun part! After you create your wireframe, obtain approvals, and set up your site, you need to gather the files you'll need to create the pages, including text, images, buttons, video, and animations. You will import some of these pages from other software programs, and some you will create in Dreamweaver. For example, you can create text in a word-processing program and import or paste it into Dreamweaver, or you can create and format text in Dreamweaver.

Images, tables, colors, and horizontal rules all contribute to making a page attractive and interesting, but they can increase file size.

Figure 14 *The Striped Umbrella website wireframe*

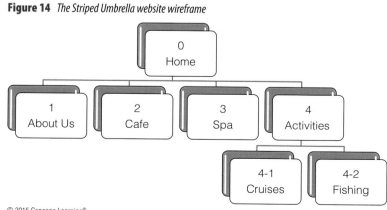

© 2015 Cengage Learning®

In choosing your page elements, carefully consider the file size of each page. A page with too many graphic elements might take a long time to load, which could cause visitors to leave your site.

Testing the Pages

Once all your pages are completed, you need to test the site to make sure all the links work and that everything looks good. It is important to test your web pages using different browser software. The four most common browsers are Mozilla Firefox, Google Chrome, Apple Safari, and Microsoft Internet Explorer. Test your site using different versions of each browser, because older versions may not support the latest web technology. Websites today are viewed with a variety of devices, screen sizes, and screen resolutions, so you should test your site using a variety of sizes, including mobile, tablet, and desktop. Some users may have small monitors, while others may have large, high-resolution monitors. Also consider connection download time. Although most people use high-speed connections with cable modems or DSL (digital subscriber line), some in rural areas still use slower dial-up modems. Testing is a continuous process, for which you should allocate plenty of time.

Modifying the Pages

Modifying and testing pages in a website is an ongoing process. After you create a website, you'll probably find that you need to keep changing it, especially when information on the site needs to be updated. Each time you make a change, such as adding a new button or image to a page, you should test the site again.

Publishing the Site

Publishing a website refers to the process of transferring all the files for the site to a **web server**, a computer that is connected to the Internet with an IP (Internet Protocol) address, so that it is available for viewing on the Internet. A website must be published so that Internet users can view it. There are several options for publishing a website. For instance, many **Internet Service Providers (ISPs)** provide space on their servers for customers to publish websites, and some commercial websites provide limited free space for their users. Although publishing happens at the end of the site development process, it's a good idea to set up web server access in the planning phase. Use the Files panel to transfer your files using the Dreamweaver FTP capability. **FTP (File Transfer Protocol)** is the process of uploading and downloading files to and from a remote site.

Managing a Project with a Team

When working with a site development team, it is especially important to define clear goals for the project and a list of objectives to accomplish those goals. Your plan should be finalized after conferring with both the clients and other team members to make sure that the purpose, scope, and objectives are clear to everyone. Establish the **deliverables**, or products that will be provided to the client at the product completion such as new pages or graphic elements, and a timeline for their delivery. You should present the web pages at strategic times in the development process to your team members and to your clients for feedback and evaluation. Analyze all feedback objectively, incorporating both the positive and the negative comments to help you make improvements to the site and meet the clients' expectations and goals.

A common pitfall in team management is **scope creep**. Scope creep means making impromptu changes or additions to a project without corresponding increases in the schedule or budget. Proper project control and communication between team members and clients can minimize scope creep and achieve the successful and timely completion of a project.

Select the location for your website

1. Open or expand the Files panel if necessary to view the contents.

   TIP If the Background File Activity dialog box opens, select Close. It is just indicating the status of any current file activity.

2. Select the **drive or folder** that is currently displayed in the pop-up menu in the Files panel to display a menu of storage locations. See Figure 15.

3. Navigate to and select the **drive or folder** (or subfolder) in the list where you will store your folders and files for your websites.

   You will store all of the folders and files you create inside this drive or folder.

   You selected the drive or folder where you will create your website.

Figure 15 *Selecting a drive in the Files panel*

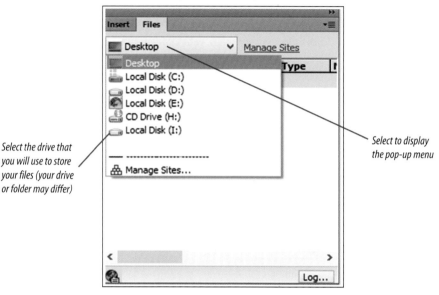

Select the drive that you will use to store your files (your drive or folder may differ)

Select to display the pop-up menu

Understanding IP Addresses and Domain Names

To be accessible over the Internet, a website must be published to a web server with a permanent IP address. An **IP address** is an assigned series of numbers, separated by periods, that designates an address on the Internet. To access a web page, you can enter either an IP address or a domain name in the address text box of your browser window. A **domain name** is a web address that is expressed in letters instead of numbers and usually reflects the name of the business represented by the website. For example, the domain name of the Adobe website is www.adobe.com, but the IP address is 192.150.16.117.

Because domain names use descriptive text instead of numbers, they are easier to remember. Compare an IP address to your Social Security number and a domain name to your name. Both your Social Security number and your name are used to refer to you as a person, but your name is much easier for your friends and family to use than your Social Security number. You can type the IP address or the domain name in the address text box of the browser window to access a website. The domain name is also referred to as a **URL** or Uniform Resource Locator.

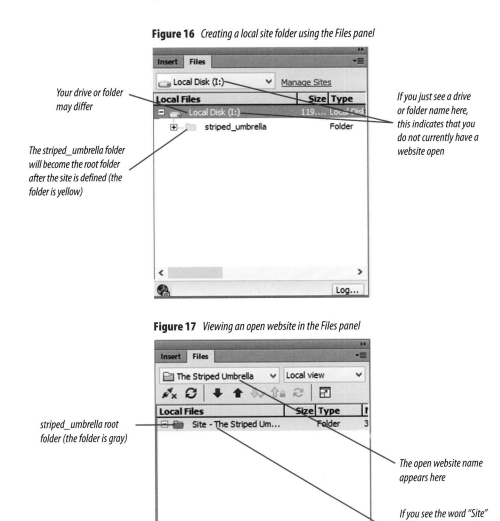

Figure 16 *Creating a local site folder using the Files panel*

Your drive or folder may differ

If you just see a drive or folder name here, this indicates that you do not currently have a website open

The striped_umbrella folder will become the root folder after the site is defined (the folder is yellow)

Figure 17 *Viewing an open website in the Files panel*

striped_umbrella root folder (the folder is gray)

The open website name appears here

If you see the word "Site" here, this indicates that you do have a website open

Create a local site folder

1. Verify that the drive or folder where you want to store your site is selected in the Files panel, right-click (Windows) or control-click (Macintosh) the **drive or folder**, then select **New Folder**.

2. Type **striped_umbrella** to rename the folder, then press **[Enter]**.

   The folder is renamed striped_umbrella, as shown in Figure 16. You have not created a website yet. You have just created the folder that will serve as the local site folder after you set up the site.

   The folder color is currently yellow (Mac users will see blue folders), but after you set up the site in the next section, it will change to gray. Notice the difference between Figure 16 and Figure 17. In Figure 16, you have only created the local site folder, not the website, and the color of the folder is yellow. In Figure 17, The Striped Umbrella website has been created and is open, so the local site folder is gray.

You created a new folder to serve as the local site folder for The Striped Umbrella website.

Set up a website

1. Select **Site** on the Menu bar, then select **New Site**.

2. Select **Site** in the category list in the Site Setup for Unnamed Site dialog box (if necessary), then type **The Striped Umbrella** in the Site name text box.

TIP You can use uppercase letters and spaces in the site name because it is not the name of a folder or a file.

3. Select the **Browse for folder button** 📁 next to the Local Site Folder text box, in the Choose Root folder dialog box, navigate to and select the **drive and folder** where your website files will be stored, then select the **striped_umbrella folder**.

4. Select **Select Folder** (Win) or **Choose** (Mac). See Figure 18.

You created a website and set it up with the name The Striped Umbrella. You then told Dreamweaver the folder name and location to use for the local site folder.

Figure 18 *Site Setup for The Striped Umbrella dialog box*

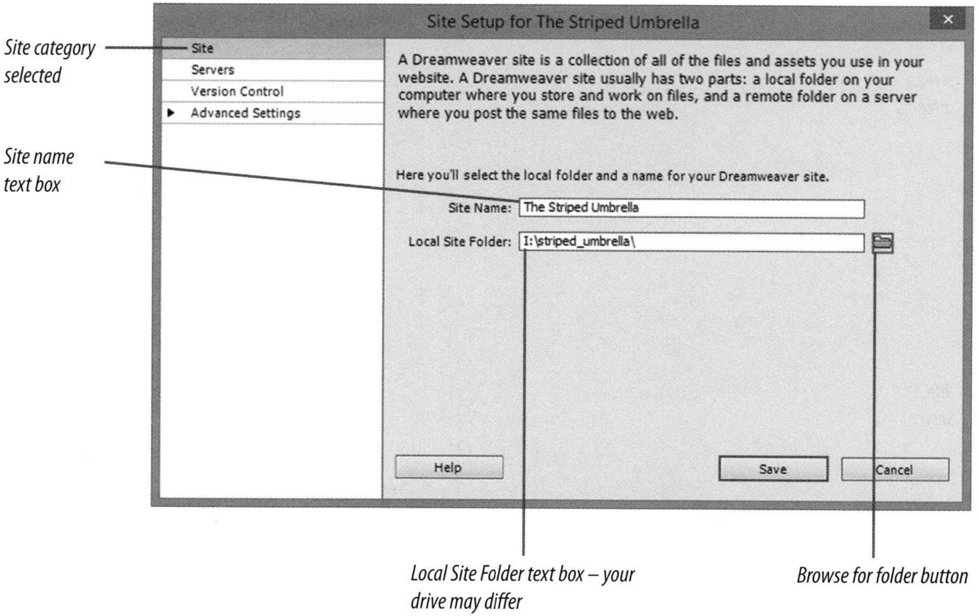

Site category selected

Site name text box

Local Site Folder text box – your drive may differ

Browse for folder button

Understanding the Process of Publishing a Website

Before publishing a website so that web users can access it, you should first create a **local site folder**, also called the **local root folder**, to house all the files for your website, as you did on page 1-23. This folder usually resides on your hard drive. Next, you need to gain access to a remote server. A **remote server** is a web server that hosts websites and is not directly connected to the computer housing the local site. Many Internet Service Providers, or ISPs, provide space for publishing websites on their servers. Once you have access to a remote server, you can then use the Servers category in the Site Setup dialog box to enter information such as the FTP host, host directory, login, and password. After entering this information, you can then use the Put File(s) button in the Files panel to transfer the files to the designated remote server. Once the site is published to a remote server, it is called a **remote site**.

Figure 19 *Adding a server for Remote Access for The Striped Umbrella website*

Servers category

Add new Server icon

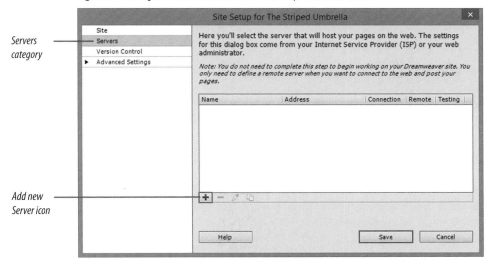

Figure 20 *Entering server information for The Striped Umbrella website*

Enter Server name here

Choices for publishing a website

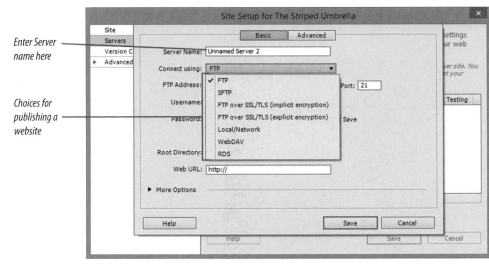

Set up web server access

1. Select **Servers** in the Category list, then select the **Add new Server icon** ✚, as shown in Figure 19.

   TIP If you do not have the information to publish your website, skip step 2 and continue to step 3. You can specify this information later.

2. Select the **Connect using: list arrow**, choose the method you will use to publish your website, as shown in Figure 20, enter any necessary information in the Site Setup for The Striped Umbrella dialog box based on the setting you chose, then select **Save**.

   TIP Your network administrator or web hosting service will give you the necessary information to publish your website.

3. Select **Save** to close the Site Setup dialog box.

You set up the remote access information to prepare you for publishing your website.

Add a Folder
AND PAGES

What You'll Do

In this lesson, you will use the Files panel to create a new folder and new pages for the website.

Adding a Folder to a Website

After setting up a website, you need to create folders to organize the files that will make up the site. Creating a folder called **assets** is a good beginning. There is nothing magic about the word "assets," though. You can name your folder anything that makes sense to you, as long as you follow proper folder naming conventions such as avoiding the use of spaces. You can use the assets folder to store all non-HTML files, such as images or sound files. Many designers name this folder "images" and use additional folders to store other types of supporting files. After you create the assets folder, it is a good idea to set

---

DESIGNTIP

Creating an Effective Navigation Structure

When you create a website, it's important to consider how your users will navigate from page to page within the site. A menu bar, or navigation bar, is a critical tool for moving around a website, so it's important that all text, buttons, and icons used in a menu bar have a consistent look across all pages. If you use a complex menu bar, such as one that incorporates JavaScript, it's a good idea to include plain text links in another location on the page for accessibility. Otherwise, users might become confused or lost within the site.

A navigation structure can include more links than those included in a menu bar, however. For instance, it can contain other sets of links that relate to the content of a specific page and which are placed at the bottom or sides of a page in a different format. No matter which navigation structure you use, make sure that every page includes a link back to the home page. Don't make users rely on the Back button on the browser toolbar to find their way back to the home page. It's possible that the user's current page might have opened as a result of a search and selecting the Back button will then take the user out of the website.

it as the default location to store the website images. This saves a step when you import new images into the website.

Creating the Home Page

The **home page** is the first page that users see when they visit your site. Most websites contain many other pages that all connect back to the home page. The home page filename usually has the name index.html (.htm), or default.html (.htm).

Adding Pages to a Website

Websites might be as simple as one page or might contain hundreds of pages. When you create a multi-page website, you can begin by adding blank pages and saving them in the website folder structure within the local site folder. Once you add and name all the website pages, you can then add text and graphics to each one. This method enables you to set up the navigation structure of the website at the beginning of the development process and view how each page is linked to others. When you are satisfied with the overall structure, you can then add content to each page. This is strictly a personal preference, however; you can also add and link pages as you create them, and that will work fine, too.

You have a choice of several default document types you can generate when you create new HTML pages. The default document type is designated in the Preferences dialog box. HTML5 is the default document type when you install Dreamweaver, but you can change it to any other document type. We will use HTML5 as our standard document type for the files we create in each lesson.

Using the Files Panel for File Management

You should use the Files panel to add, delete, move, or rename files and folders in a website. It is important that you perform these file-maintenance tasks in the Files panel rather than in Windows Explorer (Win) or in the Finder (Mac). Working outside of Dreamweaver, such as in Windows Explorer, can cause linking errors. You cannot take advantage of the simple, yet powerful, Dreamweaver site-management features unless you use the Files panel for all file-management activities. You can use Windows Explorer (Win) or the Finder (Mac) only to create the local site folder or to move or copy the local site folder of a website to another location. If you move or copy the local site folder to a new location, you will have to set up the site again in the Files panel, as you did in Lesson 3 of this chapter.

Setting up a site is not difficult and will become routine for you after you practice a bit. If you are using Dreamweaver on multiple computers, such as in labs or at home, you will have to set up your sites the first time you change to a different computer. Use Creative Cloud to sync your site files when you work with your files on more than one device. See the Creative Cloud introduction at the beginning of this book for more information on syncing.

Add a folder to a website (Windows)

1. Right-click **Site - The Striped Umbrella** in the Files panel, then select **New Folder**.

2. Type **assets** in the folder text box, then press **[Enter]**.

   TIP To rename a folder, select the folder name, pause, click once, when highlighted, type the new name and press [Enter].

3. Compare your screen to Figure 21.

You used the Files panel to create a new folder in the striped_umbrella folder and named it "assets".

Add a folder to a website (Macintosh)

1. Press and hold **[control]**, select the **striped_umbrella folder**, then select **New Folder**.

2. Type **assets** in the new folder name text box, then press **[return]**.

   TIP To rename a folder, select the folder name, pause, click once, when highlighted type the new name and press **[return]**.

3. Compare your screen to Figure 22.

You used the Files panel to create a new folder in the striped_umbrella folder and named it "assets".

Figure 21 *The Striped Umbrella site in Files panel with assets folder created (Windows)*

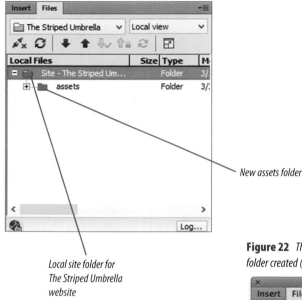

New assets folder

Local site folder for
The Striped Umbrella
website

Figure 22 *The Striped Umbrella site in Files panel with assets folder created (Macintosh)*

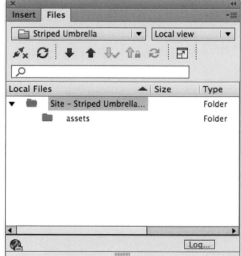

Source: Apple Inc.

Getting Started with Dreamweaver

Figure 23 *Site Setup for The Striped Umbrella dialog box with the assets folder set as the default images folder*

Local Info in the Advanced Settings category

Default Images folder text box

Browse for folder button

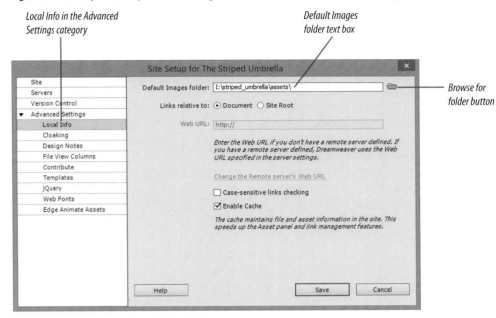

Set the default images folder

1. Select the **Site pop-up menu** in the Files panel, select **Manage Sites**, then select the **Edit the currently selected site button** ✐.

2. Select **Advanced Settings** in the category list in the Site Setup dialog box, then select **Local Info** if necessary.

3. Select the **Browse for folder button** 🗁 next to the Default Images folder text box.

4. If necessary, navigate to your striped_umbrella folder, double-click the **assets folder**, then select the **Select Folder** (Win) or double-click the **assets folder** (Mac).

   Compare your screen to Figure 23.

5. Select **Save**, then select **Done**.

You set the assets folder as the default images folder so that imported images will be automatically saved in it.

Create the home page

1. Open **dw1_2.html** from the drive and folder where you store your Data Files.

2. Select **File** on the Menu bar, select **Save As**, navigate to your striped_umbrella folder, select **dw1_2.html** in the File name text box (Win) or select **dw1_2** in the Save As text box (Mac), then type **index**.

   Mac users should be careful not to remove the .html extension.

3. Select **Save**, then select **No** when asked to update links.

   As shown in Figure 24, the drive where the local site folder is stored, the local site folder name, and the page's filename appear on the title bar (Win), to the right of the document tab. This information is called the path, or location of the open file in relation to other folders in the website.

   The banner image is no longer visible because although you saved the .html file under a new name in the website's local site folder, you have not yet copied the related files into the website's local site folder. The banner image is still linked to the Data Files folder. You will fix this in the next set of steps.

   Two cascading style sheet files and a javascript file are linked to this page to provide the formatting. Since you have not yet copied these files into the local site folder, the page appears with unformatted text. If you select a related file's tab, a warning appears above the Document window telling you that the file is not in the correct folder. You will also fix this in the next set of steps.

   You opened a file, then saved it with the filename index.html.

Figure 24 *index.html saved in the striped_umbrella local site folder*

Banner will not be visible because the path to it is inside one of the cascading style sheets; until it is copied to the site, it will not be visible

Path for file (Win)   Root folder   File renamed index.html

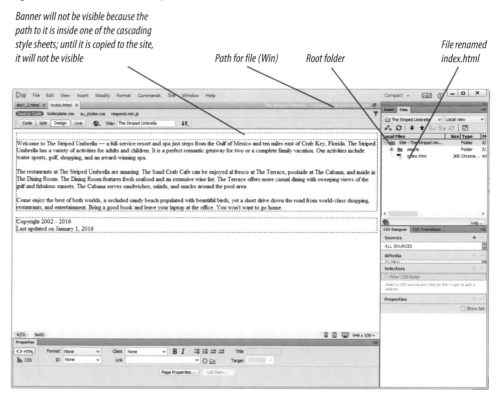

Related and Dependent Files for The Striped Umbrella Website

Files linked to an HTML page, and necessary to make the page display or work correctly, are called **dependent files**. Files that are used as images, background images, videos, etc, are stored in the website and are listed in the Assets panel. Files that are used for styling the content or enabling functions such as Javascript are called **related files**. They are stored in the website and can be opened and edited from the Related files toolbar. Both the terms dependent files and related files are also collectively referred to as supporting files. The supporting files for The Striped Umbrella site are listed in Table 2 on the next page.

Figure 25 *The index page with related files' formatting applied*

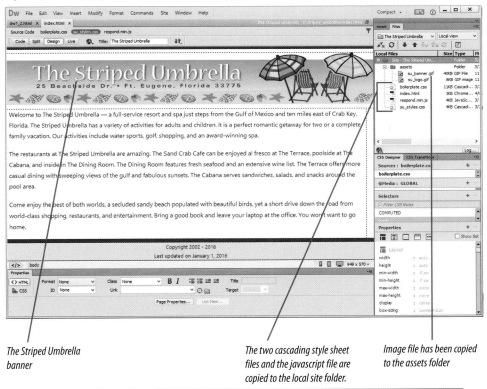

The Striped Umbrella banner

The two cascading style sheet files and the javascript file are copied to the local site folder.

Image file has been copied to the assets folder

TABLE 2: SUPPORTING FILES FOR THE STRIPED UMBRELLA WEBSITE	
File Name	**Function**
su_banner.gif	The image background for the banner
su_logo.gif	The image background for the mobile banner
boilerplate.css	Provides styles for the page; automatically generated
su_styles.css	Provides custom formatting; automatically generated; user assigns name
respond.min.js	Provides code for displaying the page on different sized media; automatically generated

Saving files in the site folder

1. Open your file management program, browse to the chapter_1 data files folder, then select and copy the files **boilerplate.css**, **respond.min.js**, and **su_styles.css** to your striped_umbrella local site folder.

   The index page contains links to these three files. Even though they are listed on the Related files toolbar, until they are copied to the same folder as the index page, they will be broken links and will not work when the site is published.

2. Repeat Step 1 to copy the **su_banner.gif** and **su_logo.gif** file from the Data Files chapter_1/assets folder to the striped_umbrella/assets folder.

   Now that the related files are copied to the website folder, the page formatting is applied, as shown in Figure 25.

3. Return to Dreamweaver, double-click the **assets folder** in the Files panel to expand it if necessary, then notice that all files are now listed in the Files panel.

   Don't concern youself now with the details of how this works. We will learn more about cascading style sheets as we go.

TIP Until you copy all supporting files needed to a website local site folder, the related HTML file will appear without complete formatting.

You copied the linked related files for The Striped Umbrella index page to the local site folder.

Add pages to a website (Windows)

1. Select the **plus sign** to the left of the assets folder (if necessary) to open the folder and view its contents, su_banner.gif and su_logo.gif.

   TIP If you do not see a file listed in the assets folder, select the Refresh button 🔁 on the Files panel toolbar.

2. Right-click The Striped Umbrella **local site folder**, select **New File**, type **about_us** to replace untitled, then press **[Enter]**.

   Each new file is a page in the website. This page does not have page content or a page title yet.

   TIP If you create a new file in the Files panel, use care to make sure the .html file extension is not deleted or that the file does not end up with a double file extension.

3. Repeat Step 2 to add five more blank pages to The Striped Umbrella website, naming the new files **spa.html**, **cafe.html**, **activities.html**, **cruises.html**, and **fishing.html**.

   TIP Make sure you add the new files to the site folder, not the assets folder. If you accidentally add them to the assets folder, just drag them to the site folder.

4. Select the **Refresh button** 🔁 on the Files panel to list the files alphabetically, then compare your screen to Figure 26.

5. Select **File**, **Save**, to save the index.html file, if necessary. Close both open files, select **File** on the Menu bar, then select **Exit**.

   TIP If you are prompted to save changes to the dw1_1.html file, select No.

You added the following six pages to The Striped Umbrella website: about_us, activities, cafe, cruises, fishing, and spa.

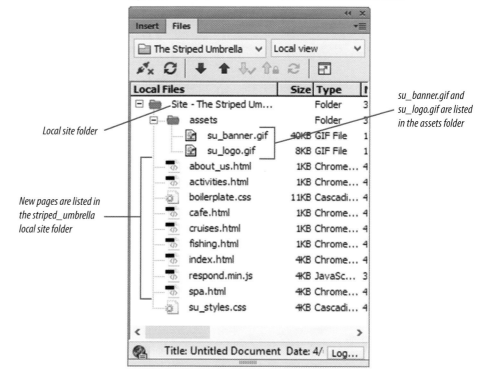

Figure 26 *New pages added to The Striped Umbrella website (Windows)*

Local site folder

su_banner.gif and su_logo.gif are listed in the assets folder

New pages are listed in the striped_umbrella local site folder

---

DESIGNTIP

Adding Page Titles

When you view a web page in a browser, its page title appears in the browser window page tab. (The page title is different from the filename, the name used to save the page on a computer.) The page title reflects the page content and sets the tone for the page. It is especially important to use words in your page title that are likely to match keywords users might enter when using a search engine. Search engines compare the text in page titles to the keywords typed into the search engine. When a page tab displays "Untitled Document," the designer has neglected to give the page a title. This is like giving up free "billboard space" and looks unprofessional. You'll learn more about page titles in Chapter 2.

Figure 27 *New pages added to The Striped Umbrella website (Macintosh)*

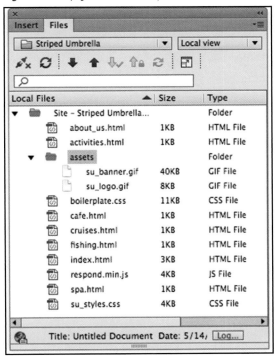

Source: Apple Inc.

POWER USER SHORTCUTS	
To do this:	**Use this shortcut:**
Open a file	[Ctrl][O] (Win) or ⌘ [O] (Mac)
Close a file	[Ctrl][W] (Win) or ⌘ [W] (Mac)
Create a new file	[Ctrl][N] (Win) or ⌘ [N] (Mac)
Save a file	[Ctrl][S] (Win) or ⌘ [S] (Mac)
Get Dreamweaver Help	[F1]
Show/Hide panels	[F4]
Switch between Code view and Design view	[Ctrl][`] (Win) or [command] [`] (Mac)

© 2015 Cengage Learning®

Add pages to a website (Macintosh)

1. Select the **triangle** to the left of the assets folder to open the folder and view its contents.

   TIP If you do not see a file listed in the assets folder, select the Refresh button ↻ on the Files panel.

2. [control]-click the **striped_umbrella local site folder**, select **New File**, type **about_us** to replace untitled, then press **[return]**.

   TIP If you create a new file in the Files panel, use care to make sure the .html file extension is not deleted or that the file does not end up with a double file extension.

3. Repeat Step 2 to add five more blank pages to The Striped Umbrella website, naming the new files **spa.html**, **cafe.html**, **activities.html**, **cruises.html**, and **fishing.html**.

   TIP Make sure to add the new files to the site folder, not the assets folder. If you accidentally add them to the assets folder, just drag them to the site folder.

4. Select the **Refresh button** ↻ to list the files alphabetically, then compare your screen to Figure 27.

5. Select **File**, **Save**, to save the index.html file, then close both open files.

6. Select **Dreamweaver** on the Menu bar, and then select **Quit Dreamweaver**.

   TIP If you are prompted to save changes, select No.

You added six pages to The Striped Umbrella website: about_us, activities, cafe, cruises, fishing, spa.

Explore the Dreamweaver workspace.

1. Start Dreamweaver.
2. Create a new HTML document.
3. Change the view to Code view.
4. Change the view to Code and Design views.
5. Change the view to Design view.
6. Collapse the panels to icons.
7. Expand the panels.
8. Undock the Files panel and float it to the middle of the document window. Dock the Files panel back to its original position.
9. View the Insert panel.
10. Close the page without saving it.

View a web page and use Help.

1. Open the file dw1_3.html from the location where you store your Data Files.
2. Locate the following page elements: a banner, an image, and text.
3. Change the view to Code view.
4. Change the view to Design view.
5. Use the Dreamweaver Online Help command to search for information on docking panels.
6. Display and read one of the topics you find.
7. Close the Learn & Support / Dreamweaver Help window.
8. Close the page without saving it.

Plan and set up a website.

1. Use the Files panel to select the drive and folder where you store your website files.
2. Create a new local site folder in this folder or drive called **blooms**.
3. Create a new site called **Blooms & Bulbs**.
4. Specify the blooms folder as the local site folder.
5. Use the Servers Info category in the Site Setup for Blooms & Bulbs dialog box to set up web server access. (*Hint*: Skip this step if you do not have the necessary information to set up web server access.)
6. Select Save to close the Site Setup dialog box.

Add a folder and pages.

1. Create a new folder in the blooms local site folder called **assets**.
2. Edit the site to set the assets folder as the default location for the website images.
3. Open the file dw1_4.html from where you store your Data Files, save this file in the blooms local site folder as **index.html**, then select No to updating the links.
4. In your file manager, locate the data files bb_styles.css, boilerplate.css, respond.min.js, blooms_banner.jpg, blooms_banner_tablet.jpg, and blooms_logo.jpg.
5. Copy the blooms_banner.jpg, blooms_banner_tablet.jpg, and blooms_logo.jpg files to the website assets folder, then copy the two style sheet files and the javascript file to the website local site folder.
6. Return to the index page and verify that the banner background is displayed and the styles are applied.
7. Create seven new pages in the Files panel, and name them: **plants.html**, **workshops.html**, **newsletter.html**, **annuals.html**, **perennials.html**, **water_plants.html**, and **tips.html**.
8. Refresh the view to list the new files alphabetically, then compare your screen to Figure 28.
9. Close all open pages.

Figure 28 *Completed Skills Review*

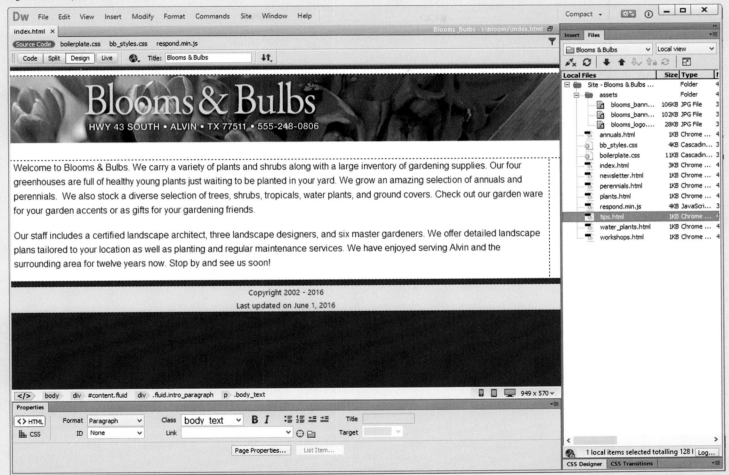

You have been hired to create a website for a travel outfitter called TripSmart. TripSmart specializes in travel products and services. In addition to selling travel products, such as luggage and accessories, they organize trips and offer travel advice. Their clients range from college students to families to vacationing professionals. The owner, Thomas Howard, has requested a dynamic website that conveys the excitement of traveling.

1. Using the information in the preceding paragraph, create a wireframe for this website, using either a pencil and paper or a program such as Microsoft Word. Include the home page with links to four child pages named **catalog.html**, **newsletter.html**, **services.html**, and **tours.html**. Include two child pages under the tours page named **egypt.html** and **argentina.html**.

2. Use either your file manager or the Dreamweaver Files panel to create a new local site folder named **tripsmart** in the drive and folder where you store your website files.

3. Start Dreamweaver, if necessary, then create a site with the name **TripSmart**. Set the tripsmart folder as the local site folder for the site.

4. Create an assets folder and set it as the default location for images.

5. Open the file dw1_5.html from where you store your Data Files, then save it in the tripsmart local site folder as **index.html**. (Remember not to update links.)

6. Locate the following files from your Chapter 1 data files folder: tripsmart_banner.jpg, tripsmart_logo.gif, boilerplate.css, respond.min.js, and tripsmart_styles.css.

7. Copy the two image files to the site assets folder, then copy the two style sheet files and javascript file to the local site folder.

8. Create six additional pages for the site, and name them as follows: **catalog.html**, **newsletter.html**, **services.html**, **tours.html**, **egypt.html**, and **argentina.html**. Use your wireframe and Figure 29 as a guide.

9. Refresh the Files panel.

10. Close all open pages.

Figure 29 *Completed Project Builder 1*

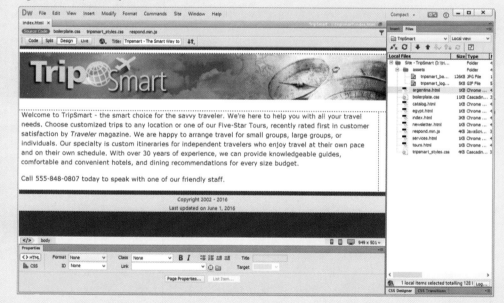

Your company has been selected to design a website for a catering business called Carolyne's Creations. In addition to catering, Carolyne's services include cooking classes and daily specials available as take-out meals. She also has a retail shop that stocks gourmet treats and kitchen items.

1. Create a wireframe for this website that includes a home page and child pages named **shop.html, classes.html, catering.html,** and **recipes.html**.

Create two more child pages under the classes.html page called **children.html** and **adults.html**.

2. Use your file manager or the Dreamweaver Files panel to create new local site folder for the site in the drive and folder where you save your website files, then name it **cc**.

3. Create a website with the name **Carolyne's Creations**, using the cc folder for the local site folder.

4. Create an assets folder for the site and set the assets folder as the default location for images.

5. Open dw1_6.html from the where you store your Data Files then save it as **index.html** in the cc folder.

6. Copy the files cc_banner.jpg, cc_banner_tablet.jpg, and cc_logo.gif from the data files folder to the cc/assets folder.

7. Copy the files boilerplate.css, cc_styles.css, and respond.min.js from the data files folder to the local site folder.

8. Using Figure 30 and your wireframe as guides, create the additional pages shown for the website.

9. Refresh the Files panel to sort the files alphabetically.

10. Close all open pages.

Figure 30 *Completed Project Builder 2*

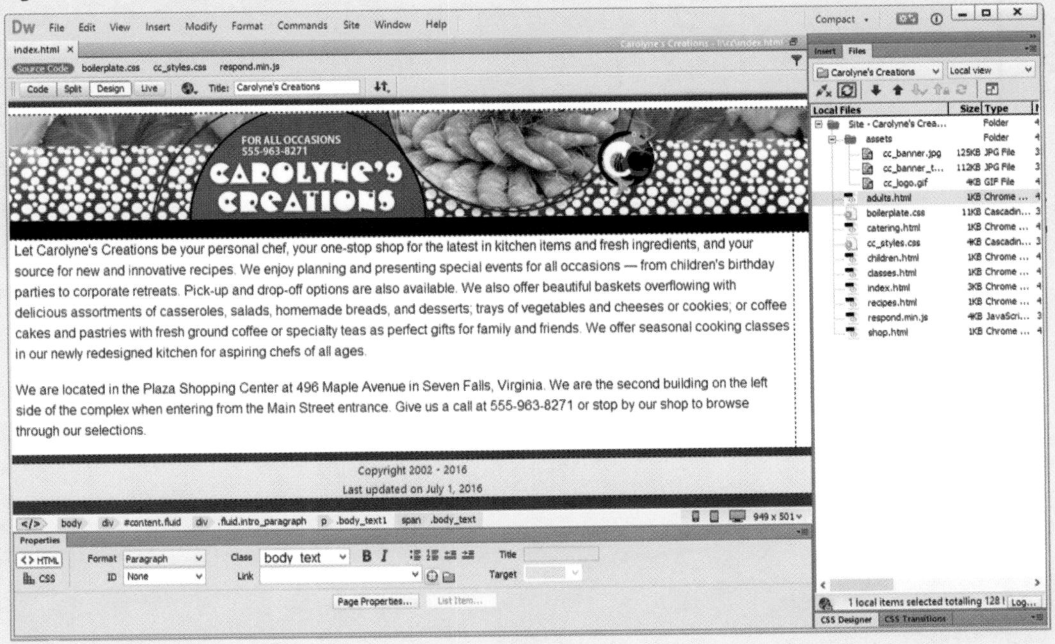

Figure 31 shows the Department of Defense website, a past selection for the Adobe Site of the Day. To visit the current Department of Defense website, connect to the Internet, then go to www.defense.gov. The current page might differ from the figure because dynamic websites are updated frequently to reflect current information. The main navigation structure is under the banner. The page title is United States Department of Defense (defense.gov). You have not yet learned how to create a new page with a Fluid Grid Layout, so you can either create a simple HTML page now and convert it to a Fluid Grid Layout later, or use one of your website index pages as a template.

Go to the Adobe Dreamweaver CC Showcase at www.adobe.com/products/dreamweaver/showcase.html, then visit one of the sites listed. (After you select the PDF associated with a site, you will see a link to the site listed.) Explore the site and answer the following questions:

1. Do you see page titles for each page you visit?
2. Do the page titles accurately reflect the page content?
3. Is the navigation structure clear?
4. How is the navigation structure organized?
5. Why do you think this site was featured?

Figure 31 *Design Project*

Source: *United States Department of Defense*

The Portfolio Project will be an ongoing project throughout the book, in which you will plan and create an original website without any Data Files supplied. The focus of the site can be on any topic, organization, sports team, club, or company that you would like. You will build on this site from chapter to chapter, so you must do each Portfolio Project assignment in each chapter to complete your website. When you finish this book, you should have a completed site that would be an excellent addition to a professional portfolio.

1. Decide what type of site you would like to create. It can be a personal site about you, a business site that promotes a fictitious or real company, or an informational site that provides information about a topic, cause, or organization.
2. Write a list of questions and answers about the site you have decided to create.
3. Create a wireframe for your site to include at least four pages. The wireframe should include the home page with at least three child pages under it.
4. Create a local site folder and an assets folder to house the assets, then set up your site using the local site folder as the website local site folder and the assets folder as the default images folder.
5. Create a blank page named **index.html** as a placeholder for the home page.
6. Begin collecting content, such as pictures or text to use in your website. You can use a digital camera to take photos, use a scanner to scan pictures, or create your own graphics using a program such as Adobe Photoshop, Adobe Edge Animate, or Adobe Fireworks. Gather the content in a central location that will be accessible to you as you develop your site.

CHAPTER 2 DEVELOPING A
WEB PAGE

1. Create head content and set page properties
2. Create, import, and format text
3. Add links to web pages
4. Use the History panel and edit code
5. Modify and test web pages

DEVELOPING A
WEB PAGE

Introduction

The process of developing a web page requires a lot of thought and planning. Besides developing the page content, you also need to write descriptive head content. Head content does not appear on the page but in the HTML code; it contains information search engines use to help users find your website. Next, choose the page background and text colors using style sheets. Then add the page content, style it attractively, and add links to let users navigate between the site pages. Finally, to ensure that all links work correctly and are current, test them regularly. You will learn about each of these processes as you work through this book.

Understanding Page Layout

Before you add content to a page, consider the following guidelines for laying out pages:

Use white space effectively. A room with too much furniture makes it difficult to appreciate the individual pieces. The same is true of a web page. Too many text blocks, links, animations, and images can be distracting. Consider leaving white space on each page. **White space**, which is not necessarily white, is the area on a page with no content.

Limit media elements. Too many media elements, such as images, video clips, or sounds, can result in a page that that looks too cluttered and takes too long to load. Users might leave your site before the entire page finishes loading. Use media elements only if they serve a purpose.

Keep it simple. Often the simplest websites are the most effective and are also the easiest to create and maintain. A simple, well-designed site that works well is far superior to a complex one that contains errors.

Use an intuitive navigation structure. Make sure your site's navigation structure is easy to use. Users should always know where they are in the site and be able to easily find their way back to the home page. If users get "lost," they might leave the site rather than struggle to find their way around.

Apply a consistent theme. To help give your website pages a consistent appearance, consider designing your pages using a common theme. Consistency in the use of colors and fonts, the placement of the navigation links, and the overall page design gives a website a unified look and promotes greater ease of use and accessibility. Style sheets and pre-developed page layouts called **templates** can make this easier.

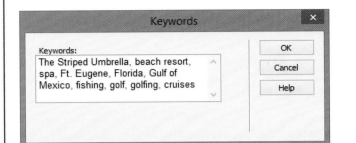

Keywords

Keywords:
The Striped Umbrella, beach resort, spa, Ft. Eugene, Florida, Gulf of Mexico, fishing, golf, golfing, cruises

OK
Cancel
Help

Description

Description:
The Striped Umbrella is a full-service resort and spa just steps from the Gulf of Mexico in Ft. Eugene, Florida.

OK
Cancel
Help

CSS Designer | CSS Transitions

Sources + −

ALL SOURCES
boilerplate.css
su_styles.css

@Media + −

GLOBAL
only screen and (min-width :...
only screen and (min-width :...

Selectors + −

🔍 Filter CSS Rules

img, object, embed, video
.ie6 img
.fluid
.fluidList
.gridContainer
.header_div

Properties + −

☐ Show Set

border-collapse : →|+ +||+
border-spacing : 0 px   0 px

☐ Background
background-color : ☐ ▾ #FFFFFF

background-image

url   Enter file path
gradient 🞩 none

background-position : 0 %   0 %
background-size : auto   auto

background-dip : border-box

background-repeat : ▦▦ ▬▬ ▦ ▪

background-origin : padding-box

Create Head Content and
SET PAGE PROPERTIES

What You'll Do

In this lesson, you will learn how to enter titles, keywords, and descriptions in the head content section of a web page. You will also change the background color for a web page.

Creating the Head Content

A web page is composed of two distinct sections: the head content and the body. The **head content** includes the page title that appears in the title bar of the browser and some important page elements, called meta tags, that are not visible in the browser.

Meta tags are HTML codes that include information about the page, such as keywords and descriptions. Meta tags are read by screen readers for users who have visual impairments. **Keywords** are words that relate to the content of the website. For instance, the words "beach" and "resort" would be appropriate keywords for The Striped Umbrella website. A **description** is a short paragraph that describes the content and features of the website. Search engines find web pages by matching the title, keywords, and description in the head content of web pages with keywords that users enter in search engine text boxes. Therefore, it is important to include concise, useful information in the head content. The **body** is the part of the page that appears in a browser window. It contains all the page content that is visible to users, such as text, images, and links.

QUICK TIP

Don't confuse page titles with filenames, the names used to store files on the server.

Setting Web Page Properties

When you create a web page, begin by choosing properties that control the way the page appears in a browser, such as the **background color**, the color that fills the entire page. The background color should complement the colors used for text, links, and images on the page. You can also use a background image to fill an entire page or a section of a page, called a CSS layout block. A **CSS layout block** is a section of a web page that is defined and formatted using a Cascading Style Sheet, a set of formatting characteristics you can apply to text, links, and other page elements. For example, the best way to set a page background color is to modify the background-color code in a style sheet. You will learn more about CSS as you work through each chapter. If you use the Page Properties dialog box to set page properties such as the background color, Dreamweaver automatically creates a style that modifies the HTML tag to include the properties you added.

A strong contrast between the text color and the background color makes it easier for users to read your text. One of the Web Content Accessibility Guidelines (WCAG), Version 2.0, from the World Wide Web Consortium (W3C) states that contrast makes it easier for users to see content. You can choose a light background color with dark text, or a dark background color with light text. A white background with dark text, though not terribly exciting, provides good contrast and is easiest for most users to read.

Another design decision you need to make is whether to change the **default font** and **default link colors**, which are the colors used by the browser to display text, links, and visited links. The default color for **unvisited links**, or links that the user has not clicked yet, is blue. Unvisited links are usually simply called **links**. The default color for **visited links**, or links that have been previously clicked, is purple. You change the text and link colors in the CSS Designer panel. You can choose colors from the color picker, as shown in Figure 1.

Choosing Colors to Convey Information

Before 1994, colors appeared differently on different types of computers. In 1994, Netscape developed the first web-safe color palette, a set of colors that appears consistently in all browsers and on Macintosh, Windows, and UNIX platforms. The evolution of video cards has made this less relevant today, but use of appropriate colors is an important factor in creating accessible pages. Be sure

to use only colors that provide good contrast on your pages. Dreamweaver lets you choose from three color notation schemes: RGBa, HEX, and HSLa. You can use any of the three notations to name a color. You will use HEX values to specify your color choices in the exercises in this book. You select colors using the color picker, shown in Figure 1. You can also type color values directly in your style sheet code in Code view.

Another WCAG guideline states that color should never be the only visual means of conveying information. For example, don't refer to a page object solely by the color, like the "red" box.

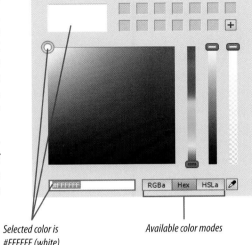

Figure 1 *Color picker showing color modes*

Selected color is #FFFFFF (white)

Available color modes

Edit a page title

1. Start Dreamweaver, select the **Site list arrow** on the Files panel, then select **The Striped Umbrella** if necessary.

2. Double-click **index.html** in the Files panel to open The Striped Umbrella home page.

   The page title The Striped Umbrella appears in the Title text box in the Document toolbar.

3. Click after the end of The Striped Umbrella text in the Title text box in the Document toolbar, press **[Spacebar]**, type **beach resort and spa, Ft. Eugene, Florida,** press **[Enter]** (Win) or **[return]** (Mac), then click in the title text box.

   Compare your screen with Figure 2. The new title is better, because it incorporates the words "beach resort" and "spa" and the location of the resort—words that potential customers might use as keywords when using a search engine.

TIP To view hidden text in the Title box, click in the title and scroll using the left and right keyboard arrow keys.

You opened The Striped Umbrella website, opened the home page, and changed the page title.

Figure 2 *The new title appears in the Title text box*

Click in the title and scroll with an arrow key to see the rest of the title

Designing Appropriate Content for Your Target Audience

When you begin developing the content for your website, you need to decide what content to include and how to arrange each element on each page. Design the content with the target audience in mind. What is the age group of your audience? What reading level is appropriate? Should you use a formal or informal tone? Should the pages be simple, consisting mostly of text, or rich with images and media files? Evaluate the font sizes, the number and size of images and animations, the reading level, and the amount of technical expertise necessary to navigate your site, and make sure they fit your audience. Usually, the first page that your audience will see when they visit your site is the home page. Design the home page so that users will understand your site's purpose and feel comfortable finding their way around your site's pages.

To ensure that users do not get "lost" in your site, design all the pages with a consistent look and feel. You can use templates and Cascading Style Sheets to maintain a common look for each page. **Templates** are web pages that contain the basic layout for each page in the site, such as the location of a company logo or a menu of buttons.

Figure 3 *Insert panel displaying the Common category*

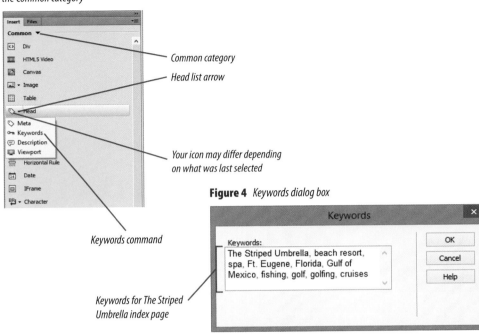

Common category

Head list arrow

Your icon may differ depending on what was last selected

Keywords command

Keywords for The Striped Umbrella index page

Figure 4 *Keywords dialog box*

Enter keywords

1. Select the **Insert panel list arrow**, then on the dropdown menu, select the **Common category** (if it is not already selected).

2. Select the **Head list arrow**, as shown in Figure 3, then select **Keywords**.

TIP Some buttons on the Insert panel include a list arrow indicating that there is a menu of choices available. The button that you selected last will appear on the Insert panel until you select another.

3. Type **The Striped Umbrella**, **beach resort**, **spa**, **Ft. Eugene**, **Florida**, **Gulf of Mexico**, **fishing**, **golf**, **golfing**, **cruises** in the Keywords text box, as shown in Figure 4, then select **OK**.

You added keywords relating to the resort to the head content of The Striped Umbrella home page.

Enter a description

1. Select the **Head list arrow** on the Insert panel, then select **Description**.

2. In the Description text box, type **The Striped Umbrella is a full-service resort and spa just steps from the Gulf of Mexico in Ft. Eugene, Florida**.

   Your screen should resemble Figure 5.

3. Select **OK**.

4. Select the **Show Code view button** `Code` on the Document toolbar, then click on the page to deselect the text, if necessary.

   The title, keywords, and description tags appear in the HTML code in the document window, as shown in Figure 6. The code in Figure 6 has been collapsed between lines 10 and 27 to display the title, keywords, and description tags. Your line numbers may differ, but should all fall between the <head> tags.

TIP You can enter and edit the title tag and the meta tags directly in the code in Code view.

5. Click the **Show Design view button** `Design` to return to Design view.

You added a description of The Striped Umbrella resort to the head content of the home page. You then viewed the page in Code view and located the head content in the HTML code.

Figure 5 *Description dialog box*

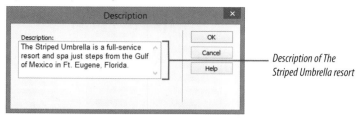

Description of The
Striped Umbrella resort

Figure 6 *Head content displayed in Code view*

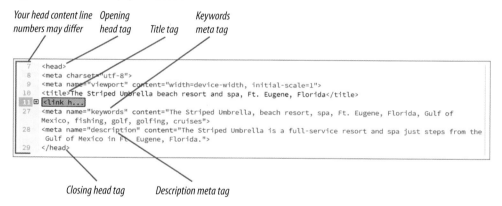

Your head content line numbers may differ   Opening head tag   Title tag   Keywords meta tag

Closing head tag   Description meta tag

Using Descriptions for POWDER Authentication

A website description can be stored in an XML file to provide POWDER authentication. **XML** stands for Extensible Markup Language, a type of file that is used to develop customized tags to store information. **POWDER** is the acronym for **Protocol for Web Description Resources**. This is an evaluation system for web pages developed with the World Wide Web Consortium (W3C) that provides summary information about a website. Examples include the date the site was created, the name of the person or company responsible for the content on the site, and a description of the content. It is designed to help users determine if a site would be considered a trustworthy resource of value and interest. It replaces the previous system called PICS, or Platform for Internet Content Selection.

Figure 7 *Resizing the CSS Designer panel*

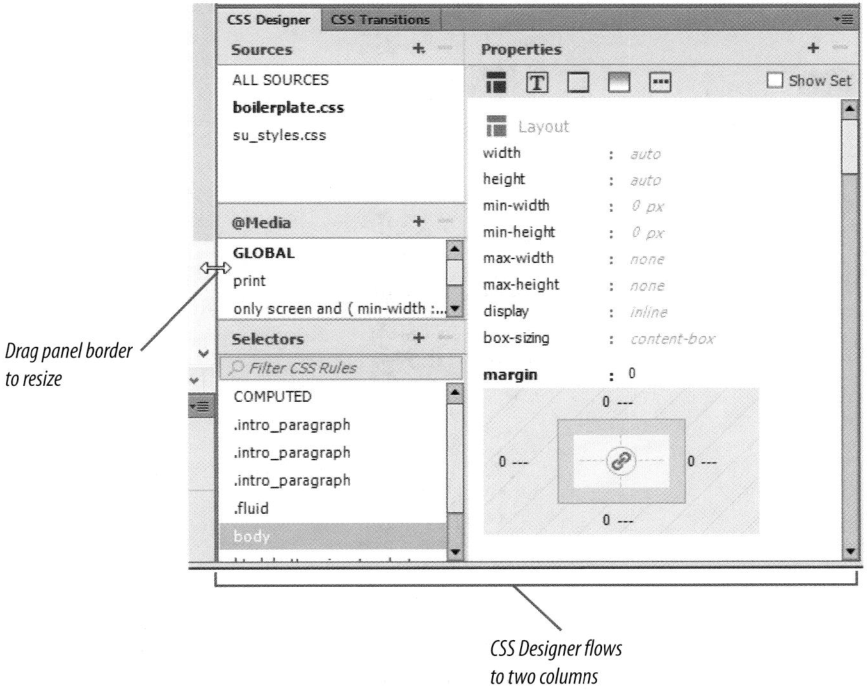

Drag panel border to resize

CSS Designer flows to two columns

Expand the CSS Designer panel

1. Place the pointer over the CSS Designer panel group title bar, then drag it to the Document window to float it.

2. Place your pointer over the left side of the panels, then drag to increase the width of the panels until the CSS Designer panel flows into two columns, as shown in Figure 7.

   It is much easier to use CSS Designer if you spread it over a two-column layout. There will be no instructions in this book to dock the CSS Designer, but you may keep it docked if you prefer.

   TIP Resize any docked panels in Dreamweaver by dragging a left panel border to the right or left to decrease or increase the width of the panels.

3. Select the Files panel tab if necessary, then notice that with the CSS Designer panel floated, the Files panel can show all of the website files without scrolling.

   The Insert panel also has room to show all commands without scrolling.

   (continued)

Understanding CSS Designer

The new CSS Designer panel lets you create and set properties for styles used to position and format page content across a website. Depending on the size of the Dreamweaver program and Document windows, CSS Designer will appear in one or two columns. The two-column layout is easier to use. The CSS Designer panel is divided into four panes: Sources, @Media, Selectors, and Properties. The Sources pane lists the style sheet files used to format the website pages. The @Media pane lists the device categories that could be used to view the pages, such as mobile and tablet sizes. The Selectors pane lists the selectors that are included in the style sheet highlighted in the Sources pane and @Media pane. The Properties pane lists the properties of the highlighted selector in the Selectors pane.

---

4. Select **su_styles.css** in the Sources pane, then select **.fluid** in the Selectors pane.

   The Properties pane now displays the properties and values for the .fluid style. The .fluid style is used to position and format the page content, including the page background.

5. Scroll down the Properties pane in the right column until you see the Background category, then select the **Set background color box** next to the background-color property, as shown in Figure 8.

   The color picker opens, as shown in Figure 9, and you see that the current background color is white. The color value for white is shown as a hexadecimal: #FFFFFF.

   (continued)

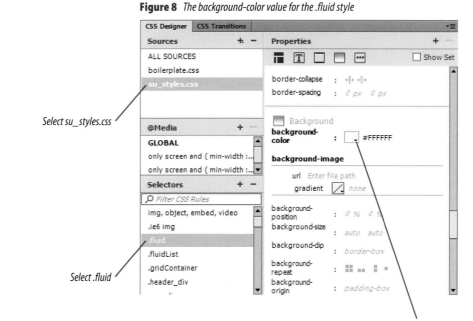

Figure 8 *The background-color value for the .fluid style*

Select su_styles.css

Select .fluid

Select the background-color box

Understanding Hexadecimal Values

Each color is assigned a **hexadecimal RGB value**, a value that represents the amount of red, green, and blue present in the color. For example, white, which is made of equal parts of red, green, and blue, has a hexadecimal value of FFFFFF. This is also called an RGB triplet in hexadecimal format (or a **hex triplet**). Each pair of characters in the hexadecimal value represents the red, green, and blue values. The hexadecimal number system is based on 16, rather than 10 in the decimal number system. Because the hexadecimal number system includes only numbers up to 9, values after 9 use the letters of the alphabet. "A" represents the number 10 in the hexadecimal number system. "F" represents the number 15. The hexadecimal values can be entered in the code using a form of shorthand that shortens the six characters to three characters when the color is represented by three repeating numbers. For instance: FFFFFF become FFF; 0066CC becomes 06C. The number value for a color is preceded by a pound sign (#) in HTML code.

Figure 9 *The color picker*

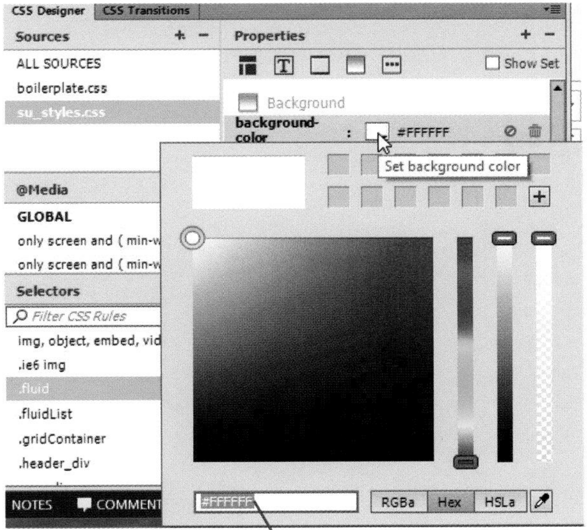

Current background
color is #FFFFFF

Figure 10 *Reverting to the original color using the color picker*

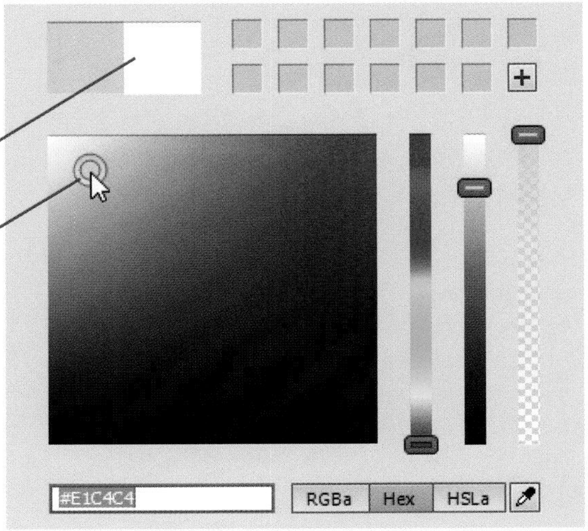

Revert to the original
color box

Use the pointer to
select a new color

6. Select a different color in the color picker, then click in the Document window to close the color picker.

   The page background changes to the new color you selected.

7. Select the **Set background color box** again, then type **#FFFFFF** in the Color value text box.

   The page background changes back to white.

TIP You can also use the Revert to the original color box, as shown in Figure 10, to change a color back to the original color as long as you do not close the color picker after you select the new color.

8. Click in the Design view window to close the color picker.

9. Select **boilerplate.css** in the CSS Designer Source pane, select **GLOBAL** in the @Media pane, then select **body** in the Selectors pane.

10. Select the **background-color property** in the Properties pane, select the **Remove CSS Property button** 🗑, select **File** on the Menu bar, then select **Save All** to save your work.

   Removing this property will allow the .fluid selector's white page background property to format the background.

TIP When making changes to related files, such as a style sheet, use the File, Save All command to be sure all files that may have been changed are saved.

You edited the .fluid selector in the su_styles.css file to add a white page background, then removed the page property in the boilerplate.css file to prevent a potential style conflict.

Create, Import,
AND FORMAT TEXT

What You'll Do

In this lesson, you will create a new page to replace the blank spa page, enter and format text, import text, set text properties, and check the spelling on the Striped Umbrella home page.

Creating and Importing Text

Most information in web pages is presented in the form of text. You can type text directly on a page in Dreamweaver, import, or copy and paste it from another software program. (Macintosh users do not have the option to import text. They must open a text file, copy the text, then paste it into an HTML document.) When using a Windows computer to import text from a Microsoft Word file, it's best to use the Import Word Document command. Not only will the formatting be preserved, but Dreamweaver will generate clean HTML code. **Clean HTML code** is code that does what it is supposed to do without using unnecessary instructions, which take up memory.

When you format text, it is important to keep in mind that your site users must have the same fonts installed on their computers as the fonts you use. Otherwise, the text might appear incorrectly. To avoid font compatibility and accessibly issues, you can use TypeKit, a company acquired by Adobe in 2011, that provides access to web fonts through the Adobe Creative Cloud. TypeKit offers fonts called Adobe Edge Web fonts through a subscription-based service that can be read correctly by all browsers and devices. TypeKit

is part of your Creative Cloud subscription. Creative Cloud users have access to most of the fonts on TypeKit at no additional charge.

> **QUICK TIP**
>
> To learn more about TypeKit, go to typekit.com.

If text does not have a font specified, the default font on the user's computer will be used to display the text. Keep in mind that some fonts might not appear the same on both a Windows and a Macintosh computer. The way fonts are **rendered** (drawn) on the screen differs because Windows and Macintosh computers use different technologies to render them. If you are not using embedded fonts, it is wise to stick to the standard fonts that work well with both systems. Test your pages using both operating systems.

Formatting Text Two Ways: HTML vs. CSS

Because text is more difficult and tiring to read on a computer screen than on a printed page, you should make the text in your website attractive and easy to read. One way to do this is to format text by changing its font, size, and color. Previously web designers used the Property inspector to apply formatting attributes, such as font type, size, color, alignment, and indents. This created HTML tags in the code that directed the way the fonts would appear in a browser. **Tags** are the parts of the code that specify the appearance for all page content when viewed in a browser.

Today, the accepted method is to create Cascading Style Sheets (CSS) to format and place web page elements. **Cascading Style Sheets** are sets of formatting attributes that you use to format web pages to provide a consistent presentation for content across the site. Cascading Style Sheets make it easy to separate page content from the page design. The content is placed in the body section on web pages, and the styles are placed in either an external style sheet file or in the page head content. Separating content from design is preferable because editing content and formatting content are two separate tasks. So when you use CSS styles, you can update or change the page content without disturbing the page formatting.

You can apply some formatting without creating styles by using the Bold and Italic HTML tags. You can also use HTML heading tags, which determine the relative size and boldness of text, and which help to show the importance of text relative to the rest of the text on the page.

To apply CSS or HTML formatting, you use the Property inspector, which has a panel for each method: the CSS Property inspector and the HTML Property inspector. You display them by clicking the CSS or the HTML button on the left side of the Property inspector. Some coding options are unique to each one and some are available on both. For instance, HTML heading tags are only available on

the HTML Property inspector. Font tags are only available on the CSS Property inspector. Regardless of which Property inspector you use, CSS styles will be created when you format page objects.

Because CSS is a lot to learn when you are just beginning, we are going to begin by using a few HTML tags for formatting. Then in Chapter 3, we will use the preferred method, CSS.

Changing Fonts

You can format your text with different fonts by choosing a font combination from the Font list in the CSS Property inspector. A **Font-combination** is a set of font choices that specify which fonts a browser should use to display the text on your web page. Font combinations ensure that if one font is not available, the browser will use the next one specified in the font combination. For example, if text is formatted with the font combination Arial, Helvetica, sans serif, the browser will first look on the user's system for Arial. If Arial is not available, then it will look for Helvetica. If Helvetica is not available, then it will look for a sans-serif font to apply to the text. Using fonts within the default settings is wise, because fonts set outside the default settings might not be available on all users' computers. Remember that TypeKit has greatly expanded your font choices with the ability to embed new fonts into web pages.

Changing Font Sizes

There are two ways to change the size of text using the Property inspector. When the CSS option is selected, you can select a numerical value for the size from 9 to 36 pixels (or type a smaller or larger number). Or you can use a size expressed in words from xx-small to larger, which sets the size of selected text relative to other text on the page. Font sizes are not available on the HTML Property inspector.

Formatting Paragraphs

The HTML Property inspector lets you format blocks of text as paragraphs or as different sizes of headings. To format a paragraph as a heading, click anywhere in the paragraph, and then select the heading size you want from the Format list in the HTML Property inspector. The Format list contains six different heading formats. Heading 1 is the largest size, and Heading 6 is the smallest size. Browsers display text formatted as headings in bold, setting them off from paragraphs of text. It is considered good practice to use headings because they give users an idea of the importance of the heading relative to other text on the page. Text with a level 1 heading would be at a higher importance level than text with a level 2 heading. You can also align paragraphs with the alignment buttons on the CSS Property inspector and indent paragraphs using the Blockquote and Remove Blockquote buttons on the HTML Property inspector. It is better practice, however, to use styles to align text.

Enter text

1. Position the insertion point directly after "want to go home." at the end of the paragraph, press **[Enter]** (Win) or **[return]** (Mac), then type **The Striped Umbrella**.

Pressing [Enter] (Win) or [return] (Mac) creates a new paragraph.

TIP If the new text does not assume the formatting attributes as the paragraph above it, click the Show Code and Design views button Split , position the insertion point right after the period after "home", then go back to the page in Design view and insert a new paragraph.

2. Press and hold **[Shift]**, press **[Enter]** (Win) or **[return]** (Mac), then type **25 Beachside Drive**.

Pressing and holding [Shift] while you press [Enter] (Win) or [return] (Mac) creates a line break. A **line break** places a new line of text on the next line down without creating a new paragraph. Line breaks are useful when you want to add a new line of text directly below the current line of text and keep the same formatting.

3. Add the following text below the 25 Beachside Drive text, using line breaks after each line:

Ft. Eugene, Florida 33775

555-594-9458

4. Compare your screen with Figure 11. Your lines may wrap differently depending on your Document window size.

You entered text for the address and telephone number on the home page.

Figure 11 *Entering the address and telephone number on The Striped Umbrella home page*

Come enjoy the best of both worlds, a secluded sandy beach populated with beautiful birds, yet a short drive down the road from world-class shopping, restaurants, and entertainment. Bring a good book and leave your laptop at the office. You won't want to go home.

Pressing [Enter] (Win) or [return] (Mac) creates a new paragraph

The Striped Umbrella
25 Beachside Drive
Ft. Eugene, Florida 33775
555-594-9458

Single-spaced lines created by using line breaks

TABLE 1: HTML FORMATTING TAGS	
HTML tag	**Represents**
<p> </p>	Opening and closing paragraph tag
 	Line break tag (does not require a closing tag)
<em> </em>	Opening and closing italic (emphasis) tag
<strong> </strong>	Opening and closing bold tag
<u> </u>	Opening and closing underline tag

© 2015 Cengage Learning®

Using Keyboard Shortcuts

When working with text, the keyboard shortcuts for Cut, Copy, and Paste are useful. These are [Ctrl][X] (Win) or ⌘ [X] (Mac) for Cut, [Ctrl][C] (Win) or ⌘ [C] (Mac) for Copy, and [Ctrl][V] (Win) or ⌘ [V] (Mac) for Paste. You can view all Dreamweaver keyboard shortcuts using the Keyboard Shortcuts dialog box, which lets you view existing shortcuts for menu commands, tools, or miscellaneous functions, such as copying HTML or inserting an image. You can also create your own shortcuts or assign shortcuts that you are familiar with from using them in other software programs. To view or modify keyboard shortcuts, select the Keyboard Shortcuts command on the Edit menu (Win) or Dreamweaver menu (Mac), then select the shortcut key set you want. Each chapter in this book includes Power User shortcuts, a list of keyboard shortcuts relevant to that chapter.

Figure 12 *Formatting the address on The Striped Umbrella home page*

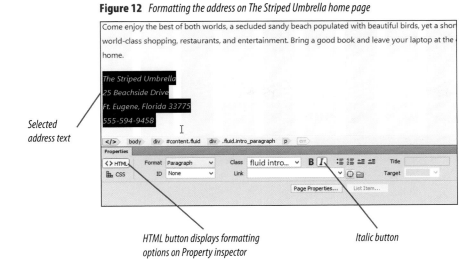

Selected address text

HTML button displays formatting options on Property inspector

Italic button

Figure 13 *Viewing the HTML code for the address and phone number*

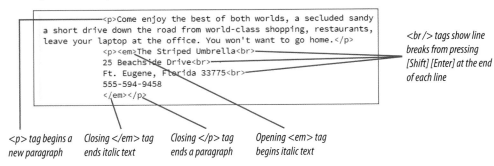

 tags show line breaks from pressing [Shift] [Enter] at the end of each line

<p> tag begins a new paragraph

Closing </em> tag ends italic text

Closing </p> tag ends a paragraph

Opening <em> tag begins italic text

Format text

1. Select the entire address and telephone number, then select the **HTML button** ⟨⟩ HTML in the Property inspector (if it is not already selected) to change to the HTML Property inspector, as shown in Figure 12.

2. Select the **Italic button** *I* in the Property inspector to italicize the text, then click after the text to deselect it.

3. Select the **Show Code view button** Code to view the HTML code, as shown in Figure 13.

   It is always helpful to learn what the HTML code means. Refer to Table 1 to locate some basic HTML formatting tags. As you edit and format your pages, read the code to see how it appears for each element. The more familiar you are with the code, the more comfortable you will feel with Dreamweaver and web design. A strong knowledge of HTML is a necessary skill for professional web designers.

4. Select the **Show Design view button** Design to return to Design view.

5. Save your work.

You changed the Property inspector options from CSS to HTML, then formatted the address and phone number for The Striped Umbrella by changing the font style to italic.

Add an image to a new page

1. Select **File** on the Menu bar, select **Save As**, then type **spa** in the File name text box.

2. Select **Save**, then select **Yes** (Win) or **Replace** (Mac) to overwrite the existing blank spa page.

   The new spa page is identical to the index page. You will replace the content from the index page with content for the spa page. Meanwhile, the formatting will remain identical to give a consistent look between these two pages.

3. Close the index page, select all of the text on the spa page except the address lines, phone number, and footer, then delete it. See Figure 14.

4. Place the insertion point in front of the first address line, select the **Insert panel menu**, select **Common** if necessary, select the **Image list arrow**, then click **Image**.

5. Browse to and open the Chapter 2 data files assets folder, select **sea_spa_logo.png**, select **OK** (Win) or **Open** (Mac), then verify that sea_spa_logo.png has been copied to the assets folder in the Files panel.

   The logo appears on the page, as shown in Figure 15.

   TIP You can also drag an image from the Files panel onto the page if it is already saved in the local site folder.

6. With the logo selected, type **The Sea Spa logo** in the Alt text box on the Property inspector, as shown in Figure 15.

   You will learn more about accessibility attributes for images in Chapter 4.

   (continued)

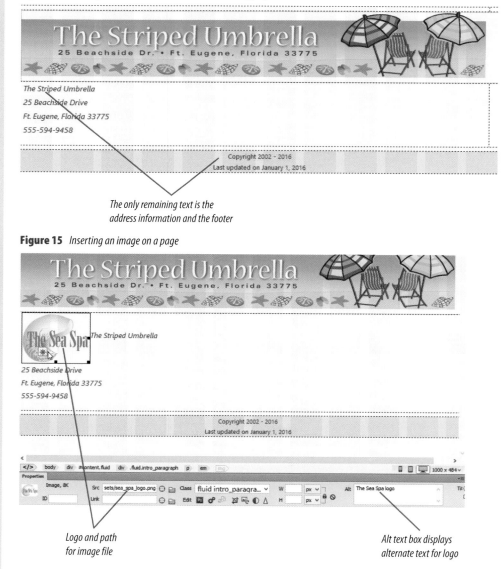

Figure 14 *Creating a new HTML document from an existing page*

The only remaining text is the
address information and the footer

Figure 15 *Inserting an image on a page*

Logo and path
for image file

Alt text box displays
alternate text for logo

Figure 16 *Image file added to the Striped Umbrella assets folder*

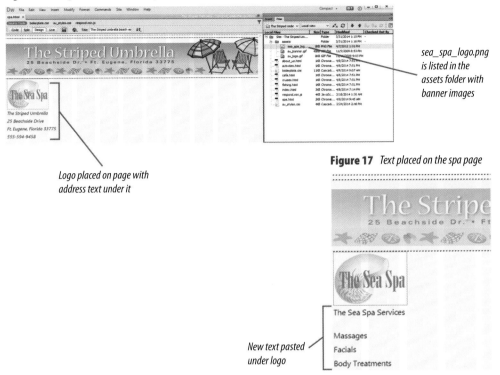

sea_spa_logo.png is listed in the assets folder with banner images

Logo placed on page with address text under it

Figure 17 *Text placed on the spa page*

New text pasted under logo

The Sea Spa Services

Massages
Facials
Body Treatments

7. Click to place the insertion point to the immediate right of the logo image, press **[Enter]** (Win) or **[Return]** (Mac) to force the text under the image, if necessary, then save your work.

A copy of the sea_spa_logo.png file appears in the assets folder, along with the banner images, as shown in Figure 16.

You created a new file from the index page file to replace the blank spa file, then deleted existing text and inserted the spa logo under the banner image, which automatically saved it in the site assets folder.

Copy and paste text

1. Open your file management program, navigate to the **chapter_2 folder** from the location where you store your Data Files, then open the file **spa.txt**.

Notepad (Win) or TextEdit (Mac) opens to display the text file.

2. Select all of the text, copy it, then close Notepad (Win) or TextEdit (Mac).

3. Return to Dreamweaver, click to place the insertion point to the right of the spa logo, then press **[Enter]** (Win) or **[return]** (Mac) to create a paragraph break.

4. Select **Edit** on the Menu bar, then select **Paste**.

The text is pasted under the spa logo, as shown in Figure 17.

You copied text and pasted it on the spa page.

Choosing Filenames for Web Pages

When you choose a name for a web page, you should use a short, simple descriptive name that reflects the contents of the page. For example, if the page is about your company's products, you could name it products.html. You should also follow some general rules for naming web pages, such as naming the home page index.html. Most file servers look for the file named index.html or default.html to use as the initial page for a website. Do not use spaces, special characters, or punctuation in filenames for files or folders that you will use in your site. Use underscores rather than spaces for readability; for example: use sea_spa_logo.png rather than sea spa logo.png. Just to be totally safe for all file servers, use only letters, numbers, or underscores in file or folder names. Many designers also avoid the use of uppercase letters.

Set text properties

1. Scroll up the page and select the text **The Sea Spa Services**.

2. Select the **Format list arrow** in the HTML Property inspector, then select **Heading 1**.

   The Heading 1 format is applied to the paragraph. Even a single word is considered a paragraph if there is a paragraph break (also known as a hard return) after it. The HTML code for a Heading 1 tag is <h1>. The tag is then closed with </h1>. For headings, the level of the heading tag follows the h, so the code for a Heading 2 tag is <h2>.

3. Select the text **Massages**, **Facials**, and **Body Treatments**, select the **Format list arrow** in the HTML Property inspector, select **Heading 2**, then click outside the heading to deselect the text.

   The H1 and H2 tags make the text a little large for the page, but it is more in keeping with semantic markup to begin with level 1 headings and work down. **Semantic markup** means coding to emphasize meaning. You can change the size of the text for each heading using style sheets if you want to change the default settings. We will do this in Chapter 3.

4. Click after the word "Treatments", if necessary, select the **Show Code and Design views button** Split on the Document toolbar, then compare your screen to Figure 18.

   The word "Massages" after the words "Body Treatments" may be in a different position on your screen. Figure 18 was sized down, so your page will be wider than the figure shows.

   (continued)

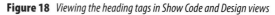

Figure 18 *Viewing the heading tags in Show Code and Design views*

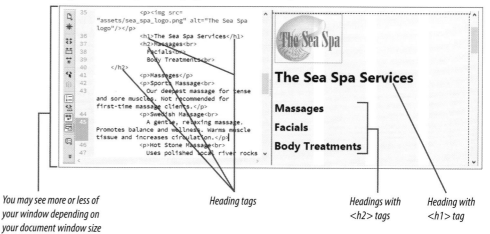

You may see more or less of your window depending on your document window size

Heading tags

Headings with <h2> tags

Heading with <h1> tag

Importing and Linking Microsoft Office Documents (Windows)

Adobe makes it easy to transfer data between Microsoft Office documents and Dreamweaver web pages. When importing a Word or Excel document, select File on the Menu bar, point to Import, then select either Word Document or Excel Document. Select the file you want to import, then select the Formatting list arrow to choose among importing Text only; Text with structure (paragraphs, lists, and tables); Text, structure, basic formatting (bold, italic); or Text, structure, full formatting (bold, italic, styles) before you select Open. The option you choose depends on the importance of the original structure and formatting. Always use the Clean Up Word HTML command from the Commands menu after importing a Word file.

You can also create a link to a Word or Excel document on your web page. To do so, browse to locate the Word or Excel document you want to add as a link, then drag the file name to the location on the page where you would like the link to appear. (If the document is located outside the site, you can browse for it using the Site list arrow on the Files panel, File Explorer, or Mac Finder.) Next, select the Create a link option button in the Insert Document dialog box, then save the file in your site root folder so it will be uploaded when you publish your site. If it is not uploaded, the link will be broken.

Figure 19 *Check Spelling dialog box*

Check Spelling ×

Word not found in dictionary:

masage.   Add to Personal

Change to: massage.

Suggestions: massage.   Ignore
              manage.
              ma-sage.   Change ——— *Select "Change" to*
              mas-age.   *correct spelling*
              mas age.   Ignore All
              ma sage.
              sage.   Change All

                              Close   Help

Checking for Spelling Errors

It is important to check for spelling and grammatical errors before publishing a page. A page that is published with errors will likely cause the user to judge the site as unprofessional and carelessly made, and to question the accuracy of the page content. If you have text in a word processing file that you plan to import into Dreamweaver, check the spelling in the word processor first. Then check the spelling in the imported text again in Dreamweaver. This allows you to add words such as proper names to the Dreamweaver dictionary so the program will not flag them again. Select the Add to Personal button in the Check Spelling dialog box to add a new word to the dictionary. Even though you might have checked a page using the Check Spelling feature, you still must proofread the content yourself to catch usage errors such as misuse of "to," "too," and "two."

TIP If your <h1> tag is before the image tag rather than before "The Sea Spa Services" heading, cut and paste it to match the code in Figure 18.

You applied two heading formats, then viewed the HTML code.

Check spelling

1. Select the **Show Design view button** `Design` to return to Design view.

2. Place the insertion point in front of the text "The Sea Spa Services".

   It is a good idea to start a spelling check at the top of the document because Dreamweaver searches from the insertion point down. If your insertion point is in the middle of the document, you will receive a message asking if you want to check the rest of the document. Starting from the beginning saves time.

3. Select **Commands** on the Menu bar, then select **Check Spelling**.

   The word "masage" is highlighted on the page as a misspelled word and suggestions are listed to correct it in the Check Spelling dialog box, as shown in Figure 19.

4. Select **massage.** in the Suggestions list if necessary, then select **Change**.

   The word is corrected on the page. If the Check Spelling dialog box highlights "exfoliating" select Ignore. If it stops on any other correctly spelled words, select Ignore.

5. Select **OK** to close the Dreamweaver dialog box stating that the Spelling Check is completed.

6. Save and close the spa page.

You checked the spa page for spelling errors.

Add Links
TO WEB PAGES

What You'll Do

In this lesson, you will open the home page and add links to the About Us, Spa, Cafe, and Activities pages. You will then insert an email link at the bottom of the page.

Adding Links to Web Pages

Links, or hyperlinks, provide the real power for web pages. Links make it possible for users to navigate all the pages in a website and to connect to other pages anywhere on the web. Users are more likely to return to websites that have a user-friendly navigation structure. Users also enjoy websites that have interesting links to other web pages or other websites.

To add links to a web page, first select the text or image that you want to serve as a link, and then, in the Link text box in the Property inspector, specify a path to the page to which you want to link.

When you create links on a web page, it is important to avoid **broken links**, or links that cannot find their intended destinations. You can accidentally cause a broken link by typing the incorrect address for the link in the Link text box. Broken links can also be caused by companies merging, going out of business, or simply moving their website addresses.

In addition to adding links to your pages, you should provide a **point of contact**, or a place on a web page that provides users with a means

of contacting the company. A common point of contact is a **mailto: link**, which is an email address that users with questions or problems can use to contact someone at the company's headquarters.

Using Menu Bars

A **menu bar**, or **navigation bar**, is an area on a web page that contains links to the main pages of a website. Menu bars are usually located at the top or side of each page in a website and can be created with text, images, or a combination of the two. Menu bars are the backbone of a website's navigation structure, which includes all navigation aids for moving around a website. To make navigating a website as easy as possible, you should place menu bars in the same position on each page. The web page in Figure 20 shows a menu bar that contains a set of main links with additional links that appear when a user moves a mouse pointer over each main link (known as a **rollover**). HTML5 includes code to identify a navigation section of a page with the <nav> HTML tag. You can create a simple menu bar by typing text representing each of your site's pages at the top of your web

Developing a Web Page

page, formatting the text, and then adding links to each of the text references. It is always a good idea to provide plain text links like this for accessibility, regardless of the type of navigation structure you choose to use. For example, if you use Javascript for your navigation links, it is a good idea to include a duplicate set of text with links to the same pages. Most websites have links at the bottom of each page for accessing company contact information, copyright, and terms of use statements.

Following WCAG Accessibility for Navigation

The WCAG guidelines list ways to ensure that all users can successfully and easily navigate a website. It states: "Provide ways to help users navigate, find content, and determine where they are." Suggestions include limiting the number of links on a page, using techniques to allow users to quickly access different sections of a page, and making sure that links are readable and easily distinguishable.

Figure 20 *The CIA website*

Source: Central Intelligence Agency

Create a menu bar

1. Open **index.html**.

2. Place the insertion point in front of the word "Welcome" in the first paragraph.

3. Select the **Structure category** in the Insert panel, then select **Navigation**.

   The Insert Navigation dialog box opens.

4. Select the list arrow in the Class list box, then select **intro_paragraph**.

   The intro_paragraph style is the same style used in the three paragraphs.

5. Verify that the Insert as Fluid Element check box is checked, as shown in Figure 21, then select **OK**.

   A new section is created on the page, as shown in Figure 22. This section will be coded as an HTML5 navigation element.

6. Select the placeholder text if necessary, then type Home - About Us - Spa - Cafe - Activities, as shown in Figure 23.

TIP Be careful not to delete the HTML tags around the placeholder text. Backspace over the placeholder text if necessary to prevent deleting the tags, even leaving one letter as a temporary placeholder, then deleting it.

TIP An asterisk after the filename in the title bar indicates that you have altered the page since you last saved it. After you save your work, the asterisk no longer appears.

You inserted code to identify an HTML5 navigation element.

Figure 21 *The Insert Navigation dialog box*

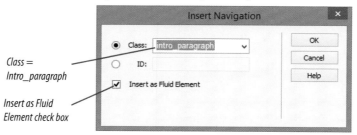

Class =
Intro_paragraph

Insert as Fluid
Element check box

Figure 22 *Viewing the navigation placeholder text*

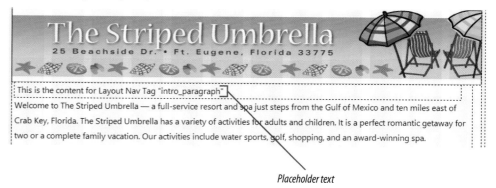

This is the content for Layout Nav Tag "intro_paragraph"

Welcome to The Striped Umbrella — a full-service resort and spa just steps from the Gulf of Mexico and ten miles east of Crab Key, Florida. The Striped Umbrella has a variety of activities for adults and children. It is a perfect romantic getaway for two or a complete family vacation. Our activities include water sports, golf, shopping, and an award-winning spa.

Placeholder text

Figure 23 *HTML5 links added to page*

Home - About Us - Spa - Cafe - Activities

Welcome to The Striped Umbrella — a full-service resort and spa just steps from the Gulf of Mexico and ten miles east of Crab Key, Florida. The Striped Umbrella has a variety of activities for adults and children. It is a perfect romantic getaway for two or a complete family vacation. Our activities include water sports, golf, shopping, and an award-winning spa.

New navigation text

Figure 24 *Selecting text for the Home link*

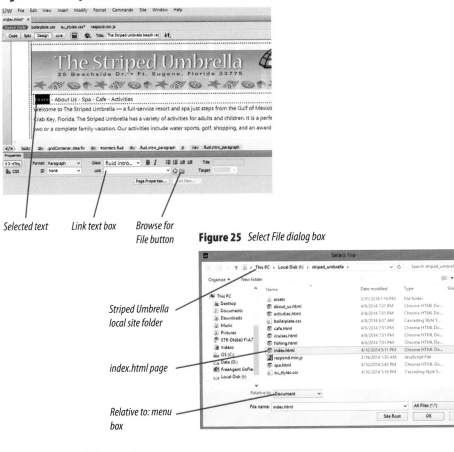

Selected text   Link text box   Browse for File button

Figure 25 *Select File dialog box*

Striped Umbrella local site folder

index.html page

Relative to: menu box

Figure 26 *Links added to menu bar*

Menu bar with links added

Add links to web pages

1. Double-click **Home** to select it, as shown in Figure 24.

2. Select the **Browse for File button** 📁 next to the Link text box in the HTML Property inspector, then navigate to the striped_umbrella local site folder if necessary.

3. Verify that the link is set **Relative to Document** in the Relative to: list.

4. Select **index.html** as shown in Figure 25, select **OK** (Win) or **Open** (Mac), then click anywhere on the page to deselect Home.

TIP Your file listing might differ depending on your view settings.

Home now appears in blue with an underline, indicating it is a link. If users select the Home link, a new page will not open, because the link is on the home page. It might seem odd to create a link to the same page on which the link appears, but this will be helpful when you copy the menu bar to other pages in the site. Always provide users a link to the home page.

5. Repeat Steps 1–4 to create links for About Us, Spa, Cafe, and Activities to their corresponding pages in the striped_umbrella site folder.

6. When you finish adding the links that link to the other four pages, deselect all, then compare your screen to Figure 26.

You created a link for each of the five menu bar elements to their respective web pages in The Striped Umbrella website.

Create an email link

1. Place the insertion point after the last digit in the telephone number, then insert a line break.

2. Select **Email Link** in the Common category on the Insert panel to insert an email link.

3. Type **Club Manager** in the Text text box, type **manager@stripedumbrella.com** in the Email text box, as shown in Figure 27, then select **OK** to close the Email Link dialog box.

TIP If the text does not retain the formatting from the previous line, use the Edit, Undo command to undo Steps 1–3. Switch to Code view and place the insertion point immediately to the right of the telephone number, then repeat the steps in Design view.

4. Save your work.

The text "mailto:manager@stripedumbrella.com" appears in the Link text box in the HTML Property inspector. See Figure 28. When a user clicks this link, a blank email message window opens in the user's default email software, where the user can type a message.

TIP You must enter the correct email address in the Email text box for the link to work. However, you can enter any descriptive name, such as customer service or Bob Smith in the Text text box. You can also enter the email address as the text if you want to show the actual email address on the web page.

You inserted an email link to serve as a point of contact for The Striped Umbrella.

Figure 27 *Email Link dialog box*

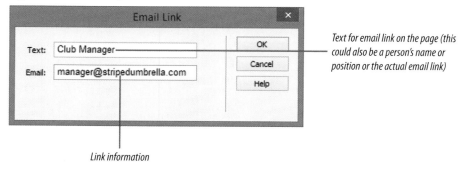

Text for email link on the page (this could also be a person's name or position or the actual email link)

Link information

Figure 28 *mailto: link on the Property inspector*

mailto: link

Figure 29 *The Assets panel URLs category*

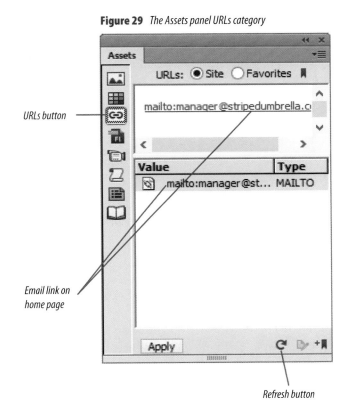

URLs button

Email link on home page

Refresh button

View the email link in the Assets panel

1. Select **Window** on the Menu bar, then select **Assets**.

   The Assets panel opens.

2. Select the **URLs button** ⊖ to display the URLs in the website.

3. Click the **Refresh button** C at the bottom of the Assets panel, if necessary, to view the code for the link, then compare your screen to Figure 29.

   URL stands for Uniform Resource Locator. The URLs listed in the Assets panel show all of the external links, or links pointing outside of the website. An email link is outside the website, so it is an external link. You will learn more about URLs and links in Chapter 5. The links you created to the site pages are internal links (inside the website), and are not listed in the Assets panel.

4. Close the Assets panel.

You viewed the email link on the home page in the Assets panel.

Use the History
PANEL AND EDIT CODE

What You'll Do

In this lesson, you will use the History panel to undo formatting changes you make to the menu bar. You will then use the Code Inspector to view the HTML code for the menu bar, then change the font size for the code. You will also insert a date object and then view it using Code and Design views.

Using the History Panel

Throughout the process of creating a web page, you will make mistakes along the way. Fortunately, you have a tool named the History panel to undo your mistakes. The **History panel** records each editing and formatting task you perform and displays them in a list in the order in which you completed them. Each task listed in the History panel is called a **step**. You can drag the **slider** on the left side of the History panel to undo or redo steps, as shown in Figure 30. You can also click in the bar to the left of a step to undo all steps below it. You click the step to select it. By default, the History panel records 20 steps. You can change the number of steps the History panel records in the General category of the Preferences dialog box. However, keep in mind that setting this number too high will require additional memory and could affect Dreamweaver's performance.

QUICK TIP

Another quick way to undo and redo steps is with the keyboard shortcuts [Control][Z] (undo) and [Control][Y] (redo). The Mac shortcuts are [command][Z] and [command][Y]. However, if you clear the History panel you are also resetting the memory for keyboard shortcuts to that point, so [Control][Z], etc will no longer work for the steps you performed.

Viewing HTML Code in the Code Inspector

If you enjoy writing code, you occasionally might want to make changes to web pages by writing the code rather than using the panels and tools in Design view. Often it is actually easier to make editing or formatting

Understanding Other History Panel Features

Dragging the slider up and down in the History panel is a quick way to undo or redo steps. However, the History panel offers much more. It has the capability to "memorize" certain tasks and consolidate them into one command. This is a useful feature for steps that you perform repetitively on web pages. The History panel does not show steps performed in the Files panel or any program-wide changes, such as editing preferences or changing panel arrangements.

corrections in the code. You can view the code in Dreamweaver using Code view, Code and Design views, or the Code Inspector. The **Code Inspector**, shown in Figure 31, is a separate window that displays the current page in Code view. The advantage of using the Code Inspector is that you can see a full-screen view of your page in Design view while viewing the underlying code in a floating window that you can resize and position wherever you want.

You can add advanced features, such as JavaScript functions, to web pages by copying and pasting code from one page to another using the Code Inspector. A **JavaScript** function is a block of code that adds dynamic content such as rollovers or interactive forms to a web page. A rollover is a special effect that changes the appearance of an object when the mouse moves over it.

Figure 30 *The History panel*

Figure 31 *The Code Inspector*

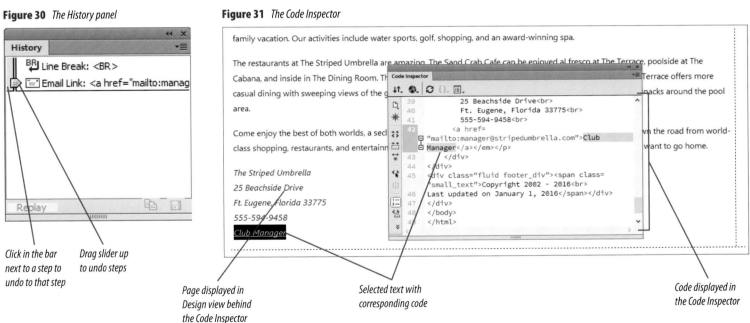

Click in the bar next to a step to undo to that step

Drag slider up to undo steps

Page displayed in Design view behind the Code Inspector

Selected text with corresponding code

Code displayed in the Code Inspector

Use the History panel

1. Select **Window** on the Menu bar, then select **History**.

   The History panel opens and displays steps you have recently performed.

2. Select the **Panel options button**, ≡ select **Clear History**, as shown in Figure 32, then select **Yes** to close the warning box.

3. Select the **five links** in the menu bar on the index page.

   The Property inspector shows the properties of the selected text.

4. Select the **Bold button** B on the Property inspector, select the **Italic button** I, then compare your Property inspector to Figure 33.

5. Drag the **slider** on the History panel up to the top of the panel, as shown in Figure 34.

   The two steps in the History panel appear gray, indicating that these steps have been undone. The menu bar links are no longer bold or italicized.

6. Right-click (Win) or Control-click (Mac) the **History panel title bar**, then select **Close** to close the History panel.

You formatted the menu bar made some formatting changes to it, then used the History panel to undo the changes.

Figure 32 *Clearing the History panel*

You may see different steps depending on your keystrokes — Panel options button — Clear History command

Figure 33 *Property inspector settings for menu bar*

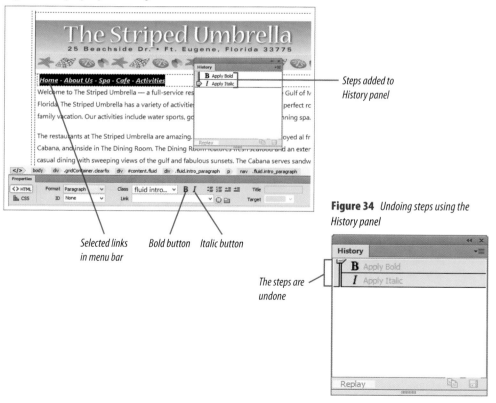

Steps added to History panel

Selected links in menu bar   Bold button   Italic button

Figure 34 *Undoing steps using the History panel*

The steps are undone

Developing a Web Page

Figure 35 *Viewing the View Options menu*

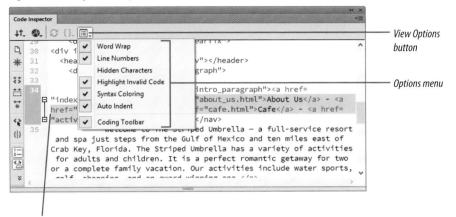

View Options button

Options menu

Code for menu bar

Use the Code Inspector

1. Select the links in the menu bar if necessary, select **Window** on the Menu bar, then select **Code Inspector**.

   Because the menu bar links on the page are selected, the corresponding code is highlighted in the Code Inspector.

   TIP You can also press [F10](Win) or [fn][option][F10] (Mac) to display the Code Inspector.

2. Select the **View Options button** 🔳 on the Code Inspector toolbar to display the View Options menu, then if **Word Wrap** is unchecked, select it once to activate it.

   The Word Wrap feature forces text to stay within the confines of the Code Inspector window, allowing you to read without scrolling sideways.

3. Repeat Step 2 to activate Line Numbers, Highlight Invalid Code, Syntax Coloring, Auto Indent, and Coding Toolbar as shown in Figure 35.

You viewed code in the Code Inspector and set code viewing options.

POWER USER SHORTCUTS	
To do this:	**Use this shortcut:**
Select All	[Ctrl][A] (Win) or ⌘ [A] (Mac)
Copy	[Ctrl][C] (Win) or ⌘ [C] (Mac)
Cut	[Ctrl][X] (Win) or ⌘ [X] (Mac)
Paste	[Ctrl][V] (Win) or ⌘ [V] (Mac)
Line Break	[Shift][Enter] (Win) or [Shift][return] (Mac)
Show or hide the Code Inspector	[F10] (Win) or [fn][option][F10] (Mac)
Preview in browser	[F12] (Win) or [fn][option][F12] (Mac)
Check spelling	[Shift][F7] (Win) or [fn][Shift][F7] (Mac)

View HTML5 nav tags

1. Locate the beginning tag for the menu bar, <nav class="fluid intro_paragraph">, as shown in Figure 36.

   The nav tag was added to the menu bar when you used the Insert panel to add a Navigation element in the Structure category. The nav tag is an HTML5 tag that tells screen readers that the text following the opening tag provides navigation links for the site. You will learn more about links and navigation in Chapter 5. Before we look at it, let's change the size of the font for better readability.

2. Select **Edit** on the Menu bar (Win) or **Dreamweaver** (Mac), then select **Preferences**.

3. Select **Fonts** in the Category column, select the **drop-down Size menu** next to Code view, then select **12pt (Medium)**, as shown in Figure 37.

4. Select **Apply**, select **Close** to close the Preferences dialog box, then notice how much easier it is to read the code now, as shown in Figure 38.

   The increased font size will also apply to Code view.

5. Close the Code Inspector.

You read information about the menu bar nav code, then increased the font size for the Code Inspector and Code view.

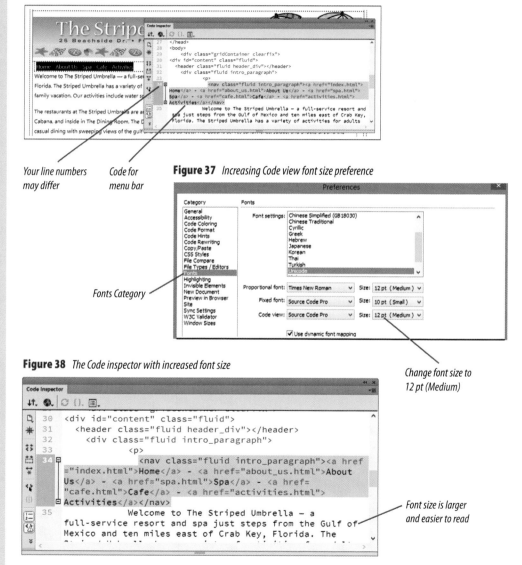

Figure 36 *Viewing the menu bar code in the Code Inspector*

Your line numbers may differ

Code for menu bar

Figure 37 *Increasing Code view font size preference*

Fonts Category

Change font size to 12 pt (Medium)

Figure 38 *The Code inspector with increased font size*

Font size is larger and easier to read

Figure 39 *Insert Date dialog box*

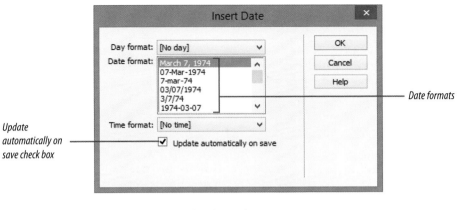

Date formats

Update automatically on save check box

Insert a date object

1. Scroll down the page, if necessary, to select **January 1, 2016**, then press **[Delete]** (Win) or **[delete]** (Mac).

2. Select **Date** in the Common category in the Insert panel, then select **March 7, 1974** if necessary in the Date format list.

3. Check the **Update automatically on save check box**, as shown in Figure 39, select **OK**, then deselect the text.

4. Change to Code and Design views.

   The code has changed to reflect the date object, which is set to today's date, as shown in Figure 40. (Your date will be different.) The new code is highlighted with a light yellow background, indicating that it is a date object, automatically coded by Dreamweaver, rather than a date that has been manually typed on the page by the designer or developer.

5. Return to Design view, then save all files.

You inserted a date object that will be updated automatically when you open and save the home page.

Figure 40 *Viewing the date object code*

Code for date object (deselect the text to see the yellow highlighting)

```
46   Last updated on
47      <!-- #BeginDate format:Am1 -->April
11, 2014<!-- #EndDate -->
48   </span></div>
49   </div>
50   </body>
51   </html>
```

Using Smart Design Principles in Web Page Layout

As you view your pages in the browser, take a critical look at the symmetry of the page. Is it balanced? Are there too many images compared to text, or vice versa? Does everything "heavy" seem to be on the top or bottom of the page, or do the page elements seem to balance with the weight evenly distributed between the top, bottom, and sides? Use design principles to create a site-wide consistency for your pages. Horizontal symmetry means that the elements are balanced across the page. Vertical symmetry means that they are balanced down the page. Diagonal symmetry balances page elements along the invisible diagonal line of the page. Radial symmetry runs from the center of the page outward, like the petals of a flower. These principles all deal with balance; however, too much balance is not good, either. Sometimes it adds interest to place page elements a little off center or to have an asymmetric layout. Color, white space, text, and images should all complement each other and provide a natural flow across and down the page. The **rule of thirds**—dividing a page into nine squares like a tic-tac-toe grid—states that interest is increased when your focus is on one of the intersections in the grid. The most important information should be at the top of the page where it is visible without scrolling, or "above the fold," as they say in the newspaper business.

Modify and Test WEB PAGES

What You'll Do

In this lesson, you will preview the home page in the browser to check for typographical errors, grammatical errors, broken links, and overall appearance. After previewing, you will make slight formatting adjustments to the page to improve its appearance.

Testing and Modifying Web Pages

Testing web pages is a continuous process. You never really finish a website, because there are always additions and corrections to make. As you add and modify pages, you must test each page as part of the development process. The best way to test a web page is to preview it in Live view or in a browser to make sure that all text and image elements appear the way you expect them to. You should also test your links to make sure they work properly. You need to proofread your text to make sure it contains all the necessary information for the page with no typographical or grammatical errors. Designers typically view a page in a browser, return to Dreamweaver to make necessary changes, and then view the page in a browser again. They repeat this process many times before the page is ready for publishing. In fact, it is sometimes difficult to stop making improvements to a page and move on to another project. You need to strike a balance among quality, creativity, and productivity.

Testing a Web Page Using Different Browsers and Screen Sizes

Because users access the Internet using a wide variety of computer systems, it is important to design your pages so that all browsers and screen sizes can display them well. You should test your pages using different browsers and a wide variety of screen sizes to ensure the

DESIGN TIP

Using "Under Construction" or "Come Back Later" Pages

Many people are tempted to insert an unfinished page as a placeholder for a page that they intend to finish later. Rather than have real content, these pages usually contain text or an image that indicates the page is not finished, or "under construction." You should not publish a web page that has a link to an unfinished page. It is frustrating for users to click a link for a page they want to open only to find an "under construction" note or image displayed. You want to make the best possible impression on your users. If you cannot complete a page before publishing it, at least provide enough information on it to make it "worth the trip."

best view of your page by the most people possible. Most web users today use a screen resolution above 1024 by 768. Very few users use a resolution below this, so design your pages for this higher resolution. However, you'll also need to accommodate users who will view your pages with laptops, tablets, and cell phones, so make sure your pages look good at these sizes, as well. To view your page using different screen sizes, select the Mobile size, Tablet size, and Desktop size buttons on the status bar.

To view your pages using several different browsers, select the Preview/Debug in Browser button on the Document toolbar, select Edit Browser List, then use the Add button to add additional browsers installed on your computer to the list. You can also designate which browser to use as the default browser, the browser which opens when you press the F12 key. Remember also to check your pages using Windows and Macintosh platforms. Some page elements such as fonts, colors, table borders, layers, and horizontal rules might not appear consistently in both.

Using Style Sheets for Responsive Design

Most websites today are written using responsive design. **Responsive design** means using style sheets to control how pages look on different devices. For instance, you might design a page with a different banner when it is viewed on a desktop than on a mobile device, as shown in Figure 41.

With the Dreamweaver Fluid Grid Layouts, you can use percents rather than specific measurements to control how large or small page elements appear. **Fluid Grid Layouts** is a tool that uses a combination of style sheets and page elements that work together to adapt page content to flexible column grid layouts: one for mobile devices, one for tablet devices, and one for desktop devices. It is poor design practice not to provide pages that can be viewed and navigated easily whatever size screen is used.

Style sheets are used with **Media Queries** to identify which device is calling up the page, then apply the appropriate code for optimum viewing. When Fluid Grid Layouts and Media Queries are used to create pages, the designer can determine the values to use for each layout: Mobile, Tablet, and Desktop. One style sheet controls the styles for all three devices by providing separate sets of styles for each device. You will build on your understanding of responsive design as you go through each chapter.

Figure 41 *Comparing a desktop design to a mobile design*

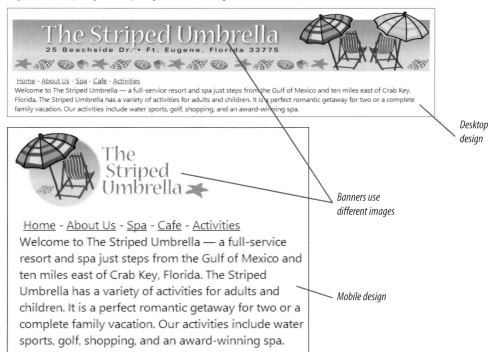

Desktop design

Banners use different images

Mobile design

Modify a web page

1. Select the **Desktop size button** 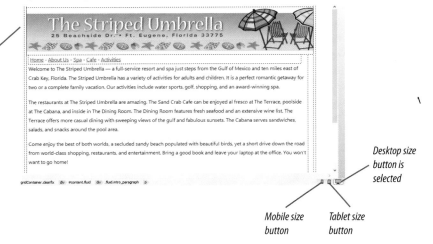 on the status bar to see how the page would appear on a desktop computer using the default desktop settings, as shown in Figure 42.

   A user viewing this page on a desktop will see the full Striped Umbrella banner.

2. Replace the period after the last sentence, "You won't want to go home." with an exclamation point.

3. Select the **Tablet size button** ▢ on the Status bar.

   Scroll up if necessary, then notice the page width is narrower and the banner does not display the rightmost umbrella and chair.

4. Select the **Mobile size button** ▢ .

   The banner is replaced with a smaller version, as shown in Figure 43.

5. Return to Desktop size, then save your work.

You viewed the home page using three different window sizes and made a simple edit.

Figure 42 *Using the Desktop size button to preview the index page*

Full banner is displayed

Desktop size button is selected

Mobile size button

Tablet size button

Figure 43 *Using the Mobile size button to preview the index page*

A smaller banner image is used for the mobile design

Mobile size button is selected

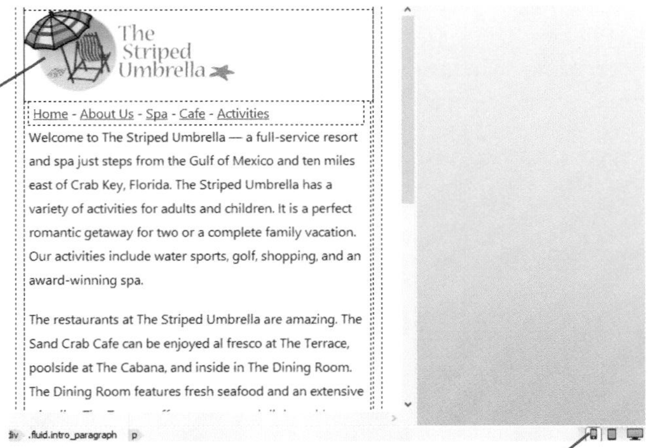

Figure 44 *Viewing The Striped Umbrella home page in the Firefox browser*

Visited links

Edited text

Choosing a Window Size

Today, most users use a screen resolution of 1024 × 768 or higher. Because of this, more content can be displayed at one time on a computer monitor. People tend to use their "screen real estate" in different ways. Some people might use their whole screen to view pages on the Internet. Others might choose to allocate a smaller area of their screen to the browser window. The ideal web page will not be so small that it tries to spread out over a larger screen size or so large that the user has to use horizontal scroll bars to read the page content. The WCAG guideline 1.4.8 states that " … Text can be resized without assistive technology up to 200 percent in a way that does not require the user to scroll horizontally to read a line of text on a full-screen window." Achieving the best balance and meeting accessibility guidelines is one of the design decisions that you must make during the planning process.

Test web pages by viewing them in a browser

1. Select the **Preview/Debug in browser button** 🔁 on the Document toolbar, then choose your browser from the menu that opens.

   The Striped Umbrella home page opens in your default browser.

2. Select each link on the menu bar, then after each selection, use the Back button on the browser toolbar to return to the home page.

   Pages with no content at this point will appear as blank pages. Compare your screen to Figure 44. The links in Figure 44 have all been selected, which made them visited links. So they appear in purple rather than blue, the color of unvisited links.

3. Close your browser window, then close all open pages in Dreamweaver.

You viewed The Striped Umbrella home page in your browser and tested each link on the menu bar.

Create head content and set page properties.

1. Open the Blooms & Bulbs website.
2. Open the index page.
3. Edit the page title on the Document toolbar so it reads **Blooms & Bulbs - Your Complete Garden Center**.
4. Insert the following keywords: **garden, plants, nursery, flowers, landscape, bulbs, Blooms & Bulbs, Alvin, Texas**.
5. Insert the following description: **Blooms & Bulbs is a premier supplier of plants, trees, and shrubs for both professional and home gardeners**.
6. Switch to Code view to view the HTML code for the head content, then switch back to Design view.
7. Increase the width of the CSS Designer panel to display it across two columns.
8. Select bb_styles.css in the Sources pane, then select .fluid in the Selectors pane.
9. Scroll to find and select the set background color box, then experiment with a different color for the page background.
10. Return the background color to #FFFFFF (white), then save all files.

Create, import, and format text.

1. Create a new paragraph after the second paragraph of text and type the following text, inserting a line break after each line.
   Blooms & Bulbs
   Highway 43 South
   Alvin, Texas 77511
   555-248-0806

2. Verify that the HTML button is selected in the Property inspector, and select it if it is not.
3. Italicize the name, address and phone number lines.
4. Change to Code view to view the formatting code for the italicized text.
5. Return to Design view, then save your work.
6. Save the index page as **tips.html**, overwriting the original blank tips page.
7. Close the index page, select all of the text on the page except the address and phone number lines and footer, then delete it.
8. Place the insertion point in front of the first address line, then use the Image command on the Insert panel to insert the file butterfly.jpg. from the folder where you store your Data Files.
9. With the logo selected, add appropriate alternate text, place the insertion point to the right of the logo, then enter a paragraph break.
10. Open your file management program, navigate to the chapter_2 folder from the location where you store your Data Files, then open the file gardening_tips.txt.
11. Select all of the text, copy it, then close Notepad (Win) or TextEdit (Mac).
12. Return to Dreamweaver, click to place the insertion point to the right of the butterfly logo.
13. Paste the copied text at the insertion point, then save your work.
14. Select the Seasonal Gardening Checklist heading, then use the Property inspector to apply a Heading 1 format.
15. Select the Basic Gardening Tips heading, then apply the Heading 1 format.

16. Place the insertion point at the top of the document, then check the page for spelling errors.
17. Make any necessary corrections, save your work, then close the tips page.

Add links to web pages.

1. Open the index page.
2. Place the insertion point in front of the word "Welcome" in the first paragraph.
3. Use the Structure category in the Insert panel to insert a Fluid Element Navigation element with the Class intro_paragraph.
4. Select the placeholder text if necessary, then type **Home - Featured Plants - Garden Tips - Workshops - Newsletter**. (*Hint*: Be careful not to delete the tags for the menu bar. Backspace over the placeholder text if necessary to prevent deleting the div itself, even leaving one letter as a temporary placeholder, then deleting it.)
5. Use the Property inspector to link Home on the menu bar to the index.html page in the Blooms & Bulbs website.
6. Link Featured Plants on the menu bar to the plants.html page.
7. Link Garden Tips on the menu bar to the tips.html page.
8. Link Workshops on the menu bar to the workshops.html page.
9. Link Newsletter on the menu bar to the newsletter.html page.
10. Create a line break after the telephone number and then use the Insert panel to create an email link, with **Customer Service** as the text and **mailbox@ bloomsandbulbs.com** as the email address. (*Hint:* If your text does not retain the formatting from the previous line, reapply the settings.)

11. Save your work.
12. View the email link in the Assets panel, refreshing it if necessary, then view the Files panel.

Use the History panel and edit code.

1. Open the History panel, then clear its contents.
2. Select the five links in the menu bar.
3. Use the HTML Property inspector to make the link text bold and italic.
4. Use the History panel to remove the bold and italic formatting.
5. Close the History panel.
6. Open the Code Inspector and verify that Word Wrap is selected.
7. View the code for the menu bar links in the Code Inspector, then close the Code Inspector.
8. Delete the current date in the Last updated on statement on the home page and replace it with a date using the March 7, 1974 format that will update automatically when the file is saved.
9. Examine the code for the date at the bottom of the page to verify that the code that forces it to update on save is included in the code. (*Hint*: The code should be highlighted with a light yellow background if it is not selected, or a blue background if it is selected (Win) or gray (Mac).)
10. Return to Design view, then save your work.

Modify and test web pages.

1. View the index page with the Tablet size and Mobile size settings, then return to Desktop size.
2. View the page in your browser. (If you see a message about allowing blocked content, select Allow.)

3. Verify that all links work correctly, then close the browser.
4. On the home page, add the text "**We are happy to deliver or ship your purchases.**" to the end of the first paragraph.

5. Save your work, then view the pages in your browser, comparing your pages to Figure 45 and Figure 46.
6. Close your browser, use Code view to delete any extra spaces between page elements, then save and close all open pages.

Figures 45 & 46 *Completed Skills Review, home page and tips page*

You have been hired to create a website for TripSmart, a travel outfitter. You have created the basic framework for the website and are now ready to format and edit the home page to improve the content and appearance.

1. Open the TripSmart website, then open the home page.

2. Enter the following keywords: **TripSmart, travel, trips, vacations, Fayetteville, Arkansas, and tours**.

3. Enter the following description: **TripSmart is a comprehensive travel service. We can help you plan trips, make travel arrangements, and supply you with travel gear.**

4. Change the page title to **TripSmart - Serving all your travel needs**.

5. Use the Insert panel to add an HTML5 menu bar with a class selector name of your choice above the first paragraph with the following text: **Home, Catalog, Services, Tours,** and **Newsletter**. Between each item, use a hyphen with a space on either side to separate the items.

6. Replace the date in the last updated statement with a date that will update automatically on save.

7. Add a paragraph break after the last paragraph, then type the following address, using line breaks after each line:
TripSmart
1106 Beechwood
Fayetteville, AR 72704
555-848-0807

8. Insert an email link in the line below the telephone number, using **Contact Us** for the text and **mailbox@tripsmart.com** for the email link.

9. Italicize TripSmart, the address, phone number, and email link.

10. Link the menu bar entries to index.html, catalog.html, services.html, tours.html, and newsletter.html.

11. View the HTML code for the page, then return to Design view.

12. Save your work.

13. View the page in Mobile size, Tablet size, and Desktop size, then test the links in your browser window.

14. Compare your page to Figure 47, close the browser, then close all open pages.

Figure 47 *Completed Project Builder 1*

Your company has been selected to design a website for a catering business named Carolyne's Creations. You are now ready to add content to the home page and apply formatting options to improve the page's appearance, using Figure 48 as a guide.

1. Open the Carolyne's Creations website, then open the home page.

2. Edit the page title to read **Carolyne's Creations: Premier Gourmet Food Shop**.

3. Add the description **Carolyne's Creations is a gourmet food shop. We offer cooking classes, take-out meals, and catering services. We also have a retail side that stocks gourmet items and kitchen accessories**.

4. Add the keywords **Carolyne's Creations, gourmet, catering, cooking classes, kitchen accessories, take-out, Seven Falls, Virginia**.

5. Place the insertion point in front of the sentence in the second paragraph beginning "Give us a call" and type **We also have a pick-up window on the right side of the building for take-out orders**.

6. Add the following address below the second paragraph using line breaks after each line:
   Carolyne's Creations
   496 Maple Avenue
   Seven Falls, Virginia 52404
   555-963-8271

7. Enter another line break after the telephone number and type **Email**, add a space, then add an email link using **Carolyne Kate** for the text and

carolyne@carolynescreations.com for the email address.

8. Insert a Navigation element, add text to serve as links to the website's main pages, then create links from each menu bar element to its corresponding web page. See Figure 48.

9. Replace the date that follows the text "Last updated on" with a date object using a format of your choice that will automatically update on save, then save your work.

10. Save your work, view the completed page in Mobile size, Tablet size, Desktop size, and in your default browser, then test each link.

11. Close your browser.

12. Close all open pages.

Figure 48 *Completed Project Builder 2*

Fernando Padilla is looking for a durable laptop case that he can use for the frequent trips he takes with his laptop. He is searching the Internet looking for one that is attractive, strong, and that provides quick access for removing the laptop for airport security. He knows that websites use keywords and descriptions in order to receive "hits" with search engines. He is curious about how they work. Follow the steps below and write your answers to the questions.

1. Connect to the Internet, then go to **www.sfbags.com** to view the WaterField Designs website's home page, as shown in Figure 49.
2. View the page source by selecting View on the Menu bar, then selecting Source (Internet Explorer) or Tools > Web Developer > Page Source (Mozilla Firefox).
3. Can you locate a description and keywords? If so, what are they?

4. How many keyword terms do you find?
5. Is the description appropriate for the website? Why or why not?
6. Look at the numbers of keyword terms and words in the description. Is there an appropriate number?

7. Use a search engine such as Google at www.google.com, then type the words **laptop bag** in the Search text box.
8. Click a link in the list of results and view the source code for that page. Do you see keywords and a description? Do any of them match the words you used in the search?

Figure 49 *Design Project*

Source: Waterfield Designs

In this assignment, you will continue to work on the website you defined in Chapter 1. In Chapter 1, you created a wireframe for your website with at least four pages. You also created a local site folder for your site and an assets folder to store the site asset files. You set the assets folder as the default storage location for your images. You began to collect information and resources for your site and started working on the home page. You have not yet learned how to create a new page with a Fluid Grid Layout, so you can either create a simple HTML page now and convert it to a Fluid Grid Layout later, or use one of your website index pages as a template.

1. Think about the head content for the home page. Add the title, keywords, and a description.
2. Create the main page content for the home page.
3. Add the address and other contact information to the home page, including an email address.
4. Consult your wireframe and design the menu bar.
5. Link the menu bar items to the appropriate pages.
6. Add a last updated on statement to the home page with a date that will automatically update when the page is saved.
7. Edit the page content until you are satisfied with the results. You will format the content after you have learned to use Cascading Style Sheets in the next chapter.
8. Verify that all links, including the email link, work correctly.
9. When you are satisfied with the home page, review the checklist questions shown in Figure 50, then make any necessary changes.
10. Save your work.

Figure 50 *Portfolio Project*

> ### Website Checklist
> 1. Does the home page have a page title?
> 2. Does the home page have a description and keywords?
> 3. Does the home page contain contact information, including an email address?
> 4. Does the home page have a menu bar that includes a link to itself?
> 5. Does the home page have a "last updated on" statement that will automatically update when the page is saved?
> 6. Do all paths for links and images work correctly?
> 7. Does the home page look good using at least two different browsers and screen resolutions?

CHAPTER 3 **WORKING WITH TEXT AND CASCADING STYLE SHEETS**

1. Create unordered and ordered lists
2. Create a Cascading Style Sheet and apply, edit and add rules
3. Understand related files and media queries
4. Add Adobe Edge Web fonts
5. Use coding tools to view and edit rules

WORKING WITH TEXT AND
CASCADING STYLE SHEETS

Introduction

Most web pages depend largely on text to convey information. Dreamweaver provides many tools for working with text that you can use to make your web pages attractive and easy to read. These tools can help you format text quickly and make sure it has a consistent look across all your web pages.

Using Cascading Style Sheets

You can save time and ensure that all your page elements have a consistent appearance by using **Cascading Style Sheets (CSS)**. CSS are sets of formatting instructions, usually stored in a separate file, that control the appearance and position of text and graphics on a web page or throughout a website. CSS are a great way to define consistent formatting attributes for page elements such as paragraph text, lists, and table data. You can then apply the formatting attributes to any element in a single document or to all of the pages in a website.

Formatting Text as Lists

If a web page contains a large amount of text, it can be difficult for users to digest it all. You can break up the monotony of large blocks of text by dividing them into smaller paragraphs or by organizing them as lists. You can create three types of lists in Dreamweaver: unordered lists, ordered lists, and definition lists.

Lists are also excellent for creating simple navigation bars. You can format list items to look like buttons by applying styles to assign background colors to each list item. You can even create rollover effects for list items by having the background color change when the user rolls the mouse over them. This technique gives your links a more professional look than plain text links. Cascading Style Sheets are indeed a powerful tool. This chapter will focus on using Cascading Style Sheets to format text.

Create Unordered
AND ORDERED LISTS

What You'll Do

Body Treatments

- Salt Glow
  Imported sea salts are massaged into the skin, exfoliating and cleansing the pores.
- Herbal Wrap
  Organic lavender blooms create a detoxifying and calming treatment to relieve aches and pains.
- Seaweed Body Wrap
  Seaweed is a natural detoxifying agent that also helps improve circulation.

Call The Sea Spa desk for prices and reservations. Any of our services can be personalized according to your needs. Our desk is open from 7:00 a.m. until 9:00 p.m. Call 555-594-9458, extension 39.

Questions You May Have

1. How do I schedule Spa services?
   Please make appointments by calling The Club desk at least 24 hours in advance. Please arrive 15 minutes before your appointment to allow enough time to shower or use the sauna.
2. Will I be charged if I cancel my appointment?
   Please cancel 24 hours before your service to avoid a cancellation charge. No-shows and cancellations without adequate notice will be charged for the full service.
3. Are there any health safeguards I should know about?
   Please advise us of medical conditions or allergies you have. Heat treatments like hydrotherapy and body wraps should be avoided if you are pregnant, have high blood pressure, or any type of heart condition or diabetes.
4. What about tipping?
   Gratuities are at your sole discretion, but are certainly appreciated.

In this lesson, you will create an unordered list of spa services on the spa page. You will also copy and paste text with questions and format them as an ordered list.

Creating Unordered Lists

Unordered lists are lists of items that do not need to appear in a specific sequence, such as a grocery list, which often lists items in a random order. Items in unordered lists are usually preceded by a **bullet**, a small dot or similar icon. Unordered lists that contain bullets are sometimes called **bulleted lists**. Although you can use paragraph indentations to create an unordered list, bullets can often make lists easier to read. To create an unordered list, first select the text you want to format as an unordered list, then use the Unordered List button in the HTML Property inspector to insert bullets at the beginning of each paragraph of the selected text.

Formatting Unordered Lists

In Dreamweaver, the default bullet style is a round dot. To change the bullet style to a different symbol, use Cascading Style Sheets. You can create a rule to modify the <ul> tag

Figure 1 *Using CSS to format all lists in a website*

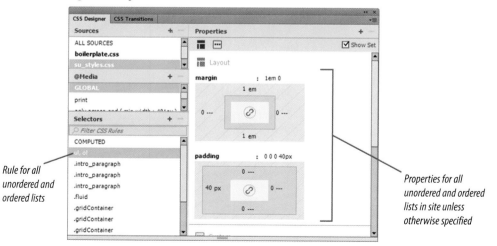

Rule for all unordered and ordered lists

Properties for all unordered and ordered lists in site unless otherwise specified

Working with Text and Cascading Style Sheets

that will apply to all lists in a website, as shown in Figure 1 or you can create a rule for a particular unordered list, such as a list of navigation elements, shown in Figure 2. You will learn about Cascading Style Sheets in the next lesson.

Creating Ordered Lists

Ordered lists, which are sometimes called **numbered lists**, are lists of items that are presented in a specific sequence and that are preceded by sequential numbers or letters. An ordered list is appropriate for a list in which each item must be executed according to its specified order. A list that provides numbered directions for driving from Point A to Point B or a list that provides instructions for assembling a bicycle are both examples of ordered lists.

Formatting Ordered Lists

You can format an ordered list to show different styles of numbers or letters by using Cascading Style Sheets, as shown in Figure 3. You can apply numbers, Roman numerals, decimals, lowercase letters, or uppercase letters to an ordered list.

Creating Definition Lists

Definition lists are similar to unordered lists but have a hanging indent and are not preceded by bullets. They are often used with terms and definitions, such as in a dictionary or glossary. To create a definition list, select the text to use for the list, select Format on the Menu bar, point to List, and then select Definition List.

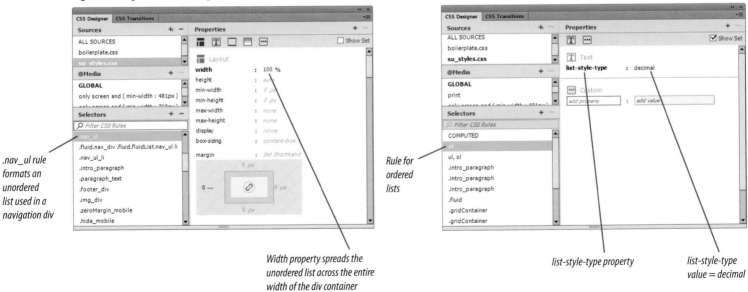

Figure 2 *Using CSS to format navigation elements as an unordered list*

Figure 3 *Using CSS to format ordered lists in a website*

.nav_ul rule formats an unordered list used in a navigation div

Rule for ordered lists

Width property spreads the unordered list across the entire width of the div container

list-style-type property

list-style-type value = decimal

Create an unordered list

1. Open the spa page in The Striped Umbrella website.

2. Select the three items and their descriptions under the Massages heading.

3. Select the **HTML button** ⟨⟩ HTML in the Property inspector to switch to the HTML Property inspector if necessary, select the **Unordered List button** ≣ to format the selected text as an unordered list, click anywhere to deselect the text, then compare your screen to Figure 4.

   Each spa service item and its description are separated by a line break. That is why each description is indented under its corresponding item, rather than formatted as a new list item. You must enter a paragraph break to create a new list item.

4. Repeat Step 3 to create unordered lists with the three items under the Facials and Body Treatments headings, being careful not to include the contact information in the last paragraph on the page as part of your last list.

TIP Pressing [Enter] (Win) or [return] (Mac) once at the end of an unordered list creates another bulleted item. To end an unordered list, press [Enter] (Win) or [return] (Mac) twice.

(continued)

Figure 4 *Creating an unordered list*

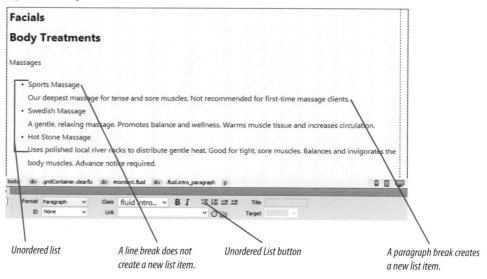

Unordered list

A line break does not create a new list item.

Unordered List button

A paragraph break creates a new list item.

Coding for the Semantic Web

You may have heard the term "semantic web." The word "semantics" refers to the study of meanings of words or sentences. So the term "semantic web" refers to the way page content can be coded to convey meaning to other computer programs such as search engines. One example is to use the <em> tag which means "emphasis" rather than the <i> tag which means "italic" to show emphasis. Another example would be to use font size attributes such as <small> or <medium> rather than using font size attributes expressed in pixels. Cascading Style Sheets are used to define the appearance of semantic tags. For instance, you can specify the attributes of the <h1> heading tag by choosing the Selector Type: Tag (redefines an HTML element) rules in the New CSS Rules dialog box. CSS and semantic coding work together to enhance the meaning of the page content and provide well-designed pages that are attractive and consistent throughout the site. An ideal website would incorporate semantic coding with external style sheets to format all website content. This approach will enable "Semantic Web" programs to interpret the content presented, make it easier for web designers to write and edit, and enhance the overall experience for site users.

Figure 5 *Viewing the three unordered lists*

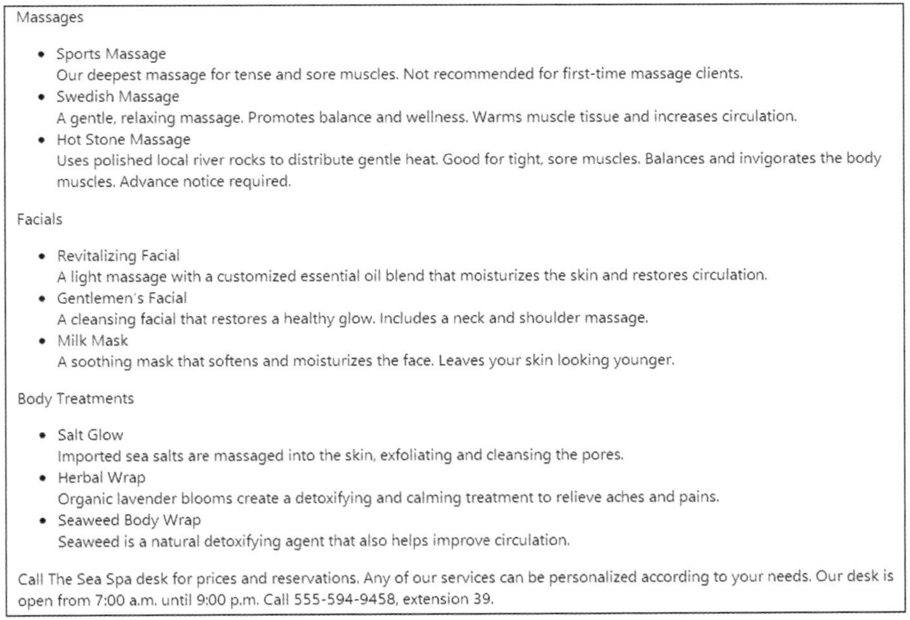

Massages
Sports Massage
Our deepest massage for tense and sore muscles. Not recommended for first-time massage clients.
Swedish Massage
A gentle, relaxing massage. Promotes balance and wellness. Warms muscle tissue and increases circulation.
Hot Stone Massage
Uses polished local river rocks to distribute gentle heat. Good for tight, sore muscles. Balances and invigorates the body muscles. Advance notice required.
Facials
Revitalizing Facial
A light massage with a customized essential oil blend that moisturizes the skin and restores circulation.
Gentlemen's Facial
A cleansing facial that restores a healthy glow. Includes a neck and shoulder massage.
Milk Mask
A soothing mask that softens and moisturizes the face. Leaves your skin looking younger.
Body Treatments
Salt Glow
Imported sea salts are massaged into the skin, exfoliating and cleansing the pores.
Herbal Wrap
Organic lavender blooms create a detoxifying and calming treatment to relieve aches and pains.
Seaweed Body Wrap
Seaweed is a natural detoxifying agent that also helps improve circulation.
Call The Sea Spa desk for prices and reservations. Any of our services can be personalized according to your needs. Our desk is open from 7:00 a.m. until 9:00 p.m. Call 555-594-9458, extension 39.

Figure 6 *HTML tags in Split view for unordered lists*

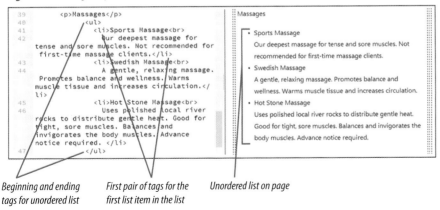

<p>Massages</p>
<ul>
<li>Sports Massage
Our deepest massage for tense and sore muscles. Not recommended for first-time massage clients.</li>
<li>Swedish Massage
A gentle, relaxing massage. Promotes balance and wellness. Warms muscle tissue and increases circulation.</li>
<li>Hot Stone Massage
Uses polished local river rocks to distribute gentle heat. Good for tight, sore muscles. Balances and invigorates the body muscles. Advance notice required. </li>
</ul>
Massages
Sports Massage
Our deepest massage for tense and sore muscles. Not recommended for first-time massage clients.
Swedish Massage
A gentle, relaxing massage. Promotes balance and wellness. Warms muscle tissue and increases circulation.
Hot Stone Massage
Uses polished local river rocks to distribute gentle heat. Good for tight, sore muscles. Balances and invigorates the body muscles. Advance notice required.
Beginning and ending tags for unordered list
First pair of tags for the first list item in the list
Unordered list on page

5. Save your work, then compare your page to Figure 5.
6. Position the insertion point to the left of the first item in the first unordered list, then select the **Show Code and Design views button** Split on the Document toolbar to view the code for the unordered list, as shown in Figure 6.

   A pair of HTML tags surrounds each type of element on the page. The first tag in each pair begins the code for a particular element, and the last tag ends the code for the element. For instance, the tag <ul>begins the unordered list, and the</ul>tag ends it. The tags <li>and</li> surround each item in the list.

TIP Depending on your Document window size, you may have to scroll to locate the code for the unordered list.

7. Select the **Show Design view button** Design on the Document toolbar.

You opened the spa page in Design view and formatted three spa services lists as unordered lists. You then viewed the HTML code for the unordered lists in Show Code and Design views (Split view).

Create an ordered list

1. Place the insertion point at the end of the last paragraph after the words "extension 39", then press **[Enter]** (Win) or **[return]** (Mac).

2. Open your file management program, browse to the location where you store your Data Files, then open **questions.txt**. Select all, copy, then paste the copied text on the page at the insertion point location.

   The inserted text appears under the last paragraph.

3. Select the text beginning with "How do I schedule" and ending with the last sentence of the pasted text.

4. Select the **Ordered List button** ⅈ≡ in the HTML Property inspector to format the selected text as an ordered list.

5. Deselect the text, delete any unwanted paragraph returns before the contact information, then compare your screen to Figure 7.

You pasted text on the spa page. You also formatted selected text as an ordered list.

Figure 7 *Creating an ordered list*

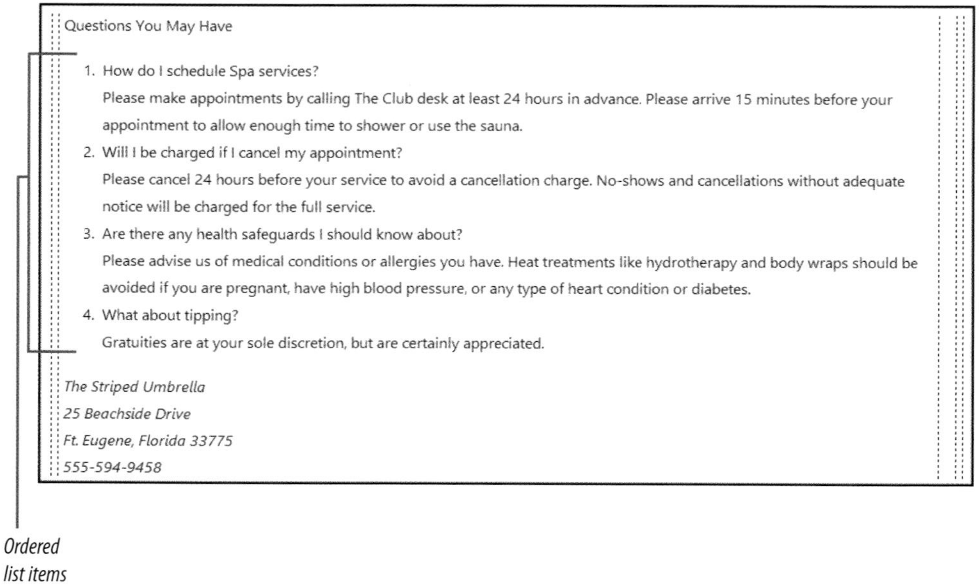

Questions You May Have

1. How do I schedule Spa services?
   Please make appointments by calling The Club desk at least 24 hours in advance. Please arrive 15 minutes before your appointment to allow enough time to shower or use the sauna.
2. Will I be charged if I cancel my appointment?
   Please cancel 24 hours before your service to avoid a cancellation charge. No-shows and cancellations without adequate notice will be charged for the full service.
3. Are there any health safeguards I should know about?
   Please advise us of medical conditions or allergies you have. Heat treatments like hydrotherapy and body wraps should be avoided if you are pregnant, have high blood pressure, or any type of heart condition or diabetes.
4. What about tipping?
   Gratuities are at your sole discretion, but are certainly appreciated.

The Striped Umbrella
25 Beachside Drive
Ft. Eugene, Florida 33775
555-594-9458

Ordered list items

Figure 8 *Formatting a list heading*

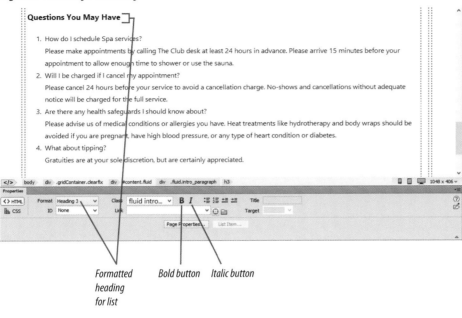

Formatted
heading
for list

Bold button   Italic button

Format an ordered list heading

1. Place the insertion point in the heading "Questions You May Have," then use the HTML Property inspector to apply the **Heading 3** format, as shown in Figure 8.

TIP You could show emphasis by using the Bold button **B** or the Italic button *I* on the HTML Property inspector, as shown in Figure 8, but using the heading code shows the significance (semantics) of the phrase more clearly. It shows that the phrase is a heading related to the text that follows it. The three headings on the page are formatted with three different heading tags that indicate their order of importance on the page: Heading 1 first, then Heading 2, followed by Heading 3.

2. Save your work.

You formatted the "Questions You May Have" heading.

Create a Cascading Style Sheet and APPLY, EDIT AND ADD RULES

What You'll Do

In this lesson, you will create a Cascading Style Sheet file for The Striped Umbrella website. You will also create a rule named list_headings and apply it to the list item headings on the spa page.

Understanding Cascading Style Sheets

Cascading Style Sheets (CSS) are made up of sets of formatting attributes called **rules**, which define the formatting attributes for page content. Rules can then be used to point to an HTML element and "style" it with the formatting attributes defined in the rule. Style sheets are classified by where the code is stored. The code can be saved in a separate file (an **external style sheet**), as part of the head content of an individual web page (an **internal or embedded style**), or as part of the body of the HTML code (an **inline style**). External CSS are saved as files with the .css extension and are stored in the website's directory structure. Figure 9 shows external style sheets named su_styles.css and boilerplate.css listed in the Files panel. External style sheets are the preferred method for creating and using styles.

CSS are also classified by their type. A **Class type** can be used to format any page element. An **ID type** and a **Tag type** are used to redefine an HTML tag. A **Compound** type is used to format a selection. In this chapter, we will use the class type and the tag type, both stored in an external style sheet file.

Using CSS Designer

You use buttons on the CSS Designer panel to create, edit, and apply rules. To add a rule, use the Sources pane to select the style sheet to which you want to add the new rule. Each rule you create is added to the selected style sheet. The tag generated by a rule is called a selector. A **selector** "selects" HTML elements and applies the rule to style the HTML element. Next, select the Add Selector button at the top of the Selectors pane, then either accept the default name in the New Selector text box that appears (based on the location of the insertion point) or type a different selector name. Once you add a new selector to a style sheet, it appears in a list in CSS Designer. To apply a selector, select the HTML element to which you want to apply the selector, and then choose a rule from the Targeted Rule list in the CSS Property inspector. You can apply CSS rules to elements on a single web page or to all of the pages in a website. When you edit a rule, such as changing the font size it specifies, all page elements formatted with that rule are automatically updated. Once you create an external CSS, you should attach it to the remaining pages in your website.

Use CSS Designer to manage your styles. The Properties pane displays properties for a selected rule at the bottom of the panel, or a second column when CSS Designer is expanded to two columns. You can easily change a property's value by selecting an option from a drop-down menu to the right of the property name.

Understanding the Advantages of Using Style Sheets

You can use CSS styles to save an enormous amount of time. Being able to define a rule and then select and apply it to page elements on all the pages of your website means that you can make hundreds of formatting changes in a few minutes. In addition, style sheets create a more uniform look from page to page and they generate cleaner code. Using style sheets separates the content itself from the way the content is presented. By separating the two processes, you can concentrate on either editing the content or modifying the design without affecting the other. Pages formatted with CSS styles are more compliant with current accessibility standards than those with manual formatting. When you create a Fluid Grid Layout page, a style sheet is automatically generated to define the rules, properties, and values used to position page elements for displaying the page in a Mobile, Tablet, or Desktop size. You will learn more about using style sheets for page layout in Chapter 5.

QUICK TIP

For more information about CSS terminology and the relationships between CSS selectors and Cascading Style Sheets, visit www.w3.org/Style.

Understanding CSS Code

You can see the properties for a CSS rule by looking at the style sheet code. A CSS rule consists of two parts: the selector and the declaration. As you learned earlier, a selector is the name of the tag to which the style declarations have been assigned. A selector consists of the selector's name, followed by declarations using the format [property]: [value]. When there is more than one property, each property is separated by a semicolon. For example, Figure 10 shows the code for an unordered list that will be used for styling navigation bar elements. The width property is set to 100% and the margin-left property to zero. In this example, the selector name is .nav_ul. There are two properties in this selector: width and margin-left. The property(s) and value(s) together comprise the declaration.

When you create a new external CSS file, you will see the file name listed as a related files document in the Related Files toolbar at the top of the Document window. Select the file name to open the contents of the file in the Document window. As you make changes to the CSS file, be sure to save it.

Figure 9 *Cascading Style Sheet files created in striped_umbrella site root folder*

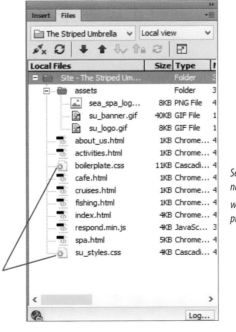

Cascading Style
Sheet files

Figure 10 *Viewing the selector and declaration for an unordered list rule*

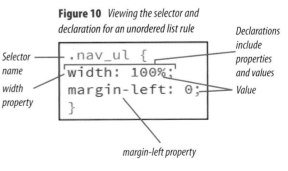

Selector name

width property

Declarations include properties and values

Value

margin-left property

Create a Cascading Style Sheet and add a rule

1. Select the **CSS button** ᚎ CSS in the Property inspector to switch to the CSS Property inspector, as shown in Figure 11.

2. If the CSS Designer panel is not open, select **Window** on the Menu bar, then select **CSS Designer** to open it or select the **CSS Designer panel tab**.

3. Resize the CSS Designer panel to display it in two columns, select the **Add CSS Source button** ╬ in the Sources pane, then select **Create a New CSS File**, as shown in Figure 12.

    The Create a New CSS File dialog box opens.

TIP You can also choose to attach an existing style sheet file or create internal styles directly in the page code.

4. Select **Browse**, navigate to the striped_umbrella site root folder, type **headings** in the File name text box in the Save Style Sheet File As dialog box, as shown in Figure 13, select **Save**, then select **OK** to close the Create a New CSS File dialog box.

    The new style sheet file named headings.css is saved in the local site folder.

(continued)

Figure 11 *CSS Property inspector*

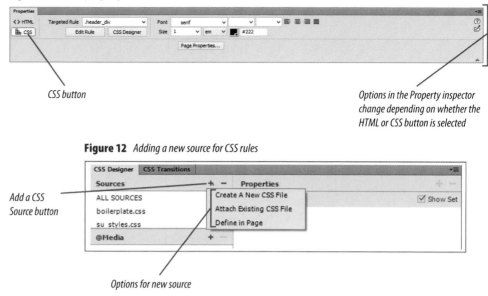

CSS button

Options in the Property inspector change depending on whether the HTML or CSS button is selected

Figure 12 *Adding a new source for CSS rules*

Add a CSS Source button

Options for new source

Figure 13 *Save Style Sheet File As dialog box*

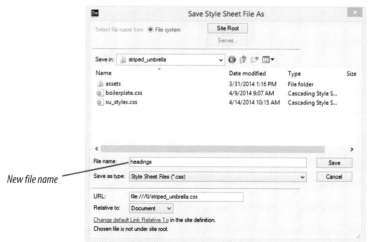

New file name

Figure 14 *CSS Designer with .list_headings rule listed in the headings.css file*

Select headings.css

.list_headings selector

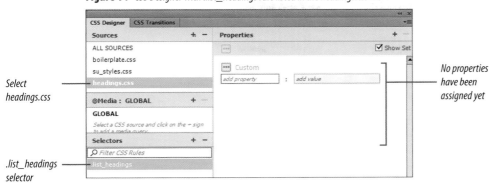

No properties have been assigned yet

Figure 15 *CSS Designer with properties and values displayed for .list_headings rule*

Text button

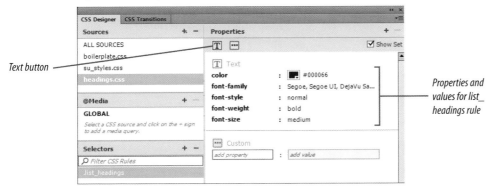

Properties and values for list_ headings rule

5. Select **headings.css** in the Sources pane, then select the **Add Selector button** + in the Selectors pane.

6. Replace the placeholder selector name with **.list_headings**, compare your screen with Figure 14, then press **[Enter]** (Win) or **[return]** (Mac).

   The .list_headings selector appears in the Selectors pane. It is the only selector in the new headings.css style sheet. Next, you define the rule properties

TIP Class selector names are preceded by a period in the code and in the CSS panel.

7. Uncheck the **Show Set check box** in the Properties pane, if necessary, to view all properties (set and not set).

8. Select the **Text button** T in the Properties pane, then select and assign values to the following properties: color to **#000066;** font-family to **Segoe, Segoe UI, DejaVu Sans, Trebucket MS, Verdana, sans serif;** font-style to **normal**, font-weight to **bold**; and font-size to **medium**.

9. Select the **Show Set check box** to see only the properties and values you selected in Step 8, compare your screen to Figure 15, then save all files.

   If you don't see the properties listed, select the Text button on the Properties toolbar. These are all text properties.

You created a Cascading Style Sheet file named headings.css and a rule named .list_headings within the style sheet.

Apply a rule

1. Place the insertion point anywhere in the paragraph heading "Massages," select the **Targeted Rule list arrow** in the Property inspector, then select **.list_headings**, as shown in Figure 16. Notice the new style sheet, headings.css, appears in the Related Files toolbar.

2. Repeat Step 1 to apply the list_headings rule to each of the spa services unordered list headings, place the insertion point anywhere in the document to deselect the text, then compare your screen to Figure 17.

TIP   You can use the keyboard shortcut [Ctrl][Y] (Win) or [Command][Y] (Mac) to repeat the previous action.

You applied the list_headings rule to each of the Spa Services category headings.

Figure 16   *Applying a CSS rule to selected text*

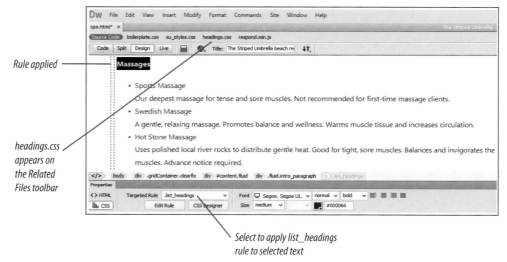

Rule applied

headings.css appears on the Related Files toolbar

Select to apply list_headings rule to selected text

Figure 17   *Unordered list with list_headings rule applied*

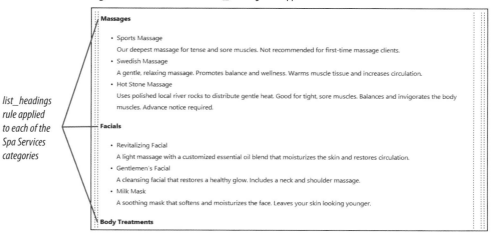

list_headings rule applied to each of the Spa Services categories

Working with Text and Cascading Style Sheets

Figure 18 *Editing a rule*

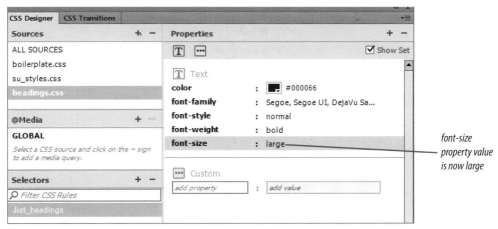

font-size
property value
is now large

1. Select **headings.css** in the Sources pane if necessary, select **.list_headings** in the CSS Designer Selectors pane.

The rule's properties and values appear in the Properties pane.

2. Select the **medium value** in the font-size property, select **large**, as shown in Figure 18, then compare your screen to Figure 19.

All of the text to which you applied the list_headings rule is larger, reflecting the changes you made to the list_headings rule.

TIP If you position the insertion point in text that has a class CSS rule applied to it, that rule is displayed in the Targeted Rule text box in the CSS Property inspector or the Class text box in the HTML Property inspector.

3. Select **File** on the menu bar, then select **Save All** to save the spa page and the style sheet file.

You edited the list_headings rule to change the font size to large. You then viewed the results of the edited rule in the unordered list.

Figure 19 *Viewing the changes made to the list_headings rule*

Headings
with the
list_headings
rule applied
are now larger

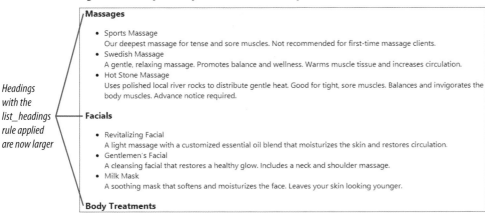

View code with the Code Navigator

1. Point to the Massages heading, then [Alt]-click (Win) or [Command] [Option]-click (Mac) to display the Code Navigator.

   A window opens, as shown in Figure 20, with a list of the three style sheets in the local site folder that have been used to style the page. The rules used in each style sheet are listed under each file name. The boilerplate.css file provides the overall basic structure for the page. The headings.css file only has one rule, .list_headings, the rule you created to style the headings in the three unordered lists. The su_styles.css file provides code for modifying the page content to display on mobile, tablet, and desktop devices.

   TIP [Control][Alt][N] (Win) or [Command][Option][N] (Mac) also opens the Code Navigator.

2. Position the mouse pointer over the list_headings rule name until you see a box with the rule's properties, as shown in Figure 21.

   TIP You can disable the Code Navigator by selecting the Disable check box as shown in Figure 21.

   You displayed the Code Navigator to view the properties of the list_headings rule.

Figure 20 *Viewing the style sheet file names in the Code Navigator*

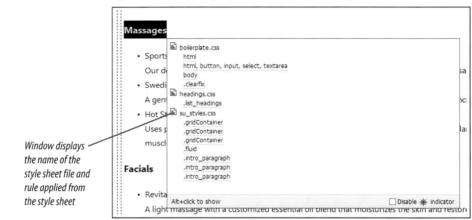

Window displays the name of the style sheet file and rule applied from the style sheet

Figure 21 *Viewing the rule properties and values in the Code Navigator*

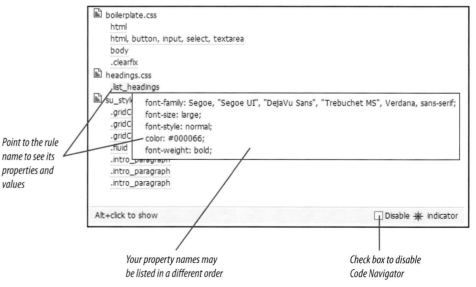

Point to the rule name to see its properties and values

Your property names may be listed in a different order

Check box to disable Code Navigator

Figure 22 *Using Code and Design views to view rule properties*

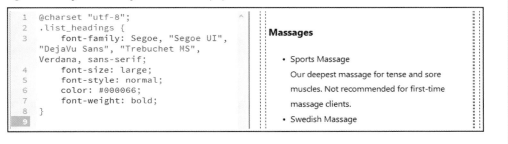

Figure 23 *Editing a rule in Code view*

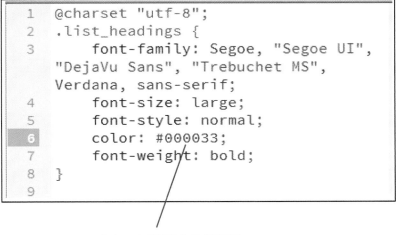

Replace color "000066" with "000033"

Use the Code Navigator to edit a rule

1. Select **.list_headings** in the Code Navigator. The document window splits into two panes. The left pane displays the code for the CSS file and the right section displays the HTML page in Design view, as shown in Figure 22.

   Your properties may be listed in a different order. The order of the code in Code view matches the order in which the properties were added.

TIP The default setting for Show Code and Design views in Dreamweaver CC splits the two windows vertically, rather than horizontally. To view the two windows split horizontally on the screen, select View on the Menu bar, then select Split Vertically to uncheck the option and split the screens horizontally.

2. Type directly in the code to replace the color "000066" with the color "000033" as shown in Figure 23.

TIP You can also edit the rule properties in the CSS Designer Properties pane.

3. Save all files.

4. Select the **Show Design view button** Design .

   The font color has changed in Design view to reflect the new shade of blue in the rule.

You changed the color value in the .list_headings color property.

Add a tag selector to an existing style sheet

1. Select **.headings.css** in the CSS Designer Sources pane, then select the **Add Selector** button ✛ in the Selectors pane.

2. Type **h1** in the Selector Name text box, or type **h** and select **h1** out of the code hints list, as shown in Figure 24, then press [**Enter**] (Win) or [**return**] (Mac).

    The h1 rule is listed in the Selectors pane.

    When you create a rule to modify an HTML tag, you do not type a period in front of the rule name. The tag is the rule name.

3. Deselect the **Show Set check box** in the Properties pane if necessary.

    When a rule does not have properties assigned, there is nothing to show in the Properties pane when Show Set is selected. Unchecking the Show Set check box displays a list by category of all property names available to use to format a rule.

4. Select the **Text button** ⊤ in the Properties pane.

    A list of text properties and their default values appears in the Properties pane.

    (continued)

Figure 24 *Creating a tag selector*

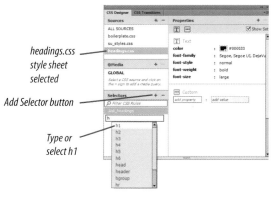

headings.css style sheet selected

Add Selector button

Type or select h1

Figure 25 *CSS Rule Definition for h1 in heading.css*

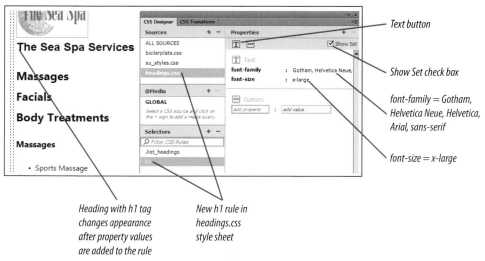

Text button

Show Set check box

font-family = Gotham, Helvetica Neue, Helvetica, Arial, sans-serif

font-size = x-large

Heading with h1 tag changes appearance after property values are added to the rule

New h1 rule in headings.css style sheet

Figure 26 *Viewing the h2 headings with new rules applied*

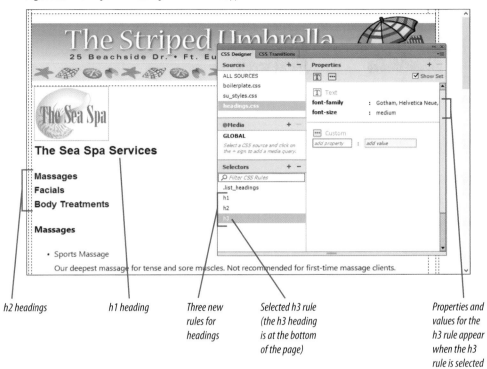

h2 headings   h1 heading   Three new
                             rules for
                             headings

Selected h3 rule
(the h3 heading
is at the bottom
of the page)

Properties and
values for the
h3 rule appear
when the h3
rule is selected

5. Select the **font-family value** (default font), then select **Gotham, Helvetica Neue, Helvetica, Arial, sans-serif**.

6. Select the **font-size value** (medium), then select **x-large**.

   The Sea Spa Services heading on the page changes in appearance to reflect the new h1 properties specified in the new rule.

7. Select the **Show Set** check box to display only the properties you have assigned to the h1 tag, as shown in Figure 25.

8. Repeat Steps 1 through 7 to create a new tag selector that redefines the h2 tag with a font-family of **Gotham, Helvetica Neue, Helvetica, Arial, sans-serif** and a font-size of **large**.

9. Repeat Steps 1 through 7 to create a new tag selector that redefines the h3 tag with a font-family of **Gotham, Helvetica Neue, Helvetica, Arial, sans-serif** and a font-size of **medium**.

10. Save all files, then compare your screen to Figure 26.

You added three tag selectors to your style sheet that modify the appearance of the h1, h2, and h3 tags.

Transitioning to a Real-World Work Process

As you learn Dreamweaver throughout the chapters in this book, you practice its many features in a logical learning sequence. You will develop an understanding of both current concepts like CSS3 and older, but still used, features such as HTML formatting and embedded styles. Once you learn Dreamweaver and start using it to create your own websites, you would ideally format all pages with rules from one external style sheet. You would move all of the embedded styles in the predesigned CSS layouts to the external style sheet because the embedded styles on each page would be redundant. After you have worked through this book, you should have the skills and understanding to design sites built entirely and efficiently with CSS.

Understand Related Files and
MEDIA QUERIES

What You'll Do

Understanding External and Embedded Style Sheets

When you are first learning about CSS, the terminology can be confusing. In the last lesson, you learned that external style sheets are separate files in a website, saved with the .css file extension. You also learned that CSS can be part of an HTML file, rather than a separate file. These are called internal, or embedded, style sheets. Some external CSS files are created by the web designer. Other external CSS files are created by Dreamweaver, such as the boilerplate.css file, generated when a new Fluid Grid Layout page is first created. Embedded style sheets are created automatically in Dreamweaver if the designer does not create them, using default names for the rules. The code for these rules resides in the head content for that page. These rules are automatically named style1, style2, and so on. You can rename the rules as they are created to make them more recognizable for you to use, for example, paragraph_text, subheading, or address. Embedded style sheets apply only to a single page, although you can copy them into the code in other pages or move them to an external style sheet. Remember that style sheets can be used to format much more than

text objects. They can be used to set the page background, link properties, or determine the appearance of any page element. Figure 27 shows the Related Files toolbar, showing the names of the style sheets used to format the open Striped Umbrella spa page. Selecting the file name in the Related Files toolbar opens the file in the Document window, as shown in Figure 27.

When you have several pages in a website, you will probably want to use the same styles for each page to ensure that all your elements have a consistent appearance. To attach a style sheet to another document, select the **Add CSS Source button** in the CSS Designer Sources pane, then select **Attach Existing CSS File** to open the Attach Existing CSS File dialog box, make sure the Add as Link option is selected, browse to locate the file you want to attach, and then select OK. The rules contained in the attached style sheet will appear in CSS Designer and you can use them to apply rules to all page elements. External style sheets can be attached, or linked, to any page. Style sheets are extremely powerful; if you decide to edit a rule, the changes will automatically be made to every object on every page that it formats.

Understanding Related Page Files

When an HTML file is linked to a Cascading Style Sheet or other files necessary to display the page content, these files are called **related files.** When a file that has related files is open in the Document window, each related file name is displayed in the Related Files toolbar above the Document window. When an HTML document has a linked CSS file but the CSS file is not available, the page file will appear in the browser, but will not be formatted correctly, because the link is broken. It takes both the HTML file and the CSS file working together to display the content properly. When you upload HTML files, remember also to upload all related page files. Other examples of related page files are Flash player, video files, and JavaScript files.

When an HTML file with a linked CSS file is open in Dreamweaver, the name of the CSS file appears in the Related Files toolbar. When you select the CSS filename, the screen changes to Split view, with the right side displaying the open HTML page in Design view and the left side displaying the CSS file. If you select "Source Code," the first filename listed on the Related Files toolbar, the code for the top level document (open HTML file) will appear on the left side of the Document window. You can edit both Code view windows by typing directly in the code.

Understanding Fluid Grid Layout Code

When a web page is opened in a browser, the style sheet detects the device being used using **Media queries.** Media queries act as traffic policemen. When they detect a mobile device, they direct the device to use the code for mobile devices; when they detect a tablet device, they direct the tablet to use the code for tablets, and so forth. Each set of codes is designed for optimum viewing on each device.

Figure 27 *Viewing an open style sheet file using the Related Files toolbar*

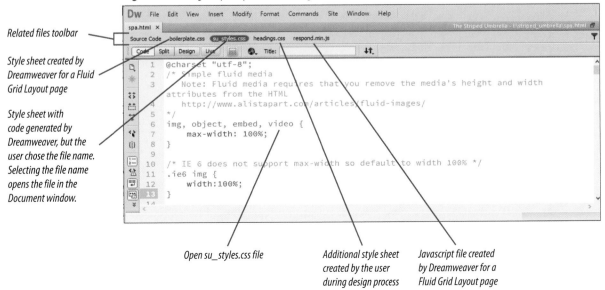

Related files toolbar

Style sheet created by Dreamweaver for a Fluid Grid Layout page

Style sheet with code generated by Dreamweaver, but the user chose the file name. Selecting the file name opens the file in the Document window.

Open su_styles.css file

Additional style sheet created by the user during design process

Javascript file created by Dreamweaver for a Fluid Grid Layout page

Examining Media Queries code

1. With the spa page open, select the **su_styles.css** file name on the Related Files toolbar.

   The code for the su_styles.css file opens in the Document window, as shown in Figure 28. Since the file is open in the Document window, the only style sheet file listed in CSS Designer now is su_styles.css, as shown in Figure 29.

   TIP The code in Figure 28 was resized to increase readability. Your lines may wrap differently.

2. Scroll to locate the comment line (in light gray text) "/* Mobile Layout: 480px and below. */" (on or around line 45).

   The lines of code following this comment are applied when a mobile device reads the page.

   TIP Figure 28 was captured with several blocks of code collapsed to point out the beginnings of each different device section, since the entire file is too long to fit on the page. To quickly locate the referenced code, use the Find command.

3. Scroll to locate the comment line (in light gray text) "/* Tablet Layout: 481px to 768 px. Inherits styles from: Mobile Layout. */" (on or around line 123).

   The lines of code following this comment are applied when a tablet device reads the page.

4. Scroll to locate the comment line (in light gray text) "/* Desktop Layout: 769px to a max of 1232px. Inherits styles from: Mobile Layout and Tablet Layout. */" (on or around line 165).

   The lines of code following this comment are applied when a desktop device is reading the page.

   (continued)

Figure 28 *Viewing the styles for each device in the su_styles.css file*

Comment tells you that this code begins the code for mobile devices

Comment tells you that this code begins the code for tablet devices

Comment tells you that this code begins the code for desktop devices

Figure 29 *Viewing CSS Designer with the su_styles.css file selected in the Related Files toolbar*

su_styles is the only file listed in CSS Designer

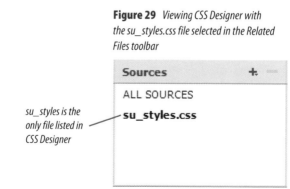

Figure 30 *Viewing the selectors for Tablet devices*

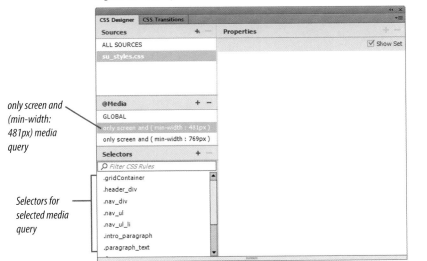

only screen and (min-width: 481px) media query

Selectors for selected media query

5. Select **su_styles.css** in the Sources pane if necessary, then select **only screen and (min-width: 481px)** in the @Media pane.

   The selectors for Tablet size devices are listed in the Selectors pane, as shown in Figure 30. When you select a Media Query, the selectors for that query appear in the Selectors pane.

6. Select **only screen and (min-width: 769px)** in the @Media pane.

   The selectors for Desktop size devices appear in the Selectors pane.

7. Select **Global** in the @Media pane.

   Selectors that are used globally for all devices and those used for Mobile size devices are listed in the Selectors pane.

8. Return to Design view.

You viewed the su_styles.css media queries and their selectors in CSS Designer.

Media Queries and Inherited Styles

When media queries are used in style sheets, it is important to understand how they work. You learned that each section of the code contains styles for different media devices. However, not every style is used with the same properties and values for every device. Rather, styles can be customized for each device.

Any style listed in the Global section applies to the page regardless of what device is used. The styles that apply to mobile devices are also included as global selectors. The global styles are **inherited**, or applied to every other device unless otherwise specified. For instance, the global style for a heading might be a medium-size font used for mobile devices. To specifiy a larger heading font for tablet devices, that same style name can be redefined in the media query section for tablet devices. It can be specified even larger for desktops to use by redefining it in the desktop media query section. Another example: you can start with a global style to use a small banner in a mobile device, a wider banner in a tablet device, and an even wider banner in a desktop device by using a background image property for a header div.

Add Adobe Edge
WEB FONTS

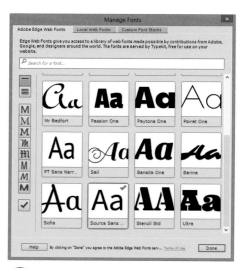

In this lesson, you will add an Adobe Edge Web Font to your list of available fonts to use in The Striped Umbrella website.

Choosing Fonts

There are two classifications of fonts: sans-serif and serif. Sans-serif fonts are fonts without any extra decorative strokes (serifs). They are often used for small blocks of text such as headings and subheadings. The headings in this book use a sans-serif font. Examples of sans-serif fonts include Arial, Verdana, and Helvetica. Serif fonts are more ornate and contain small extra strokes at the tops and bottoms of the characters. Serif fonts are considered easier to read in larger blocks of text and printed material, because the extra strokes lead your eye from one character to the next. Examples of serif fonts include Times New Roman, Times, and Georgia. The text you are reading now is in a serif font. Many designers feel that a sans-serif font is preferable when the content of a website is primarily intended to be read on the screen, but that a serif font is preferable if the content will be printed. When you choose fonts, keep in mind the amount of text each page will contain and whether most users will read the text on-screen or print it. A good rule of thumb is to limit each website to no more than three font variations.

Using Adobe Edge Web Fonts

With Adobe's purchase of Typekit in 2011, access to fonts for web page design changed dramatically. Previously, you specified font families for font-face properties, a user's device searched for the fonts in its system files, then applied the first one it found to the page text. An example of a font-family is Segoe, Segoe UI, DejaVu Sans, Trebuchet MS, Verdana, sans-serif. In this example, a device would first look for the Segoe font, then work down the list looking for each font name. If none of the fonts listed were found, the user's device would apply a default sans-serif. These fonts were hosted locally, meaning the user's device located the fonts in the device system and applied the formatting.

With Typekit, you are provided with an extensive library of Adobe Edge Web Fonts that is available to use free of charge with a Creative Cloud subscription. **Typekit** is a repository of over a thousand font families that you can use both in web and print projects. Once you choose a font family, those fonts are integrated into the Dreamweaver font menus for instant access. Typekit fonts are stored on the Creative Cloud with embedded instructions in the page code for each device calling up the page, as shown in Figure 31. Adobe Edge Web Fonts are hosted remotely, meaning that a remote website (Adobe Typekit) locates the fonts and applies the formatting.

To add an Adobe Edge Web Font to a website, click the current font family list, select the font-family property value list box, select Manage Fonts, then in the Manage Fonts dialog box, select the Adobe Edge Web Fonts tab, as shown in Figure 32. You can then search for a font, or use the font categories in the toolbar on the left side of the page to filter fonts as you browse through the font library.

Adding an Adobe Edge Web Font to a Page

Once you select a new Adobe Edge Web font, you will see it listed in the Dreamweaver menus that allow you to choose fonts. Select a selector's property in your style sheet for which you want to specify a font, then select the Adobe Edge Web font from the font list. The code will then be embedded in the head content of the page and will be used to format text styled by that selector. For more about Typekit, see the Creative Cloud introduction at the front of this book.

Figure 31 *Embedded Adobe Edge Web Fonts code*

```
30    <script src=
      "http://use.edgefonts.net/source-sans-pro:n2:default.js"
      type="text/javascript"></script>
31    </head>
32    <body>
```

Figure 32 *The Manage Fonts Dialog box*

Adobe Edge Web Fonts tab

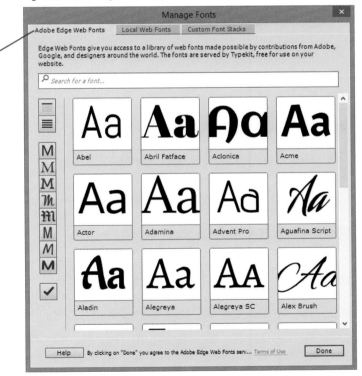

Add an Adobe Edge Web font

1. Select **headings.css** in the CSS Designer Sources pane, then select **h1** in the Selectors pane.

2. Select the **font-family list box**, then select **Manage Fonts**.

3. Select the **Adobe Edge Web Fonts** tab if necessary, then select the **List of fonts recommended for Headings** button ▭.

4. Scroll down and select the **Source Sans Pro** font, as shown in Figure 33, then select **Done**.

   The font is added to your list of available fonts, but was not changed in the property value.

5. Select the **font-family list box** again, then select **source-sans-pro**.

   The h1 font-family property value is now source-sans-pro and The Sea Spa Services heading changes to the font source-sans-pro, as shown in Figure 34. Notice also that a font-weight and a font-size value were added when you chose the font. (Refresh the CSS Designer panel by toggling the Show Set checkbox if you don't see them listed.)

TIP To see the font exactly as it will appear in a browser, use Live view to view the page.

You selected an Adobe Edge Web font for the h1 tag in the headings.css style sheet.

Figure 33 *Selecting an Adobe Edge Web font*

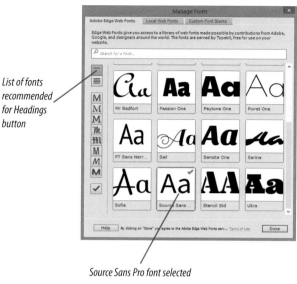

List of fonts recommended for Headings button

Source Sans Pro font selected

Figure 34 *Viewing the Edge Web font value for the h1 tag*

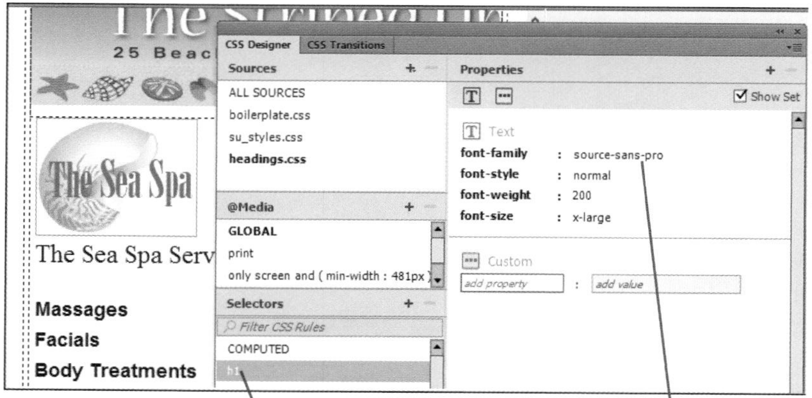

h1 tag

font-family = source-sans-pro

Working with Text and Cascading Style Sheets

Figure 35 *Correcting script errors*

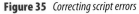

Clean Up Web
Fonts Script
Tag (Current
Page)

| Commands | Site | Window | Help |

Edit Command List...

Check Spelling   Shift+F7

Apply Source Formatting

Apply Source Formatting to Selection

Clean Up HTML...

Clean Up Word HTML...

Clean Up Web Fonts Script Tag (Current Page)

Externalize JavaScript...

Remove FLV Detection

Optimize Image...

Sort Table...

Figure 36 *Adobe Edge Web Fonts script tag added to head section*

```
29  <script>var __adobewebfontsappname__="dreamweaver"</script>
30  <script src="http://use.edgefonts.net/source-sans-pro:n2:default.js" type=
    "text/javascript"></script>
31  </head>
32  <body>
```

Script added to spa
page to link font

View the embedded code for an Adobe Edge Web font

1. Change to Code view, select **Commands** on the Menu bar, then select **Clean Up Web Fonts Script Tag (Current Page)**, as shown in Figure 35, if necessary.

   This command updates the script tag to add new fonts recently selected, as shown in Figure 36.

2. Return to Design view, then save all pages.

You used the Clean Up Web Fonts Script Tag (Current Page) command on the spa page to locate and correct any errors found in the code.

Use Coding Tools to
VIEW AND EDIT RULES

What You'll Do

In this lesson, you will collapse, then expand the code for the index page to view the code for the embedded and external styles. You will then move embedded styles to the external style sheet file.

Coding Tools in Dreamweaver

In Code view, you can see the Coding toolbar, shown in Figure 37. It contains a number of handy tools that help you navigate through and view your code in different ways. It has buttons that expand or collapse code, buttons for changing the way the code is displayed, and buttons for inserting and removing comments. The Coding toolbar appears on the left side of the Document window. Although you cannot move it, you can hide it, using the Toolbars command on the View menu in Code view.

As you learned in Chapter 2, you can customize the way your page code appears in Code view. You can wrap the lines of code, display or hide line numbers and hidden characters, or highlight invalid code so you can fix it. You can also have different code types appear in different colors, indent lines of code, and display syntax error alerts. In Chapter 2, you viewed these options using the View Options button on the Code Inspector toolbar. You can also view and change them on the Code View options menu under the View menu on the Menu bar.

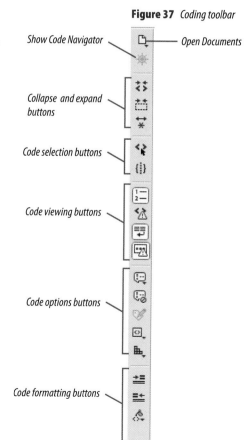

Figure 37 *Coding toolbar*

Show Code Navigator — Open Documents

Collapse and expand buttons

Code selection buttons

Code viewing buttons

Code options buttons

Code formatting buttons

Using Coding Tools to Navigate Code

As your pages get longer and the code more complex, it is helpful to collapse sections of code, much as you can collapse and expand panels, folders, and styles. Collapsing code lets you temporarily hide code between two different sections of code that you would like to read together. To collapse selected lines of code, you can select the minus sign (Win) or the triangle (Mac) next to the line number. You can also use the Collapse Full Tag or Collapse Selection buttons on the Coding toolbar. This will allow you to look at two different sections of code that are not adjacent to each other.

Adding comments is an easy way to add documentation to your code, which is especially helpful when you are working in a team environment and other team members will be working on pages with you. For example, you might use comments to communicate instructions like "Do not alter code below this line." or "Add final schedule here when it becomes available." Comments are not visible in the browser.

Using Code Hints to Streamline Coding

If you are typing code directly into Code view, Dreamweaver can speed your work by offering you code hints. **Code hints** are lists of HTML tags that appear as you type, similar to other auto-complete features that you have probably used in other software applications. As you are typing code, Dreamweaver will recognize the tag name and offer you choices to complete the tag simply by double-clicking a tag choice in the menu, as shown in Figure 38. You can also add your own code hints to the list using JavaScript. Code hints are stored in the file CodeHints.xml.

Converting Styles

You can also convert one type of style to another. For instance, you can move an embedded style to an external style sheet or an inline style to either an embedded style or a style in an external style sheet. To do this, select the style in Code view, right-click the code, point to CSS Styles, then select Move CSS Rules. You can also move styles in the CSS Styles panel by selecting the style, right-clicking the style, and choosing the action you want from the shortcut menu.

Figure 38 *Using code hints*

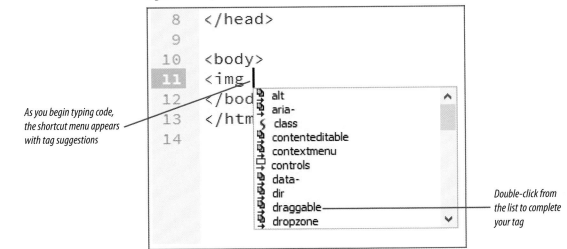

As you begin typing code, the shortcut menu appears with tag suggestions

Double-click from the list to complete your tag

Collapse code

1. Verify that the spa page is open, then select **Source Code** in the Related Files toolbar to change to Split view.

2. Scroll up the page, if necessary, to display the code that begins the head section (<head>).

   The code will probably be on or close to line 7 in the head section.

3. Select this line of code, then drag down to select all of the code down to and including the ending tag for the head section (</head>) on or around line 31, as shown in Figure 39.

TIP If your code is in a slightly different order, scroll to find the meta tags to select them.

4. Click the **minus sign** (Win) or **vertical triangle** (Mac) in the first or last line of selected code to collapse all of the selected code.

   You can now see code above and below the collapsed code section as shown in Figure 40. The plus sign (Win) or horizontal triangle (Mac) next to the line of code indicates that there is hidden code. You also see a gap in the line numbers where the hidden code resides.

You collapsed a block of code in Code view to be able to see two non-adjacent sections of the code at the same time.

Figure 39 *Selecting lines of code on the index page to collapse*

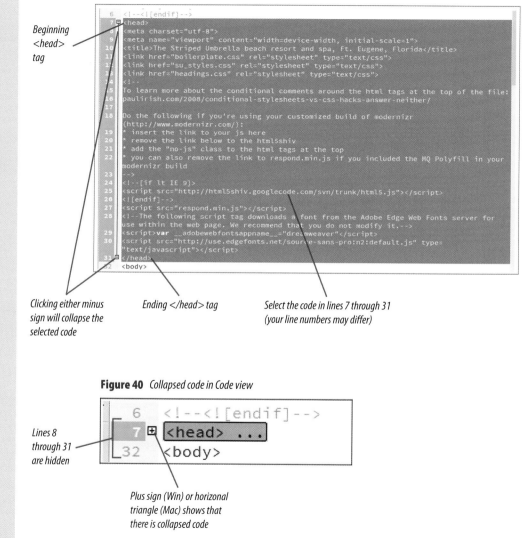

Beginning <head> tag

Clicking either minus sign will collapse the selected code

Ending </head> tag

Select the code in lines 7 through 31 (your line numbers may differ)

Figure 40 *Collapsed code in Code view*

Lines 8 through 31 are hidden

Plus sign (Win) or horizonal triangle (Mac) shows that there is collapsed code

Working with Text and Cascading Style Sheets

Figure 41 *Expanded code for index page*

```
8   <!--<![endif]-->
7   <head>
8   <meta charset="utf-8">
9   <meta name="viewport" content="width=device-width, initial-scale=1">
10  <title>The Striped Umbrella beach resort and spa, Ft. Eugene, Florida</title>
11  <link href="boilerplate.css" rel="stylesheet" type="text/css">
12  <link href="su_styles.css" rel="stylesheet" type="text/css">
13  <link href="headings.css" rel="stylesheet" type="text/css">
14  <!--
15  To learn more about the conditional comments around the html tags at the top of the file:
16  paulirish.com/2008/conditional-stylesheets-vs-css-hacks-answer-neither/
17
18  Do the following if you're using your customized build of modernizr (http://www.modernizr.com/):
19  * insert the link to your js here
20  * remove the link below to the html5shiv
21  * add the "no-js" class to the html tags at the top
22  * you can also remove the link to respond.min.js if you included the MQ Polyfill in your modernizr build
23  -->
24  <!--[if lt IE 9]>
25  <script src="http://html5shiv.googlecode.com/svn/trunk/html5.js"></script>
26  <![endif]-->
27  <script src="respond.min.js"></script>
28  <!--The following script tag downloads a font from the Adobe Edge Web Fonts server for use within the web page. We
    recommend that you do not modify it.-->
29  <script>var __adobewebfontsappname__="dreamweaver"</script>
30  <script src="http://use.edgefonts.net/source-sans-pro:n2:default.js" type="text/javascript"></script>
31  </head>
32  <body>
```

Code is expanded again

Expand code

1. Click the **plus sign** (Win) or **horizontal triangle** (Mac) on line 7 to expand the code.

2. Compare your screen to Figure 41, then click in the page to deselect the code.

   All line numbers are visible again.

You expanded the code to display all lines of the code again.

POWER USER SHORTCUTS	
To do this:	**Use this shortcut:**
Switch views	[Ctrl][`] (Win) or [control][`] (Mac)
Indent text	[Ctrl][Alt][]] (Win) or ⌘ [option][]] (Mac)
Outdent text	[Ctrl][Alt][[] (Win) or ⌘ [option][[] (Mac)
Align Left	[Ctrl][Alt][Shift][L] (Win) or ⌘ [option][shift][L] (Mac)
Align Center	[Ctrl][Alt][Shift][C] (Win) or ⌘ [option][shift][C] (Mac)
Align Right	[Ctrl][Alt][Shift][R] (Win) or ⌘ [option][shift][R] (Mac)
Align Justify	[Ctrl][Alt][Shift][J] (Win) or ⌘ [option][shift][J] (Mac)
Bold	[Ctrl][B] (Win) or ⌘ [B] (Mac)
Italic	[Ctrl][I] (Win) or ⌘ [I] (Mac)
Refresh	[F5]

Move style from one style sheet to another

1. Return to Design view, then open CSS Designer if necessary.

2. Select **headings.css** in the Sources pane.

3. Select **.list_headings**, as shown in Figure 42, then drag and drop it on top of **su_styles.css** in the Sources pane.

   The .list_headings rule is moved from the headings.css file to the su_styles.css file, as shown in Figure 43.

4. Repeat step 3 to move the h1, h2, and h3 rules to the su_styles.css file.

   All rules have been moved out of the headings.css file and it is no longer needed.

5. Select **headings.css** in the Sources pane, then select the **Remove CSS Source button** — in the Sources pane.

   The headings.css file is no longer listed as a source in the Sources pane.

(continued)

Figure 42 *Selecting the .list_headings rule to move to a different style sheet*

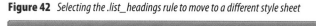

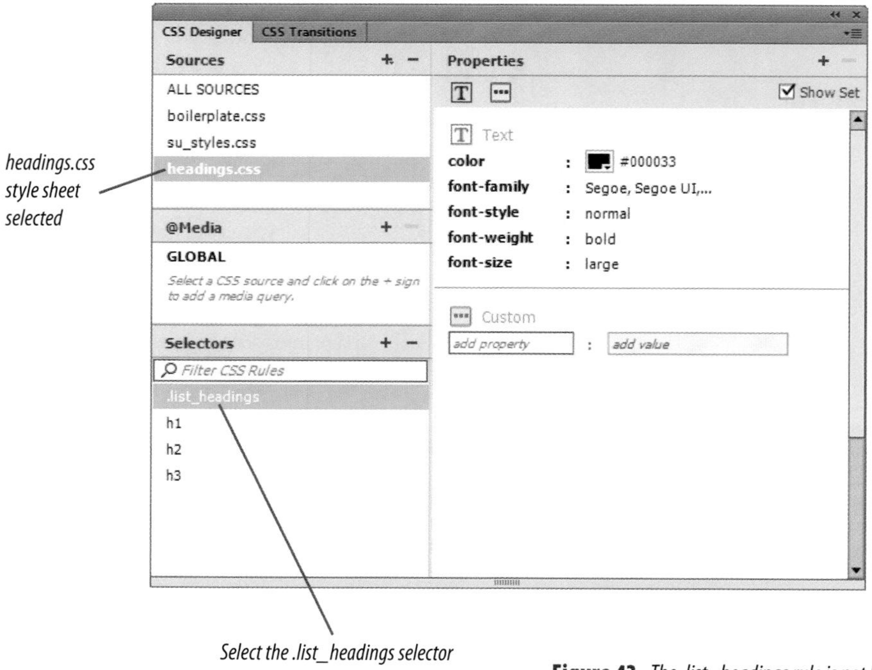

headings.css style sheet selected

Select the .list_headings selector

The list_headings style has been moved to the su_styles.css file and no longer appears in the headings.css file

Figure 43 *The .list_headings rule is not listed*

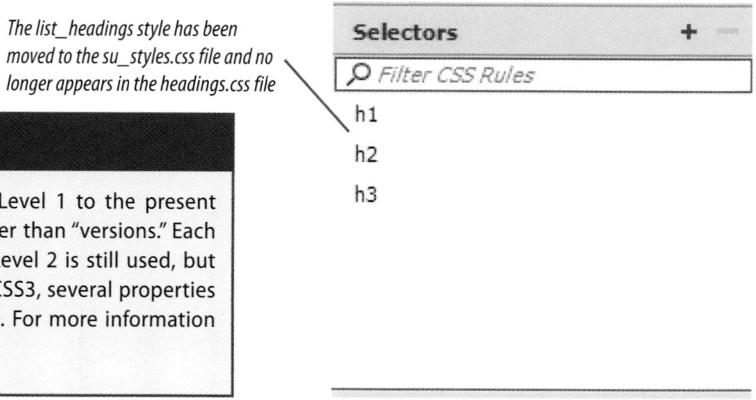

Selectors	+
🔍 *Filter CSS Rules*	
h1	
h2	
h3	

The Evolution of CSS3

The use of Cascading Style Sheets has evolved over the years from CSS Level 1 to the present CSS Level 3. Cascading Style Sheets revisions are referenced by "levels" rather than "versions." Each new level builds on the previous level. CSS Level 1 is obsolete today. CSS Level 2 is still used, but CSS Level 3 is the latest W3C (World Wide Web Consortium) standard. With CSS3, several properties are available that promote website accessibility such as the @font-face rule. For more information about CSS3, go to www.w3.org/TR/CSS/.

Figure 44 *Selecting the code to move*

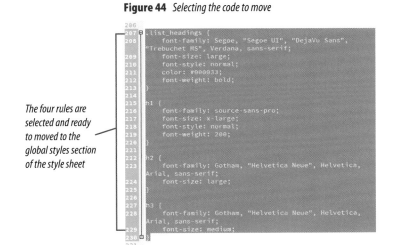

The four rules are selected and ready to moved to the global styles section of the style sheet

Figure 45 *Viewing the four rules moved to the global styles section of the su_styles.css file*

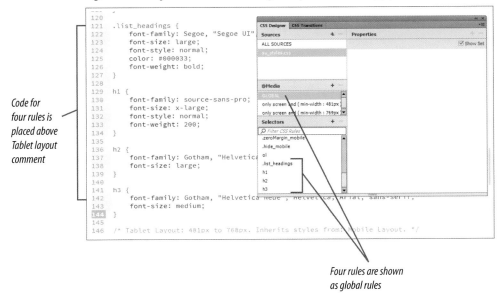

Code for four rules is placed above Tablet layout comment

Four rules are shown as global rules

6. Select **su_styles.css** on the Related files toolbar, then scroll to the bottom of the file to locate the code for the four styles that you just moved from the headings.css file, then select those lines of code, as shown in Figure 44.

7. Right-click the selected code, then select **Cut**.

8. Scroll to place the insertion point above the comment "/* Tablet Layout: 481px to 768px. Inherits styles from: Mobile Layout. */", right-click, then select **Paste**.

   The code for the four styles now is categorized as GLOBAL codes that can be used for all devices, as shown in Figure 45.

9. Switch to Code view on the Spa page, scroll to find the link in the head section to the headings.css file, then delete it.

10. Delete the **headings.css** file in the Files panel.

11. Return to Design view, then save and close all open files.

You moved three embedded rules to the su_styles.css style sheet. You then moved the code from the bottom of the style sheet to the global styles section of the code. Finally, you deleted the headings.css source, which was now empty.

Create unordered and ordered lists.

1. Open the Blooms & Bulbs website.
2. Open the tips page.
3. Select the text items below the Seasonal Gardening Checklist heading and format them as an unordered list. (*Hint*: There are no paragraph breaks between each item. To correct this, enter a paragraph break between each line, then remove any extra spaces.)
4. Select the lines of text below the Basic Gardening Tips heading and format them as an ordered list. (Refer to the Step 3 hint if each line does not become a separate list item.)
5. Save your work.

Create a Cascading Style Sheet and apply, edit, and add rules.

1. Create a new CSS file named **headings.css**.
2. Create a new global selector in the headings.css style sheet named **.bullet_term**.
3. Choose the following text properties and values for the .bullet_term selector: color: #333333; font-weight: bold; font-size: medium.
4. Apply the bullet_term rule to the names of the seasons in the Seasonal Gardening Checklist: Fall, Winter, Spring, and Summer.

5. Edit the bullet_term rule by changing the font size to large.
6. Create a new global selector to modify the h1 tag in the headings.css file with the following property and value: font-size = large.
7. Save your work.

Understand related files and media queries.

1. Select the bb_styles.css file in the Related files toolbar.
2. Change to Code view, then locate each block of code that lists the global, tablet, and desktop selectors.
3. Return to Design view.

Add Adobe Edge Web fonts.

1. Select the headings.css in the CSS Designer Sources pane, then select h1 in the Selectors pane.
2. Select the font-family list box in the Properties pane, then select Manage Fonts.
3. Select the font Lobster Two from the list of fonts recommended for headings.
4. Set the lobster-two font for the h1 font-family value.
5. Use the Clean Up Web Fonts Script Tag (Current Page), then save your work.
6. View the tips page in Live view to view the new h1 font.

Use coding tools to view and edit rules.

1. Open the index page, then change to Code view.
2. Display the code for the head section of the page.
3. Collapse all of the selected code.
4. Expand the code.
5. Use CSS Designer to attach the headings.css file to the index page, then select headings.css in the CSS Designer Sources pane.
6. Select the .bullet_term selector, then drag and drop it to bb_styles.css in the Sources pane.
7. Repeat Step 6 to move the h1 rule to the bb_styles.css file.
8. Select headings.css in the Sources pane, then delete it as a source in the Sources pane.
9. Select bb_styles.css on the Related files toolbar, scroll to the bottom of the file to locate the code for the two styles that you just moved from the headings.css file, then select and cut those lines of code.
10. Scroll to place the insertion point above the comment "/* Tablet Layout: 481px to 768px. Inherits styles from: Mobile Layout. */", right-click, then paste the code you just cut.
11. Go to the tips page code and remove the link to the headings.css file if you find one there, then select and delete the headings.css file in the Files panel.
12. Check the code for the index and tips page for a link to the headings.css file. If you see one, delete it and save the page.
13. Save all open files, change to Design view, compare your pages to Figures 46 and 47, then close all open files.

Figure 46 & 47 *Completed Skills Review*

Home - Featured Plants - Garden Tips - Workshops - Newsletter

Welcome to Blooms & Bulbs. We carry a variety of plants and shrubs along with a large inventory of gardening supplies. Our four greenhouses are full of healthy young plants just waiting to be planted in your yard. We grow an amazing selection of annuals and perennials. We also stock a diverse selection of trees, shrubs, tropicals, water plants, and ground covers. Check out our garden ware for your garden accents or as gifts for your gardening friends. We are happy to deliver or ship your purchases.

Our staff includes a certified landscape architect, three landscape designers
plans tailored to your location as well as planting and regular maintenance
surrounding area for twelve years now. Stop by and see us soon!

Blooms & Bulbs
Highway 43 South
Alvin, TX 77501
555-248-0806
Customer Service

Copyright 2002 - 201
Last updated on April 17

We have lots of tips we would like to share with you as you prepare your gardens this season. Remember, there is always something to be done for your gardens, no matter what the season. Our experienced staff is here to help you plan your gardens, select your plants, prepare your soil, assist you in the planting, and maintain your beds. Check out our calendar for a list of our scheduled workshops. Our next workshop is "Attracting Butterflies to Your Garden." All workshops are free of charge and on a first-come, first-served basis! They fill up quickly, so be sure to reserve your spot early.

Seasonal Gardening Checklist

- **Fall** – The time to plant trees and spring-blooming bulbs. Take the time to clean the leaves and dead foliage from your beds and lawn.
- **Winter** – The time to prune fruit trees and finish planting your bulbs. Don't forget to water young trees when the ground is dry.
- **Spring** – The time to prepare your beds, plant annuals, and apply fertilizer to established plants. Remember to mulch to maintain moisture and prevent weed growth.
- **Summer** – The time to supplement rainfall so that plants get one inch of water per week. Plant your vegetable garden and enjoy bountiful harvests until late fall.

Basic Gardening Tips

1. Select plants according to your climate.
2. In planning your garden, consider the composition, texture, structure, depth, and drainage of your soil.
3. Use compost to improve the structure of your soil.
4. Choose plant foods based on your garden objectives.
5. Generally, plants should receive one inch of water per week.
6. Use mulch to conserve moisture, keep plants cool, and cut down on weeding.

Use Figure 48 as a guide to continue your work on the TripSmart website that you began in Project Builder 1 in Chapter 1, and continued to work on in Chapter 2. (Your finished pages will look different if you choose different formatting options.) You are now ready to create some rules to use for the text on the newsletter and index pages.

1. Open the TripSmart website.
2. Open dw3_1.html from where you store your Data Files and save it in the tripsmart site folder as **newsletter.html**, overwriting the existing newsletter.html file and not updating the links.
3. Create an unordered list from the text beginning "Be organized." to the end of the page except for the contact information.
4. Create a new CSS file named **headings.css.**
5. Create a new selector in the headings.css style sheet named **.list_terms**.
6. Choose properties and values of your choice for the .list_terms selector.
7. Apply the .list_terms rule to each of the item names in the list such as "Be organized."
8. Close the dw3_1.html page, then save the newsletter page and the style sheet.
9. Select the headings.css file in the CSS Designer Sources pane, then create a tag selector to format the h1 tag with properties and values of your choice. If you like, you can choose an Edge Web font.

10. Apply the h1 format to the Ten Tips for Stress-Free Travel heading, use the Clean Up Web Fonts Script Tag (Current Page) if you used an Edge Web font, return to Design view, then save your work.
11. View the newsletter page in Live view to view the new h1 font.
12. Move the two selectors in the headings.css file to the tripsmart_styles.css file, being sure to place them above the comment "/* Tablet Layout: 481px to 768px. Inherits styles from: Mobile Layout. */".
13. Select and delete the headings.css file in the Files panel.
14. Delete the headings.css source in the CSS Designer Sources pane, then save and preview the newsletter page in your browser, using Figure 48 as an example.
15. Close your browser, then close all open files.

Figure 48 *Sample Project Builder 1*

Working with Text and Cascading Style Sheets

In this exercise, you continue your work on the Carolyne's Creations website that you started in Project Builder 2 in Chapter 1, and continued to build in Chapter 2. You are now ready to add a page to the website that will showcase a recipe. Figure 49 shows a possible solution for the page in this exercise. Your finished pages will look different if you choose different formatting options.

1. Open the Carolyne's Creations website.
2. Open dw3_2.html from the location where you store your Data Files, save it to the website site folder as **recipes.html**, overwriting the existing file and not updating the links. Close the dw3_2.html file.
3. Format the list of ingredients on the recipes page as an unordered list.
4. Create a new CSS Styles file named **headings.css**, then add a new tag selector rule that defines the properties for a Heading 1 rule and another one that defines the properties for a Heading 2 rule, using appropriate formatting options. Use Adobe Edge Web fonts if you like.
5. Apply the <h1> format to the "Caramel Coconut Pie" heading and the <h2> rule to the "Ingredients" and "Directions" headings, then save your work.

6. Move the two new selectors to the cc_styles.css file, then delete the headings.css source in the CSS Designer Sources pane, and also in the Files panel.
7. Save all open files, then preview the page in the browser.
8. Close your browser, then close all open pages.

Figure 49 *Sample Project Builder 2*

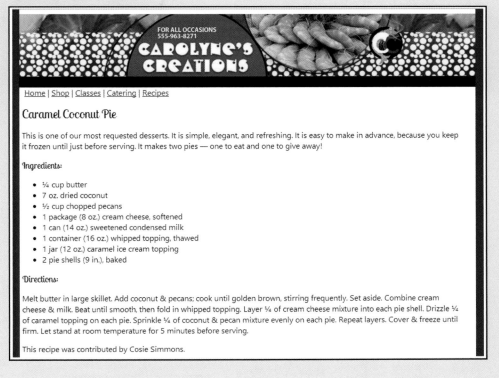

Home | Shop | Classes | Catering | Recipes

Caramel Coconut Pie

This is one of our most requested desserts. It is simple, elegant, and refreshing. It is easy to make in advance, because you keep it frozen until just before serving. It makes two pies — one to eat and one to give away!

Ingredients:

- ¼ cup butter
- 7 oz. dried coconut
- ½ cup chopped pecans
- 1 package (8 oz.) cream cheese, softened
- 1 can (14 oz.) sweetened condensed milk
- 1 container (16 oz.) whipped topping, thawed
- 1 jar (12 oz.) caramel ice cream topping
- 2 pie shells (9 in.), baked

Directions:

Melt butter in large skillet. Add coconut & pecans; cook until golden brown, stirring frequently. Set aside. Combine cream cheese & milk. Beat until smooth, then fold in whipped topping. Layer ¼ of cream cheese mixture into each pie shell. Drizzle ¼ of caramel topping on each pie. Sprinkle ¼ of coconut & pecan mixture evenly on each pie. Repeat layers. Cover & freeze until firm. Let stand at room temperature for 5 minutes before serving.

This recipe was contributed by Cosie Simmons.

Charles Chappell is a sixth-grade history teacher. He is reviewing educational websites for information he can use in his classroom.

1. Connect to the Internet, then navigate to the Library of Congress website at www.loc.gov. The Library of Congress website is shown in Figure 50.

2. Which fonts are used for the main content on the home page—serif or sans-serif? Are the same fonts used consistently on the other pages in the site?

3. Do you see ordered or unordered lists on any pages in the site? If so, how are they used?

4. Use the View > Source (IE) or the Tools > Web Developer > Page Source (Firefox) command to view the source code to see if a style sheet was used.

5. Do you see the use of Cascading Style Sheets noted in the source code?

Figure 50 *Design Project*

Source: Library of Congress

In this assignment, you will continue to work on the website that you started in Chapter 1, and continued to build in Chapter 2. No Data Files are supplied. You are building this site from chapter to chapter, so you must do each Portfolio Project assignment in each chapter to complete your website.

You continue building your website by designing and completing a page that contains a list, headings, and paragraph text. During this process, you will develop a style sheet and add several rules to it

1. Consult your wireframe and decide which page to create and develop for this chapter.
2. Plan the page content for the page and make a sketch of the layout. Your sketch should include at least one ordered or unordered list, appropriate headings, and paragraph text. Your sketch should also show where the paragraph text and headings should be placed on the page and what rules should be used for each type of text. You should plan on creating at least two CSS rules.
3. Create the page using your sketch for guidance.
4. Create a Cascading Style Sheet for the site and add to it the rules you decided to use. Apply the rules to the appropriate content.
5. Attach the style sheet to the index page you developed in Chapter 2.
6. Preview the new page in a browser, then check for page layout problems and broken links. Make any necessary corrections in Dreamweaver, then preview the page again in the browser. Repeat this process until you are satisfied with the way the page looks in the browser.
7. Use the checklist in Figure 51 to check all the pages in your site.
8. Close the browser, then close all open pages.

Figure 51 *Portfolio Project*

Website Checklist

1. Does each page have a page title?
2. Does the home page have a description and keywords?
3. Does the home page contain contact information?
4. Does every completed page in the site have consistent navigation links?
5. Does the home page have a last updated statement that will automatically update when the page is saved?
6. Do all paths for links and images work correctly?
7. Is there a style sheet with at least two rules?
8. Did you apply the rules to all text blocks?
9. Do all pages look good using mobile, tablet, and desktop sizes?

© 2015 Cengage Learning®

CHAPTER **4** ADDING IMAGES

1. Insert and align images using CSS
2. Enhance an image and use alternate text
3. Insert a background image and perform site maintenance
4. Add graphic enhancements

DREAMWEAVER

4
ADDING IMAGES

Introduction

The majority of web page information appears in the form of text. But pages are much more interesting if they also include images that enhance or illustrate the information. A well-designed web page usually includes a balanced combination of text and images. Dreamweaver provides many tools for working with images that you can use to make your web pages attractive and easy to understand.

Using Images to Enhance Web Pages

Images make web pages visually stimulating and more exciting than pages that contain only text. However, you should use images with an eye on both the purpose of each page and the overall design plan. There is a fine balance between using too many images that overwhelm the user and not providing enough images to enhance the text. There are many ways to work with images so that they complement the content of pages in a website. For instance, a research website would probably need few graphics other than charts, because the content emphasis would

be on text. A photographer's website, on the other hand, would be rich in high-quality photographs to display the photographer's expertise. You can use specific file formats used to save images for websites to ensure maximum quality with minimum file size.

Graphics Versus Images

Two terms that designers sometimes use interchangeably are graphics and images. For the purposes of discussion in this text, we will use the term **graphics** to refer to the appearance of most non-text items on a web page, such as photographs, logos, menu bars, animations, charts, background images, and drawings. Files for items such as these are called graphic files. They are referred to by their file type, or graphic file format, such as JPEG (Joint Photographic Experts Group), GIF (Graphics Interchange Format), or PNG (Portable Network Graphics). We will refer to the actual pictures that you see on the pages as images. But don't worry about which term to use. Many people use one term or the other according to habit or region, or use them interchangeably.

Insert and
ALIGN IMAGES USING CSS

What You'll Do

In this lesson, you will insert an image on the about_us page in The Striped Umbrella website. You will then adjust the alignment of the image on the page to make the page more visually appealing.

Understanding Graphic File Formats

When you choose graphics to add to a web page, it's important to use graphic files in the appropriate file format. Keep in mind the different types of devices that may be used to view the pages, such as tablets or other mobile devices. The three primary graphic file formats used in web pages are **GIF** (Graphics Interchange Format), **JPEG** or **JPG** (Joint Photographic Experts Group), and **PNG** (Portable Network Graphics). GIF files download quickly, making them ideal to use on web pages. Though limited in the number of colors they can represent, GIF files have the ability to show transparent areas. JPG files can display many colors. Because they often contain many shades of the same color, photographs are often saved in JPG format. Files saved with the PNG format can display many colors and use various degrees of transparency, called **opacity**. The PNG format gives greater color depth when designing for mobile devices.

Understanding the Assets Panel

When you add a graphic to a website, Dreamweaver automatically adds it to the Assets panel. The **Assets panel** displays all the assets (images, videos, audio files) in a website. The Assets panel contains eight category buttons that you use to view your assets by category. These include Images, Colors, URLs, SWF, Movies, Scripts, Templates, and Library. To view a particular type of asset, click the appropriate category button.

The Assets panel is divided into two panes. When you select the Images button, the lower pane displays a list of all the images in your site and is divided into five columns. Resize the Assets panel to see all five columns, by dragging a side or corner of the panel border.

The top pane displays a thumbnail of the selected image in the list. You can view assets in each category in two ways. You can use the Site option button to view all the assets in a website, or you can use the Favorites option button to view those assets that you have designated as **favorites**, or assets that you expect to use repeatedly while you work on the site. You can use the Assets panel to add an asset to a web page by dragging the asset from the Assets panel to the page or by using the Insert button on the Assets panel.

Aligning Images

When you insert an image on a web page, you need to position it in relation to other page elements such as text or other images. Positioning an image is also called **aligning** an image. By default, when you insert an image in a paragraph, its bottom edge aligns with the baseline of the first line of text or any other element in the same paragraph. When you first place images on a page, they do not include code to align them, so they appear at the insertion point, with no other page elements next to them. You add alignment settings using CSS. By adding a new rule to modify the <img> tag, you can add an alignment property and value. If you use an external style sheet, the <img> tag will apply globally to all images on pages with a link to the style sheet. If you want to align some images differently than others, create specific rules for each device when using fluid grid layouts. However, as you create these rules, remember the rules of inheritance: tablet and desktop selectors inherit global (mobile) properties, but if you modify the tablet properties, the desktop selectors then inherit the tablet properties, unless you specify otherwise, as shown in Figure 1.

Selecting Images for a Responsive Design

It is important to visualize how your images will look when displayed in multiple devices. Experiment with the images you select by using the Mobile, Tablet, and Desktop size buttons to see how they will look on the finished page. One way to allow for attractive placement of images is to avoid setting specific sizes for image heights and widths on a page. If you do set image sizes, use percents so the image can adjust proportionally to the screen size. Still another method is to specify different images for each device. The Striped Umbrella website has a different image used as the banner background for the mobile size page. The tablet size page uses the same banner image as the desktop size, but not all of the umbrellas on the right side of the banner are visible when the window width is reduced to tablet size. Try each of these methods and see which best fits your design needs.

Figure 1 *Rules of inheritance for selectors*

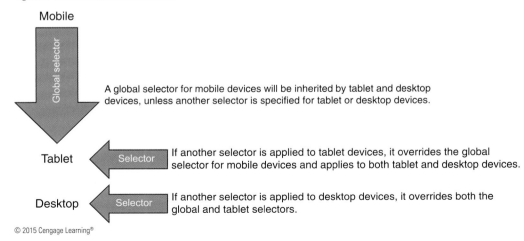

Mobile

Global selector

A global selector for mobile devices will be inherited by tablet and desktop devices, unless another selector is specified for tablet or desktop devices.

Tablet — Selector

If another selector is applied to tablet devices, it overrides the global selector for mobile devices and applies to both tablet and desktop devices.

Desktop — Selector

If another selector is applied to desktop devices, it overrides both the global and tablet selectors.

© 2015 Cengage Learning®

Insert an image

1. Open The Striped Umbrella website, then open dw4_1.html from the drive and folder where you store your Data Files.

   Notice that the page is not formatted, as shown in Figure 2. This is because the page cannot find the style sheet. The style sheet is in the local site folder, but not in the Data Files folder. When you save the file without updating links, the link to the style sheet will find the style sheet and apply the selectors to the page elements. If you update links, the link to the style sheet will be broken and the page will remain unformatted.

2. Save the file as **about_us.html** in the local site folder, select **Yes** (Win) or **Replace** (Mac) to overwrite the existing file, select **No** to Update Links, then close dw4_1.html.

   The new about_us page is now formatted with the website style sheets since the link to the su_styles.css file can now find the file in the local site folder.

3. In the Property inspector, select the **HTML button** `<> HTML`, if necessary, then apply the Heading 1 tag to the text "Welcome guests!"

4. Place the insertion point before "When" in the first paragraph, switch to Code view to place your insertion point before the opening <p> tag for the first paragraph, if necessary, return to Design view, select the **Images list arrow** in the Common category in the Insert panel, then select **Image** to open the Select Image Source dialog box.

(continued)

Figure 2 *The about_us page before the CSS file is linked to apply formatting*

Welcome guests!

When you arrive at The Striped Umbrella, check in at The Club House. Look for the signs that will direct you to registration. Our beautiful club house is the home base for our registration offices, The Sand Crab Cafe, and The Sea Spa. Registration is open from 8:00 a.m. until 6:00 p.m. Please call to make arrangements if you plan to arrive after 6:00 p.m. The cafe and spa hours are both posted and listed in the information packet that you will receive when you arrive. The main swimming pool is directly behind The Club House. A lifeguard is on duty from 8:00 a.m. until 9:00 p.m. The pool area includes a wading pool, a lap pool, and a large pool with a diving board. Showers are located in several areas for your use before and after swimming. We also provide poolside service from the cafe for snacks and lunch.

Text is not yet formatted since the links to the style sheets cannot find the style sheets to apply the styles

Figure 3 *Striped Umbrella about_us page with the inserted image*

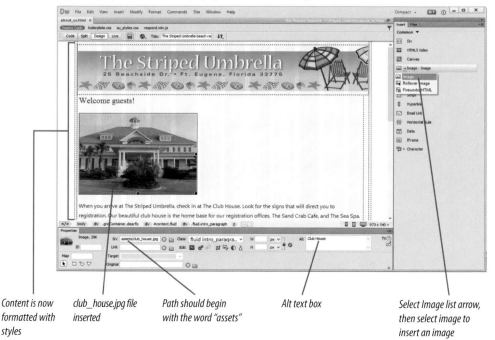

Content is now formatted with styles

club_house.jpg file inserted

Path should begin with the word "assets"

Alt text box

Select Image list arrow, then select image to insert an image

Figure 4 *Image files for The Striped Umbrella website listed in Assets panel*

Images button

Thumbnail of selected image

List of images in The Striped Umbrella website

Refresh Site List button

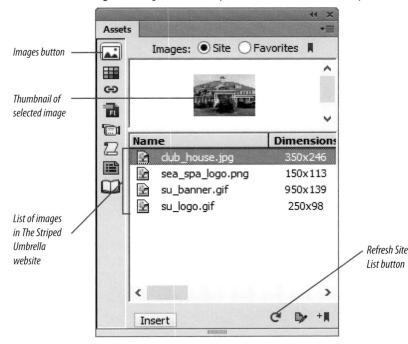

Organizing Assets for Quick Access

Your can organize the assets in the Assets panel in two ways, using the Site and Favorites options buttons. The Site option lists all of the assets in the website in the selected category in alphabetical order. But in a complex site, your asset list can grow quite large. To avoid having to scroll to search for frequently used items, you can designate them as Favorites. To add an asset to the Favorites list, right-click (Win) or [control]-click (Mac) the asset name in the Site list, and then select Add to Favorites. When you place an asset in the Favorites list, it still appears in the Site list. To delete an asset from the Favorites list, select the Favorites option button in the Assets panel, select the asset you want to delete, and then press [Delete] or [Backspace] (Win) or [control][delete] (Mac), or the Remove from Favorites button on the Assets panel. If you delete an asset from the Favorites list, it still remains in the Site list. You can further organize your Favorites list by creating folders for similar assets and grouping them inside the folders.

5. Navigate to the assets folder in the drive and folder where you store your Data Files, double-click **club_house.jpg**, type the alternate text **Club House** in the Alt text box in the Property inspector, open the Files panel if necessary, then verify that the file was copied to your assets folder in the striped_umbrella site root folder.

6. If the text appears on the same line as the image, place the insertion point before "When" again, press **[Enter]** (Win) or **[return]** (Mac), then select the club house image.

   The paragraph now begins under the club house image, as shown in Figure 3.

7. Open the **Assets panel**, select the **Images button** in the Assets panel (if necessary), then select the **Refresh Site List button** in the Assets panel to update the list of images in The Striped Umbrella website.

   The Assets panel displays a list of all the images in The Striped Umbrella website, as shown in Figure 4. If you don't see the new image listed, press and hold [CTRL] (Win) or ⌘ (Mac) before you select the Refresh Site List button.

8. Close the Assets panel.

You inserted one image on the about_us page and verified that it was copied to the assets folder of the website.

Create a global class selector for images

1. Open CSS Designer and expand the width to display two columns, if necessary.

2. Select **su_styles.css** in the Sources pane, then select **GLOBAL** in the @Media pane.

   You are creating a new global rule that will apply to all images that you want to control the float, or position in relation to other page elements next to them. Remember that global rules are used to style page elements for the mobile size display and are inherited by the tablet and desktop size devices unless otherwise specified.

3. Select the **Add Selector button** ✚ in the Selectors pane, then type **.img_float** in the selector name text box and press **[Enter]** (Win) or **[return]** (Mac).

   TIP When you add a new class selector, remember to type a period before all class selector names.

4. Select the **.img_float** selector in the Selectors pane if necessary, then uncheck the **Show Set** check box in the Properties pane if necessary.

5. Select the **Layout button** 🔳 in the Properties pane, if necessary, then scroll down to select the **none button** ◲ beside the float property, as shown in Figure 5.

   (continued)

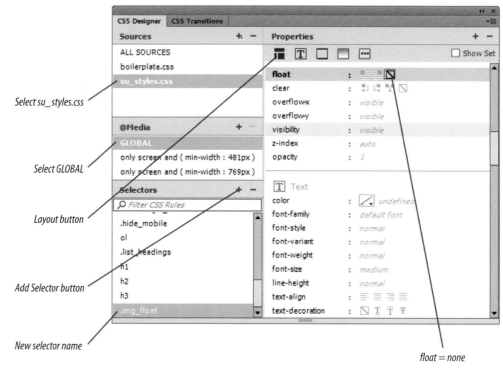

Figure 5 *Selecting the float property for the .img_float selector*

Select su_styles.css

Select GLOBAL

Layout button

Add Selector button

New selector name

float = none

Figure 6 *Viewing only the GLOBAL .img_float selector's set properties*

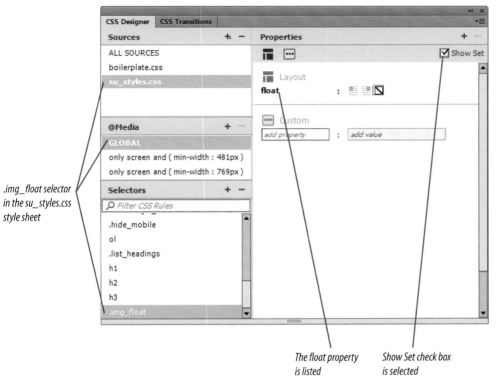

.img_float selector
in the su_styles.css
style sheet

The float property
is listed

Show Set check box
is selected

The default value for the float property is none. The float property is used to force other page elements to display to the right or to the left of another page element. The none value means that no other page element will appear beside an image with this selector applied. The left value means an image styled with this selector will "float" to the left of other page elements if space is available. The right value means an image styled with this selector will "float" to the right of other page elements if space is available.

6. Select the **Show Set check box** to see the new selector, as shown in Figure 6, then uncheck it again.

   The Show Set check box allows you to quickly see only the properties that have been set for a selector.

7. Save all files.

You added a global selector named .img_float to set the float property to none selector.

Create a tablet size selector for images

1. Select **su_styles.css** in the Sources pane, then select **only screen and (min-width : 481px)** in the @Media pane.

   You are going to modify the .img_float selector for viewing on a tablet size device.

2. Select the **Add Selector button** + in the Selectors pane, then type **.img_float** in the selector name text box and press **[Enter]** (Win) or **[return]** (Mac) twice.

3. Select the **.img_float** selector in the Selectors pane if necessary, then uncheck the **Show Set** check box in the Properties pane if necessary.

4. Select the **Layout button** in the Properties pane if necessary, then scroll down to select the **left button** beside the float property, as shown in Figure 7.

   An image styled with this selector will "float" to the left of other page elements when viewed on a tablet-size or desktop-size device. The global .img_float selector will no longer apply to images with this selector when they are viewed on a tablet-size or desktop-size device, because this selector will now take precedence. Desktop devices will inherit the tablet selector properties and values unless otherwise specified.

   (continued)

Figure 7 *Selecting the float property for the tablet size img selector*

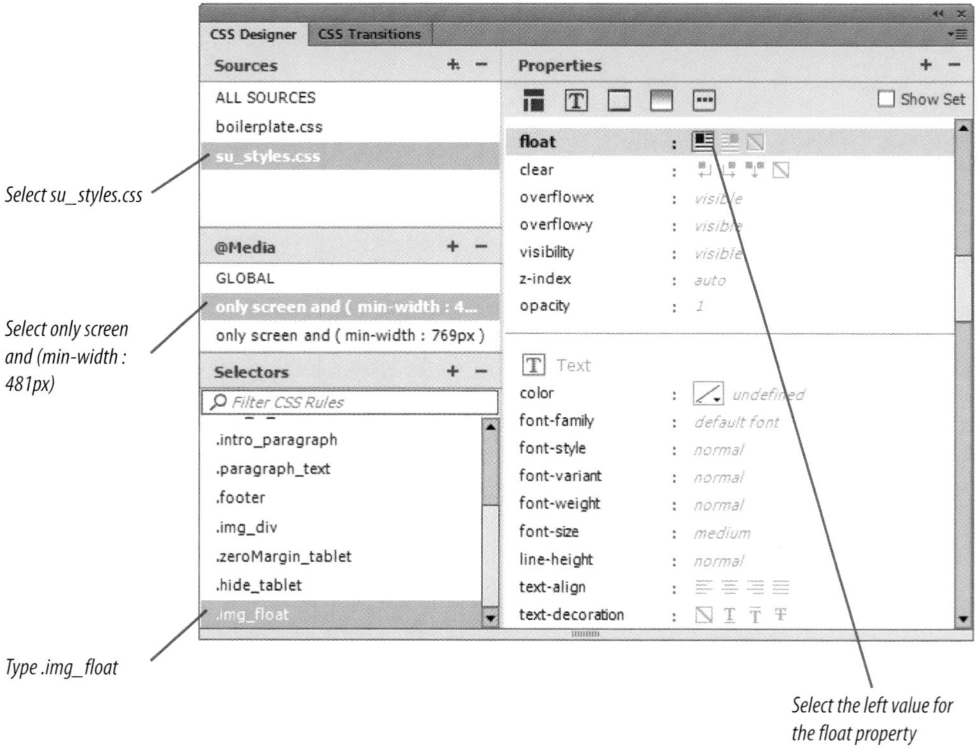

Select su_styles.css

Select only screen and (min-width : 481px)

Type .img_float

Select the left value for the float property

Figure 8 *Viewing the tablet size img selector's set float property*

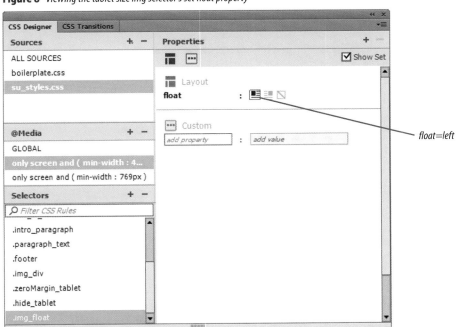

float=left

5. Select the **Show Set check box** to see the new selector, as shown in Figure 8, then uncheck it again.

   The Show Set check box allows you to quickly see only the properties that have been set for a selector.

6. Save all files.

You set the float property to left for the tablet size img selector.

Apply a selector and view the pages in three device sizes

1. On the about_us page, select the **club house** image if necessary, select the **Class list arrow** on the Property inspector, then select **img_float**, as shown in Figure 9.

   The img_float selector is applied to the club house image. The paragraph of text moves up and to the right of the club house image.

2. Select the **Mobile size** button 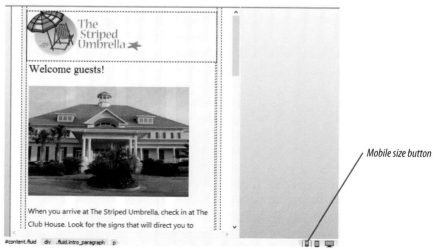 on the Status bar.

   The paragraphs of text are below the club house image when viewed in mobile size, as shown in Figure 10, because the img_float global selector has a float value of none.

   (continued)

Figure 9 *Applying the img_float selector to the club house image*

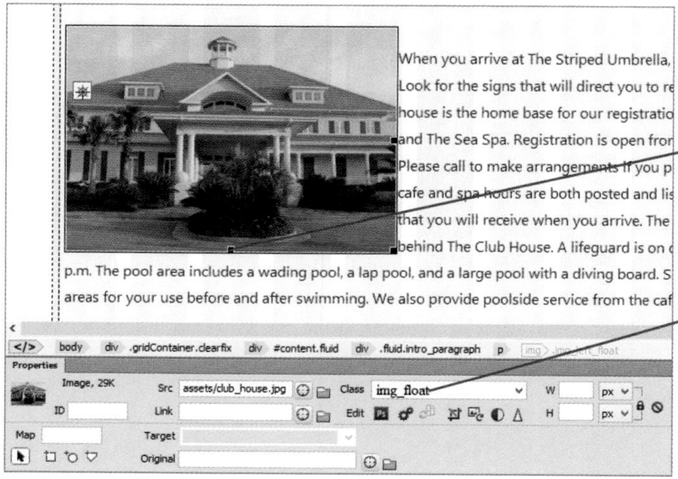

Club house image is selected

img_float selector is selected

Figure 10 *Viewing the about us page in mobile size*

Mobile size button

Figure 11 *Viewing the about us page in tablet size*

Figure 12 *Viewing the about us page in desktop size*

Desktop size button

Tablet size button

Figure 13 *Viewing the two new rules in the su_styles.css file*

Mobile rule

Tablet rule

3. Select the **Tablet size** button  on the Status bar.

   The first paragraph of text floats up to the right side of the image when the screen is wider, as shown in Figure 11, because the tablet size img_float selector has a float value of left.

4. Select the **Desktop size** button on the Status bar.

   With the inherited tablet size img_float selector, the first paragraph of text floats up to the right side of the image with longer lines of text filling the empty space when the screen is wider, as shown in Figure 12.

5. Select **su_styles.css** in the Related Files toolbar, then scroll to locate the two image_float rules.

   Each rule is in a separate section of the file, as shown in Figure 13: one in the mobile layout (global) section of code, and one in the tablet layout section of code. Because the desktop layout inherits the tablet size img_float selector, it does not have an img_float selector listed.

   The two sections of code have been collapsed to show each of the rules in the same figure.

6. Return to Design view.

You applied the img_float selector to the club house image, then viewed the results in three device sizes.

Enhance an Image and
USE ALTERNATE TEXT

What You'll Do

In this lesson, you will use CSS to add borders to images, add horizontal and vertical space to set them apart from the text, and then add or edit alternate text for each image on the page.

Enhancing an Image

After you place an image on a web page, you have several options for enhancing it, or improving its appearance. To make changes to the image itself, such as removing scratches from it, or erasing parts of it, you need to use an external image editor such as Adobe Fireworks or Adobe Photoshop.

You can use Dreamweaver to enhance how images appear on a page. For example, you can modify the brightness and contrast, add borders around an image or add horizontal and vertical space. **Borders** are frames that surround an image. Horizontal and vertical space is blank space above, below, and on the sides of an image that separates the image from text or other elements on the page. Adding horizontal or vertical space is the same as adding white space, and helps images stand out on a page. You add horizontal and vertical space with the CSS margin properties and add borders with the CSS borders properties. The Department of Transportation website,

---

DESIGNTIP

Resizing Graphics Using an External Editor

Each image on a web page takes a specific number of seconds to download, depending on the size of the file. Larger files (in kilobytes, not width and height) take longer to download than smaller files. It's important to use the smallest acceptable size for an image on a page. If you need to reduce the file size, use an external image editor to do so, instead of resizing it in Dreamweaver. Decreasing the size of an image using the H (height) and W (width) settings in the Property inspector does not reduce the file size or the time it will take the file to download. Ideally you should use images that have the smallest file size and the highest quality possible, so that each page downloads as quickly as possible.

as shown in Figure 14, uses horizontal and vertical space around the images to help make these images more prominent. Adding horizontal or vertical space does not affect the width or height of the image. You can also add spacing around web page objects by using "spacer" images, or transparent images that act as placeholders.

Using Alternate Text

One of the easiest ways to make your web page user-friendly and accessible to people of all abilities is to use alternate text. Alternate text is descriptive text that appears in place of an image while the image is downloading or not displayed. **Screen readers**, devices used by persons with visual impairments to convert written text on a computer monitor to spoken words, can "read" alternate text aloud and make it possible for users to have an image described to them in detail. You should also use alternate text when inserting form objects, text displayed as graphics, buttons, frames, and media files. Without alternate text assigned to these objects, screen readers will not be able to read them.

One of the default preferences in Dreamweaver is to prompt you to enter alternate text whenever you insert media on a page. You can set alternate text options in the Accessibility category of the Preferences dialog box. You can program some browsers to display only alternate text and to download images manually. Earlier versions of some browsers used to show alternate text when the pointer was placed over an image, such as Internet Explorer versions before version 8.0.

The use of alternate text is the first checkpoint listed in the Web Content Accessibility Guidelines (WCAG), Version 2.0, from the World Wide Web Consortium (W3C). The 12 WCAG guidelines are grouped together under four principles: perceivable, operable, understandable, and robust. The first guideline under perceivable states that a website should

"Provide text alternatives for any non-text content so that it can be changed into other forms people need, such as large print, Braille, speech, symbols, or simpler language." To view the complete set of accessibility guidelines, go to the Web Accessibility Initiative page at w3.org/WAI/. You should always strive to meet these criteria for all web pages.

Figure 14 *Department of Transportation website*

Source: United States Department of Transportation

Add a border

1. Select **su_styles** in the CSS Designer Sources pane, select **GLOBAL** in the @Media pane, then select **img_float** in the Selectors pane.

   Since the image property you are going to create will apply to all device-size layouts, it can be defined once in the GLOBAL media selector. The tablet and desktop size layouts will inherit this image property.

2. Select the **Border button** ☐ in the Properties pane, then select the **All sides button** ☐ .

3. Select the **width value** text box, then select **thin**.

4. Select the **style value** text box, then select **solid**.

5. Select the **default color text box** ☐ , use the Color picker to select a **dark gray color**, then compare your screen to Figure 15.

   Your color value will probably have a different HEX value.

6. Select the **Mobile size button** ☐ on the Status bar, select the **Tablet size button** ☐ , then select the **Desktop size button** ☐ .

   The thin gray border surrounds the image in each layout, as shown in Figure 16, since the image border property was inherited by the tablet and desktop layouts.

   You edited the img_float global selector by adding a border.

Figure 15 *The img_float border values in the CSS Designer Properties pane*

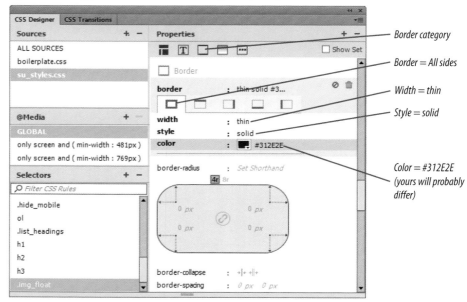

Border category
Border = All sides
Width = thin
Style = solid
Color = #312E2E
(yours will probably differ)

Figure 16 *Viewing the image_float border in the Desktop-size layout*

Welcome guests!

Thin border frames image

When you arrive at The Stripe
Look for the signs that will dir
house is the home base for ou
and The Sea Spa. Registration
Please call to make arrangem
cafe and spa hours are both p
that you will receive when you
directly behind The Club Hous

until 9:00 p.m. The pool area includes a wading pool, a lap pool, and a large pool

Adding Images

Figure 17 *Setting the margin property value for the img_float selector*

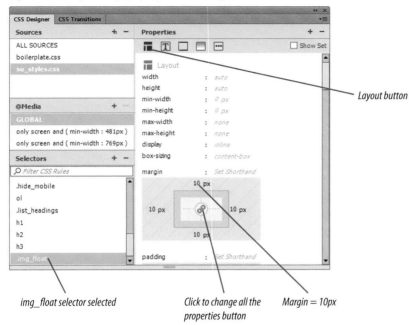

Layout button

img_float selector selected

Click to change all the
properties button

Margin = 10px

Figure 18 *Viewing the image with a border and margins*

The club house
image has a margin
around all sides

Add horizontal and vertical space

1. With the img_float global selector selected in the Selectors pane, select the **Layout button** ▀▀ , then select the **Click to change all the properties button** ⟨⟩ in the middle of the margin properties diagram.

2. Select the **top margin property**, then type **10px**, then press [Enter] (Win) or [return] (Mac) as shown in Figure 17.

   By selecting the Click to change all the properties button, the 10 px margin is applied to all four sides of the image, as shown in Figure 18. The text is easier to read, because it is not so close to the edge of the image. Since you made these changes to the global img_float rule, they will also be inherited by the tablet and desktop size devices.

TIP If you don't want to set the same margin value to all sides, deselect the Click to change all the properties button, then select and change each value independently.

3. Save all files.

You added horizontal and vertical spacing to the img_float selector with the margin property.

Edit image settings

1. Select the **club house image** on the about_us page.

   The club_house image is a jpg, which is an appropriate format to use for photographs. You can tell the image is selected when you see selection handles around it.

2. Select the **Edit Images Settings button** in the Property inspector, then select the **Preset list arrow**, as shown in Figure 19.

   You can use the Image Optimization dialog box to save a copy of the image in a different file format. File property options vary depending on which graphics format you choose. When you choose a different file format, then edit and save it, the program creates a copy and does not alter the original file. The current image file size shown at the bottom of the dialog box is 23 K.

3. Choose the **JPEG for Photos (Continuous Tones)** preset, then notice that the file size that appears at the bottom of the dialog box has increased only slightly.

   You can also use the Quality slider to change the file size after you have selected a format and preset.

4. Select **OK** to save the changes and to close the Image Optimization dialog box.

5. Navigate to the website assets folder in the Save Web Image dialog box, then select **Save** to save the about_us.jpg image.

   You experimented with the format settings in the Image Optimization dialog box, then saved the image with the JPEG for Photos (Continuous Tones) preset.

Figure 19 *Choosing a Preset in the Image Optimization dialog box*

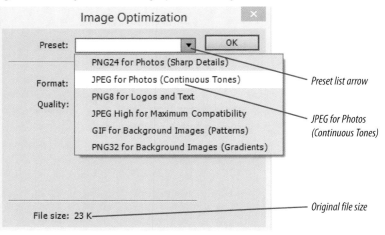

Preset list arrow

JPEG for Photos (Continuous Tones)

Original file size

Integrating Photoshop CC with Dreamweaver

Dreamweaver has many ways to integrate with Photoshop CC. For example, you can copy and paste a Photoshop PSD file directly from Photoshop into Dreamweaver. Dreamweaver will prompt you to optimize the image by choosing a file format and settings for the web. Then it will paste the image on the page. If you want to edit the image later, select the image, then select the Edit button in the Property inspector to open the image in Photoshop. (The appearance of the Edit button will change according to the default image editor you have specified.)

Photoshop users can set Photoshop as the default image editor in Dreamweaver for specific image file formats. For Windows users, select Edit on the Menu bar, select Preferences, select File Types/Editors, select Photoshop in the Editors list, then select Make Primary. If you don't see Photoshop listed, select the Add Editor button, then browse to select Photoshop. For Mac users, select Preferences, select File Types/Editors, select Photoshop in the Extensions list, then select Make Primary. If you don't see Photoshop listed, select the Add Extension button, then browse to select Photoshop. You can also edit an image in Photoshop and export an updated Smart Object instantly in Dreamweaver. A **Smart Object** is an image layer that stores image data from raster or vector images. Search the Adobe website for a tutorial on Photoshop and Dreamweaver integration. Fireworks is another commonly used default image editor. Use the same steps to select it rather than Photoshop.

Figure 20 *Alternate text setting in the Property inspector*

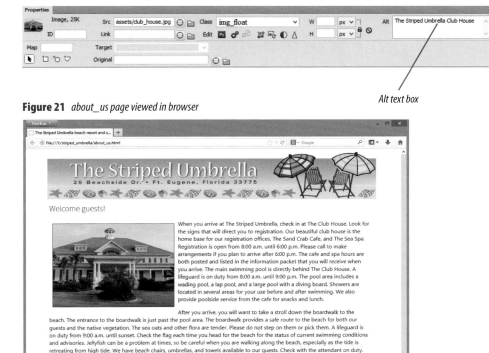

Alt text box

Figure 21 *about_us page viewed in browser*

Edit alternate text

1. Select the club house image, select **Club House** in the Alt text box in the Property inspector (if necessary), then type **The Striped Umbrella Club House** as shown in Figure 20.

2. Save your work.

3. Preview the page in your browser, compare your screen to Figure 21, then close your browser.

You edited the alternate text for the club house image.

POWER USER SHORTCUTS	
To do this:	**Use this shortcut:**
Switch views	[Ctrl][`] (Win) or ⌘ [`] (Mac)
Insert image	[Ctrl][Alt][I] (Win) or ⌘ [option][I] (Mac)
Refresh	[F5] (Win) or Refresh [fn][F5] (Mac)

© 2015 Cengage Learning®

Displaying Alternate Text in a Browser

There is a simple method you can use to force alternate text to appear in a browser when a mouse is held over an image. To do this, add a title tag to the image properties using the same text as the alt tag. Example: <img src ="assets/club_house.jpg" alt ="The Striped Umbrella Club House" title ="The Striped Umbrella Club House" class="img_float" /> This method will work in Internet Explorer and Mozilla Firefox.

Insert a Background Image and
PERFORM SITE MAINTENANCE

What You'll Do

In this lesson, you will insert a background image using an internal style. You will then move the internal selector to the su_styles.css style sheet. Last, you will edit the header background-image repeat value.

Inserting a Background Image

You can insert a background image on a web page to provide depth and visual interest to the page, or to communicate a message or mood. **Background images** are image files used in place of background colors. Although you can use background images to create a dramatic effect, you should avoid inserting them on web pages where they would not provide the contrast necessary for reading page text. Even though they might seem too plain, standard white backgrounds are usually the best choice for web pages. If you choose to use a background image on a web page, it should be small in file size. You can choose a single image that fills the page background, or you can choose a tiled image. A **tiled image** is a small image that repeats across and down a web page, appearing as individual squares or rectangles.

When you create a web page, you can use either a background color or a background image, unless you want the background color to appear while the background image finishes downloading. You can also use background images for some sections of your page and solid color backgrounds for other sections. The NASA home page shown in Figure 22 uses a night sky image for the page background, but individual sections have solid blue or white backgrounds. The banner has a dark night sky background, so NASA used white or light blue text to provide contrast. The stars in the background tie in well with the rest of the page design and help to set a dramatic mood.

Background images or background colors are inserted using CSS. To add them to a single page, use the Modify > Page Properties dialog box, which adds an internal rule to modify the body tag. To use them as a global setting for the entire site, create an external rule to modify the <body> tag.

Managing Images

As you work on a website, you might find that you have files in your assets folder that you don't use in the website. To avoid accumulating unnecessary files, it's a good idea to look at an image first, before you place it on the page, and copy it to the assets folder. If you inadvertently copy an unwanted file to the assets folder, you should delete it or move it to another location. This is a good website management practice that will prevent the assets folder from filling up with unwanted image files.

Removing an image from a web page does not remove it from the assets folder in the local site folder of the website. To remove an asset from a website, if you have a lot of files, it is faster to locate the file you want to remove in the Assets panel. You then use the Locate in Site command to open the Files panel with the unwanted file selected. If you don't have many images in your site, it is faster to locate them in the Files panel. You can then use the Delete command to remove the file from the site. If you designate frequently used image files as favorites, you can locate them quickly in the Assets panel by selecting the Favorites option.

It is a good idea to store original unedited copies of your website image files in a separate folder, outside the assets folder of your website. If you edit the original files, resave them using different names. Doing this ensures that you will be able to find a file in its original, unaltered state. You may have files on your computer that you are currently not using at all; however, you may want to use them in the future. Storing currently unused files helps keep your assets folder free of clutter. Storing copies of original website image files in a separate location also ensures that you have back-up copies in the event that you accidentally delete a file from the website.

Creating a Website Color Palette

With monitors today that display millions of colors, you are not as limited with the number of colors you can use, and you may choose to select any color you feel fits the website design and accessibility standards. You can use the eyedropper tool 🖊 in the Color picker to pick up a color from a page element, such as the background of an image. To do this, select a color box from a value in the CSS Designer properties pane, then place the pointer over a color on the page. Select the color, and this color will then replace the previous color in the color box and apply it to the page element. If you are designing pages that will be displayed with a web device such as a mobile phone, be aware that many of these devices have more limited color displays and, in these cases, it might be wise to use standard colors.

Figure 22 *NASA website*

Source: NASA

Insert a background image

1. Select **Modify** on the Menu bar, then select **Page Properties** to open the Page Properties dialog box.

2. In the Appearance (CSS) category, select **Browse** next to the Background image text box, navigate to the assets folder in the chapter_4 Data Files folder, then double-click **water.jpg**.

3. Select **OK** to close the Page Properties dialog box, then select the **Refresh** ↻ to refresh the file list in the assets folder in the Files panel. The water.jpg file is automatically copied to The Striped Umbrella assets folder.

   The white page background is replaced with a muted image of water, as shown in Figure 23. The color of the water is close to the shades of blue in the website banner, so the image fits in well with the other page colors. It doesn't interfere with the text because the body of the page is behind the container div where the content appears, and the container div has a white background.

4. Expand the CSS Designer panel if necessary, select **<style>** in the Sources pane, select **body** in the Selectors pane, select the **Show Set check box** in the Properties pane, then compare your screen to Figure 24.

   Since you used the Modify > Page Properties command to set the image background, Dreamweaver created an internal <body> rule that tells the browser to use the water.jpg file as the page background for that one page.

You created an internal style to apply an image background to the about_us page. You then viewed the CSS Designer panel. It now includes two external style sheets and an internal style sheet.

Figure 23 *The about_us page with a background image*

The water image only flows behind the container div, so does not affect contrast

Figure 24 *CSS Designer with the new embedded body rule added*

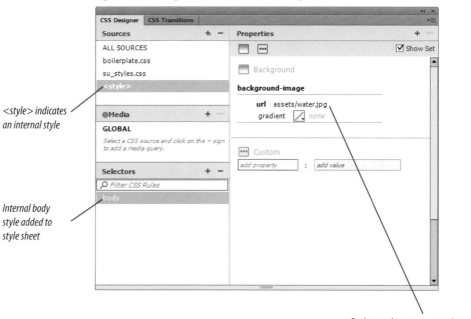

<style> indicates an internal style

Internal body style added to style sheet

Background image = assets/water.jpg

Adding Images

Figure 25 *The <style> source in the CSS Designer panel with no selectors listed*

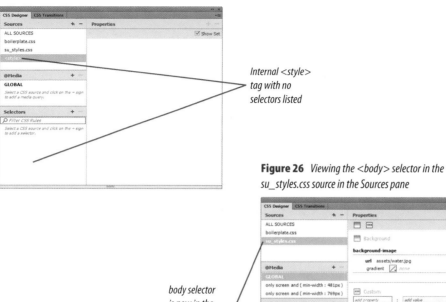

Internal <style>
tag with no
selectors listed

Figure 26 *Viewing the <body> selector in the su_styles.css source in the Sources pane*

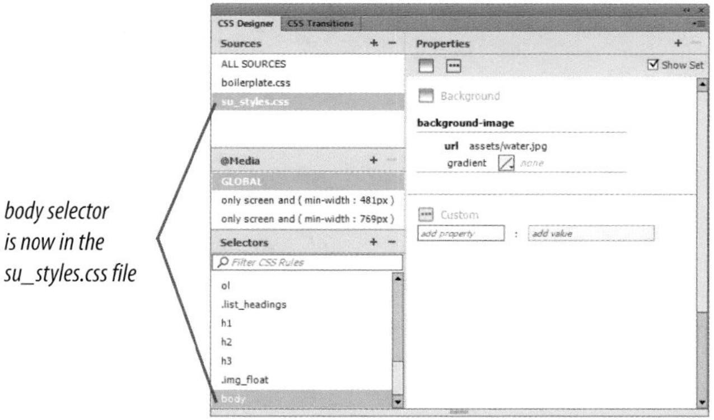

body selector
is now in the
su_styles.css file

Understanding HTML Body Tags

When you set page preferences, it is helpful to understand the HTML tags that are being generated. Sometimes it's easier to edit the code directly, rather than use menus and dialog boxes. The code for the page background color is located in the head section. If you want to change the page properties, you add additional codes to the body tag. Adding a color to the background will add a style to the page; for example, "body { background-color: #000000, }". If you insert an image for a background, the code will read "body { background-image: url(assets/water.jpg); }".

Move an internal selector to an external style sheet

1. Open the spa page.

   If you see a message above the Document window reminding you that Web Fonts are only visible in Live view; you can close the message. The water background is not behind the page content, because the internal background-image selector only applies to the about_us page.

2. Switch back to the about_us page, select **<style>** in the CSS Designer Sources pane, select **body** in the Selectors pane, as shown in Figure 24, then drag the body selector to su_styles.css in the Sources pane.

   You can only see the body selector in the Selectors pane when the about_us page is open and before you move it to su_styles.css, since it is an internal style for that page only.

3. Select **<style>** in the Sources pane, as shown in Figure 25, then select the **Delete key**.

   Since you moved the only selector in the internal style sheet, you no longer have a need for it.

4. Select **su_styles.css** in the Sources pane, select **GLOBAL** in the @**Media pane**, then scroll to and select **body** in the Selectors pane.

5. Select the **Show Set check box** if necessary, then compare your screen to Figure 26.

   You see the background-image property and value in the Properties pane.

   (continued)

---

6. Switch back to the spa page.

   The spa page now has the water image as a page background, as shown in Figure 27.

7. Open the index page.

   The index page now has the water image as a page background, as shown in Figure 28.

8. Save your work.

You moved the internal body selector to the su_styles.css file, then viewed the spa and index pages to see that the body selector was now applied to those pages.

Figure 27 *The spa page with the water background image*

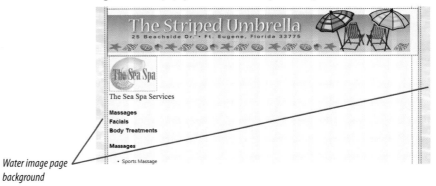

Water image page
background

Figure 28 *The index page with the water background image*

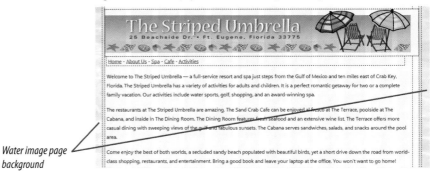
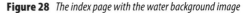

Water image page
background

Using Color in Compliance with Accessibility Guidelines

Web Content Accessibility Guidelines (WCAG), Version 2.0, from the World Wide Web Consortium (W3C), states that a website should not rely on the use of color alone. This means that if your website content depends on your user correctly seeing a color, then you are not providing for those people who cannot distinguish between certain colors or do not have monitors that display color. Be especially careful when choosing color used with text, so you provide a good contrast between the text and the background.

If you are typing in the code or in a text box, it is better to reference colors as numbers, rather than names. For example, use #FFFFFF instead of "white." Using style sheets for specifying color formats is the preferred method for coding. For more information, see the complete list of accessibility guidelines listed on the W3C website, www.w3.org.

Figure 29 *Changing the value for the background-repeat property*

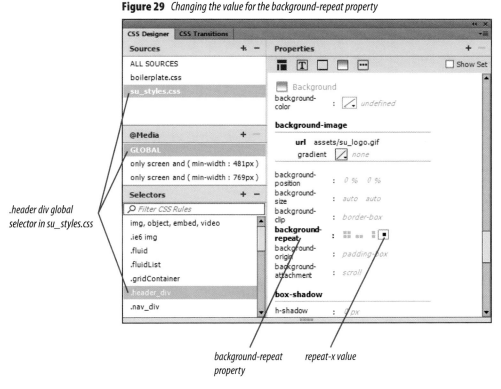

.header div global
selector in su_styles.css

background-repeat
property

repeat-x value

Figure 30 *Viewing the revised background image on the about us page*

Banner extends to fill
header div now

Edit a background-image selector

1. Select **su_styles.css** in the CSS Designer Sources pane, select **GLOBAL** in the @Media pane, then select **.header_div** in the Selectors pane.

   The .header_div selector formats the header block.

2. Uncheck the Show Set check box, if necessary, select the **Background button** [ ] in the Properties pane, then select the **no-repeat value** next to the background-repeat property, as shown in Figure 29.

3. Select **only screen and (min-width: 481ps)** in the @Media pane, select **.header_div** in the Selectors pane, then change the background repeat value to **repeat-x**.

   Changing from the no-repeat to repeat-x value will fill in the white space at the right side of the header div in the tablet and desktop sizes.

4. Save all files, then preview the about_us page in your browser.

   The banner image background fills the header, as shown in Figure 30.

5. Preview the spa and index pages to verify that the banner on those pages also fills the header div.

6. Close the spa and index pages.

You edited the .header_div global selector in the su_styles.css style sheet, then viewed the revised pages in the browser.

Add Graphic
ENHANCEMENTS

What You'll Do

In this lesson, you will use a small image to link to a larger image and add a favicon to a page.

Adding a Link to a Larger Image

Sometimes designers want to display a small image on a page with an option for the user to select it to display a larger image. You frequently see this practice on retail sites with multiple items for sale. It is done both to conserve space and to keep the page size as small as possible. These sites will display a **thumbnail image**, or small version of a larger image, so that more images will fit on the page. Another technique is to link from one image to a second image that incorporates the first image. For example, a furniture site may create a link from an image of a chair to an image of the chair in a furnished room. An additional enhancement is often added to allow users to select the larger image to magnify it even more.

To accomplish this, you need two versions of the same image using an image editor such as Photoshop: one that is small (in dimensions and in file size) and one that is large (in dimensions and in file size.) After you have both images ready, place the small image on your page, select it, then link it to the large image. When a user selects the small image in a browser, the large image opens. Another option is to place the large image on a new web page so you can also include additional descriptive text about the image or a link back to the previous page.

Adding Favicons

In most browsers today, when you add a web page to your favorites list or bookmarks, the page title will appear with a small icon that represents your site, similar to a logo, called a **favicon** (short for favorites icon). This feature was introduced in Microsoft Internet Explorer 5. Most browsers now also display favicons in the browser address bar. Favicons are a convenient way to add branding, or recognition, for your site. To create a favicon, first create an icon that is 16 pixels by 16 pixels. Second, save the file as an icon file with the .ico file extension in your site root folder. Do not save it in a subfolder such as an assets or images folder.

QUICK TIP

There are plug-ins available for Photoshop that will save files with an icon file format, or you can search the Internet for programs that will generate icons.

Third, add HTML code to the head section of your page to link the icon file. The browser will then find the icon and load it in the address bar when the page loads.

QUICK **TIP**

The Firefox and Opera browsers can read a .jpg or a .png file, in addition to an .ico file.

Figure 31 shows a favicon in the Department of Education website. Notice that the favicon is displayed on the page tab. The design of the favicon ties in with the large logo at the top of the page. This is an attractive touch to complete a well-designed site.

Adding a No Right-Click Script

On most websites, users are able to save an image on a page by right-clicking an image, then selecting Save on the shortcut menu. If you would like to prevent viewers from having this option, you can add a **no right-click script**, or JavaScript code that will not allow users to display the shortcut menu by right-clicking an image. To do this, locate JavaScript code that will add this option and copy and paste it into the head content of your page. To locate JavaScript code, use a search engine to search the Internet with a term such as "no right-click script." You will find scripts that prevent users from saving any image on the page, or all content of any kind on the page. Some scripts return a message in the browser such as "This function is disabled," and some do not return a message at all. These scripts will keep many users from saving your images, but they will not stop the most serious and knowledgeable perpetrators.

You can also protect website images by inserting the image as a table, cell, or CSS block background and then placing a transparent image on top of it. When a user attempts to save it with the shortcut menu, they will only save the transparent image.

Figure 31 *U. S. Department of Education website*

Favicon displayed on the page tab

Favicon is a smaller version of the logo used on the page

Source: U. S. Department of Education

Use an image to link to another image

1. Place the insertion point at the end of the last paragraph after the word "beachwear", insert a paragraph break, insert the image **map_small.jpg** from the assets folder where you store your Data Files, then type **Map to The Striped Umbrella** in the Alt text box in the Property inspector.

2. Select the map_small image, click the **Browse for File button** 📁 next to the Link text box in the Property inspector, navigate to the assets folder in the drive and folder where you store your Data Files, select **map_large.jpg**, then click **OK**.

   The small map image now links to the large map image, so users can select the small version to view the large version.

3. Place the insertion point after the last paragraph, insert a paragraph break, type **Select the map below to view a larger image.**, then compare your screen to Figure 32.

4. Save your work, then preview the page in your browser.

5. Select the **small map image** to view the large map image in a separate window, use the Back button to return to the about_us page, then close the browser.

6. Open the Files panel if necessary, and verify that both map images were copied to the assets folder, as shown in Figure 33.

You inserted a small image on the page and linked it to a larger image.

Figure 32 *The about_us page with an image linking to a larger image*

Figure 33 *The assets folder with two map images added*

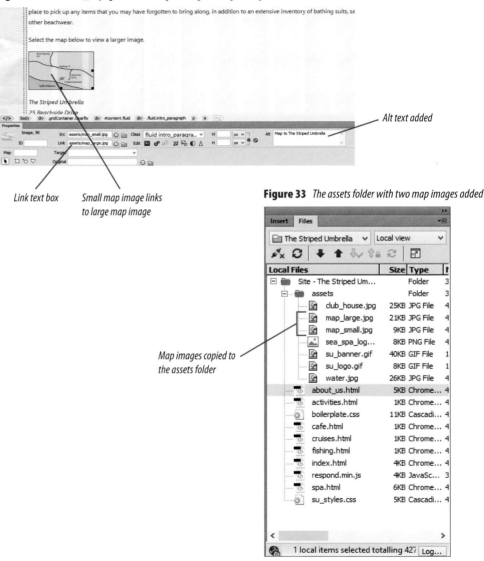

Alt text added

Link text box

Small map image links to large map image

Map images copied to the assets folder

Figure 34 *Copying the favicon.ico file in the data files folder*

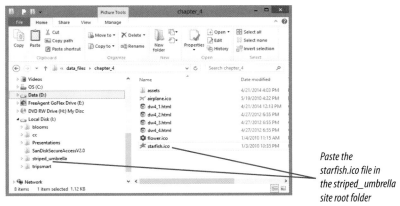

Paste the
starfish.ico file in
the striped_umbrella
site root folder

Figure 35 *Adding code to link the favicon*

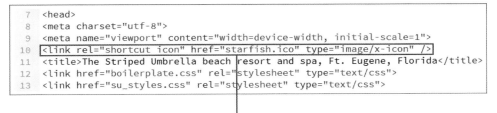

```
7    <head>
8    <meta charset="utf-8">
9    <meta name="viewport" content="width=device-width, initial-scale=1">
10   <link rel="shortcut icon" href="starfish.ico" type="image/x-icon" />
11   <title>The Striped Umbrella beach resort and spa, Ft. Eugene, Florida</title>
12   <link href="boilerplate.css" rel="stylesheet" type="text/css">
13   <link href="su_styles.css" rel="stylesheet" type="text/css">
```

Type this code above the <title> tag

Figure 36 *Viewing a favicon in the Firefox browser*

Starfish favicon

Insert a favicon on a page

1. Open File Explorer (Win) or Finder (Mac), then browse to the chapter_4 folder in the drive and folder where your Data Files are stored.

2. Right-click the file **starfish.ico**, copy it, browse to your site root folder, (not the assets folder) then paste the **starfish.ico** file into the site root folder, as shown in Figure 34, then close File Explorer (Win) or Finder (Mac).

3. Switch to Code view in Dreamweaver, insert a blank line above the line of code for the page title, then insert this code directly above the <title> tag: **`<link rel="shortcut icon" href="starfish.ico" type="image/x-icon" />`** as shown in Figure 35.

4. Save your work, then preview the about_us page in the browser.

   The favicon will appear on the page tab in browsers that use tabbed pages, as shown in Figure 36.

TIP Internet Explorer may not display the favicon until the website is published to a server.

5. Copy the code for the favicon link, then paste it into the code for the index and spa pages.

6. Save your work, close all open pages, then exit Dreamweaver.

You copied a favicon to the site root folder, then added code to the About Us page to direct browsers to display the favicon in the title bar when the page is viewed in a browser. Then you copied the code to link the favicon to the index and spa pages.

Insert and align Images using CSS.

1. Open the Blooms & Bulbs website, open dw4_2.html from the drive and folder where you store your Data Files, then save it as **plants.html** in the Blooms & Bulbs website, overwriting the existing plants.html file. Do not update links.
2. Close dw4_2.html.
3. Select the heading "Featured Spring Plant: Roses!" and use the HTML Property inspector to apply the Heading 1 format.
4. On the plants page, change to Code view and verify that the Adobe Edge Web font code is in the head section.
5. If it is not, open the tips page, change to Code view, copy the code for the Edge Web font in the head section, close the tips page, then paste the code you copied in Step 4 to the head section in the code for the plants page.
6. In Design view, place the insertion point in front of the first paragraph that begins with "Who", then insert the file rose.jpg from the assets folder in the drive and folder where you store your Data Files.

TIP Switch to Code view to verify that your insertion point is before the opening <p> tag for the first paragraph.

7. Refresh the Files panel to verify that the image was copied to the assets folder.
8. Add a new global class selector to the bb.styles style sheet named **.img_float**. (Remember to type the period in the selector name.)

9. Set the float property to none.
10. Add a new class selector named **.img_float** in tablet media with the float property set to left.
11. Select the rose image on the page, then apply the img_float selector to it.
12. Save all files, then view the page in mobile, tablet, and desktop views. Notice that the text does not wrap (falls below) the image in mobile view, but wraps around the image in tablet and desktop views.

Enhance an image and use alternate text.

1. Edit the img_float global selector to add a border to all sides of an image with the following settings: Style=solid; Width=thin; Color=#333333.
2. Edit the global img_float margin property to add a 10 px margin to all sides.
3. Add the alternate text "**Rose bloom**" to the rose image.
4. Save your work.

Insert a background image and perform site maintenance.

1. Use the Modify menu to insert the lady_in_red.jpg file as a background image from the assets folder where you store your Data Files.
2. Save your work.
3. Preview the web page in your browser, then close your browser.

4. Move the <body> tag code from the internal style sheet to the bb.styles.css file, then remove the <style> source in the CSS Designer Sources pane.
5. Save your work, verify that the image page background appears on the index and tips pages, then close the index and tips pages.
6. View the colors used in the site in the Assets panel.
7. Edit the desktop size .header_div selector to set the background-repeat value to repeat-x, then save your work.

Add graphic enhancements.

1. Insert the file two_roses.jpg from your Data Files assets folder at the beginning of the second paragraph.
2. Create a new global class selector in bb_styles.css named **.img_float_right**.
3. Use the same properties you used for the .img_float global class selector.
4. Repeat Steps 2 and 3 to add a tablet class selector named **.img_float_right** with the float set to right.
5. Apply the .img_float_right selector to the two_roses image, then add appropriate alternate text.
6. Use the Link text box on the Property inspector to link the two_roses image to the two_roses_large.jpg file in the assets folder where you store your Data Files.
7. Add the sentences **You must see a close-up of these beauties! Select the image to enlarge it**. at the end of the last paragraph.

8. Save your work, preview the page in the browser, then select the two_roses image to view the larger version of the image.

9. Use the Back button to return to the plants page, then close the browser.

10. Open File Explorer (Win) or Finder (Mac), browse to the folder where you store your Data Files, then copy the file flower.ico.

11. Paste the file flower.ico in the blooms site root folder.

12. Close File Explorer (Win) or Finder (Mac), then switch to Code view for the plants page.

13. Insert a blank line above the title tag, then type this code directly above the <title> tag:

    ```
    <link rel="shortcut icon"
    href="flower.ico" type="image/
    x-icon" />
    ```

14. Verify that you entered the code correctly, copy the new line of code, then switch back to Design view.

15. Paste the same code you typed in Step 13 to the index and tips pages, then save all files.

16. Preview the plants, tips, and index pages in mobile, tablet, and desktop views, and the browser, compare your screen to Figure 37, then close the browser.

17. Figures 38a, 38b, and 38c on the next two pages show the plants page in the mobile, tablet, and desktop sizes.

18. Close all open files.

Figure 37 *Completed Skills Review viewed in a browser*

Figure 38a *Mobile view*

Featured Spring Plant: Roses!

Who can resist the romance of roses? Poets have waxed poetically over them throughout the years. Many persons consider the beauty and fragrance of roses to be unmatched in nature. The varieties are endless, ranging from floribunda to hybrid teas to shrub roses to climbing roses. Each variety has its own personality and preference in the garden setting. The Candy Cane Floribunda is a beautiful rose with

Figure 38b *Tablet view*

Featured Spring Plant: Roses!

Who can resist the romance of roses? Poets have waxed poetically over them throughout the years. Many persons consider the beauty and fragrance of roses to be unmatched in nature. The varieties are endless, ranging from floribunda to hybrid teas to shrub roses to climbing roses. Each variety has its own personality and preference in the garden setting. The Candy Cane Floribunda is a beautiful rose with cream, pink, and red stripes and swirls. They have a heavy scent that will remind you of the roses you received on your most special occasions. These blooms are approximately four inches in diameter. They bloom continuously from early summer to early fall. The plants grow up to four feet tall and three feet wide. They are shipped bare root in February.

For ease of growing, Knock Out® roses are some of our all-time favorites. Even beginners will not fail with these garden delights. They are shrub

Figure 38c *Desktop view*

Blooms & Bulbs

HWY 43 SOUTH • ALVIN • TX 77511 • 555-248-0806

Featured Spring Plant: Roses!

Who can resist the romance of roses? Poets have waxed poetically over them throughout the years. Many persons consider the beauty and fragrance of roses to be unmatched in nature. The varieties are endless, ranging from floribunda to hybrid teas to shrub roses to climbing roses. Each variety has its own personality and preference in the garden setting. The Candy Cane Floribunda is a beautiful rose with cream, pink, and red stripes and swirls. They have a heavy scent that will remind you of the roses you received on your most special occasions. These blooms are approximately four inches in diameter. They bloom continuously from early summer to early fall. The plants grow up to four feet tall and three feet wide. They are shipped bare root in February.

For ease of growing, Knock Out® roses are some of our all-time favorites. Even beginners will not fail with these garden delights. They are shrub roses and prefer full sun, but can take partial shade. They are disease resistant and drought tolerant. You do not have to be concerned with either black spot or dead-heading with roses such as the Knock out®, making them an extremely low-maintenance plant. They are also repeat bloomers, blooming into late fall

Use Figures 39a, 39b, and 39c. as guides to continue your work on the TripSmart website that you began in Project Builder 1 in Chapter 1, and continued to work on in Chapters 2 and 3. You are now ready to begin work on the destinations page that showcases one of the featured tours to Egypt. You want to include some colorful pictures on the page.

1. Open the TripSmart website.
2. Open dw4_3.html from the drive and folder where you store your Data Files and save it in the tripsmart site root folder as **tours.html**, overwriting the existing tours.html file and not updating the links. Close the dw4_3.html file.
3. Apply the Heading 1 format to the "Destination: Egypt" heading.
4. Insert statues.jpg from the assets folder in the drive and folder where you store your Data Files to the left of the sentence beginning "We have a really special", then add appropriate alternate text.
5. Insert nile.jpg from the assets folder in the drive and folder where you store your Data Files to the left of the sentence beginning "To provide the finest", then add appropriate alternate text.
6. Create one or more new rules in the tripsmart_styles.css file to add alignment, spacing, and borders of your choice to each new image.
7. If you would like, use the existing rules in the style sheet to add any additional formatting to the page to enhance the appearance or copy any rules from other websites that you would like to reuse.

8. Copy the file airplane.ico from the folder where you store your data files to your site root folder.
9. Add appropriate code to the head content to link the favicon to the page, then copy the code to the index and newsletter pages.
10. Save your work, then preview the tours, index, and newsletter pages in your browser and in mobile, tablet, and desktop sizes.
11. Close your browser, then close all open files.

Figure 39a *Mobile view*

Figure 39b *Tablet view*

Destination: Egypt

We have a really special trip planned for next November. Egypt - the land of kings and pharaohs! This ten-day adventure will begin in Cairo as we visit the Giza Plateau to see the pyramids of Cheops, Chepheren, and Mycerinus. We will also visit the Great Sphinx and the Egyptian Museum of Antiquities before we leave Cairo for our cruise along the Nile. We board the Egyptian Queen at Luxury and enjoy stops along the way to the Valley of the Kings, the Valley of the Queens, the Ptolemaic temple, the Temple of Horus, and the Temple of Philae on the island of Agilika. When we return to Cairo, you will have the opportunity to do some shopping in the famous Khan El-Khalili Bazaar and enjoy an unforgettable performance of the El-Tannoura Egyptian Heritage Dance Troup.

To provide the finest in personal attention, this tour will be limited to no more than twenty people. The price schedule is as follows: Land Tour and Supplemental Group Air, $5,500.00; International Air, $1,350.00; and Single Supplement, $1,000.00. Entrance fees, hotel taxes, and services are included in

Figure 39c *Desktop view*

Destination: Egypt

We have a really special trip planned for next November. Egypt - the land of kings and pharaohs! This ten-day adventure will begin in Cairo as we visit the Giza Plateau to see the pyramids of Cheops, Chepheren, and Mycerinus. We will also visit the Great Sphinx and the Egyptian Museum of Antiquities before we leave Cairo for our cruise along the Nile. We board the Egyptian Queen at Luxury and enjoy stops along the way to the Valley of the Kings, the Valley of the Queens, the Ptolemaic temple, the Temple of Horus, and the Temple of Philae on the island of Agilika. When we return to Cairo, you will have the opportunity to do some shopping in the famous Khan El-Khalili Bazaar and enjoy an unforgettable performance of the El-Tannoura Egyptian Heritage Dance Troup.

To provide the finest in personal attention, this tour will be limited to no more than twenty people. The price schedule is as follows: Land Tour and Supplemental Group Air, $5,500.00; International Air, $1,350.00; and Single Supplement, $1,000.00. Entrance fees, hotel taxes, and services are included in the Land Tour price. Ship gratuities are also included for the Egyptian Queen crew and guides. A deposit of $500.00 is required at the time the booking is made. Trip insurance and luggage insurance are optional and are also offered for an extra charge. A passport and visa will be required for entry into Egypt. Call us at 555-555-0807 for further information and the complete itinerary from 8:00 a.m. to 6:00 p.m. (Central Standard Time).

In this exercise, you continue your work on the Carolyne's Creations website that you started in Project Builder 2 in Chapter 1, and continued to build in Chapters 2 and 3. You are now ready to add a new page to the website that will display featured items in the kitchen shop. Figures 40a, 40b, and 40c show a possible solution for this exercise. Your finished page will look different if you choose different formatting options.

1. Open the Carolyne's Creations website.
2. Open dw4_4.html from the drive and folder where you store your Data Files, save it to the site root folder as **shop.html**, overwriting the existing file and not updating the links.
3. Insert peruvian_glass.jpg from the assets folder in the drive and folder where you store your Data Files, in a location of your choice on the page, and add appropriate alternate text.
4. Add a rule to the cc_styles style sheet that adds alignment and spacing to the Peruvian glass image, then apply the new selector to the glass image.
5. Apply the Heading 1 format to the page heading "June Special: Peruvian Glasses".

6. If you would like a different mobile banner, replace cc_logo.gif with cc_banner_mobile.jpg in the global .header_div selector only. (*Hint:* It is the background image.)

7. Save the shop page, then preview it in the browser and mobile, tablet, and desktop sizes.
8. Close your browser, then close all open pages.

Figure 40a *Mobile view*

Adding Images

Figure 40b *Tablet view*

Figure 40c *Desktop view*

Patsy Broers is working on a team project to design a website for her high school drama department. She has been assigned the task of gathering images to add interest and color.

1. Connect to the Internet, then navigate to the National Oceanic and Atmospheric Administration at noaa.gov, shown in Figure 41.
2. Do you see a favicon used on the page?
3. Are any of the images on the page used as links to other images or pages?
4. Is a background image used for any of the page objects?
5. How do the images, horizontal and vertical spacing, color, and text work together to create an attractive and interesting experience for viewers?

Figure 41 *Design Project*

Source: National Oceanic and Atmospheric Administration

In this assignment, you will continue to work on the website that you started in Chapter 1, and continued to build in Chapters 2 and 3. No Data Files are supplied. You are building this site from chapter to chapter, so you must do each Portfolio Project assignment in each chapter to complete your website.

You continue building your website by inserting appropriate images on a page and enhancing them for maximum effect.

1. Consult your wireframe and decide which page to create and develop for this chapter.
2. Plan the page content and make a sketch of the layout. Your sketch should include several images and a background color or image.
3. Create the page using your sketch for guidance.
4. Access the images you gathered, and place them on the page so that the page matches the sketch you created in Step 2. Add a background image if you want, and appropriate alternate text for each image.
5. Create rules in your style sheet to position and format your images.

6. Identify any files in the Assets panel that are currently not used in the site. Decide which of these assets should be removed, then delete these files.
7. Preview the new page in a browser, then check for page layout problems and broken links. Make any necessary corrections in Dreamweaver, then preview the page again in the browser, mobile, tablet, and desktop sizes. Repeat this process until you are satisfied with the way the page looks in the browser.
8. Use the checklist in Figure 42 to check all the pages in your site.
9. Close the browser, then close the open pages.

Figure 42 *Portfolio Project checklist*

Website Checklist

1. Does each page have a page title?
2. Does the home page have a description and keywords?
3. Does the home page contain contact information?
4. Does the home page have a last updated statement that will automatically update when the page is saved?
5. Do all paths for links and images work correctly?
6. Do all images have alternate text?
7. Are there any unnecessary files you can delete from the assets folder?
8. Is there a style sheet with at least two selectors?
9. Did you apply the selectors to all text?
10. Did you use selectors to position and format images?
11. Do all pages look good using at least two different browsers and mobile, tablet, and desktop sizes?

© 2015 Cengage Learning®

CHAPTER 5

WORKING WITH LINKS
AND NAVIGATION

1. Create external and internal links
2. Use IDs to navigate to specific page locations
3. Create, modify, and copy a menu bar
4. Create an image map
5. Manage website links
6. Incorporate Web 2.0 technology

5

WORKING WITH LINKS
AND NAVIGATION

Introduction

What makes websites so powerful are the links, or hyperlinks, that connect one page to another within a website or to any page on the Web. Although you can enhance a website with graphics, animations, movies, and other features to make it visually attractive, the links you include are a site's most essential components. Links that connect the pages within a site are important because they help users navigate between the pages of the site. If it's important to keep users within your site, link only to pages within your website and avoid including links to external sites. For example, e-commerce sites only link to other pages in their own site to discourage shoppers from leaving.

In this chapter, you will create links to other pages in The Striped Umbrella website and to other sites on the Web. You will insert a menu bar, and check the site links to make sure they all work correctly. You will also learn about Web 2.0 and social networking, an area of the Internet that has exploded over the years. **Social networking** refers to the grouping of individual web users who connect and interact with other users in online communities. **Online communities**, or virtual communities, are social websites you can join, such as Facebook and Twitter, where you can communicate with others by posting messages or media content such as images or videos. You will learn about how you can connect your website to these communities.

Understanding Internal and External Links

Web pages contain two types of links: internal links and external links. **Internal links** are links to web pages within the same website, and **external links** are links to web pages in other websites or to email addresses. Both internal and external links have two important parts that work together. The first part of a link is displayed on a web page, for example, text, an image, or a button that is used for a link. The second part of a link is the **path**, or the name and location of the web page or file that users select to open the target for the link. Setting and maintaining the correct paths for all of your links is essential to avoid having broken links in your site, which can cause a user to leave the site.

Insert

Structure ▼

`<•>`	Div
ul	Unordered List
ol	Ordered List
li	List Item
	Header
H1 ▾	Heading
P	Paragraph
	Navigation
	Aside
	Article

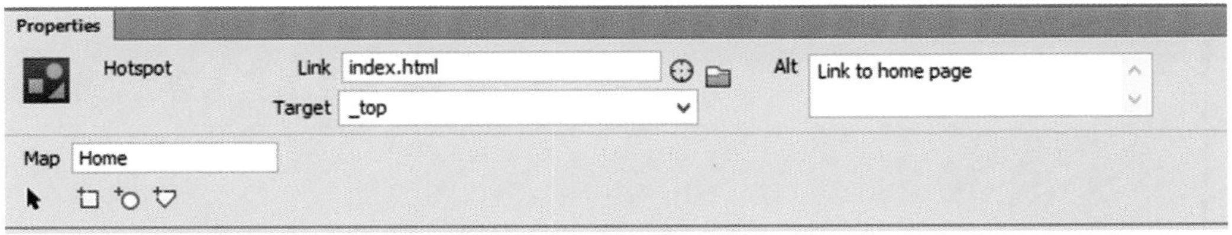

Properties

Hotspot

Link index.html   Alt Link to home page

Target _top

Map Home

Properties

<•> HTML

Format None   Class fluid header...   *B* *I*   Title

CSS   ID banner   Link   Target

Page Properties...   List Item...

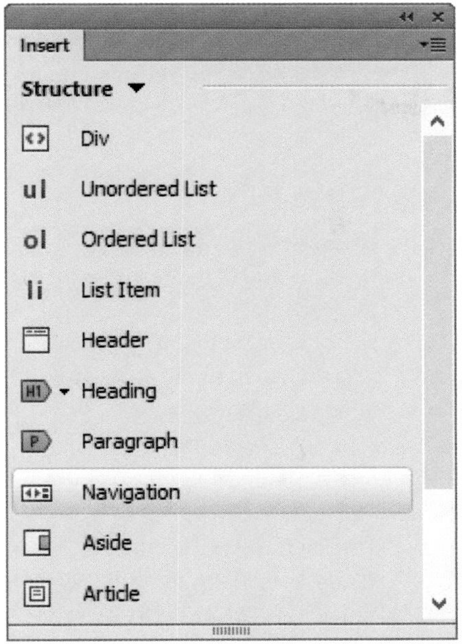

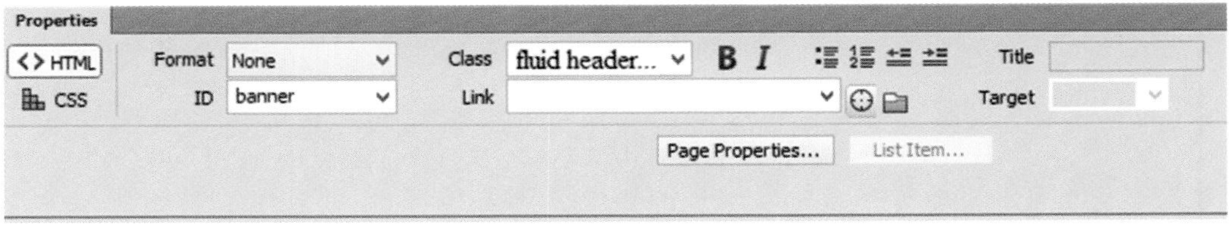

Create External and
INTERNAL LINKS

What You'll Do

In this lesson, you will create external links on The Striped Umbrella activities page that link to websites related to area attractions. You will also create internal links to other pages within The Striped Umbrella website.

Creating External Links

If one of the objectives of your site is to provide users with additional research sources for information not provided within the site, external links are one way to meet that objective. To create an external link, first select the text or object that you want to serve as a link, then type the absolute path to the destination web page in the Link text box in the Property inspector. An **absolute path** is a path used for external links that includes the complete address for the destination page, including the protocol (such as http://) and the complete **URL** (Uniform Resource Locator), or address, of the destination page. When necessary, the web page filename and folder hierarchy are also part of an absolute path. Figure 1 shows an example of an absolute path showing the protocol,

URL, and path, which in this case is a single folder name. Paths can contain several folder levels and a file name, depending on how the destination page is stored on the server. An example of the code for the external link to the United States Army website would be <a href="http://www.army.mil"> The United States Army website</a>.

Creating Internal Links

Each page in a website usually focuses on an individual information category or topic. You should make sure that the home page provides links to each major page in the site, and that all pages in the site contain numerous internal links so that users can move easily from page to page. To create an internal link, you first select the text element or image that you want to use to make a link, and then use the Browse

Figure 1 *An example of an absolute path*

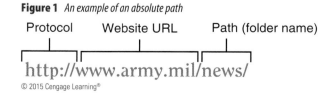

© 2015 Cengage Learning®

for File button next to the Link text box in the HTML Property inspector to specify the relative path to the destination page. A **relative path** is a type of path that references web pages and media files within the same website. Relative paths include the filename and folder location of a file. An example for the code for a relative internal link would be <a href="news.html">News</a>.

Figure 2 shows an example of a relative path. Table 1 describes absolute and relative paths. Relative paths can either be site-root relative or document-relative. The internal links that you will create in this lesson will be document-relative. You can also use the Point to File button in the HTML Property inspector to select the file you want to link to, or drag the file you want to use for the link from the Files panel into the Link text box in the Property inspector.

You should take great care in managing your internal links to make sure they work correctly and are timely and relevant to the page content. Design the navigation structure of your website so that users are never more than a few clicks or taps away from the page they are seeking.

Figure 2 *An example of a relative path*

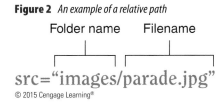

© 2015 Cengage Learning®

TABLE 1: DESCRIPTION OF ABSOLUTE AND RELATIVE PATHS		
Type of path	**Description**	**Example**
Absolute path	Used for external links and specifies protocol, URL, and filename of the destination page	http://www.yahoo.com/recreation
Relative path	Used for internal links and specifies location of file relative to the current page	spa.html or assets/heron.gif
Site Root-relative path	Used for internal links when publishing to a server that contains many websites or where the website is so large it requires more than one server	/striped_umbrella/activities.html
Document- relative path	Used in most cases for internal links and specifies the location of a file relative to the current page	cafe.html or assets/heron.gif

© 2015 Cengage Learning®

Create an external link

1. Open The Striped Umbrella website, open dw5_1.html from the drive and folder where you store your Chapter 5 Data Files, then save it as **activities.html** in the striped_umbrella local site folder, overwriting the existing activities page, but not updating links.

2. Close the dw5_1.html page.

   The page code picks up the links to the style sheet from the website now and formats the page, but the links to the images are broken because these images have not yet been copied to the website assets folder.

3. Select the first broken image link, select the **Browse for File button** [icon] next to the Src text box, then select **family_sunset.jpg** in the Data Files assets folder to save the image in your assets folder.

4. Select the image, then use the Property inspector to apply the **img_float** rule, as shown in Figure 3.

5. Repeat Step 3 for the second broken image link, linking it to two_dolphins_small.jpg.

6. Create a new global selector in CSS Designer in the su_styles.css file named **.img_float_right** with the following properties and values:

   All margins: **10px**;

   Float: **none**;

   Border-width: **thin**;

   Border-style: **solid**;

   Border-color: **#312E2E**;

7. Repeat step 6 to create a selector in the su_styles.css file for tablet size devices named **.img_float_right** with the float property set to **right**.

(continued)

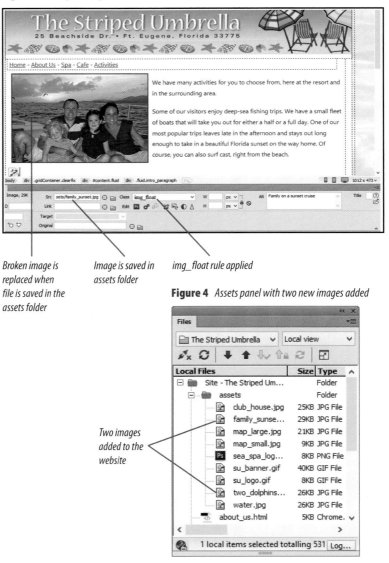

Figure 3 *Saving an image file in the assets folder*

Broken image is replaced when file is saved in the assets folder

Image is saved in assets folder

img_float rule applied

Figure 4 *Assets panel with two new images added*

Two images added to the website

Figure 5 *Creating an external link to the Blue Angels website*

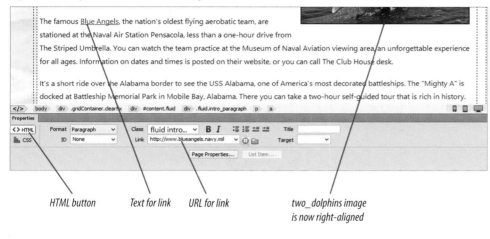

HTML button   Text for link   URL for link   two_dolphins image
is now right-aligned

Typing URLs

Typing URLs in the Link text box in the Property inspector can be tedious. When you need to type a long and complex URL, it is easy to make mistakes and create a broken link. You can avoid such mistakes by copying and pasting the URL from the Address text box (Internet Explorer) or Location bar (Mozilla Firefox) to the Link text box in the Property inspector. Copying and pasting a URL ensures that the URL is entered correctly.

This selector will inherit the global .img_float_right selector, except with the float set to right for tablet and desktop sizes.

8. Apply the .img_float_right selector to the two_dolphins_small.jpg, then refresh the files panel if necessary.

   The two new files are copied into the assets folder, as shown in Figure 4.

9. Scroll down, then select the text "Blue Angels" in the first line of the third to last paragraph.

10. Select the **HTML button** `</> HTML` in the Property inspector to switch to the HTML Property inspector if necessary, place the insertion point in the Link text box, type **http://www.blueangels.navy.mil**, press **[Enter]** (Win) or **[return]** (Mac), click on or tap the link to deselect it, then compare your screen to Figure 5.

11. Repeat Steps 9 and 10 to create a link for the USS Alabama text in the next paragraph: **http://www.ussalabama.com**.

12. Save your work, preview the page in your browser, test all the links to make sure they work, then close your browser.

TIP You must have an active Internet connection to test the external links. If selecting a link does not open a page, make sure you typed the URL correctly in the Link text box.

You opened The Striped Umbrella website, replaced the existing activities page, then imported images into the site. You created a new selector similar to the img_float selector but with a right alignment rather than a left alignment. You applied a different selector to each image. You added two external links to other sites, then tested each link in your browser.

Create an internal link

1. Select the text "fishing excursions" in the third paragraph.

2. Select the **Browse for File button** 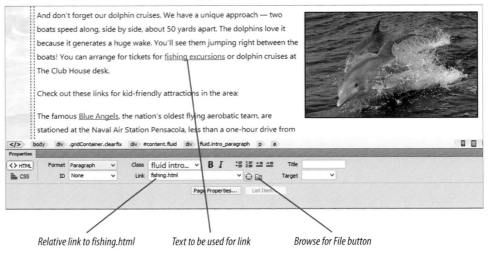 next to the Link text box in the HTML Property inspector, navigate to the site root folder, then double-click **fishing.html** in the Select File dialog box to set the relative path to the fishing page.

   The filename fishing.html appears in the Link text box in the Property inspector, as shown in Figure 6. (The link is deselected in the figure for readability.)

   TIP Pressing [F4] will hide or redisplay all panels, including the Property inspector and the panels on the right side of the screen.

3. Select the text "dolphin cruises" in the same sentence.

4. Select the **Browse for File button** next to the Link text box in the HTML Property inspector, then double-click **cruises.html** in the Select File dialog box to specify the relative path to the cruises page.

   The words "dolphin cruises" are now a link to the cruises page.

5. Save your work, preview the page in your browser, verify that the internal links work correctly, then close your browser.

   The fishing and cruises pages do not have page content yet, but serve as placeholders until they do.

   You created two internal links on the activities page, then tested the links in your browser.

Figure 6 *Creating an internal link on the activities page*

And don't forget our dolphin cruises. We have a unique approach — two boats speed along, side by side, about 50 yards apart. The dolphins love it because it generates a huge wake. You'll see them jumping right between the boats! You can arrange for tickets for fishing excursions or dolphin cruises at The Club House desk.

Check out these links for kid-friendly attractions in the area:

The famous Blue Angels, the nation's oldest flying aerobatic team, are stationed at the Naval Air Station Pensacola, less than a one-hour drive from

Relative link to fishing.html   *Text to be used for link*   *Browse for File button*

Using Case-Sensitive Links

When you hear that text is "case sensitive," it means that the text will be treated differently when it is typed using uppercase letters rather than lowercase letters, or vice-versa. With some operating systems, such as Windows, it doesn't matter which case you use when you enter URLs. However, with other systems, such as UNIX, it does matter. To be sure that your links will work with all systems, use lowercase letters for all URLs. This is another good reason to select and copy a URL from the browser address bar, and then paste it in the Link text box or Dreamweaver code when creating an external link. You won't have to worry about missing a case change.

Figure 7 *Assets panel with four external links*

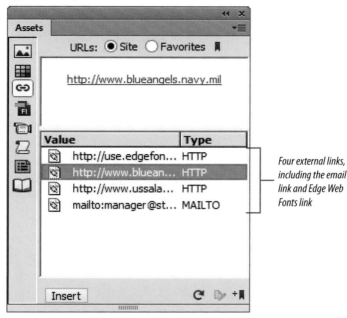

Four external links, including the email link and Edge Web Fonts link

View links in the Assets panel

1. Open the Assets panel.
2. Select the **URLs button** ⊖ in the Assets panel.
3. Select the **Refresh Site List button** ⟳ if necessary to see the links listed.

   Four links appear in the Assets panel: one external link for the email link on the home page; one external link to the Adobe Edge Web Fonts site; and two external links, to the Blue Angels and USS Alabama websites on the activities page, as shown in Figure 7. Notice that the internal links do not appear in the Assets panel. The Assets panel shows the links for the entire site, not just for the open page.
4. Close the Assets panel.
5. Close the activities page.

You viewed the external links on the activities page in the Assets panel.

Use IDs to Navigate
TO SPECIFIC PAGE LOCATIONS

What You'll Do

 In this lesson, you will assign four IDs to page elements on the spa page: one for the top of the page and three for each of the spa services lists. You will then create internal links to each ID.

Inserting Page Markers with IDs

Some web pages have so much content that users must scroll repeatedly to get to the bottom of the page and then back up to the top of the page. To make it easier for users to navigate to specific areas of a page without scrolling, you can use a combination of internal links and targets to designated locations on a page. A **target** is the location on a web page that a browser displays when users select an internal link. For example, you can assign an ID called "top" to a page element such as an image or div, at the top of a web page, and then create a link to it from the bottom of the page.

You can also assign IDs to page elements in strategic places on a web page, such as at the beginning of paragraph headings. The Neighbor's Mill website shown in Figure 8 uses a div with the ID "wrap" at the top of each page and a text link at the bottom of each page that links to it. This gives users a way to

quickly return to the top of a page after they have scrolled down through the page content.

To assign an ID to a page element, select a tag you intend to use for a link. For instance, if you want to link to the top of a page, select a tag such as an image or div that is at the top of the page, then assign an ID to it if it does not have one. If it does have one, use the assigned ID for your target. You should choose short names that describe the named location on the page.

Creating Internal Links to IDs

Once you assign an ID to a page element, you can create an internal link to it using one of two methods. You can select the text or image on the page that you want to use to make a link, and then drag the Point to File button from the Property inspector to the location of the ID on the page. Or, you can select the text or image to which you want to use to make a link, then type # followed by the ID name (such as "#top") in the Link text box in the Property inspector.

Figure 8 *Neighbor's Mill website with a link to the top of a page*

Div with ID at the top of the page

Text link to div with ID at the top of the page

Source: Neighbor's Mill Bakery & Cafe

Assign IDs to tags

1. Open dw5_2.html, save it as **spa.html**, replacing the spa page, but not updating links, then close dw5_2.html.

2. Place the insertion point in the div containing the background banner image.

   The Class text box in the Property inspector shows that the class tag for this div is fluid header_div.

3. Type **banner** in the ID text box, replacing None, in the Property inspector, as shown in Figure 9.

TIP When typing ID names, use lowercase letters, no spaces, and no special characters. Also, avoid using a number as the first character.

4. Scroll down the spa page to the list of massages, select the **Massages** heading, type **massages** in the ID text box in the Property inspector, then press **[Enter]** (Win) or **[return]** (Mac)

(continued)

Figure 9 *Adding an ID to a div tag*

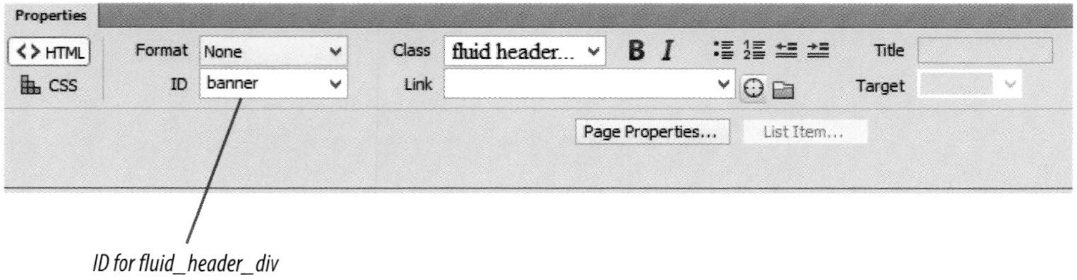

ID for fluid_header_div

Using Visual Aids

The Visual Aids submenu on the View menu gives you several choices for displaying page elements in Design View, such as Invisible Elements, which include comments, line breaks, and embedded styles. Other options in the Visual Aids submenu are CSS Layout Backgrounds, CSS Layout Box Model, CSS Layout Outlines, Table Widths, Table Borders, Image Maps, and Invisible Elements. The Hide All option hides all of these page elements. In later chapters, as you work with each page object that these refer to, you will see the advantages of displaying them. The CSS options allow you to see the formatting properties for CSS layout blocks such as the outline, background color, and margins.

Figure 10 *The Massages heading in Split view*

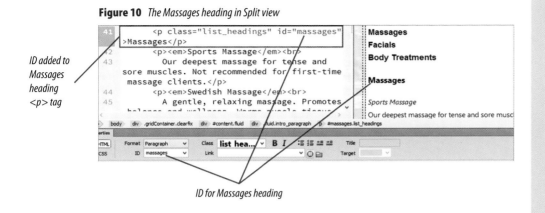

ID added to Massages heading <p> tag

ID for Massages heading

5. Deselect the Massages heading, place the insertion point inside the heading, switch to Show Code and Design views, then locate the id="massages" tag that you added to the Massages heading, as shown in Figure 10.

6. Return to Design view, scroll down to the Facials heading, select the **Facials heading**, type **facials** in the ID text box in the Property inspector, then press **[Enter]** (Win) or **[return]** (Mac).

7. Scroll down to the Body Treatments heading, select the **Body Treatments** heading, type **body_treatments** in the ID text box in the Property inspector, then press **[Enter]** (Win) or **[return]** (Mac).

8. Save your work.

You assigned four IDs to four spa page tags: one to the banner in the div at the top of the page and one to each of the three spa treatment headings.

Create an internal link to an ID

1. Select the word **Massages** just under The Sea Spa Services heading and type **#massages** in the Link text box in the Property inspector, as shown in Figure 11.

   The word "Massages" is now linked to the massages ID for the Massages heading. When users select the word "Massages" at the top of the page, the browser will display the Massages heading at the top of the browser window. The Link text box on the Property inspector now reads #massages.

   TIP An ID name is always preceded by a pound (#) sign in the Link text box in the Property inspector.

2. Repeat Step 1 to create internal links for the Facials and Body Treatments headings to **#facials** and **#body_treatments**.

   (continued)

Figure 11 *Linking the Massages heading to the massages ID*

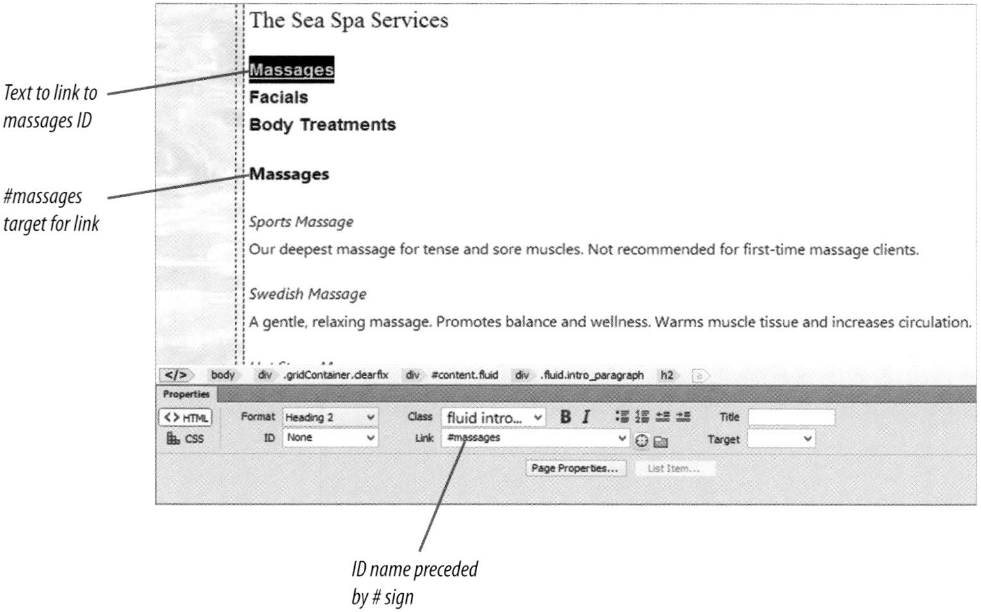

Text to link to massages ID

#massages target for link

ID name preceded by # sign

Figure 12 *Spa page with internal links to IDs*

Internal links to IDs

3. Scroll down to the bottom of the page, then place the insertion point at the end of the last sentence on the page, after the word "appreciated."

4. Press **[Enter]** (Win) or **[return]** (Mac) to insert a paragraph break, then type **Return to top of page**.

5. Select the text "Return to top of page", then enter **#banner** in the Link text box in the Property inspector.

6. Save your work, preview the page in your browser, as shown in Figure 12, then test the links to each ID, using the Back button to return to the links.

   When you select the Body Treatments link in the browser, the associated target ID may appear in the middle of the page instead of at the top. This happens because the spa page is not long enough to position this ID at the top of the page.

7. Close your browser.

You created internal links to the ID names for the Spa Services headings and to the top of the spa page. You then previewed the page in your browser and tested each link.

Create, Modify, and
COPY A MENU BAR

What You'll Do

 In this lesson, you will create a menu bar on the spa page that can be used to link to each main page in the website. The menu bar will have five elements: Home, About Us, Cafe, Spa, and Activities. You will also copy the new menu bar to other pages in the website. On each page you will modify the appropriate element state to reflect the current page.

Creating a Menu Bar

To make your website more visually appealing, you can add special effects. For example, you can create a menu bar with rollover images rather than with plain text links. One way to do this is to use HTML5 <nav> tags to create navigation buttons that link to the pages in your website. To do this, you first insert a navigation tag using the Insert panel. Next, you select the placeholder text for each button and type replacement names to use for each of your links, called **items**, using list items in an unordered list. Once your navigation elements are in place, use CSS styles to modify both the navigation bar code and the unordered list items code. With a little patience and creativity, you can create an attractive, interactive menu bar.

You can add special effects for menu bar items by changing the characteristics for each item's state. A **state** is the condition of the item relative to the pointer. You can create a rollover effect for each menu item by using different background and text colors for each state to represent how the menu item appears when the users move their pointer over it or away from it. You can also create special effects for web page links. The United States Botanic Garden website shown in Figure 13 uses several different types of links: plain text links, links created as list items, and links created with images. They also use a CSS3 mega drop-down menu. A **mega menu** is a type of menu that uses sub-menus to group related pages under a main menu item. When you select a main menu item, a second menu drops down with additional menu items to choose from. When the pointer moves away from the main menu item, the sub-menu closes. This is a way to provide a hierarchy of links, yet conserve space on the page by not making them all visible all of the time.

You insert a menu bar on a web page using the Insert Navigation command in the Structure category on the Insert panel. Dreamweaver adds the menu bar links to the page and adds JavaScript code and CSS styles to the code to make the links respond to user input. In the code, the links are placed within <nav> tags, which clearly indicate to screen readers that this is a navigational element, a semantic markup that helps provide accessibility.

There are other methods that you can use to create a menu bar with images, such as an image map. You will learn about image maps in Lesson 4.

Copying and Modifying a Menu Bar

After you create a menu bar, you can save time by copying and pasting it to the other main pages in your site. Make sure you place the menu bar in the same position on each page. This practice ensures that the menu bar will look the same on each page, making it easier for users to navigate to all the pages in your website. If you are even one line or one pixel off, the menu bar will appear to "jump" as it changes position from page to page. When you learn to use templates, you can create a main page template with a menu bar, then base the rest of your pages on the template. This makes it easy to provide continuity across the site and is easier to update when changes are needed.

Figure 13 *United States Botanic Garden website*

Links created as list items

Images used for links

Source: United States Botanic Garden

Create a menu bar

1. Change to Code view, place the insertion point in front of the opening <h1> tag before the page heading "The Sea Spa Services", then return to Design view.

2. With the insertion point in front of The Sea Spa Services, press **[Enter]** (Win) or **[return]** (Mac), select the **Structure category** on the Insert panel, then select **Navigation**.

3. In the Insert Navigation dialog box, type **menu_bar** in the Class text box, verify that **Insert as Fluid Element** is checked, as shown in Figure 14, then select **OK** to close the dialog box.

   The placeholder text for the menu bar appears inside a layout box outline under the banner on the page, as shown in Figure 15.

   You created a navigation bar element on the spa page.

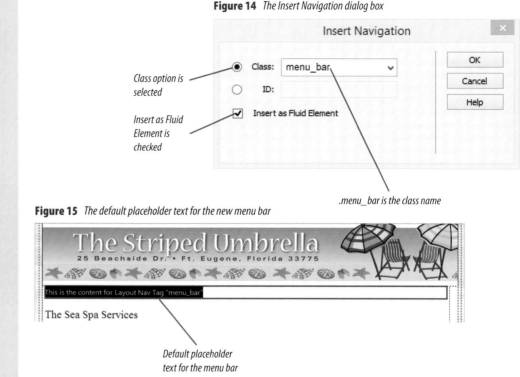

Figure 14 *The Insert Navigation dialog box*

Class option is selected

Insert as Fluid Element is checked

.menu_bar is the class name

Figure 15 *The default placeholder text for the new menu bar*

Default placeholder text for the menu bar

Understanding the Web Accessibility Initiative - Accessible Rich Internet Applications Suite

The Web Accessibility Initiative Accessible Rich Internet Applications Suite (WAI-ARIA) is a resource for applying best practices when adding advanced user interface controls to a website. Functions such as drag-and-drop or browsing through a menu can be difficult for users who rely on assistive devices to navigate a site. WAI-ARIA, at w3.org/TR/wai-aria/, provides guidelines and techniques for planning and implementing accessible content. It also provides presentations, handouts, and tutorials for developers who are interested in learning how to provide content that all users can easily navigate, such as providing alternative keyboard navigation for web objects primarily designed to function using mouse clicks or screen taps. The information offered through WAI-ARIA is developed by the Protocols and Formats Working Group (PFWG), a part of the World Wide Web Consortium (W3C).

Figure 16 *The default placeholder text for the menu bar selected*

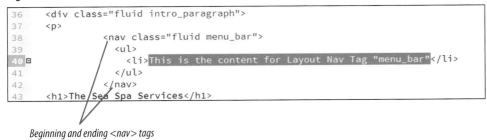

This is the content for Layout Nav Tag "menu_bar"

The Sea Spa Services

Massages

Facials

Body Treatments

Massages

Sports Massage

Unordered List button

Add items to a menu bar

1. Click in the default menu bar text, select the text, then select the **Unordered list button** :≡ on the Property inspector, as shown in Figure 16.

2. Switch to Code view, then verify that the selected placeholder text is between the beginning and ending unordered list tag. If it is not, cut and paste it as shown in Figure 17. If you don't see a <p> tag before the opening <nav> tag, place the insertion point in front of the opening <nav> tag, and type **<p>**.

3. Return to Design view, reselect the placeholder text if necessary, type **Home**, press **[Enter]** (Win) or **[return]** [Mac], then continue by adding About Us, Sand Crab Cafe, Sea Spa, and Activities to serve as the five links in the menu bar.

   The default placeholder text for the menu bar is replaced with text to use for the links to the five main pages in the website.

   (continued)

Figure 17 *The unordered list item in Code view*

```
36    <div class="fluid intro_paragraph">
37    <p>
38            <nav class="fluid menu_bar">
39            <ul>
40              <li>This is the content for Layout Nav Tag "menu_bar"</li>
41            </ul>
42            </nav>
43    <h1>The Sea Spa Services</h1>
```

Beginning and ending <nav> tags

Lesson 3   Create, Modify, and Copy a Menu Bar

DREAMWEAVER 5-19

4. Use the Property inspector to link each item as follows: Home: **index.html**; About Us: **about_us.html**; Sand Crab Café: **café.html**; The Sea Spa: **spa.html**; and Activities: **activities.html**.

5. Compare your page to Figure 18, then save your work.

You created an unordered list from the five menu items, then linked each item to its page.

Figure 18 *The menu bar items linked to their pages*

Unordered list items with links added

Inserting a Fireworks Menu Bar

Another option for adding a menu bar to your page is to create a menu bar in Adobe Fireworks and import it onto an open page in Dreamweaver. Adobe Fireworks is a bitmap and vector graphics editor used for creating website images and designs. To do this you first create a menu bar in Fireworks and export the file to a Dreamweaver local site folder. This file contains the HTML code that defines the menu bar properties. Next, open the page you want to insert it on in Dreamweaver, then use the Insert, Image, Fireworks HTML command to place the HTML code on the page. You can also use Dreamweaver to import rollover images and buttons created in Fireworks.

Figure 19 *The ul li a properties*

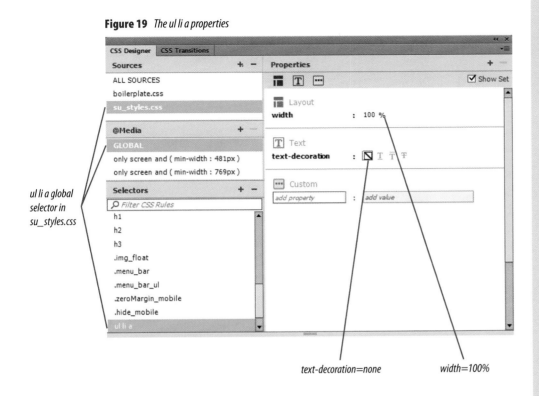

ul li a global
selector in
su_styles.css

text-decoration=none   width=100%

Use CSS to format a menu bar

1. If necessary, place the insertion point in the menu bar, select **su_styles.css** in the Sources pane in CSS Designer, select **GLOBAL** in the @Media pane, select the **Add Selector button** ✚ , then verify that ul li a is the selected name in the selectors pane, and then press **[Enter]** (Win) or **[return]** [Mac].

   The suggested name is based on the location of the insertion point. In this case, ul li a indicates that the insertion point was in an unordered list, it's in a list item, and is a link. This is a standard HTML tag, and these tags do not have to begin with a period, as do the custom tags that you create.

2. Add the following properties and values in the Properties pane:

   width = **100%;**

   text-decoration = **none;**

   Setting the width to 100% tells the selector to occupy 100% of its space, and setting the text decoration to none removes the underline from the links.

3. With the ul li a selector still highlighted, select the **Show Set check box** in the Properties pane and compare your screen to Figure 5-19.

   (continued)

4. Create a new global tag selector in the su_styles.css file named **li**, and then set the list item Display property to **inline**.

Even though you see the word "inline" in light gray text in the Display property value text box, it is serving as a property value placeholder. To make sure it is actually assigned as a property value, it must be selected. This insures that the inline display value will be added to the li tag selector and will be listed as a li property value when the Show Set checkbox is selected in the Properties pane.

5. Select the su_styles.css GLOBAL **menu_bar selector**, then set the following property and value:

text-align = **center**;

The menu bar is now horizontal instead of vertical on the page, as shown in Figure 21.

6. Save your work, then preview the page in a browser.

7. Close the browser.

You used CSS to assign properties to menu bar elements.

Figure 20 *The li selector display property set to inline*

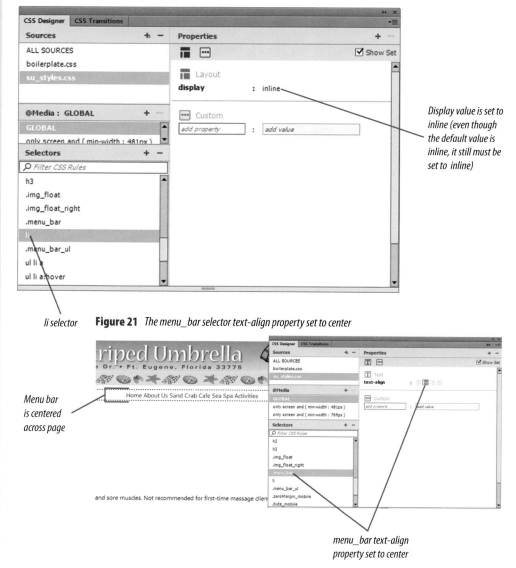

Display value is set to inline (even though the default value is inline, it still must be set to inline)

li selector

Figure 21 *The menu_bar selector text-align property set to center*

Menu bar is centered across page

menu_bar text-align property set to center

Figure 22 *Choosing a background color for the menu bar*

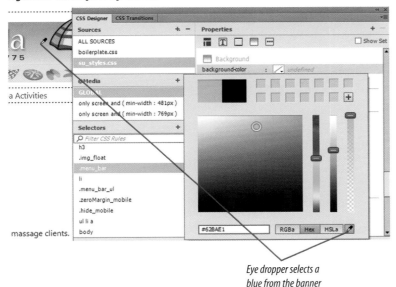

Eye dropper selects a
blue from the banner

Figure 23 *Adding left and right padding properties to the ul li a selector*

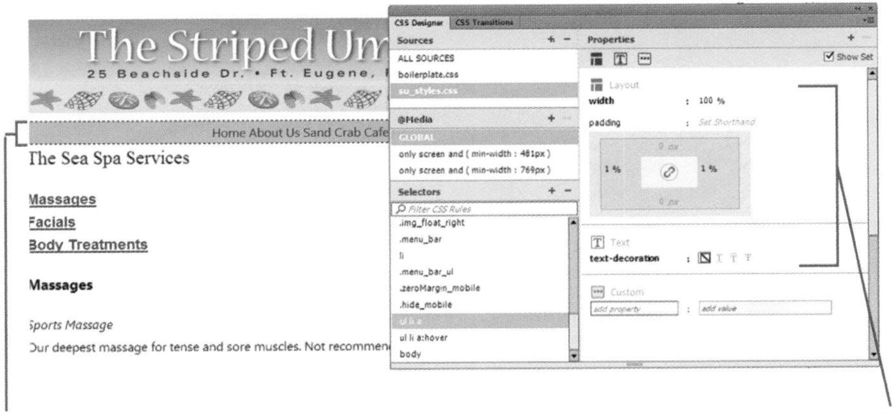

Settings add some
space between
the links

Properties added
to the ul li a
global selector

Edit CSS menu bar selectors

1. Select the GLOBAL selector **menu_bar** in CSS Designer if necessary, then select the **background-color box** to open the color picker.

2. Select the **Eyedropper tool**, select a shade of blue from the banner background, as shown in Figure 22, then move the pointer over the page and click to close the color picker.

   The menu bar now has a blue background that blends with the banner.

3. Select the GLOBAL selector **ul li a** in CSS Designer then add the following properties and values:

   left padding =**1%**

   right padding = **1%**

4. Show the ul li a set properties, compare your screen to Figure 23, save your work, preview the page in the browser, then close the browser.

   These settings put some space between the links. However, the navigation bar is not the same width as the banner because the container it is in, the .intro_paragraph selector, needs an adjustment.

   (continued)

5. Select the **GLOBAL .intro_paragraph selector** in the su_styles.css file, then change the width to **100%** and the padding to **0px** on all sides.

Changing the container width spreads the banner across the container so its edges line up with the banner edges, as shown in Figure 24.

6. Select the **su_styles.css file** on the Related Files toolbar, then scroll to locate the ul li a selector, which is toward the end of the Mobile Layout section, around line 160.

This selector is inherited by the other device sizes, but the rule is not duplicated in the other sections of the code. Therefore, if you want to change a property or value, you must duplicate the code for the other two device sizes, then modify the property values that you want to change for those devices.

7. Copy all of the code for this selector, including its brackets, then paste it into the Tablet Layout: 481px to 768px section of the code (which begins around line 180), before the closing bracket for that section, and then paste it into the Desktop Layout: 769 px to a max of 1232 px section (which begins around line 233).

8. Modify the desktop size ul li a selector to set the padding to **4%** for the left side and **4%** for the right side.

Adjusting the padding percentages increases the space between the menu bar items to better fit the display size.

9. Save your work, select **Source Code** on the Related files toolbar to return to the spa page, change to Design view, then view the menu bar using Live view in all three screen sizes.

(continued)

Figure 24 *Adjusted menu bar width*

The menu bar width is now equal to the width of the banner

Figure 25 *A menu element with the pointer over it changes color*

Menu item changes colors when the pointer is placed over it

Working with Links and Navigation

Figure 26 *Copying the code for the new menu bar*

```
37      <div class="fluid intro_paragraph">
38        <p>
39          <nav class="fluid menu_bar">
40          <ul>
41          <li><a href="index.html">Home</a></li>
42          <li><a href="about_us.html">About Us</a></li>
43          <li><a href="cafe.html">Sand Crab Cafe</a></li>
44          <li><a href="spa.html">Sea Spa</a></li>
45          <li><a href="activities.html">Activities</a></li>
46        </ul></nav>
47          <h1>The Sea Spa Services</h1>
```

Copy the selected code for the menu bar, including the <p> tag on the line above it

Figure 27 *Selecting the original menu bar before replacing it*

```
36      <div class="fluid intro_paragraph">
37      <nav class="fluid intro_paragraph">
38          <a href="index.html">Home</a> - <a href="about_us.html">About Us</a> - <a href=
        "spa.html">Spa</a> - <a href="cafe.html">Cafe</a> - <a href="activities.html">
        Activities</a></nav>
39          <a href="assets/family_sunset.jpg"><img src="assets/family_sunset.jpg" alt="Family
        on a sunset cruise" class="img_float"/></a>
```

Select the original menu bar, then replace it with the new code

Figure 28 *The activities page with the completed menu bar*

Now all of the menu items fit on the screen, regardless of the display size. Finally, you will adjust the menu bar appearance when a user points to an item in a browser.

10. Add one more global selector in the su_styles.css file named **ul li a:hover** with the following properties: Set the text color value to the **brown starfish color**, using the Color picker and the Eye Dropper; then set the background-color value to the **sand color**.

11. Save all files, then go to Live view and hover the pointer over a menu bar item as shown in Figure 25.

You used global selectors to format menu bar spacing and colors.

Copy and paste a menu bar

1. Change to Code view, then select the code for the menu bar, as shown in Figure 26.

2. Select **Edit** on the Menu bar, then select **Copy**.

3. Double-click **activities.html** on the Files panel to open the activities page.

4. Switch to Code view if necessary, select the code for the five links on the Activities page as shown in Figure 27, select **Edit** on the Menu bar, select **Paste**, return to Design view, compare your screen to Figure 28, save the page, then test the links in Live view.

5. Repeat Step 4 to replace the original menu bar on the index page and add the new menu bar to the about_us page, then save your work.

6. Preview the activities page in your browser, test the menu bar on the home, about_us, spa, and activities pages, then close your browser. Close all open pages.

You copied the menu bar on the spa page to three additional pages in The Striped Umbrella website.

Create an IMAGE MAP

What You'll Do

In this lesson, you will create an image map by placing a hotspot on The Striped Umbrella banner on the about_us page that will link to the home page.

Understanding Image Maps

Another way to create links for web pages is to combine them with images by creating an image map. An **image map** is an image that has one or more hotspots placed on top of it. A **hotspot** is a selectable area on an image that, when the user selects it, links to a different location on the page or to another web page. For example, see the National Park Service website shown in Figure 29. When you select a state, you link to information about national parks in that state.

You can create hotspots by first selecting the image on which you want to place a hotspot, and then using one of the hotspot tools in the Property inspector to define its shape.

There are several ways to create image maps to make them user-friendly and accessible. One way is to be sure to include alternate text for each hotspot. Another is to draw the hotspot boundaries a little larger than they need to be to cover the area you want to set as a link. This allows users a little leeway when they place their mouse over the hotspot by creating a larger target area for them. Always assign a unique name for each image map.

Dreamweaver hotspot tools make creating image maps a snap. In addition to the Rectangle Hotspot tool, you can create any shape you need using the Circle Hotspot tool and the Polygon Hotspot tool. For instance, on a map of the United States, you can draw an outline around each state with the Polygon Hotspot tool and then make each state "selectable." You can easily change and rearrange hotspots on the image. Use the Pointer Hotspot tool to select the hotspot you would like to edit. You can drag one of the hotspot selector handles to change its size or shape. You can also move the hotspot by dragging it to a new position on the image. It is a good idea to limit the number of complex hotspots in an image because the code can become too lengthy for the page to download in a reasonable length of time.

Figure 29 *Viewing an image map on the National Park Service website*

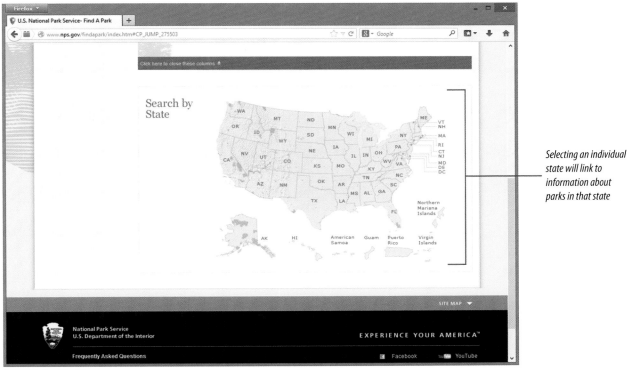

Selecting an individual state will link to information about parks in that state

Source: National Park Service

Create an image map

1. Open the about us page, place the insertion point in the banner div, change to Code view to verify that the insertion point is between the div tags, then insert the file **transparent_gif** from the assets folder in the drive and folder where you store your Chapter 5 Data Files. To make an image map, you have to select an image. Since the banner is a background image, it cannot be selected. You insert a transparent image on top of the banner background so you can create an image map over the banner.

2. Select the transparent_image on the about_us page, then select the **Rectangle Hotspot tool** in the Property inspector.

3. Drag the **pointer** to create a rectangle over the transparent image over the banner, as shown in Figure 30.

TIP To adjust the shape of a hotspot, select the Pointer Hotspot tool in the Property inspector, then drag a sizing handle on the hotspot.

4. Drag the **Point to File button** next to the Link text box in the Property inspector to the index.html file on the Files panel to link the hotspot to the index page.

5. Replace the default text "Map" with **Home** in the Map text box in the Property inspector to give the image map a unique name.

6. Select the **Target list arrow** in the Property inspector, then select **_top**.

   When the hotspot is selected, the _top option opens the home page in the same window. See Table 2 for an explanation of the four target options.

   (continued)

Figure 30 *A hotspot drawn on the transparent image over the banner background*

Transparent image

Hotspot

Rectangle Hotspot tool

TABLE 2: OPTIONS IN THE TARGET LIST	
Target	**Result**
_blank	Displays the destination page in a separate browser window
new	Displays the destination page in a new tab (CSS3)
_parent	Displays the destination page in the parent frameset (replaces the frameset)
_self	Displays the destination page in the same frame or window
_top	Displays the destination page in the whole browser window

© 2015 Cengage Learning®

Figure 31 *Hotspot properties*

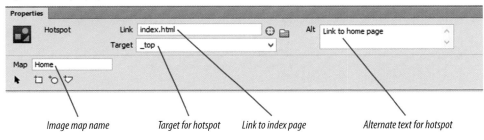

Image map name Target for hotspot Link to index page Alternate text for hotspot

7. Type **Link to home page** in the Alt text box in the Property inspector, as shown in Figure 31.

8. Save your work, preview the page in your browser, then place the pointer over the image map.

   As you place the pointer over the hotspot, the pointer turns to a pointing finger, indicating that it is a link, as shown in Figure 32.

9. Select the link to test it, close the browser, then close all open pages.

You created an image map on the banner of the about_us page using the Rectangle Hotspot tool. You then linked the hotspot to the home page.

Figure 32 *Preview of the image map on the activities page in the browser*

When pointer is over the hotspot, the link appears in the bottom-left corner of the screen in some browsers

Pointing finger indicates pointer is over the link hotspot

Manage
WEBSITE LINKS

What You'll Do

In this lesson, you will use some Dreamweaver reporting features to check The Striped Umbrella website for broken links and orphaned files.

Managing Website Links

Because the World Wide Web changes constantly, websites might be up one day and down the next. If a website changes server locations or goes down due to technical difficulties or a power failure, the links to it become broken. Broken links, like misspelled words on a web page, indicate that a website is not being maintained diligently.

Checking links to make sure they work is an ongoing and crucial task you need to perform on a regular basis. You must check external links manually by reviewing your website in a browser and selecting each link to make sure it works correctly. The Check Links Sitewide feature is a helpful tool for managing internal links. You can use it to check your entire website for the total number of links and the number of links that are broken, external, or orphaned, and then view the results in the Link Checker panel. **Orphaned files** are files that are not linked to any pages in the website.

DESIGN**TIP**

Using Good Navigation Design

As you work on the navigation structure for a website, you should try to limit the number of links on each page to no more than is necessary. Too many links may confuse users of your website. You should also design links so that users can reach the information they want within a few clicks or taps. If finding information takes more than three or four clicks or taps, the user may become discouraged or "lost" in the site. It's a good idea to provide visual clues on each page to let users know where they are, much like a "You are here" marker on a store directory at the mall, or a breadcrumbs trail. A **breadcrumbs trail** is a list of links that provides a path from the initial page you opened in a website to the page that you are currently viewing. Many websites provide a list of all the site's pages, called a **site map**. A site map is similar to an index. It lets users see how the information is divided between the pages and helps them locate the information they need quickly.

Figure 33 *Link Checker panel displaying external links*

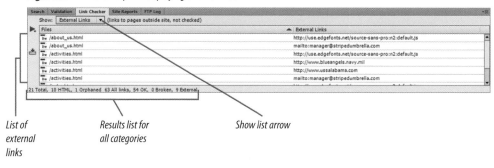

List of external links

Results list for all categories

Show list arrow

Figure 34 *Link Checker panel displaying one orphaned file*

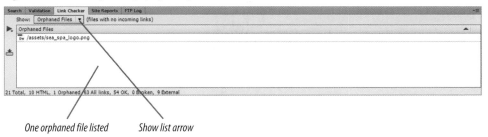

One orphaned file listed

Show list arrow

Figure 35 *Assets panel displaying links*

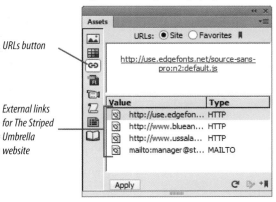

URLs button

External links for The Striped Umbrella website

Manage website links

1. Select **Site** on the Menu bar, point to **Advanced**, then select **Recreate Site Cache**.

2. Select **Site** on the Menu bar, then select **Check Links Sitewide**.

   The Results tab group opens, with the Link Checker panel in front. By default, the Link Checker panel initially lists any broken internal links found in the website. The Striped Umbrella website has no broken links.

3. Select the **Show list arrow** in the Link Checker panel, select **External Links**, then compare your screen to Figure 33.

4. Select the **Show list arrow**, then select **Orphaned Files** to view the orphaned files in the Link Checker panel, as shown in Figure 34.

   The Striped Umbrella website has one orphaned file, sea_spa_logo.png. You may use this file later, so you leave it in the assets folder. (*Hint*: if you see more orphaned files listed, recreate your site cache and try again.)

5. Right-click (Win) or Control-click (Mac) in an empty area of the Results tab group title bar, then select **Close Tab Group**.

6. Display the Assets panel if necessary, then select the **URLs button** ⊖ in the Assets panel if necessary to display the list of links in the website.

   The Assets panel displays the external links used in the website, as shown in Figure 35.

You used the Link Checker panel to check for broken links, external links, and orphaned files in The Striped Umbrella website. You also viewed the external links in the Assets panel.

Update a page

1. Open dw5_3.html from the drive and folder where you store your Data Files, then save it as **fishing.html** in the striped_umbrella local site root folder, overwriting the existing fishing page, but not updating the links.

   The page elements are updated with the website style sheets.

2. Select the broken link image placeholder, select the **Browse for File button** next to the Src text box in the Property inspector, browse to the drive and folder where you store your Data Files, open the assets folder, then select the file **fisherman.jpg** to copy the file to the striped_umbrella assets folder.

3. Deselect the image placeholder and the image appears, as shown in Figure 36.

4. Save and close the fishing page, then close the dw5_3.html page.

5. Open dw5_4.html from the drive and folder where you store your Data Files, then save it as **cruises.html** in the striped_umbrella local site folder, overwriting the existing cruises page, but not updating the links.

   The links to the website CSS files are in place and format the page elements. Since you haven't yet corrected the path for the image, you can't see the styles applied to the image yet.

   (continued)

Figure 36 *Fishing page updated*

Testing Your Website Against the Wireframe

Another test you should run regularly is a comparison of how your developing website pages are meeting the specifications of your wireframe prototype. Compare each completed page against its corresponding wireframe to make sure that all page elements have been placed in their proper locations on the page. Verify that all specified links have been included and test them to make sure that they work correctly. You might also consider hiring site-usability testers to test your site navigation. A site usability test provides impartial feedback on how intuitive and user-friendly your site is to use.

Figure 37 *Cruises page updated*

POWER USER SHORTCUTS	
To do this:	**Use this shortcut:**
Close a file	[Ctrl][W] (Win) or ⌘ [W] (Mac)
Close all files	[Ctrl][Shift][W] (Win) or ⌘ [Shift][W] (Mac)
Print code	[Ctrl][P] (Win) or ⌘ [P] (Mac)
Check page links	[Shift][F8] (Win)
Undo	[Ctrl][Z], [Alt][BkSp] (Win) or ⌘ [Z], [option][delete] (Mac)
Redo	[Ctrl][Y], [Ctrl][Shift][Z] (Win) or ⌘ [Y], ⌘ [Shift][Z] (Mac)
Refresh Design view	[F5] (Win and Mac)
Hide all visual aids	[Ctrl][Shift][I] (Win) or ⌘ [Shift][I] (Mac)
Make a link	[Ctrl][L] (Win) or ⌘ [L] (Mac)
Remove a link	[Ctrl][Shift][L] (Win) or ⌘ [Shift][L] (Mac)
Check links sitewide	[Ctrl][F8] (Win) or [fn] ⌘ [F8] (Mac)
Show Files tab group	[F8] (Win) or ⌘ [Shift][F] (Mac)

© 2015 Cengage Learning®

6. Select the broken link image placeholder, select the **Browse for File button** 📁 next to the Src text box in the Property inspector, then browse to the drive and folder where you store your Data Files, open the assets folder, then select the file **boats.jpg** to copy the file to the striped_umbrella assets folder.

TIP If you have trouble selecting the placeholder, click or tap the middle of the placeholder to select it.

7. Deselect the image placeholder and the image will appear as shown in Figure 37.

8. Add the following properties and values to the **GLOBAL.gridContainer** selector:

   border-width: **thin**;

   border-style: **solid**;

   border-color: **#272525**;

   background-color: **#FFFFFF**.

9. Save your work.

   The border properties add a thin border to set off the page area in a browser. The white background adds a little space around the page area so the text doesn't come so close to the edge of the page.

10. Preview each page in the browser, close the browser, test them in Live view in three different sizes, then close all open pages.

You added content to two previously blank pages in the website and previewed each page to check for consistent layout. You also added some properties to the GLOBAL .grid_container selector to add some white space and a border around each page.

Incorporate Web 2.0
TECHNOLOGY

What You'll Do

In this lesson, you will explore some of the Web 2.0 applications that can be used to engage website users.

What Exactly Is Web 2.0?

The term **Web 2.0** describes the evolution of web applications that facilitate and promote information sharing among Internet users. These applications not only reside on computers, but on cell phones, in cars, on portable GPS devices, and in game devices. **GPS (Global Positioning System)** devices are used to track your position through a global satellite navigation system, and are popular to use for driving directions, hiking, and map making. Web 2.0 applications do not simply display information for users to read passively; they allow users to actively contribute to the content.

RSS feeds are another easy way to share information with users. **RSS** stands for **Really Simple Syndication**. Websites use **RSS feeds** to distribute news stories, information about upcoming events, and announcements. Web users can subscribe to RSS feeds to receive regular releases of information from a site. Users can download and play these digitally broadcasted files called **podcasts (Programming On Demand)** using devices such as computers or MP3 players. Many news organizations and educational institutions publish both audio and video podcasts. Video podcasts are referred to as **vodcasts** or **vidcasts**.

Web 2.0 also includes social networking. **Social networking** refers to any web-based service that facilitates social interaction among users. Examples of social networking sites include **Facebook**, **Pinterest**, and **Match.com**. These sites allow users to set up profile pages and post information on them for others to view. Facebook pages often contain lots of text, images, and videos. Pinterest is an online pinboard for sharing crafts, recipes, and other items of interest.

A wiki is another example of a Web 2.0 application. The term **wiki** (named for the Hawaiian word for "quick") refers to a site where a user can use simple editing tools to contribute and edit the page content in a site. A good example is **Wikipedia**, an online encyclopedia. Wikipedia allows users to post new information and edit existing information on any topic. Although people have different opinions about the academic integrity of the information on Wikipedia, Wikipedia is a rich source of information. Proponents argue that its many active and vigilant users maintain its information integrity.

Blogs (web logs) are another example of a Web 2.0 application. **Blogs** are websites where the website owner regularly posts commentaries and opinions on various topics. Content can consist of text, video, or images. Users can respond to the postings and read postings by other users. **Twitter** is a website where users can post short messages, called **tweets**. Twitter is considered a blog or a micro blog, because you cannot enter more than 140 characters in each post. To use Twitter, you must first join by creating a free account. Then you can post messages about yourself, "follow" other people's tweets, and invite others to "follow" you. **Tumblr** is another popular blog where you can post and share text, photos, music, and videos.

There are many video sharing applications such as Skype, Google Video Chat, and YouTube. **Skype** and **Google Video Chat** are free applications that you use to communicate live with other people through video conferencing, using a high-speed Internet connection and a web camera, called a **web cam**. **YouTube** is a website where you can upload and share videos. To upload videos, you need to register with the site.

So how do these various Web 2.0 components relate to the process of creating websites? Most websites today engage their users in one or more of these applications. The Peace Corps website, shown in Figure 38, has links to Facebook, Twitter, YouTube, and others. When you are designing a site, one of the decisions you must make is not if, but how you

will incorporate Web 2.0 technology to fully engage your users. To incorporate one of these applications into your website, first register to set up an account on the social networking site, then place a link on one of your site's web pages (usually the home page) that links to each social networking site and opens your page. For example, if your Twitter account is located at twitter.com/your_name, add this link to your home page using the Twitter logo as a graphic link. You can download social networking sites' logos from their websites. Some applications specify how you should refer to and link to their site.

Using the applications that are a part of Web 2.0 with your website can bring your site from simply presenting information on pages for users to read to facilitating a compelling dialog between the users and the site. They will no longer be just "users," but active participants.

Web 3.0 will be the next generation of the Web. With Web 3.0, browsers will be able to handle multiple searches simultaneously. For instance, you could search for a recent Oscar best picture nominee and sushi restaurant in the vicinity of the theater where it is playing. iPhones and Google Androids come with a personal assistant you can "talk" with, rather than typing in searches. Browsers may soon be able to do this, too. The more information that is stored from your past searches, the more they will get to "know" you and be able to give responses that fit your profile.

Figure 38 *Viewing social networking links on the Peace Corps website*

Links to Facebook, Twitter, YouTube, Tumblr, LinkedIn, Pinterest, Instagram

Source: The Peace Corps

Create external and internal links.

1. Open the Blooms & Bulbs website.
2. Open dw5_5.html from the drive and folder where you store your Data Files, then save it as **newsletter.html** in the Blooms & Bulbs website, overwriting the existing file without updating the links. Close dw5_5.html.
3. Select each broken image and browse to the assets folder in the drive and folder where you store your Chapter 5 Data Files and copy the ruby_grass, trees, and plants broken images to the local site assets folder.
4. Create a new global selector to the bb_styles.css file to modify the <h2> tag as follows:

   font-color: **#003300**
   font-family: Segoe, Segoe UI, DejaVu Sans;
   Trebuchet MS; Verdana, sans-serif
   font-weight: bold
   font-size: large

5. Modify the <h1> rule (which you created in Chapter 3) as follows:

   font-size: x-large
   font-color: #003300

6. Add a new global selector to the blooms_styles.css file that modifies the <h3> tag as follows:

   font-color: #003300
   font-family: Segoe, Segoe UI, DejaVu Sans;
   Trebuchet MS; Verdana, sans-serif
   font-weight: bold
   font-size: medium

7. Apply the img_float rule to the ruby_grass and plants images.

8. Apply the img_float_right rule to the trees image.
9. Scroll to the bottom of the page, then link the National Gardening Association text to **http://www.garden.org**.
10. Link the Organic Gardening text to **http://www.organicgardening.com**.
11. Link the Southern Living text to **http://www.southernliving.com/southern**.
12. Save all files, then preview the page in your browser, verifying that each link works correctly.
13. Close your browser, returning to the newsletter page in Dreamweaver.
14. Scroll to the paragraph about gardening issues, select the gardening tips text in the last sentence, then link the selected text to the tips.html file in the blooms local site folder.
15. Change the page title on the Document toolbar to read **Blooms & Bulbs Gardening Matters**, then save your work.
16. Open the plants page and add this new paragraph to the bottom of the page: **In addition to these marvelous roses, we have many annuals, perennials, and water plants that have just arrived.**
17. Link the "annuals" text to the annuals.html file, link the "perennials" text to the perennials.html file, and the "water plants" text to the water_plants.html file.
18. Save your work, test the links in your browser, then close your browser. (*Hint*: These pages do not have content yet, but are serving as placeholders.)

Use IDs to navigate to specific page locations.

1. Switch to the newsletter page, then select the Grass heading and add the ID **grass**.
2. Select the Trees heading, then add the ID **trees**.
3. Select the Plants heading, then add the ID **plants**.
4. Select the word "grass" in the Gardening Issues paragraph and type **#grass** in the Link text box in the Property inspector.
5. Select the word "trees" in the Gardening Issues paragraph and type **#trees** in the Link text box in the Property inspector.
6. Select the word "plants" in the Gardening Issues paragraph and type **#plants** in the Link text box in the Property inspector.
7. Save your work, view the page in your browser, test all the links to make sure they work, then close your browser.

Create, modify, and copy a menu bar.

1. Change to Code view for the plants page, then place the insertion point in front of the opening <h1> tag before the page heading "Featured Spring Plant: Roses!", enter a paragraph break, then return to Design view.
2. With the insertion point in front of "Featured Spring Plant: Roses!", enter a paragraph break, select the Structure category on the Insert panel, then select Navigation.
3. Type **menu_bar** in the Class text box, verify that Insert as Fluid Element is checked, then select OK to close the Insert Navigation dialog box.

4. Select the default placeholder text in the menu_bar container, then select the Unordered List button in the Property inspector.

5. Verify in Code view that the placeholder text is between the beginning and ending unordered list item tag. If it is not, cut and paste it to that position in the code.

6. Return to Design view, select the default placeholder text, if necessary, type **Home**, press [Enter] (Win) [return] [Mac], then continue by adding **Newsletter**, **Plants**, **Tips**, and **Workshops** to serve as the five links in the menu bar.

7. Use the Property inspector to link each item as follows: Home: index.html; Newsletter: newsletter.html; Plants: plants.html; Tips: tips.html; and Workshops: workshops.html.

8. Place the insertion point in the menu bar, select bb_styles.css in the Sources pane in CSS Designer, select GLOBAL in the @Media pane, select the Add Selector button then select the ul li a default GLOBAL selector name in the Selectors pane.

9. Add the following properties and values in the Properties pane:
width = **100%**;
text-decoration = none;

10. Select the bb_styles.css GLOBAL menu_bar selector, then set the following property and value:
text-align = center;

11. Save your work, preview the page in a browser, then close the browser.

12. Select the bb_styles.css GLOBAL menu_bar selector again, then select the background-color box to open the Color picker.

13. Select the Eyedropper tool, then select a shade of light gold from the text in the banner background.

14. Create a new GLOBAL selector in the bb_styles.css file named **li**, then add the following property and value: display = inline;

15. Select the GLOBAL selector ul li a in CSS Designer then add the following properties and values:
left padding = **4%**;
right padding = **4%**;

16. Save your work, then preview the page in your browser.

17. Select the GLOBAL .intro_paragraph selector in the bb_styles.css file, then change the padding to **0px** on all sides and the width to **100%**.

18. Switch to the bb_styles.css file, then scroll to locate the ul li a selector in the code.

19. Copy all of the code for this selector, then paste it into the tablet (only screen and (min-width: 481px), and desktop (min-width: 769px), sections of the code.

20. Modify the tablet size ul li a selector code to set the padding to **1%** for the left side and **1%** for the right side.

21. Modify the global size ul li a selector to set the padding to **1%** for the left side and **1%** for the right side.

22. Modify the Tablet .header_div selector to add a height value of **110px**; then modify the .header_div background-repeat value in the Desktop selector to repeat-x.

23. Add the following properties and values to the GLOBAL .gridContainer selector:
border-width = thin;
border-style = solid;
border-color = **#272525**;
background-color = **#FFFFFF**.

Figure 39 *Completed Skills Review*

24. Add one more GLOBAL selector in the bb_styles.css file named ul li a:hover with the following properties: set the text color using the Color picker eye dropper to pick up a dark purple in a flower on the banner; then for the background color, use the Eye Dropper to pick up the light purple from a flower.
25. Save your work, then preview the page in a browser to see if you are satisfied with your menu bar color scheme. If you are not, try different colors for your ul li a:hover selector.
26. Copy the new menu bar to the index, newsletter, and tips pages.
27. Save all files, then go to Live view and point to (hover over) a menu bar item to see the rollover effect.

Create an image map.

1. On the newsletter page, place the insertion point in the banner div then insert the file transparent_gif from the assets folder in the drive and folder where you store your Chapter 5 Data Files.
2. Use the Rectangle Hotspot tool to draw an image map across the transparent image on the banner, then link it to the home page.
3. Name the image map **home** and set the target to _top.
4. Add the alternate text **Link to home page**, save the page, then preview it in the browser to test the link.
5. Close the browser.

Manage website links.

1. Use the Link Checker panel to view and fix broken links and orphaned files in the Blooms & Bulbs website. (*Hint*: Remember to recreate your site cache if you see any. That usually fixes them.)

2. Open dw5_6.html from the drive and folder where you store your Data Files, then save it as **annuals. html**, replacing the original file. Do not update links, but save the file coleus.jpg from the Chapter 5 Data Files assets folder to the assets folder of the website.
3. Close dw5_6.html.
4. Apply the img_float rule to the coleus image.
5. Repeat Steps 2 and 3 using dw5_7.html to replace perennials.html, saving the fiber_optic_grass.jpg file in the local site assets folder and using dw5_8.html to replace water_plants.html, saving the water_lily.jpg file in the local site assets folder.
6. Save your work, then preview each page in the browser, testing each link to make sure they all work correctly. As you preview each page, compare the different page sizes to the sample pages shown in Figures 40a, b, and c.
7. Close all open pages.

Figure 40a *Completed Skills Review*

Blooms & Bulbs

Home   Newsletter   Plants   Tips   Workshops

Gardening Matters

Welcome, fellow gardeners. My name is Cosie Simmons, the owner of Blooms & Bulbs. My passion has always been my gardens. Ever since I was a small child, I was drawn to my back yard where all varieties of beautiful plants flourished. A lush carpet of thick grass bordered with graceful beds is truly a haven for all living creatures. With proper planning and care, your gardens will draw a variety of birds and butterflies and become a great pleasure to you.

Gardening Issues

There are several areas to concentrate on when formulating your landscaping plans. One is your grass. Another is the number and variety of trees you plant. The third is the combination of plants you select. All of these decisions should be considered in relation to the climate in your area. Be sure and check out our gardening tips before you begin work.

Figure 40b & c *Completed Skills Review*

Welcome to Blooms & Bulbs. We carry a variety of plants and shrubs along with a large inventory of gardening supplies. Our four greenhouses are full of healthy young plants just waiting to be planted in your yard. We grow an amazing selection of annuals and perennials. We also stock a diverse selection of trees, shrubs, tropicals, water plants, and ground covers. Check out our garden ware for your garden accents or as gifts for your gardening friends. We are happy to deliver or ship your purchases.

Our staff includes a certified landscape architect, three landscape designers, and six master gardeners. We offer detailed landscape plans tailored to your location as well as planting and regular maintenance services. We have enjoyed serving Alvin and the surrounding area for twelve years now. Stop by and see us soon!

Blooms & Bulbs
Highway 43 South
Alvin, TX 77501
555-248-0806
Customer Service

Copyright 2002 - 2016
Last updated on May 2, 2014

Featured Spring Plant: Roses!

Who can resist the romance of roses? Poets have waxed poetically over them throughout the years. Many persons consider the beauty and fragrance of roses to be unmatched in nature. The varieties are endless, ranging from floribunda to hybrid teas to shrub roses to climbing roses. Each variety has its own personality and preference in the garden setting. The Candy Cane Floribunda is a beautiful rose with cream, pink, and red stripes and swirls. They have a heavy scent that will remind you of the roses you received on your most special occasions. These blooms are approximately four inches in diameter. They bloom continuously from early summer to early fall. The plants grow up to four feet tall and three feet wide. They are shipped bare root in February.

For ease of growing, Knock Out® roses are some of our all-time favorites. Even beginners will not fail with these garden delights. They are shrub roses and prefer full sun, but can take partial shade. They are disease resistant and drought tolerant. You do not have to be concerned with either black spot or dead-heading with roses such as the Knock out®, making them an extremely low-maintenance plant. They are also repeat bloomers, blooming into late fall. The shrub can grow quite large, but can be pruned to any size. Pictured here is Southern Belle. Check out all our varieties as you will not fail to have great color with these plants. You must see a close-up of these beauties! Select the image to enlarge it.

In addition to these marvelous roses, we have many annuals, perennials, and water plants that have just arrived.

Use Figures 41, 42, 43, and 44 as guides to continue your work on the TripSmart website, which you began in Project Builder 1 in Chapter 1 and developed in the previous chapters. You have been asked to create a new page for the website that lists helpful links for customers. You will add content to the destinations, eqypt, and argentina pages.

1. Open the TripSmart website.
2. Open dw5_9.html from the drive and folder where you store your Data Files, then save it as **services.html** in the TripSmart local site folder, replacing the existing file, but not updating links.
3. Close dw5_9.html.
4. Assign the **IDs reservations**, **outfitters**, **tours**, and **links** to the respective headings on the page, then link each ID to "Reservations," "Travel Outfitters," "Escorted Tours," and "Helpful Links in Travel Planning" in the first paragraph, as shown in Figure 43.
5. Link the text "on-line catalog" in the Travel Outfitters paragraph to the catalog.html page.
6. Link the text "CNN Travel Channel" under the heading Helpful Links in Travel Planning to **http://www.cnn.com/TRAVEL**.
7. Repeat Step 7 to create links for the rest of the websites listed:
   U.S. Department of State: **http://travel.state.gov**
   Yahoo Currency Converter:
   http://finance.yahoo.com/currency-converter
   The Weather Channel: **http://www.weather.com**
8. Save the services page, preview the page in the browser and test each link, then close the browser.

Figure 41 *Completed Project Builder 1*

TripSmart has several divisions of customer service to assist you in planning and making reservations for your trip, shopping for your trip wardrobe and providing expert guide services. Give us a call and we will be happy to connect you with one of the following departments: Reservations, Travel Outfitters, or Escorted Tours. If you are not quite ready to talk with one of our departments and would prefer doing some of your own research first, may we suggest beginning with our Helpful Links in Travel Planning.

Reservations

Our Reservations Department is staffed with five Certified Travel Agents, each of whom is eager to assist you in making your travel plans. They have specialty areas in Africa, the Caribbean, South America, Western Europe, Eastern Europe, Asia, Antarctica, and Hawaii and the South Pacific. They also specialize in Senior Travel, Family Travel, Student Travel, and Special Needs Travel. Call us at *(555) 848-0807* extension 75 or e-mail us at *Reservations* to begin making your travel plans now. We will be happy to send you brochures and listings of Internet addresses to help you get started. We are open from 8:00 a.m. until 6:00 p.m. CST.

Travel Outfitters

Our travel outfitters are seasoned travelers that have accumulated a vast amount of knowledge in appropriate travel clothing and accessories for specific destinations. Climate and seasons, of course, are important factors in planning your wardrobe for a trip. Area customs should also be taken in consideration so as not to offend the local residents with inappropriate dress. When traveling abroad, we always hope that our customers will represent our country well as good ambassadors. If they can be comfortable and stylish at the same time, we have succeeded! Our clothing is all affordable and packs well on long trips. Most can be washed easily in a hotel sink and hung to drip-dry overnight. Browse through our on-line catalog, then give us a call at *(555) 433-7844* extension 85. We will also be happy to mail you a catalog of our extensive collection of travel clothing and accessories.

Escorted Tours

Our Escorted Tours department is always hard at work planning the next exciting destination to offer our TripSmart customers. We have seven professional tour guides that accompany our guests from the United States point of departure to their point of return.

Our current feature package tour is to Peru. Our local escort is Don Eugene. Don has traveled Peru extensively and enjoys sharing his love for this exciting country with others. He will be assisted after arrival in Peru with the services of archeologist JoAnne Rife, anthropologist Christina Elizabeth, and naturalist Iris Albert. Call us at *(555) 848-0807* extension 95 for information on the Peru trip or to learn about other destinations being currently scheduled.

Helpful Links in Travel Planning

The following links may be helpful in your travel research. Happy surfing!

CNN Travel Channel - News affecting travel plans to various destinations

US Department of State - Travel warnings, passport information, and more

Yahoo! Currency Converter - Calculate the exchange rate between two currencies

The Weather Channel - Weather, flight delays, and driving conditions

TripSmart
1106 Beechwood
Fayetteville, AR 72704
555-848-0807
Contact Us

Copyright 2002 - 2016
Last updated on May 2, 2014

9. Enter a paragraph break before the first paragraph on the services page, change to Code view, delete the   code after the opening <p> tag, then insert a navigation bar with the class name **menu_bar**.

10. Use the Property inspector to create an unordered list from the default placeholder menu bar text, then type text for the links: **Home**, **Catalog**, **Services**, **Tours**, and **Newsletter**. (Remember to add paragraph returns after all but the last menu item.)

11. Link each item as follows: Home: index.html; Catalog: catalog.html; Services: services.html; Tours: tours.html; and Newsletter: newsletter.html.

12. Place the insertion point in the menu bar, then add a global selector in the tripsmart_styles.css source in CSS Designer, with the default selector name (ul li a).

13. Add the following properties and values in the Properties pane:
width = 100%;
text-decoration = none;

14. Select the tripsmart_styles.css GLOBAL menu_bar selector, then set the following properties and values:
text-color = (a color of your choice using the eye dropper tool)
text-align = center;
background-color = (a color of your choice using the eye dropper)

15. Save your work.

16. Create a new GLOBAL selector in the tripsmart_styles.css file named **li**, then add the following property and value:
display = inline;

17. Modify the GLOBAL selector named ul li a to add the following properties and values:
left padding = 1%;
right padding = 1%.

18. Save your work, then preview the page in the browser and test the links.

19. Switch to the tripsmart_styles.css file, then scroll to locate the ul li a selector in the code.

20. Copy the ul li a selector to the tablet and desktop section of the tripsmart_styles.css code, then select padding sizes for the ul li a selector for the mobile and tablet size sections of the code.

Figure 42 *Completed Project Builder 1*

Destinations: Egypt and Argentina

We are featuring two new trips for the coming year. The first is to Egypt. After arriving, we will check into our hotel and enjoy the sights for two days in Cairo, including the famous Egyptian Museum of Antiquities. Next, we will fly to Luxor to visit the Temple of Karnak and then boad our luxury Nile cruise boat, the Sun Queen VII. As we slowly cruise down the Nile, our stops will include Qena, the Ptolemaic Temple of Goddess Hathor in Denderah, the Edfu Temple, the Kom Ombo Temple, and the Philae Temple. We will enjoy a felucca ride around Elephantine Island, and then attend a formal farewell dinner the last night onboard our boat. We return to Cairo and enjoy a day in the market and a walking tour of the old walled city of Cairo.

Argentina is our next destination. We begin our tour in Buenos Aires on our first day with an orientation to this lovely city, including the gardens of Palermo, San Telmo, the business center, La Boca, and Recoleta Cemetery. That evening we will attend a Tango class to learn basic tango steps before having a chance to show off our talents at a dinner and tango show. The two main features for most people on this trip are the magnificient Iguassu Falls and Perito Moreno Glacier. The most adventurous can strap on trampons and trek across the glacier. A trek across a glacier with the beautiful blue Patagonia skys overhead is not to be forgotten. With luck, you will witness a calving, when ice breaks off the glacier with a crash of thunder and falls to the water.

21. Add one more selector in the tripsmart_styles.css file named **ul li a:hover** with text and background colors of your choice. Then make any other modifications to your selectors using properties and values of your choice.
22. Preview the page in a browser to text the links and evaluate your color choices.
23. When you are satisfied, copy the new menu bar to the index, newsletter, and tours pages.
24. Save all files, then go to Live view and hover over a menu bar item to see the rollover effect.
25. Place the insertion point in the banner div on the newsletter page, then insert the file transparent_gif from the assets folder in the drive and folder where you store your Chapter 5 Data Files.
26. Use the Rectangle Hotspot tool to draw an image map across the transparent image on the banner, then link it to the home page.
27. Name the image map **home** and set the target to _top.
28. Add the alternate text **Link to home page**, save the page, then preview it in the browser to test the link.
29. Close the browser.

Figure 43 *Completed Project Builder 1*

Destination: Egypt

We have a really special trip planned for next November. Egypt - the land of kings and pharaohs! This ten-day adventure will begin in Cairo as we visit the Giza Plateau to see the pyramids of Cheops, Chepheren, and Mycerinus. We will also visit the Great Sphinx and the Egyptian Museum of Antiquities before we leave Cairo for our cruise along the Nile. We board the Egyptian Queen at Luxury and enjoy stops along the way to the Valley of the Kings, the Valley of the Queens, the Ptolemaic temple, the Temple of Horus, and the Temple of Philae on the island of Agilika. When we return to Cairo, you will have the opportunity to do some shopping in the famous Khan El-Khalili Bazaar and enjoy an unforgettable performance of the El-Tannoura Egyptian Heritage Dance Troup.

To provide the finest in personal attention, this tour will be limited to no more than twenty people. The price schedule is as follows: Land Tour and Supplemental Group Air, $5,500.00; International Air, $1,350.00; and Single Supplement, $1,000.00. Entrance fees, hotel taxes, and services are included in the Land Tour price. Ship gratuities are also included for the Egyptian Queen crew and guides. A deposit of $500.00 is required at the time the booking is made. Trip insurance and luggage insurance are optional and are also offered for an extra charge. A passport and visa will be required for entry into Egypt. Call us at 555-555-0807 for further information and the complete itinerary from 8:00 a.m. to 6:00 p.m. (Central Standard Time).

30. Open the tours page, save it as the **egypt** page, overwriting the original eqypt page, then close both the tours and egypt pages.

31. Open dw5_10.html from the drive and folder where you store your Data Files, then save it as **argentina. html**, replacing the original file. Do not update links, but save the files iguazu_falls.jpg and glacier.jpg from the Chapter 5 Data Files assets folder to the assets folder of the website, then format them with an image class selector.

32. Close dw5_10.html, then open dw5_11.html, and save it as the **tours** page. Correct the links to the two images, then format them with an image class selector.

33. In the first paragraph of the tours page, add a link to the egypt page using the word "egypt" in the first paragraph, then add a link to the argentina page using "argentina" in the second paragraph.

34. Save your work, then preview each page in the browser, testing each link to make sure they all work correctly.

35. Use the Link Checker panel to view and fix broken links and orphaned files. (*Hint*: Remember to recreate your site cache if you see any. That usually fixes them.)

36. Close all open pages.

Figure 44 *Completed Project Builder 1*

Destination: Argentina

We have Argentina from north to south and exciting locations in between. We start in Buenos Aires for our arrival in country. Visit the many landmarks of Buenos Aires, including the Plaza de Mayo, Casa Rosada (Presidential Palace) and the Cabildo. Known as the "Paris of South America," the city's European influences are on display in the architecture, cuisine and other facets of daily life. Stroll the lovely parks of Palermo; the charming quarters of San Telmo, birthplace of the tango; the bustling banking and business center; the barrio of La Boca; and Recoleta Cemetery where Eva Peron is interred.

Our next stop is Iguassu Falls, a breath taking natural wonder of the world with its 275 cascades that spread across a gulf of nearly two miles. We will go on a catwalk extending 3,600 feet over Devil's Throat , a rolling cataract marking the border of Brazil and Argentina and view the many distinct falls from balconies in both countries. You will be talking about the magnificence of these massive works of nature for many years.

Barlioche, Argentina's "Little Switzerland" in Pantagonia is our next stop. This snow peaked wonderland allows viewing some of the most attractive scenery in Argentina, a panoply of lush hills, snow-topped peaks and lakes reflecting a crisp blue sky,

You are continuing your work on the Carolyne's Creations website, which you started in Project Builder 2 in Chapter 1 and developed in the previous chapters. Chef Carolyne has asked you to create a page describing her cooking classes offered every month. You will create the content for that page and individual pages describing the children's classes and the adult classes. Refer to Figures 45, 46, and 47 for possible solutions.

1. Open the Carolyne's Creations website.
2. Open dw5_12.html from the drive and folder where you store your Data Files, save it as **classes.html** in the local site folder of the Carolyne's Creations website, overwriting the existing file and not updating the links. Close dw5_12.html.
3. Select the text "adults' class" in the last paragraph, then link it to the adults.html page. (*Hint*: This page has not been developed yet.)

4. Select the text "children's class" in the last paragraph and link it to the children.html page. (*Hint*: This page has not been developed yet.)
5. Create an e-mail link from the text "Sign me up!" that links to **carolyne@carolynescreations.com**.
6. Insert the egyptian_traditional_dessert.jpg from the assets folder where you store your Data Files at the

beginning of the second paragraph, add appropriate alternate text, then choose your own alignment and formatting settings.
7. Check any other pages with images and adjust your image rules if necessary to improve the appearance of each page.

Figure 45 *Completed Project Builder 2*

Cooking Classes are fun!

Chef Carolyne loves to offer a fun and relaxing cooking school each month in her newly refurbished kitchen. She teaches an adults' class on the fourth Saturday of each month from 6:00 to 8:00 pm. Each class will learn to cook a complete dinner and then enjoy the meal at the end of the class with a wonderful wine pairing. This is a great chance to get together with friends for a fun evening.

Chef Carolyne also teaches a children's class on the second Tuesday of each month from 4:00 to 5:30 pm. Our young chefs will learn to cook two dishes that will accompany a full meal served at 5:30 pm. Children aged 5–8 years accompanied by an adult are welcome. We also host small birthday parties where we put the guests to work baking and decorating the cake! Call for times and prices.

We offer several special adults' classes throughout the year. The Valentine Chocolate Extravaganza is a particular favorite. You will learn to dip strawberries, make truffles, and bake a sinful Triple Chocolate Dare You Torte. We also host the Not So Traditional Thanksgiving class and the Super Bowl Snacks class each year with rave reviews. Watch the website for details! Prices are $40.00 for each adults' class and $15.00 for each children's class. Sign up for classes by calling 555-963-8271 or by emailing us: Sign me up! See what's cooking this month for the adults' class and children's class.

8. Create a new menu bar using selectors of your choice. Refer to Figure 45 as you work. (*Hint*: The menu bar on Figure 45 was styled with 3% padding on the left and right sides of each menu bar item.)

9. Make any other adjustment to your selectors if you like, then save your work and close the classes page. (*Hint*: If you used an Edge Webfont, use the Command, Cleanup Webfonts Script Tag (Current Page) on each page on which you used a Webfont.)

10. Open dw5_13.html from the drive and folder where you store your Data Files, then save it as **children.html,** overwriting the existing file and not updating links. Save the image children_cooking.jpg from the assets folder where you store your Data Files to the website assets folder, then make any adjustments to your selectors to enhance the design if you like.

11. Copy the menu bar from the classes page to the children page, save your work, compare your screen to Figure 46, then close the children page.

12. Repeat Steps 10 and 11 to open the dw5_14.html file and save it as **adults.html**, overwriting the existing file and saving the file egyptian_lunch from the assets folder where you save your Data Files, then use alignment settings of your choice. Compare your work to Figure 47 for a possible solution, then save and close the files.

Figure 46 *Completed Project Builder 2*

Home   Shop   Classes   Catering   Recipes

Children's Cooking Class for March:
Oven Chicken Fingers, Chocolate Chip Cookies

This month we will be baking oven chicken fingers that are dipped in a milk and egg mixture, then coated with breadcrumbs. The chocolate chip cookies are based on a famous recipe that includes chocolate chips, M&Ms, oatmeal, and pecans. Yummy! We will be learning some of the basics like how to cream butter and crack eggs without dropping shells into the batter.

We will provide French fries, green beans, fruit salad, and a beverage to accompany the chicken fingers.

Carolyne's Creations
496 Maple Avenue
Seven Falls, Virginia 52404
555-963-8271
Email <u>Carolyne Kate</u>

13. Open the index page and replace the old menu bar with the new one.
14. Repeat Step 13 to replace all old menu bars on the rest of the completed pages in the site.
15. Save all the pages, then check for broken links and orphaned files. You will see one orphaned file, cc_logo.gif. Since this is only used for a background image, it shows up as an orphaned file. Since you are using it, do not delete it.
16. Make any selector edits of your choice to improve the design of the pages.
17. Preview all the pages in your browser, check to make sure the links work correctly, close your browser, then close all open pages.

Figure 47 *Completed Project Builder 2*

Home   Shop   Classes   Catering   Recipes

Adult's Cooking Class for March: Egyptian Cuisine

The class in March will be cooking several traditional Egyptian dishes: kushari, Arabic bread, falafel, and tahini. Our dessert will be a traditional rice pudding. Egyptian cuisine is both very tasty and healthy, a typical Mediterranean diet!

Carolyne's Creations
496 Maple Avenue
Seven Falls, Virginia 52404
555-963-8271

Sherrill Simmons is a university English instructor. She would like to find new ways to engage her students through her university website. She decided to explore incorporating podcasts, FaceBook, and Twitter. She spends several hours looking at other websites to help her get started.

1. Connect to the Internet, then navigate to the Federal Bureau of Investigation website at fbi.gov, as shown in Figure 48.
2. Browse through the site and locate the link to "Podcasts & Radio." What are the options they have provided for their users to download and listen to them?

Figure 48 *Design Project*

Source: The Federal Bureau of Investigation

3. Navigate to the U.S. Navy website at navy.mil, as shown in Figure 49.
4. Describe how the Navy is using Web 2.0 technology. What do you think their purpose might be for incorporating each application?
5. Which Web 2.0 applications would you include on your website if you were Sherrill?
6. Describe how you would use each one of them to engage her students.

Figure 49 *Design Project*

Source: The United States Navy

In this assignment, you will continue to work on the website that you started in Chapter 1 and developed in the previous chapters.

You will continue building your website by designing and completing a page with a menu bar. After creating the menu bar, you will copy it to each completed page in the website. In addition to the menu bar, you will add several external links and several internal links to other pages as well as to IDs on a page. You will also link text to a named anchor. After you complete this work, you will check for broken links and orphaned files.

1. Consult your wireframe to decide which page or pages you would like to develop in this chapter. Decide how to design and where to place the menu bar, IDs, and any additional page elements you decide to use. Decide which reports should be run on the website to check for accuracy.
2. Research websites that could be included on one or more of your pages as external links of interest to your users. Create a list of the external links you want to use. Using your wireframe as a guide, decide where each external link should be placed in the site.
3. Add the external links to existing pages or create any additional pages that contain external links.
4. Create IDs to use to link to key locations on the page, such as the top of the page, then link appropriate text on the page to them.

5. Decide on a design for a menu bar that will be used on all pages of the website.
6. Create the menu bar and copy it to all finished pages on the website.
7. Think of a good place to incorporate an image map, then add it to a page. Remember if you want to create an image map over a background image, you will need to place a transparent image on top of the background image first.
8. Decide on at least one Web 2.0 application that you might like to incorporate and determine how and on what page they would be included.
9. Use the Link Checker panel to check for broken links and orphaned files.
10. Use the checklist in Figure 50 to make sure your website is complete, save your work, then close all open pages.

Figure 50 *Portfolio Project checklist*

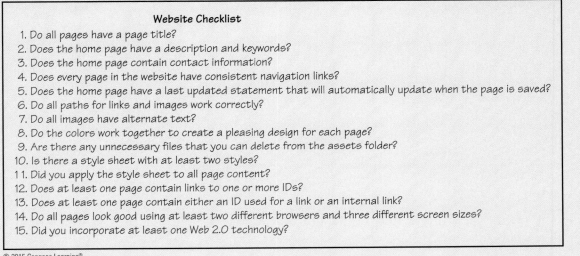

Website Checklist
1. Do all pages have a page title?
2. Does the home page have a description and keywords?
3. Does the home page contain contact information?
4. Does every page in the website have consistent navigation links?
5. Does the home page have a last updated statement that will automatically update when the page is saved?
6. Do all paths for links and images work correctly?
7. Do all images have alternate text?
8. Do the colors work together to create a pleasing design for each page?
9. Are there any unnecessary files that you can delete from the assets folder?
10. Is there a style sheet with at least two styles?
11. Did you apply the style sheet to all page content?
12. Does at least one page contain links to one or more IDs?
13. Does at least one page contain either an ID used for a link or an internal link?
14. Do all pages look good using at least two different browsers and three different screen sizes?
15. Did you incorporate at least one Web 2.0 technology?

CHAPTER 6

POSITIONING OBJECTS WITH CSS AND TABLES

1. Create a page using a Fluid Grid layout
2. Add and position divs
3. Add content to divs
4. Create a table
5. Resize, split, and merge cells
6. Insert and align images in table cells
7. Insert text and format cell content

WITH CSS AND TABLES

Introduction

To create an organized, attractive web page, you need precise control of the position of page elements. CSS page layouts can provide this control. **CSS page layouts** consist of containers formatted with CSS rules into which you place page content. These containers can accommodate images, blocks of text, videos, or any other page element. The appearance and position of the containers are set through the use of HTML tags known as **div tags**. Using div tags, you can position elements next to each other as well as on top of each other.

Another option for controlling the placement of page elements is through the use of tables. **Tables** are placeholders made up of small boxes called **cells**, into which you can insert text and graphics. Cells in a table are arranged horizontally in **rows** and vertically in **columns**. Using tables on a web page gives you control over the placement of each object on the page, similar to the way CSS layout blocks control placement. In this chapter, you use a predesigned CSS Fluid Grid page layout with one default div tag to position text and graphics. You then add a table to one of the CSS blocks.

Using Div Tags Versus Tables for Page Layout

Div tags and tables both enable you to control the appearance of content in your web pages. Unlike tables, div tags let you stack your information, allowing for one piece of information to be visible at a time. Tables are static, which makes it difficult to change them quickly as need arises. Div tags can be dynamic, changing in response to variables such as a mouse click. You can create dynamic div tags using JavaScript **behaviors**, simple action scripts that let you incorporate interactivity by modifying content based on variables like user actions. For example, you could add a JavaScript behavior to text in a div tag to make it become larger or smaller when the pointer hovers over it.

Designers previously used tables to position content on web pages. Since the inception of CSS, designers have moved to positioning most page content with CSS layouts. However, tables are still used for some layout purposes, such as arranging tabular data on a page. As a designer, you should become familiar with the tools that are available to you, including CSS and tables, then decide which tool meets current standards and is best suited for the current design challenge.

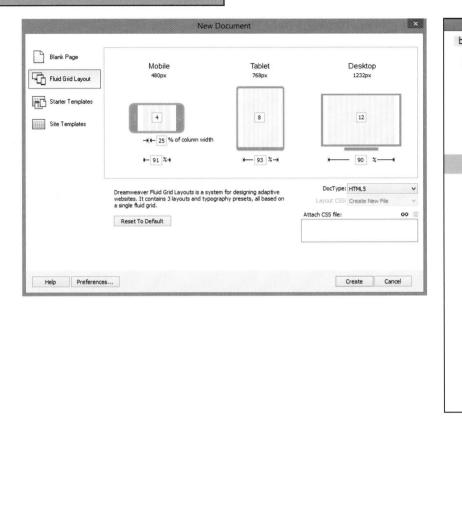

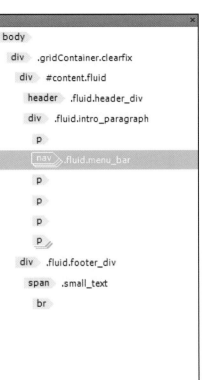

Create a Page
USING A FLUID GRID LAYOUT

What You'll Do

In this lesson, you will create a new page based on a predesigned CSS layout to become the new cafe page for the website.

Understanding Div Tags

Div tags are HTML tags that define how areas of content are formatted or positioned on a web page. For example, when you center an image on a page or inside a table cell, Dreamweaver automatically inserts a div tag in the HTML code. In addition to using div tags to align page elements, designers also use them to assign background colors or borders to content blocks, CSS styles to text, and many other properties to page elements. One type of div tag is an AP div tag. AP stands for absolutely positioned, so an **AP div tag** creates a container that has a specified, fixed position on a web page. The resulting container that an AP div tag creates on a page is called an **AP element**.

Using CSS Fluid Grid Layouts

Because building a web page using div tags can be tedious for beginning designers, Dreamweaver CC provides a default Fluid Grid layout in the New Document dialog box, as shown in Figure 1.

Fluid Grid layouts are layouts based on three device sizes: Mobile, Tablet, and Desktop.

Each device size is based on a grid system similar to column guides. CSS style sheets control the way the page content is displayed across the grids, with each grid using slightly different selector properties and values tailored to the device being used to display the page. The theory is that a designer can design a single page, but modify the way the content is displayed by changing the style sheet properties so the content will be attractive and readable regardless of the screen size used to display it.

A Fluid Grid layout contains div tags that control the placement of page content using placeholders. Each div tag container has placeholder text that appears until you replace it with your own content. Because div tags use CSS for formatting and positioning, designers prefer them for building web page content. When you use a Dreamweaver Fluid Grid layout you can be sure that your pages will appear with a consistent design when viewed in all browsers and all device sizes. Once you become more comfortable using a Fluid Grid layout, you will be able to modify the code to customize your own designs.

Viewing CSS Layout Blocks

As you design your page layouts using div tags, use Design view to see and adjust CSS content blocks. In Design view, text or images that have been aligned or positioned using div tags have a dotted border, as shown in Figure 2. In the Visual Aids list on the View menu, you can display selected features of div tag elements, such as CSS Layout Backgrounds, CSS Layout Box Model, and CSS Layout Outlines. The CSS Layout Box Model displays the padding and margins of a block element.

Figure 1 *New Document dialog box*

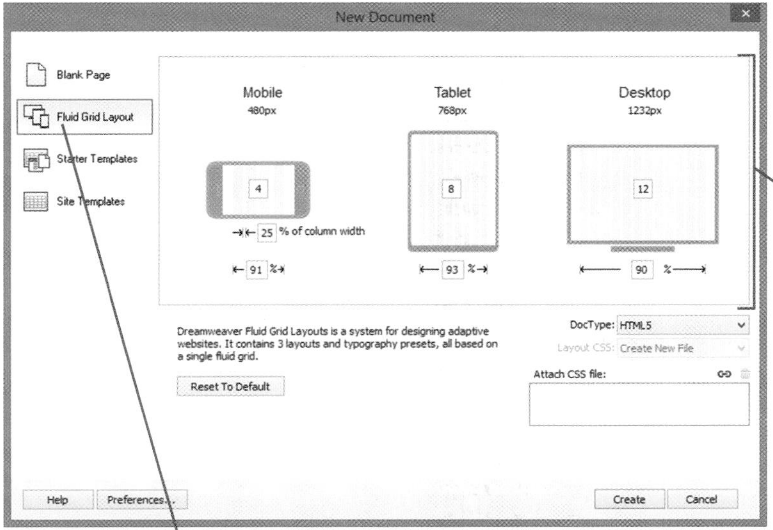

Fluid Grid Layout option

Default predesigned Fluid Grid layouts

Figure 2 *CSS blocks defined by dotted borders*

Dotted-line borders surround CSS blocks

Using Tracing Images for Page Design

Another design option for creating a page layout is to use a tracing image. A **tracing image** is an image that is placed in the background of a document. By adjusting the transparency (opacity) of the image, you can then use it to create page elements on top of it, similar to the way you would place a piece of tracing paper on top of a drawing and trace over it. The tracing image serves as a guide or pattern. You can delete it after you complete your design. To insert a tracing image, Use the Modify, Page Properties, Tracing Image dialog box or the View, Tracing Image, Load command. Browse to select the image you want to use for the tracing image, then adjust the transparency as desired.

Create a page with a Fluid Grid layout

1. Open The Striped Umbrella website.

2. Select **File** on the Menu bar, select **New**, then select **Fluid Grid Layout**, as shown in Figure 3. Fluid Grid layouts are used to create **adaptive websites**, meaning that the website appearance adapts to match the device size on which it is displayed. The dialog box shows diagrams of the three preset device sizes: Mobile, Tablet, and Desktop, and how the fluid column grid appears at each size. The three preset sizes for Mobile, Tablet, and Desktop devices are shown with a diagram of the columns that make up each grid.

3. Select the **Attach Style Sheet button** 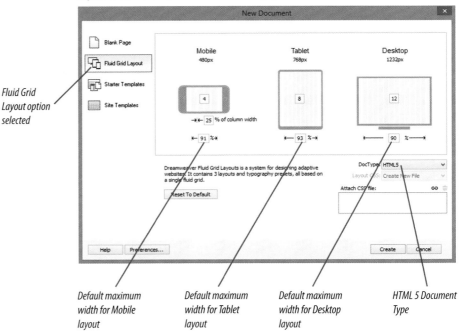 in the bottom-right corner of the dialog box, select the **Browse** button, navigate to the local site folder if necessary, select **boilerplate.css**, select **OK**, verify that the **Link** option is selected, then select **OK** to attach the boilerplate.css style sheet.

4. Select the **Attach Style Sheet button** again, then select **Browse**.

5. Select **su_styles.css**, select **OK**, verify that the **Link** option is selected, then select **OK** to close the Select Style Sheet File dialog box.

   Both style sheets that are used to style the pages in the website will be attached to the new page, as shown in Figure 4.

6. Select **Create** in the New Document dialog box, and in the File name text box in the Save As dialog box, type **su_styles_default**, then select **Save**.

   Each time you create a new Fluid Grid Layout page, Dreamweaver generates a style sheet file that defines the styles for the layout sizes for each device. When the first page was created for The Striped Umbrella website, I named this style sheet

(continued)

Figure 3 *Fluid Grid Layout selected for the new page*

Fluid Grid Layout option selected

Default maximum width for Mobile layout

Default maximum width for Tablet layout

Default maximum width for Desktop layout

HTML 5 Document Type

Using XML and XSL to Create and Format Web Page Content

You can also create information containers on your web pages using XML, Extensible Markup Language, and XSL, Extensible Stylesheet Language. **XML** is a language that you use to structure blocks of information, similar to HTML. It uses similar opening and closing tags and the nested tag structure that HTML documents use. However, XML tags do not determine how the information is formatted, which is handled using XSL. **XSL** is similar to CSS; the XSL stylesheet information formats the containers created by XML. Once the XML structure and XSL styles are in place, **XSLT**, **Extensible Stylesheet Language Transformations**, interprets the code in the XSL file to transform an XML document, much like style sheet files transform HTML files from an unformatted file to a formatted file. XSL transformations can be written as client-side or server-side transformations. To create XML documents, use the XML page type in the Blank page category in the New Document dialog box.

Figure 4 *Boilerplate.css and su_styles.css files will be attached to the new page*

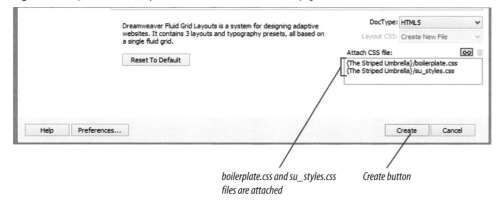

boilerplate.css and su_styles.css   Create button
files are attached

Figure 5 *New page based on a Fluid Grid layout*

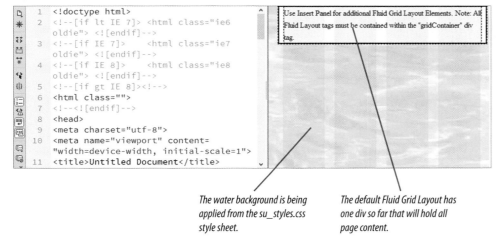

The water background is being   The default Fluid Grid Layout has
applied from the su_styles.css   one div so far that will hold all
style sheet.   page content.

su_styles.css file. You have since added styles to it and modified its styles as you've added pages and page elements. If you save over this file now, you will lose these changes. Therefore, you saved the new style sheet file as su_styles_default.css so it will not overwrite the modified file, preserving the styles you have been using. You can compare the two files if you want to see the differences between the styles that were in place when you started and the styles that you added and/or modified. We will remove the link to this new style sheet file on the new page to avoid any potential style conflicts.

The new blank page opens in Split view, as shown in Figure 5. You can tell that the page is reading the style sheet you have been using because you see the water background in Design view.

7. Save the open file as **cafe.html**, overwriting the existing blank cafe page.

8. Select **OK** to close the error message about the Edge Web Fonts, if one opens.

   The error message tells you that a selector in the su_styles.css code refers to an Adobe Edge Web font and an external link to the Typekit site.

9. Switch to Code view, select the link to the su_styles_default.css file, then delete it and return to Design view. If you see two links to the boilerplate.css file, delete one of them.

   You did not delete these files from the website; you just removed the links to them on the cafe page.

You created a new page based on a Fluid Grid layout with the two attached style sheets for The Striped Umbrella website. You renamed the new, default style sheet that was automatically generated, and saved the new document as cafe.html, overwriting the existing blank cafe page. Last, you deleted the link to the new style sheet file on the cafe page to prevent any style conflicts.

Add and Position
DIVS

What You'll Do

In this lesson, you will add three divs to the cafe page: one for a header, one for the menu bar, and one for a photo of the cafe.

Understanding How to Create a New Page with Fluid Grid Layouts

You gained understanding of the power of divs combined with style sheets as you worked through Chapters 1 through 5. You also examined how the Fluid Grid layouts and Media queries features customize web pages for specific device sizes. You created a new page based on a Fluid Grid layout in Lesson 1. Now you will learn how to add new divs to a page.

When you use Fluid Grid layouts and style sheets to design new website pages, you move from long, complicated page code to much shorter page code, because the bulk of the code moves from the pages to the style sheets.

Once you have style sheets in place to format your pages, most of the work is done. Then to add a new page, you can:

- Save an existing page with a new file name and replace the content with new content;
- Create a site template from an existing page and use it to create new pages; or
- Use the New Document dialog box to create a blank page. When you use the New Document dialog box, as you did in Lesson 1, attaching the existing style sheet files to it ensures that the new page will have a similar design as the existing pages.

Every new blank page, by default, has one div called .gridContainer.clearfix, as shown in Figure 6. This div acts as a "wrapper" inside

Using Dreamweaver New Page Options

You can use either the Welcome Screen or the New command on the File menu to create several different types of pages. The predesigned CSS page layouts make it easy to design accessible web pages based on Cascading Style Sheets, without an advanced level of expertise in writing HTML code. Predesigned templates are another time-saving feature that promotes consistency across a website. Fluid Grid layouts, Starter Templates, and Site Templates are a few of the other options. It is worth the time to explore each category to understand what is available to you as a designer. Once you have selected a page layout, you can customize it to suit your client's content and design needs.

which all other divs are placed. All Fluid Grid tags must be placed inside this div, between its opening and closing <div> tags. A new page also contains an additional div on the page, located inside the .gridContainer.clearfix div. This div has the default name "div1". You should give this div a more meaningful name, such as "header_div" or "main_content_div". Dreamweaver automatically adds the word "fluid" to the div name for each div you create in a Fluid Grid layout to help identify divs that are based on a Fluid Grid layout.

Controlling Div Placement on a Page

After you have used div tags to create divs, you can rearrange and/or resize the divs on the page. There are several tools available to help you: your style sheets, the Fluid Grid Layout guides, the Element Quick View tool, and the HUD Options mini-toolbar. Figure 7 shows the Fluid Grid Layout guides, the Element Quick View tool, and the HUD Options mini-toolbar.

Fluid Grid Layout guides are visual aids that show you the number of columns used for each view: Mobile, Tablet, and Desktop. You can turn Fluid Grid Layout guides on and off with the Hide Fluid Grid Layout Guides/Show Fluid Grid Layout Guides button on the Document toolbar, as shown in Figure 7.

Selecting the **Element Quick View button**, as shown in Figure 7, shows a visual representation of the HTML DOM structure for the page. **DOM** stands for Document Object Model, a convention that represents

Figure 6 *Code for a new blank page*

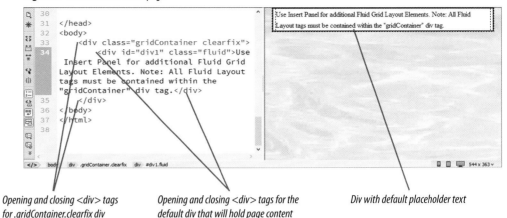

Opening and closing <div> tags for .gridContainer.clearfix div

Opening and closing <div> tags for the default div that will hold page content

Div with default placeholder text

Figure 7 *Viewing tools for managing divs*

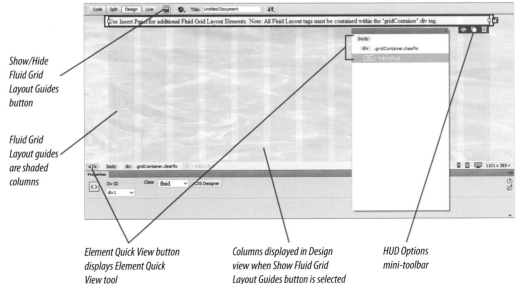

Show/Hide Fluid Grid Layout Guides button

Fluid Grid Layout guides are shaded columns

Element Quick View button displays Element Quick View tool

Columns displayed in Design view when Show Fluid Grid Layout Guides button is selected

HUD Options mini-toolbar

the order and type of elements used in a web page. The Element Quick View button lets you view each defined page element in a tree diagram so you can quickly see the order and position of each element relative to the other page elements. A folder icon represents every element. When you see multiple folder icons stacked, as shown in Figure 8, select a folder to see other elements nested inside the element. This is similar to expanding and collapsing folders in File Explorer by selecting the plus or minus sign.

When you display Fluid Grid layout guides and select a div, a mini-toolbar, sometimes referred to as a HUD and shown in Figure 7, appears next to a div border. **HUD** is an acronym for Heads Up Display. You can use the HUD to hide, duplicate, move, or delete a div. The name comes from the idea that you don't have to open panels to perform basic editing using divs; you can keep your "head up" or focused on the div itself while making changes.

These tools help you understand the relative position of each div on a page so you can easily position or change the order of the div elements.

Figure 8 *Viewing the order of page elements with Element Quick View*

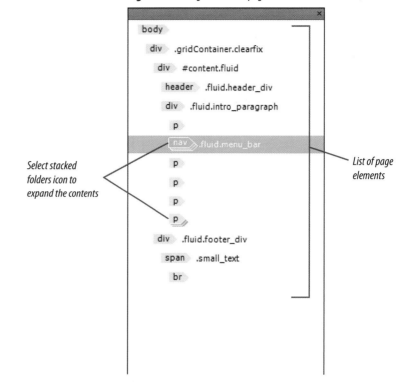

Select stacked folders icon to expand the contents

List of page elements

The Evolution of HTML5

HTML has been in existence since the early 1990s, but it wasn't until 1997 that the then current version, HTML4, became a W3C recommendation. Many HTML4 attributes such as body background, align, cell padding, and hspace are now added using CSS3. HTML5 introduced new ways to add interactivity and tags that support semantic markup, such as the <nav> tag used for navigation links. In Chapter 3 you learned about using semantic markup to incorporate meaning with your HTML markup. Other semantic HTML5 tags include <header>, <footer>, <article>, <audio>, <section>, and <video>. HTML5 is still a work in progress, but most modern browsers support it. HTML5 also introduces markup for Web applications (apps), an exploding sector of Web development.

Figure 9 *Renaming the default div id "div_1" to "content"*

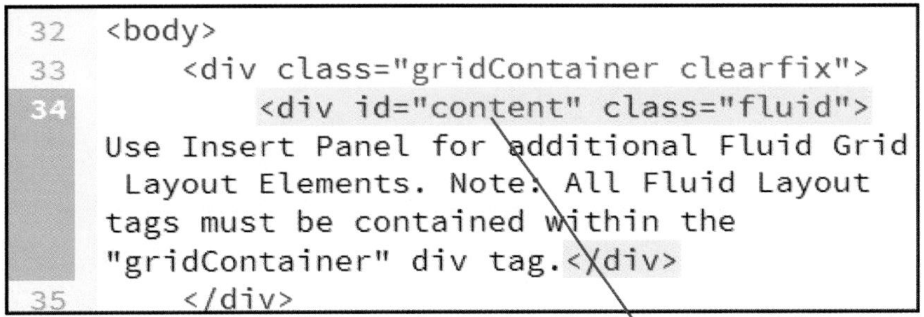

```
32    <body>
33        <div class="gridContainer clearfix">
34            <div id="content" class="fluid">
      Use Insert Panel for additional Fluid Grid
       Layout Elements. Note: All Fluid Layout
      tags must be contained within the
      "gridContainer" div tag.</div>
35        </div>
```

div id is changed to "content"

Figure 10 *Selecting the placeholder text for the content div*

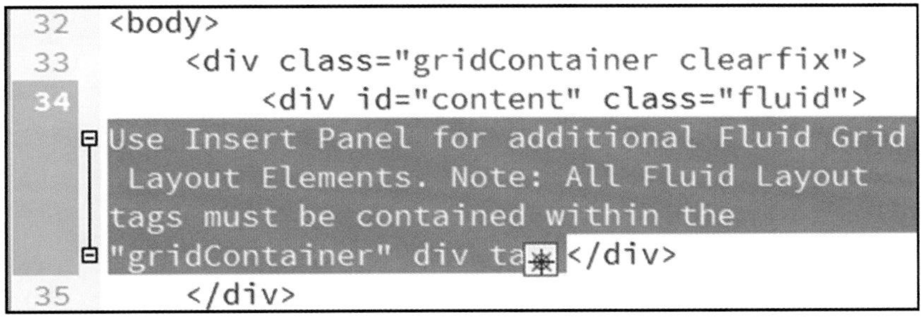

```
32    <body>
33        <div class="gridContainer clearfix">
34            <div id="content" class="fluid">
      Use Insert Panel for additional Fluid Grid
       Layout Elements. Note: All Fluid Layout
      tags must be contained within the
      "gridContainer" div ta ✳</div>
35        </div>
```

Figure 11 *Adding a class style for the header selector*

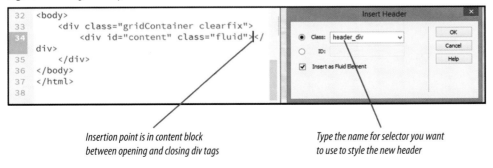

Insertion point is in content block between opening and closing div tags

Type the name for selector you want to use to style the new header

1. With the new blank cafe page open in Design view, change to Split view, then scroll to find the code for the div id="div1".

2. Select the default name **div_1**, then type **content**, as shown in Figure 6-9.

   The default name div_1 is replaced with the name content. This will match the rest of the pages in the site and allow the content div selector to apply the properties and values previously defined in the su_styles.css file.

3. In the Code view window, select the **placeholder text** in the content div, as shown in Figure 6-10, then delete it.

4. With the insertion point between the opening and closing <div> tags, select **Header** in the Structure category of the Insert panel.

5. Type **header_div** in the Insert Header dialog box, as shown in Figure 11, select **OK**, then delete the header placeholder text.

(continued)

6. Select **Refresh** on the Property inspector.

The header div is now filled with the banner background from the existing selector property in the su_styles.css file, as shown in Figure 12.

TIP You may need to select the Desktop size button on the status bar to see the banner shown.

7. Change to Design view, then select the **Element Quick View button** `</>` on the status bar.

8. Select each **stacked folder icon** to expand them, if necessary, then look at the page structure, as shown in Figure 13.

Recall that Dreamweaver adds the word "fluid" to each fluid grid selector name.

You renamed the default placeholder div on the cafe page, added a new header div inside it, then viewed the page structure with Element Quick View.

Figure 12 *Assigning the header selector to the header*

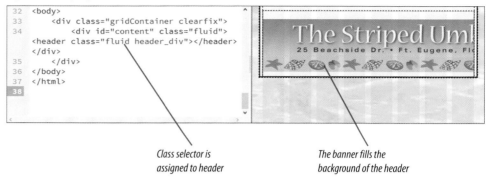

Class selector is
assigned to header

The banner fills the
background of the header

Figure 13 *Viewing the page DOM structure with Element Quick View*

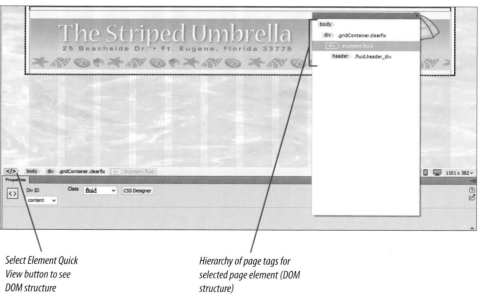

Select Element Quick
View button to see
DOM structure

Hierarchy of page tags for
selected page element (DOM
structure)

Figure 14 *Assigning a class name to a new div*

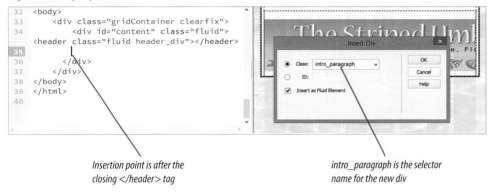

Insertion point is after the
closing </header> tag

intro_paragraph is the selector
name for the new div

Figure 15 *Viewing the new intro_paragraph div added under the header*

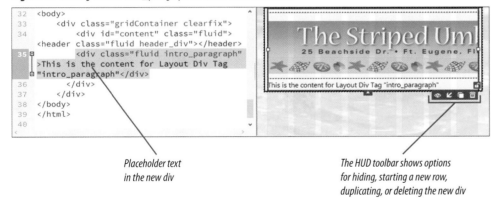

Placeholder text
in the new div

The HUD toolbar shows options
for hiding, starting a new row,
duplicating, or deleting the new div

Figure 16 *Selecting and copying the navigation code from the index page*

```
36        <div class="fluid intro_paragraph">
37        <p>
38        <nav class="fluid menu_bar">
39            <ul>
40            <li><a href="index.html">Home</a></li>
41            <li><a href="about_us.html">About Us</a></li>
42            <li><a href="cafe.html">Sand Crab Cafe</a></li>
43            <li><a href="spa.html">Sea Spa</a></li>
44            <li><a href="activities.html">Activities</a></li>
45        </ul></nav>
```

Add a new div and paste the menu bar into it

1. Change to Split view, then place the insertion point after the closing </header> tag as shown in Figure 14.

   If you find it is easier to read through your code with spaces separating each div, add a paragraph break in Code view, as shown in Figure 14. Paragraph breaks entered in Code view do not affect the page design; they just make it easier to read the code.

2. Select **Div** in the Structure category of the Insert panel, type **intro_paragraph** in the Class text box in the Insert Div dialog box, as shown in Figure 14, then select **OK**.

   The new header is placed on the page with default placeholder text, as shown in Figure 15. You are now ready to insert the website menu bar, but it will be faster to copy the menu bar code from another page.

3. Verify that the fluid grid layout guides are showing, then select the border of the new div in the Design view pane.

   The HUD toolbar appears with buttons to control the div appearance and position on the page.

4. Open the index page, switch to Code view if you prefer the full Code window, then copy the code for the menu bar beginning with the <p> tag immediately above it, as shown in Figure 16.

   (continued)

5. Switch to the cafe page in Code or Split view, place the insertion point after the closing header tag if necessary, paste the copied code, open the Property inspector if necessary, select **Refresh** in the Property inspector, then compare your screen to Figure 17.

The menu bar is placed on the cafe page.

6. Place the insertion point before the last two ending </div> tags near the bottom of the page, select **Footer** in the Structure category of the Insert panel, type **footer_div** in the class text box in the Insert Div dialog box, then select **OK**.

The new footer is placed on the page with default placeholder text, as shown in Design view in Figure 18.

TIP To quickly determine which ending </div> tag goes with which beginning <div> tag, select either the beginning or ending tag to highlight it, then scroll to find the highlighted tag that it begins or ends.

7. Close the index page, then save your work.

(continued)

Figure 17 *Pasting the menu bar from the index page to the cafe page*

```
35          <header class="fluid
    header_div"></header>
36          <p>
37          <nav class="fluid menu_bar">
38          <ul>
39          <li><a href="index.html"
    >Home</a></li>
40          <li><a href=
    "about_us.html">About Us</a></li>
41          <li><a href="cafe.html">
    Sand Crab Cafe</a></li>
42          <li><a href="spa.html">
    Sea Spa</a></li>
43          <li><a href=
    "activities.html">Activities</a></li>
44          </ul>
45          </nav>
```

Figure 18 *The footer with placeholder text on the cafe page*

Placeholder text for the footer is added automatically

Figure 19 *Setting the position for the new image_div*

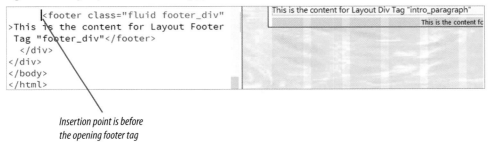

```
<footer class="fluid footer_div"
>This is the content for Layout Footer
Tag "footer_div"</footer>
  </div>
</div>
</body>
</html>
```

This is the content for Layout Div Tag "intro_paragraph"

This is the content fo

Insertion point is before
the opening footer tag

Figure 20 *Placeholder text in new div for image placement*

Figure 21 *The menu bar with updated font-family property*

Font is updated with
added property

8. In Split view, place the insertion point in front of the opening <footer> tag, as shown in Figure 19.

9. Select **Div** in the Structure category of the Insert panel, type **image_div** in the Insert Div dialog box, then select **OK**.

   This is a div that will hold a large image of the cafe.

10. Save your work, return to Design view, then compare your screen to Figure 20.

    You notice the menu bar is no longer formatted with the correct font. This is because when you created this page, the tags for the .menu_bar selector were above the div for the .intro_paragraph selector, so the .menu_bar selector does not have a font-family property assigned.

11. Select **su_styles.css** in the Sources pane in CSS Designer, select **GLOBAL** in the @Media pane, then select **.menu_bar** in the Selectors pane.

12. Select the default **font-family value**, then select **Segoe, Segoe UI, DejaVu Sans, Trebuchet MS, Verdana, sans-serif**.

TIP You may need to deselect the Show Only Set Properties checkbox to access the text properties.

   Now the menu bar elements appear in the correct font, as shown in Figure 21.

13. Save your work.

You added a new div for paragraph text to the cafe page, added navigation and footer tags, then added an additional div to use to place a large image. Last, you added a font-family property to the .menu_bar selector.

Add Content to
DIVS

What You'll Do

In this lesson, you will add text to the intro paragraph div and add an image to the image div on the cafe page. Then you will exchange the position of the two divs on the page and return them to their original positions.

Understanding Div Tag Content

As you remember, a div tag is a container that formats blocks of information on a web page, such as background colors, images, links, tables, and text. Once you have created a layout using div tags, you are ready to insert and format text. As with formatting text on a web page, you should use CSS styles to format text in div tags. You can also add all other properties such as text indents, padding, margins, and background color using CSS styles.

In this lesson, you continue to use your Fluid Grid layout to add content to the new cafe page. You have added several CSS layout blocks to the page and are ready to fill them with the cafe page content.

Writing for the Web

It doesn't matter how attractive or informative your text is if it isn't readable. Readability is determined by the complexity of your sentences, the average number of sentences per paragraph, and the average length of your words. Unless you are writing for a technical or scientific website, you should keep your reading level between the seventh and eighth grade levels to reach the largest audience. To evaluate the reading level of text on a page, copy and paste the text into Microsoft Word. Open the Word Options dialog box, select Proofing, then select the Show readability statistics check box. Next, use the Check Spelling and Grammar command and the Readability Statistics dialog box will open to show the results for your text. The grade level for the text on the index page is 7.9.

Understanding CSS Code

CSS rules can reside in the Head section of a page or in an external style sheet. The code for a CSS container begins with the class, or name of the rule, and is followed by rule properties. In Figure 22, the styles shown are from a section of the boilerplate.css file that is created by default when you create a Fluid Grid Layout page. These styles are tag selectors (meaning that they are used to modify standard HTML tags, rather than class styles you create), so they do not begin with a period in front of the name. The tag selector name is the tag itself. For instance, a selector to modify the horizontal rule tag (<hr>) is named hr. Unless otherwise specified, these tag selectors will apply to all page elements to which you apply these tags. For instance, any text surrounded by a <b> or <strong> tag will appear in bold.

In Lesson 1, you attached the boilerplate.css file to the Striped Umbrella cafe page. This CSS file contains global styles to help format page content based on Fluid Grid layouts. The selectors in this file are grouped by function with the category noted in comments. **Comments** are gray, non-executable tags proceeded by "/*". This notation tells the browser to skip over the lines of code that follow it until it comes to an ending comment tag, "*/". Comments can help you learn more about HTML code, so it is worth the time to stop and read them. Figure 22 shows selectors grouped as Link selectors and Typography selectors.

Figure 22 *Viewing the boilerplate.css code*

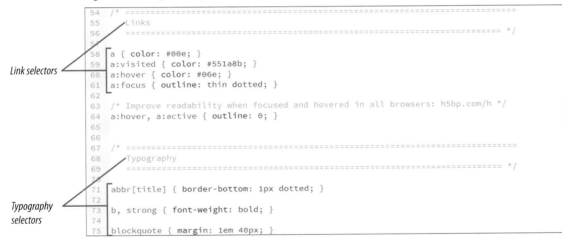

```
54  /* ========================================================================
55       Links
56       ==================================================================== */
57
58  a { color: #00e; }
59  a:visited { color: #551a8b; }
60  a:hover { color: #06e; }
61  a:focus { outline: thin dotted; }
62
63  /* Improve readability when focused and hovered in all browsers: h5bp.com/h */
64  a:hover, a:active { outline: 0; }
65
66
67  /* ========================================================================
68       Typography
69       ==================================================================== */
70
71  abbr[title] { border-bottom: 1px dotted; }
72
73  b, strong { font-weight: bold; }
74
75  blockquote { margin: 1em 40px; }
```

Link selectors

Typography selectors

Add text to a CSS container

1. With the cafe page open in Design view, delete the **placeholder** text in the intro_paragraph div, being careful not to delete a beginning or ending <div> tag.

TIP Remember that it's easier to leave at least one character in the placeholder text, then delete it after you have placed new content.

2. Open your file manager program, open the file **cafe.txt** from the drive and folder where you store your Data Files, then copy and paste the contents into the intro_paragraph div, as shown in Figure 23.

3. Close the cafe.txt file, then switch to Code view to verify that there is a <p> tag in front of the pasted text and insert one if one was not automatically added.

4. Open the index page, copy the two lines of text in the footer, then paste them in the footer on the cafe page, replacing the footer placeholder text, as shown in Figure 24.

5. Close the index page.

You replaced the placeholder text in the content div with text from the cafe.txt file, copied the footer text from the index page, then used it to replace the footer placeholder text on the cafe page.

Figure 23 *Pasting text into the content div*

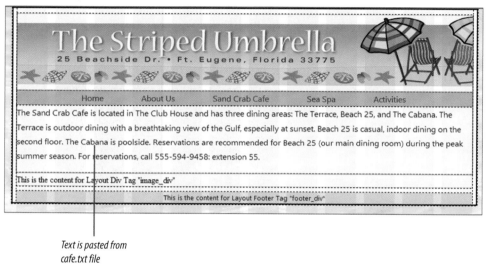

Text is pasted from cafe.txt file

Figure 24 *The footer placeholder text replaced with website footer text*

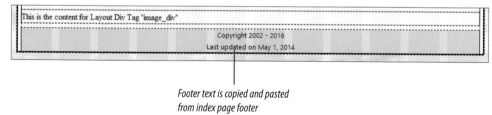

Footer text is copied and pasted from index page footer

Figure 25 *The cafe page with the cafe photo added*

Club house photo provided by Spectrum Resorts of The Beach Club in Gulf Shores, Alabama

---

Viewing Options for CSS Layout Blocks

You can view your layout blocks in Design view in several ways. You can choose to show or hide outlines, temporarily assign different background colors to each individual layout block, or view the **CSS Layout Box Model** (padding, margins, borders, etc.) of a selected layout. To change these options, use the View > Visual Aids menu, and then select or deselect the CSS Layout Backgrounds, CSS Layout Box Model, or CSS Layout Outlines menu choice.

Add an image to a CSS container

1. Place the insertion point in the img_div, then carefully delete the placeholder text (not a div tag).
2. Select the **Insert** menu, point to **Image**, then select **Image** to open the Select Image Source dialog box.
3. Navigate to the assets folder where you store your Data Files, and select the image club_house_oceanside.jpg, as shown in Figure 25.
4. Save your work, then view the Desktop, Tablet, and Mobile sizes.
5. Preview the page in your browser, then close the browser.

You added an image to the cafe page.

Reorder page elements

1. With the fluid grid layout guides displayed, place the pointer in the introductory paragraph.

   The div is selected and you see a small black triangle, called a handle, pointing downward on the bottom border of the div.

   If you don't see the black handles after you select the paragraph, check to see if your Fluid Grid Layouts are displayed.

2. Place the pointer over the handle to see the tool tip **Swap DIV.intro_paragraph with DIV. image_div**, as shown in Figure 26.

   Selecting this handle will change the position of the two divs. The image div will move above the intro_paragraph div.

3. Select the handle.

   The image div moves above the intro_paragraph div. Notice there are two handles now, as shown in Figure 27. The first one can be used to swap the image div back under the intro_paragraph div. The second one can be used to swap the image div with the footer div. The tool tips tell you where the div will go if selected.

TIP Your handles will appear side by side when there is not enough room in the Document window to show the entire div. They will appear one beneath the other if there is enough room to see the entire div.

(continued)

Figure 26 *Preparing to move the intro paragraph div*

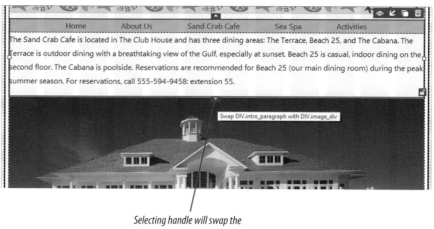

Selecting handle will swap the div according to tool tip

Figure 27 *The image div changed positions with the intro paragraph div*

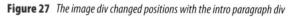

Select handles to move div up or down

Positioning Objects with CSS and Tables

Figure 28 *The intro paragraph div moved under the footer div*

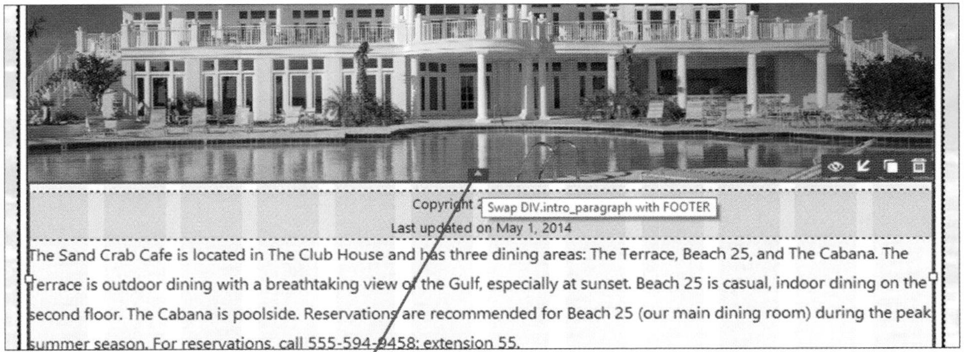

Copyright 2   Swap DIV.intro_paragraph with FOOTER
Last updated on May 1, 2014

The Sand Crab Cafe is located in The Club House and has three dining areas: The Terrace, Beach 25, and The Cabana. The Terrace is outdoor dining with a breathtaking view of the Gulf, especially at sunset. Beach 25 is casual, indoor dining on the second floor. The Cabana is poolside. Reservations are recommended for Beach 25 (our main dining room) during the peak summer season. For reservations, call 555-594-9458: extension 55.

*Select handle to swap intro
paragraph div with footer*

Figure 29 *All divs are back in their original position*

summer season. For reservations, call 555-594-9458: extension 55.

Positioning Divs Side by Side

To position two divs side by side on a page, use CSS Designer to set a width expressed in percent for each div so the two widths together are less than or equal to 100%. Next, set the float for the first div to left and the float for the second div to right.

Content for Div 1   Content for Div 2

4. Select the handle pointing downward, **Swap DIV.intro_paragraph with FOOTER**.

    Now the intro_paragraph is below the footer, as shown in Figure 28.

5. Select the handle pointing up, **Swap DIV. intro_paragraph with FOOTER**.

    The image div is back above the intro_paragraph div.

6. Select the handle pointing up, **Swap DIV.intro_paragraph with DIV.image_div**.

    Figure 29 shows the introductory paragraph above the image once again. The footer is also back at the bottom of the page.

You moved the divs on the page into different positions, then moved them back to their original positions.

Create
A TABLE

What You'll Do

In this lesson, you will create a table for the cafe page in The Striped Umbrella website to provide a grid for the cafe hours.

Understanding Table Modes

Now that you have learned how CSS can act as containers to hold information in place on web pages, let's look at tables as another layout tool. Tables are great when you need a grid layout on a page for a list of data.

Creating a Table

To create a table, select the Table button in the Common category on the Insert panel to open the Table dialog box. You can enter values for the number of rows and columns in the Table dialog box, but the rest of the table properties should be assigned using CSS. If you only plan to use one table design in a site, you can create a rule to modify the <table> tag and save it in your website style sheet.

You then use this rule to add formatting options to the table such as adding a border or table width. The **border** is the outline or frame around the table and is measured in pixels. The table width can be specified in units of measure such as pixels, or as a percentage. When the table width is specified as a percentage, the table width expands to fill up its container (the browser window, a CSS container, or another table). Setting table widths as percentages works best with Fluid Grid layouts. Table width is set using the Width property in the Box category of the relevant CSS style.

To align a table on a page or within a CSS layout block, use the Float property in the Box category. A table placed inside another table is called a **nested table**. **Cell padding** is the distance between the cell content and the **cell walls**, the lines inside the cell borders. **Cell spacing** is the distance between cells. Neither cell padding or cell spacing is supported by HTML5, however, so it's better to address spacing issues by assigning styles.

Before you create a table, you should include in your wireframe a plan for it that shows its location on the page and the placement of text and graphics in its cells. You should also decide whether to include borders around the tables. Setting the border value to 0 causes the table borders to be invisible. Users will not realize that you used a table unless they look at the code.

Setting Table Accessibility Preferences

You can make a table more accessible to visually impaired users by adding a table caption and a table header that screen readers can read. A **table caption** appears at the top of a table and describes the table contents. **Table headers** are another way to provide information about table content. Table headers can be placed at the top of columns. They are automatically centered and bold and are used by screen readers to help users identify the table content. Table captions and headers are created with the Table dialog box.

Formatting Tables with HTML5 and CSS3

Many of the HTML codes used to format tables in HTML4 are now considered to be **deprecated**, or no longer within the current standard and in danger of becoming obsolete. As you design web pages, it is best to avoid using deprecated tags because eventually they will cause problems when they are no longer supported by newer browsers. Deprecated HTML4 table tags include summary, cellpadding, cellspacing, align, width, and bgcolor.

Rather than format tables using the Table dialog box or the Property inspector, use CSS to create rules that modify table properties and content. You can either add properties to the <table> tag itself or create new class rules that you can then assign to specific tables. Use the HTML5 tags <th> and <caption>. The table header <th> tag is a type of cell that contains header information, such as column headings, that identify the content of the data cells below them. The <caption> tag is the caption, or title, of a table and describes the table content. These tags provide greater accessibility, because they are used by screen readers. They also add value as semantic markup because they help to label and describe table content.

Create a table

1. Place the insertion point in the intro_paragraph div, switch to Code view, then place the insertion point after the ending div tag for the intro_paragraph div.

2. Return to Design view, then use the Insert panel to insert a new div named **table_div**.

   Placeholder text appears in table_div, as shown in Figure 30.

3. Carefully delete the placeholder text, then select **Table** in the Common category on the Insert panel.

   The Table dialog box opens.

4. Type **5** in the Rows text box, type **3** in the Columns text box, if necessary, delete any value previously left in the Table width, Border thickness, Cell padding, or Cell spacing text boxes, then select the **Top** Header.

TIP It is better to add more rows than you think you need when you create your table. After they are filled with content, it is easier to delete rows than to add rows if you decide later to split or merge cells in the table.

5. In the Caption text box, type **The Sand Crab Cafe Hours**, compare your screen to Figure 31, then select **OK**.

   The table appears very small because the width for the table has not yet been set. You will define a new table CSS rule to use to format the table.

You created a table in a new div on the cafe page that will display the cafe hours with five rows and three columns. You used a top header and added a table caption that will be read by screen readers.

Figure 30 *New div inserted for a table*

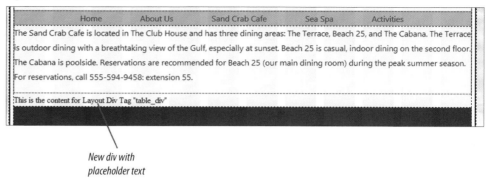

New div with placeholder text

Figure 31 *Table dialog box*

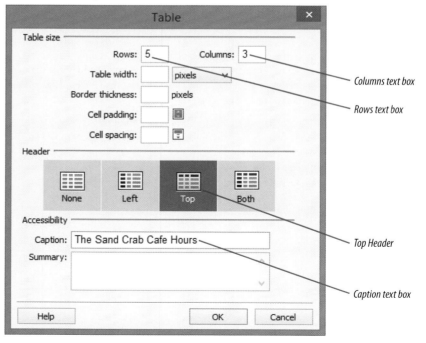

Columns text box

Rows text box

Top Header

Caption text box

Figure 32 *Setting table selector properties*

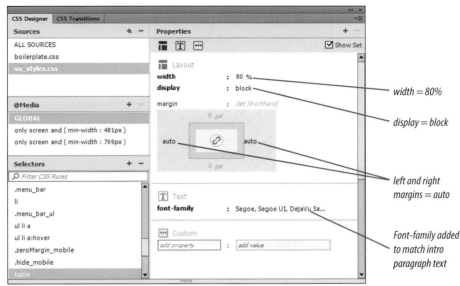

width = 80%

display = block

left and right margins = auto

Font-family added to match intro paragraph text

Set table properties

1. Use CSS Designer to add a new global tag selector in the su_styles.css file named **table**.

   This rule will format the only table in the website.

2. Select the **Layout category** in the Properties pane, then add the following properties and values as shown in Figure 32:

   width: **80%;**

   display: **block;**

   margin-left: **auto;**

   margin-right: **auto;**

   font-family: **Segoe, Segoe UI, DejaVu Sans, Trebuchet MS, Verdana, Sans-serif;**

   These settings will set the table to 80% width and centered on the page with a specified font family to match the intro paragraph text.

   The <table> selector modified the table by setting the width and alignment on the page, as shown in Figure 33.

3. Save your work.

You modified the table rule by adding table width and margin properties.

Figure 33 *Viewing the new table in the table div*

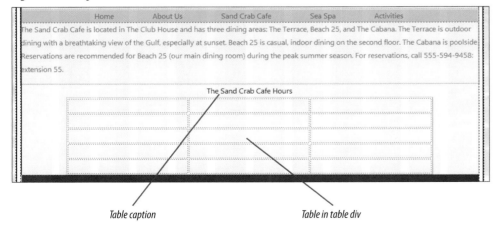

Table caption

Table in table div

Resize, Split,
AND MERGE CELLS

What You'll Do

In this lesson, you will set the width of the table cells to be split across the table in predetermined widths. You will then split one cell. You will also merge some cells to provide space for the table header.

Modifying Table Structure

To create HTML5-compliant table coding, you should resize tables, rows, and cells using Cascading Style Sheets. If you only have one table in your site, you can modify the <table> tag by assigning properties and values to set the table width. If you have multiple tables, you can create a new class rule for each table and format each individually using class rule properties. This will allow you to use multiple tables with differing widths. When you first create a table, the columns have equal widths. To widen a column and meet HTML5 standards, use the column group tag <colgroup> to set properties for an entire column or the column tag <col> to set properties for an individual cell.

Sometimes you want to adjust the cells in a table by splitting or merging them. To **split** a cell means to divide it into multiple rows or columns. To **merge** cells means to combine multiple cells into one cell. Using split and merged cells gives you more flexibility and control in placing page elements in a table and can help you create a more visually exciting layout. When you merge cells, the

Adding or Deleting a Row

As you add new content to your table, you might find that you have too many or too few rows or columns. You can add or delete one row or column at a time or several at once using commands on the Modify menu. When you add a new column or row, you must first select the existing column or row to which the new column or row will be adjacent. Because of this, it can be challenging to add or delete rows after you have split and merged cells. The Insert Rows or Columns dialog box lets you choose how many rows or columns you want to insert or delete, and where you want them placed in relation to the selected row or column. The new column or row will have the same formatting and number of cells as the selected column or row. You can also use the shortcut menu or keyboard shortcuts to add or delete rows.

HTML tag used to describe the merged cell changes from a width size tag to a column span or row span tag. For example, <td colspan="2"> is the code for two cells that have been merged into one cell that spans two columns.

QUICK TIP

You can split merged cells and merge split cells.

Understanding Table Tags

When formatting a table, it is important to understand the basic HTML table tags. The tags for creating a table are <table> </table>. The tags to create table rows are <tr></tr>. The tags used to create table data cells are <td></td>. The tags used to create table header cells are <th> </th>. Dreamweaver places the

< > code into each empty table cell at the time you create it. The < > code represents a nonbreaking space, or a space that a browser will display on the page. Some browsers collapse an empty cell, which can ruin the look of a table. The nonbreaking space holds the cell until you place content in it, when at that time it is automatically removed.

DESIGNTIP

Using Nested Tables

A nested table is a table inside a table. Place the insertion point in the cell where you want to insert the nested table, then select the Table button on the Insert panel. A nested table is a separate table that can be formatted differently from the table in which it is placed. Nested tables are useful when you want part of your table data to have visible borders and part to have invisible borders. For example, you can nest a table with red borders inside a table with invisible borders. You need to plan carefully when you insert nested tables. It is easy to get carried away and insert too many nested tables, which makes it more difficult to apply formatting and rearrange table elements. Before you insert a nested table, consider whether you could achieve the same result by adding rows and columns or by splitting cells.

Split cells

1. Place the insertion point inside the first cell in the last row, then select **\<td\>** in the tag selector.

TIP You can select the cell tag \<td\> (the HTML tag for that cell) on the tag selector to select the corresponding cell in the table. When a tag is selected, the tag color on the tag selector changes from a black to a turquoise font. You can also just place the insertion point inside the cell before you begin Step 2.

2. Select the **Splits cell into rows or columns button** ⫲ in the Property inspector.

3. Select the **Split cell into Rows option button** (if necessary), type **2** in the Number of rows text box (if necessary), as shown in Figure 34, select **OK**, then deselect the cell.

    The cell is split, as shown in Figure 35.

TIP To create a new row at the end of a table, place the insertion point in the last cell, then press [Tab].

You split a cell into two rows.

Figure 34 *Splitting a cell into two rows*

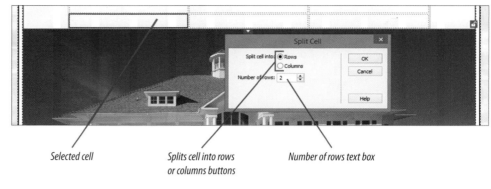

Selected cell   Splits cell into rows   Number of rows text box
                       or columns buttons

Figure 35 *Splitting one cell into two rows*

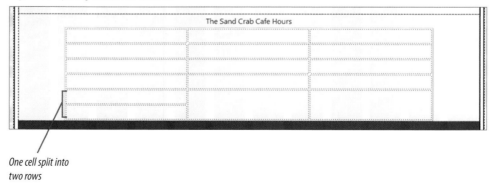

One cell split into
two rows

Figure 36 *Merging selected cells into one cell*

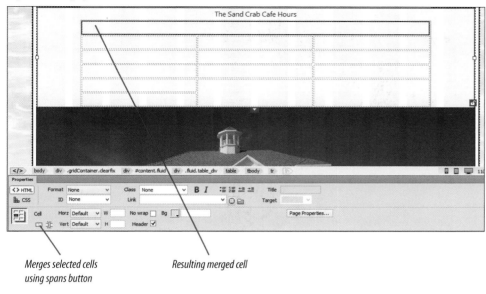

Merges selected cells using spans button

Resulting merged cell

Figure 37 *Code for merged cells*

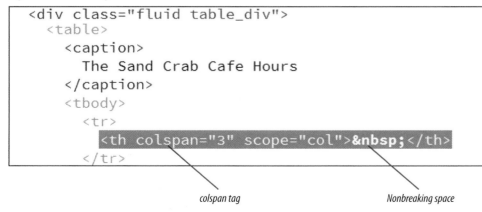

```
<div class="fluid table_div">
  <table>
    <caption>
      The Sand Crab Cafe Hours
    </caption>
    <tbody>
      <tr>
        <th colspan="3" scope="col"> </th>
      </tr>
```

colspan tag

Nonbreaking space

Merge cells

1. Place the insertion point in the first cell in the top row, then drag to the right to select the three cells in the top row.

2. Select the **Merges selected cells using spans button** 🔳 in the Property inspector.

   The three cells are merged into one cell, as shown in Figure 36. This merged cell will act as a table header. Descriptive text in this cell will spread across the table width.

   TIP You can only merge cells that are adjacent to each other.

3. Select the **Show Code view button** `Code`, then view the code for the merged cells, as shown in Figure 37.

   Notice the table tags denoting the column span (th colspan="3") and the nonbreaking space ( ) inserted in the empty cell.

4. Select the **Show Design view button** `Design`, select and merge the first cells in rows 2, 3, 4, and 5 in the left column, then save your work.

You merged three cells in the first row to make room for the table header. You then merged four cells in the left column to make room for an image.

Insert and Align
IMAGES IN TABLE CELLS

What You'll Do

The Sand Crab Cafe Hours

In this lesson, you will insert an image of a bowl of soup in the left column of the table. After placing the image, you will align it within the cell.

Inserting Images in Table Cells

You can insert images in the cells of a table using the Image command in the Images menu on the Insert panel. If you already have images saved in your website that you would like to insert in a table, you can drag them from the Assets panel into the table cells. When you add a large image to a cell, the cell expands to accommodate the inserted image. Figure 38 shows the USHorse.biz website, which uses several tables for page layout and contains images in some of the table cells. Notice that some images appear in cells by themselves, and some appear in cells containing text or other graphics. Some cells have a light background, and some have a darker background.

Aligning Images in Table Cells

You can align images both horizontally and vertically within a cell. With HTML5, it's best to align an image by creating a rule with alignment settings, then apply the rule to the image content. For example, if you

Positioning Objects with CSS and Tables

have inserted an image in a table cell, you can create a Class rule in your style sheet called something like img_table_cell, then assign a center-align property to the rule. After saving the rule, select the image, then apply the img_table_cell rule to it. It will then center-align within the table cell.

Another way to align content in table cells is to add a style to the individual cell tag that sets the cell alignment. For example, add the code "style=text-align:center" to the cell tag for the cell you want to modify to center the cell's contents.

Figure 38 *USHorse.biz website*

Source: USHorse.biz

Insert images in table cells

1. Place the insertion point in the merged cells in the left column of the table (under the merged cell in the top row).

2. Insert **shrimp_bisque.jpg** from assets folder in the drive and folder where you store your Data Files, then type **Gulf Shrimp Bisque** for the alternate text.

3. Compare your screen to Figure 39.

TIP Don't be concerned if your table spacing does not match the figure at this time. You will fix this shortly when you set the cell widths.

4. Refresh the Files panel and verify that the new image was copied to The Striped Umbrella website assets folder.

5. Save your work.

You inserted an image into a table cell on the cafe page.

Figure 39 *Image inserted into table cell*

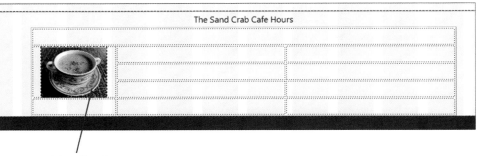

shrimp_bisque.jpg

Using Rulers, Grids, and Guides for Positioning Page Content

To help you position your page content, the View menu offers Grid and Guides choices. **Grids** provide a graph paper-like view of a page. Horizontal and vertical lines fill the page when this option is turned on. You can edit the line colors, the distance between them, whether they are composed of lines or dots, and whether or not objects "snap" to them. **Guides** are horizontal or vertical lines that you drag onto the page from the rulers. You can edit both the colors of the guides and the color of the distance, a feature that shows you the distance between two guides. You can lock the guides so you don't accidentally move them and you can set them either to snap to page elements or have page elements snap to them. To display grids or guides, select View on the Menu bar, point to Grid, then select Show Grid or point to Guides and then select Show Guides.

Figure 40 *Setting the display and margin properties for the tr td img*

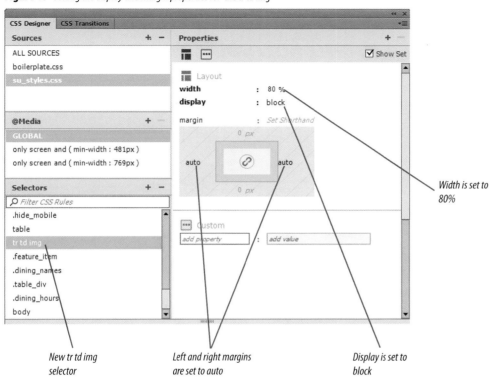

Width is set to 80%

New tr td img selector

Left and right margins are set to auto

Display is set to block

Align graphics in table cells

1. Select the **shrimp bisque image**.

2. Use CSS Designer to add a global tag selector in su_styles.css, with the name that appears as the default name after you select the Add Selector button, **tr td img**.

   You'll add properties and values to this selector to center the image in the table cell.

3. Deselect the Show Set check box if necessary, then add the following properties and values to the tr td img selector as shown in Figure 40:

   width: **80%;**

   display: **block;**

   margin-left: **auto;**

   margin-right: **auto.**

4. Save your work.

You center-aligned cell content by editing the tr td img selector.

Insert Text and Format
CELL CONTENT

What You'll Do

In this lesson, you will type the cafe hours in the table. You will also format the text to enhance its appearance on the page. Last, you will add formatting to some of the cells and cell content.

Inserting Text in a Table

You can enter text in a table either by typing it in a cell, copying it from another source and pasting it into a cell, or importing it from another program. Once you place text in a table cell, you can format it to make it more readable and more visually appealing on the page.

Formatting Cell Content

To format the contents of a cell, select the cell contents, then apply formatting to it. For example, you can select an image in a cell and add properties such as a font, font size, or background color by using a class rule. Or, you can select text in a cell and use the Blockquote or Remove Blockquote buttons in the HTML Property inspector to move the text farther away from or closer to the cell walls.

If a cell contains multiple objects of the same type, such as text, you can format each item individually by applying different CSS rules to each one.

Formatting Cells

Formatting a cell is different from formatting a cell's contents. Formatting a cell can include setting properties that visually enhance the cell's appearance, such as setting a cell width and assigning a background color. To format a cell with code that is HTML5 compliant, use tags to define a column group style <colgroup>, which will format all cells in a particular column. You can also use the column tag <col> to apply formatting styles to individual cells. Once you have created your styles, you add them to the code for the appropriate columns or cells you wish to format.

QUICK TIP

Although you can set some table and cell properties using the Property inspector, strive to use CSS Styles for all formatting tasks.

Figure 41 *Typing text into cells*

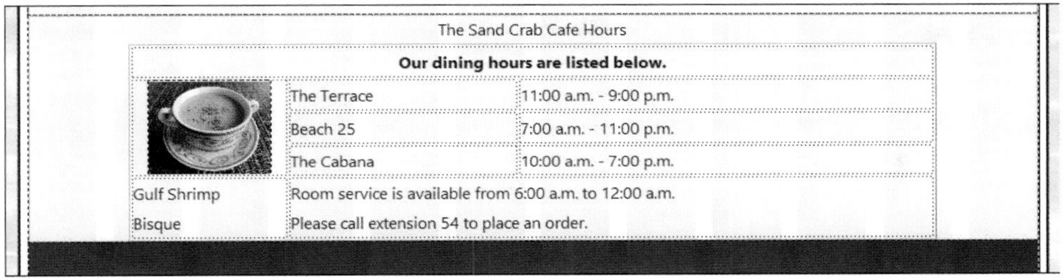

The Sand Crab Cafe Hours		
Our dining hours are listed below.		
	The Terrace	11:00 a.m. - 9:00 p.m.
	Beach 25	7:00 a.m. - 11:00 p.m.
	The Cabana	10:00 a.m. - 7:00 p.m.
Gulf Shrimp	Room service is available from 6:00 a.m. to 12:00 a.m.	
Bisque	Please call extension 54 to place an order.	

Importing and Exporting Data from Tables

You can import and export tabular data into and out of Dreamweaver. **Importing** means to bring data created in another software program into Dreamweaver, and **exporting** means to save data created in Dreamweaver in a special file format that can be opened by other programs. Files that are imported into Dreamweaver must be saved as delimited files. Tabular data is data that is arranged in columns and rows and separated by a **delimiter**: a comma, tab, colon, semicolon, or similar character. **Delimited files** are database, word processing, or spreadsheet files that have been saved as text files with delimiters such as tabs or commas separating the data. Programs such as Microsoft Access and Microsoft Excel offer many file formats for saving files. To import a delimited file, select File on the Menu bar, point to Import, then select Tabular Data. The Import Tabular Data dialog box opens, offering you formatting options for the imported table. To export a table that you created in Dreamweaver, select File on the Menu bar, point to Export, then select Table. The Export Table dialog box opens, letting you choose the type of delimiter you want for the delimited file.

Insert text

1. Place the insertion point in the cell below the bisque image type **Gulf Shrimp**, press **[Shift][Enter]** (Win) or **[shift][return]** (Mac), then type **Bisque**.

TIP If you can't see the last lines you typed, toggle Live view, or resize your screen to refresh it.

2. Place the insertion point in the top row of the table, then type **Our dining hours are listed below**.

   The text is automatically bolded because you selected the top row header when you created the table. A table's header row is bold by default.

3. Merge the two bottom-right cells in the last row, then enter the cafe dining area names, hours, and room service information in the cell rows, as shown in Figure 41. Use a line break after the first line of text in the last cell.

TIP Don't be concerned about the table appearance yet. Deselect the table as you work to refresh it to display properly.

You entered text in the table to provide information about the dining room hours.

Format cell content

1. Use CSS Designer to create a new global selector in the su_styles.css file named **.feature_item**.

2. Add the following properties and values to the Text category for the .feature_item selector, as shown in Figure 42:

   color: **#000033**;

   font-family: **lobster-two**;

   font-style: **italic**;

   font-weight: **400**;

   font-size: **large**.

   If you don't have the lobster-two font listed, use the Manage Fonts dialog box to open the Adobe Edge Web Fonts list and add it. You'll use this rule to format the name of the featured dessert.

3. Select **Gulf Shrimp Bisque** under the bisque image, select the **CSS button** [img] CSS on the Property inspector, then apply the **.feature_item rule** to the text.

4. Save your work, select **Update** in the Update Web Fonts dialog box, then select **Close** to close the Update Pages dialog box.

   Updating the script tags on the rest of the pages in the website will make the lobster-two font available for those pages, also.

You created a new rule in the su_styles.css style sheet and used it to format text in a table cell.

Figure 42 *Formatting text using a Class rule*

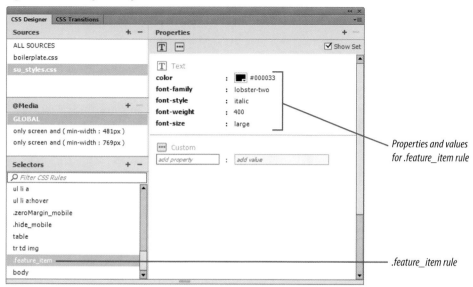

Properties and values for .feature_item rule

.feature_item rule

POWER USER SHORTCUTS	
To do this:	**Use this shortcut:**
Insert table	[Ctrl][Alt][T] (Win) or ⌘ [option][T] (Mac)
Select a cell	[Ctrl][A] (Win) or ⌘ [A] (Mac)
Merge cells	[Ctrl][Alt][M] (Win) or ⌘ [option][M] (Mac)
Split cell	[Ctrl][Alt][S] (Win) or ⌘ [option][S] (Mac)
Insert row	[Ctrl][M] (Win) or ⌘ [M] (Mac)
Insert column	[Ctrl][Shift][A] (Win) or ⌘ [Shift][A] (Mac)
Delete row	[Ctrl][Shift][M] (Win) or ⌘ [Shift][M] (Mac)
Delete column	[Ctrl][Shift][-] (Win) or ⌘ [Shift][-] (Mac)
Increase column span	[Ctrl][Shift][]] (Win) or ⌘ [Shift][]] (Mac)
Decrease column span	[Ctrl][Shift][[] (Win) or ⌘ [Shift][[] (Mac)

Figure 43 *Adding a text-align property to a class selector*

The Sand Crab Cafe Hours	
Our dining hours are listed below.	
The Terrace	11:00 a.m. - 9:00 p.m.
Beach 25	7:00 a.m. - 11:00 p.m.
The Cabana	10:00 a.m. - 7:00 p.m.
Room service is available from 6:00 a.m. to 12:00 a.m.	
Gulf Shrimp Bisque	Please call extension 54 to place an order.

Bisque text is centered in cell

Format cells

1. Place the insertion point in the cell with the bisque text.

   Notice that the .feature_item rule is applied to the text. You will modify the .feature_item rule to add an alignment value.

2. Select the **.feature_item global selector** if necessary, then add the **text-align: center** property and set the width in the Layout category to **25%**.

   The text is now centered in the cell, as shown in Figure 43.

You modified the .feature_item class global selector.

Modify table text for different device sizes

1. Switch to the su_styles.css file, then scroll to locate the global table selector code.
2. Copy the table selector code, then paste it into both the tablet and desktop sections of code.
3. Use CSS Designer to edit the global table selector font-size to small, as shown in Figure 44.
4. Edit the tablet table selector font-size to small, as shown in Figure 45.
5. Edit the desktop table selector to change the font-size to **medium**, then save your work.

You copied the global table selector to the tablet and desktop sections of the su_styles.css code, then modified the global and tablet text size.

Figure 44 *The global table selector settings*

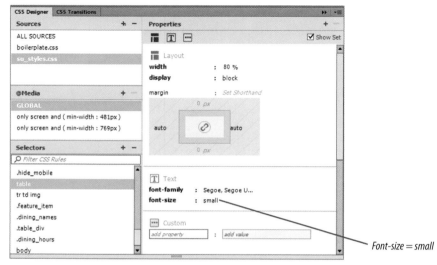

Font-size = small

Figure 45 *The tablet table selector settings*

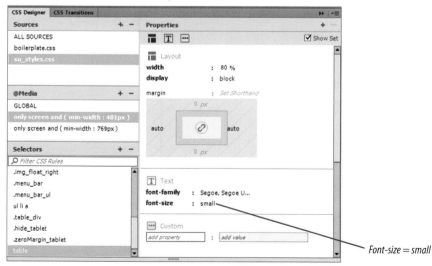

Font-size = small

Figure 46 *Placing horizontal rules in the table*

Horizontal rules added

Modify cell content

1. Place the insertion point after the word "bisque" in the bottom left cell, then press **[Tab]**.

   Pressing the Tab key while the insertion point is in the last cell of the table creates a new row. Even though it looks like the cell with the room service information is the last cell, it is not because of the merged cells.

2. Merge the cells in the new row, place the insertion point in the merged cells, select **Insert** on the Menu bar, then select **Horizontal Rule**.

3. Place the insertion point in front of the table header, insert another horizontal rule, then save your work.

4. Switch to Live view, then compare your table to Figure 46.

You added two horizontal rules to the table to set the table off from the rest of the page.

Check layout in all device sizes

1. Still in Live view, select the Desktop size button 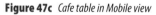, then compare your screen to Figure 47a.

    All figures shown on this page are without Fluid Grid Layout Guides shown.

2. Select the Tablet size button ▢, then compare your screen to Figure 47b.

3. Select the Mobile size button ▢, then compare your screen to Figure 47c.

4. Return to Desktop view, then turn off Live view.

5. Add the page title **The Striped Umbrella Sand Crab Cafe** in the Title text box, then save your work.

You viewed the new table using Desktop, Tablet, and Mobile size views.

Figure 47a *Cafe table in Desktop view*

Figure 47b *Cafe table in Tablet view*

Figure 47c *Cafe table in Mobile view*

Positioning Objects with CSS and Tables

Figure 48 *Validating HTML5 markup*

W3C validation
button

1. Verify that the Source Code button is selected on the Related Files toolbar.

2. Select **File** on the Menu bar, point to **Validate**, then select **Validate Current Document (W3C)**.

   Before you validate a page, be sure that the HTML file is selected on the Related Files toolbar.

3. Select **OK** to close the W3C Validator Notification dialog box.

   The Results panel shows no errors or warnings found, as shown in Figure 48.

4. Select the **panel options button**, then select **Close Tab Group**.

   The Results panel closes.

5. Close all open files.

TIP If you see any errors or warnings listed, refer to the line number that corresponds to each error, then check your code to locate and correct the error.

You validated the cafe page and the Results panel showed that no errors were found.

Validating Your Pages Against HTML5 Standards

One of the tests you should run on your web pages is to validate your page code against current HTML5 standards. Dreamweaver provides a quick way to test each page with the Validation panel in the Results panel group. When you select the W3C Validation button ▶, Dreamweaver connects to the W3C server, submits the page code, and records the results in the Validation panel. If you want to test your pages against other versions of HTML, select the Validate Current Document (W3C) button, select Settings, then choose the additional version or versions of HTML you would like to use for validation.

SKILLS REVIEW

Create a page using a Fluid Grid layout

1. Open the Blooms & Bulbs website.
2. Open the New Document dialog box to create a new Fluid Grid Layout page, and browse to attach the boilerplate.css and bb_styles.css style sheets.
3. Select Create in the New Document dialog box, type **bb_styles_default** in the File name text box in the Save As dialog box, then save the new file as workshops.html, overwriting the existing workshops page. Close the Web Fonts dialog box if it opens.
4. In Code view, delete the link to the bb_styles_default.css file, and if you have two links to the boilerplate.css file, you can delete one of them.

Add and position divs

1. In Design view, place the insertion point in the placeholder text on the page or select the #div1.fluid tag in the Tag Selector, select the default name div_1 on the HTML Property inspector, then type **content** to rename the div.
2. In Code view, select the placeholder text in the content div, then delete it.
3. With the insertion point between the opening and closing content <div> tags, use the Insert panel Structure category to insert a Header.
4. Type **header_div** in the Insert Header dialog box, change to Design view, delete the placeholder text, then select the Element Quick View button on the status bar.
5. Select any stacked folder icons to expand them, if necessary, then look at the page structure, noting each tag that has been added to the page.

6. Close Element Quick View, change to Split view, then place the insertion point after the closing </header> tag.
7. Insert a new div from the Structure category of the Insert panel, then type **intro_paragraph** in the class text box in the Insert Div dialog box and select OK.
8. Open the index page, switch to Code view if necessary, then copy the code for the menu bar beginning with the <p> tag immediately to the left of it.
9. Switch to the workshops page in Code view, place the insertion point after the closing header tag if necessary, then paste the copied code.
10. Place the insertion point before the last two ending </div> tags at the bottom of the page, insert a Footer from the Structure category on the Insert panel, type **footer_div** in the class text box in the Insert Div dialog box, then select OK.
11. Close the index page, then save your work.
12. In Split view, place your insertion point in front of the opening <footer> tag.
13. Select Div in the Structure category of the Insert panel, type **image_div** in the Insert Div dialog box, then select OK.
14. Save your work, then return to Design view.
15. In CSS Designer, select bb_styles.css in the Sources pane, select GLOBAL in the @Media pane, then select .menu_bar in the Selectors pane.
16. Select the default font-family value, then select Segoe, Segoe UI, DejaVu Sans, Trebuchet MS, Verdana, sans-serif.
17. Save your work.

Add content to divs

1. With the workshops page open, delete the placeholder text in the Intro_paragraph div, being careful not to delete a beginning or ending <div> tag.
2. Open your file manager program, open the file composting.txt from the drive and folder where you store your Data Files, then copy and paste the contents into the Intro_paragraph div.
3. Close the composting.txt file.
4. Add a paragraph break after the sentence "New Composting Workshop!" and the following paragraph if necessary.
5. Apply the H2 format to the "New Composting Workshop!" heading.
6. Open the index page, copy the two lines of text in the footer, then paste them in the footer on the workshops page, replacing the footer placeholder text. Close the index page.
7. Place the insertion point in the img_div, then carefully delete the placeholder text (being careful not to delete a div tag).
8. Use the Insert panel to insert the image shade_garden.jpg from the Chapter 6 assets folder in the location where you store your Data Files, in the image div, and add **Shade garden with water feature** as the alternate text.
9. Save your work, then view the Desktop, Tablet, and Mobile sizes.
10. Preview the page in your browser, then close the browser.
11. Place the pointer in the introductory paragraph, then verify that you have your Fluid Grid Layout guides displayed. Display them if you do not.

12. Switch to Live view, place the pointer over the triangle (handle) at the bottom of the intro_paragraph div to see the tool tip Swap DIV.intro_paragraph with DIV.image_div, then select the handle.
13. Select the handle pointing up, swap DIV.intro_paragraph with DIV.image_div, then return to Design view and turn off Live view.

Create a table

1. Place the insertion point in the intro paragraph div, switch to Code view, then place the insertion point after the ending div tag for the intro paragraph div.
2. Return to Design view, then use the Insert panel to insert a new div named **table_div**.
3. Carefully delete the div placeholder text, then insert a table from the Common category on the Insert panel.
4. In the Table dialog box, select **5** rows, **3** columns, and a **Top** header. All other values should be empty.
5. In the Caption text box, type **Blooms & Bulbs Spring Workshops**.
6. Use CSS Designer to add a new global tag selector in the bb_styles.css file named **table**.
7. Using the Layout and Text categories in the Properties pane, then add the following properties and values:
   display: **block**
   width: **80%**
   margin-left: **auto**
   margin-right: **auto**
   font-family: **Segoe, Segoe UI, DejaVu Sans, Trebuchet MS, Verdana, Sans-serif**
8. Save your work.

Resize, split, and merge cells

1. Click or tap the last cell in the last row, then split the cell into 2 rows.
2. Merge the three cells in the top row of the table.
3. Merge the second, third, fourth, and fifth cells in the first column.
4. View the cells in Code view, then return to Design view.
5. Save your work.

Insert and align images in table cells

1. In the merged cells in the first column, insert the image pink_rose.jpg from the drive and folder where your Chapter 6 Data Files are stored.
2. Use CSS Designer to add a global tag selector in the bb_styles.css file with the name **tr td img**.
3. Add the following properties to the tr td img tag:
   width: **85%**
   display: **block**
   margin-left: **auto**
   margin-right: **auto**
4. Use the Property inspector to add the alternate text **Pink Rose**.
5. Create a new global class selector in the bb_styles.css file named **.feature_flower** with the following property and value:
   width: **25%**
6. Place the insertion point in the cell with the pink rose image.
7. Select the <td> tag on the Status bar, select the Class list arrow, then select **feature_flower**.
8. Add a global class selector named **.workshop_date** with the following property:
   width: 50%
9. Place the insertion point in the first cell that will contain a workshop date, then use the Property inspector to apply the .workshop_date rule, as shown in Figure 49 on the next page.
10. Save your work.

Insert text and format cell content

1. Type **Currently Scheduled Spring Workshops - Call for Availability** in the merged cells in the top row.
2. Type the names and dates of the workshops from Figure 49 in the table cells.
3. In the last cell in the last row, type **Classes are limited to 25 members. Bring work gloves!** (Don't be concerned if your text wraps differently than the text shown in the figure. It display correctly after you adjust the font size.)
4. Place the insertion point in the last cell of the last row, press the Tab key to insert a new row, merge the three cells, then insert a horizontal rule from the Insert menu.
5. Place the insertion point in front of the table header, then insert another horizontal rule.
6. Switch to the bb_styles.css file, then scroll to locate the table selector code.
7. Copy the table selector code, then paste it into both the tablet and desktop sections of code.
8. Add a property to change the global table selector font-size to small.
9. Edit the desktop table selector font-size to medium, then save your work
10. Preview the workshops page in mobile, tablet, and desktop sizes.
11. Preview the workshops page in a browser.
12. Close all open files.

Figure 49 *Completed Skills Review*

New Composting Workshop!

Our next workshop is entitled "Everything You Need to Know About Composting." This informative workshop will be great for any gardener, whether you plan to invest in a commercial compost bin or simply start a compost pile in a corner of your garden. You will be amazed at how quickly you can produce rich, nutrient-filled compost with only a little effort. Use this black gold to amend your soil naturally, to encourage the growth of healthy plants. Not only will you create rich soil and save water—you will also reduce trash at the landfill by recycling your kitchen scraps and garden materials.

We offer this free workshop on a first-come, first-served basis. All workshop participants will receive a packet of bacteria to kick-start their composting process. Our speaker will be Ann Porter from the County Extension Office. Ann recently completed her Master Composter Certification and is eager to share her knowledge. She is an engaging speaker you will be sure to enjoy. Call 555-248-0806 today to reserve your spot!

Blooms & Bulbs Spring Workshops

Currently Scheduled Spring Workshops - Call for Availability

Composting	April 1 - 10:00 a.m. - 12:00 p.m.
Pruning	April 8 - 9:00 a.m. - 11:00 a.m.
Containers	April 15 - 1:00 p.m. - 3:00 p.m.
Going Green	April 22 - 10:00 a.m. - 12:00 p.m.
	Classes are limited to 25 members. Bring work gloves!

Copyright 2002 - 2016
Last updated on May 13, 2014

In this exercise, you continue your work on the TripSmart website that you began in Project Builder 1 in Chapter 1 and developed in the previous chapters. You are ready to begin work on a page featuring a catalog item. You plan to use a CSS Fluid Grid layout with a table to place the information on the page.

1. Open the TripSmart website.
2. Create a new Fluid Grid Layout page, and browse to attach the boilerplate.css and tripsmart_styles.css style sheets.
3. Use **tripsmart_styles_default** in the File name text box in the Save As dialog box, then save the new file as **catalog.html**, overwriting the existing catalog page.
4. Delete the link to the tripsmart_styles_default.css file in the catalog page code.
5. Place the insertion point in the placeholder text on the page, select the default name div_1 on the Property inspector, type **content** to rename the div, then delete the placeholder text in the content div.
6. With the insertion point between the opening and closing content <div> tags, insert a Header with the name **header_div**, then delete the placeholder text in the header_div.
7. Insert a new div after the closing header tag named **intro_paragraph**.
8. Open the index page, switch to Code view, copy the code for the menu bar beginning with the <p> tag immediately above it, then close the index page.

9. Switch to the catalog page, then paste the copied code after the closing header div.
10. Insert a footer before the last two ending </div> tags at the bottom of the page with the class name **footer_div**, then save your work.
11. In CSS Designer, select the global selector .menu_bar in tripsmart_styles.css, then add the default font-family value Segoe, Segoe UI, DejaVu Sans, Trebuchet MS, Verdana, sans-serif.
12. With the catalog page open, open your file manager program, open the file hiking.txt from the drive and folder where you store your Data Files, then copy and paste the contents into the intro_paragraph div.
13. Close the hiking.txt file.
14. Add a paragraph break after the sentence "Take a hike!"
15. Apply the H2 format to the "Take a hike!" heading.
16. Open the index file, copy the two lines of text in the footer, then paste them in the footer on the catalog page, replacing the footer placeholder text.
17. Save your work, close the index page, then view the Desktop, Tablet, Mobile sizes, and a browser.
18. In Code view, place the insertion point after the ending intro_paragraph div, then use the Insert panel to insert a new div named **table_div**.
19. Carefully delete the table div placeholder text, then insert a table from the Common category on the Insert panel.
20. In the Table dialog box, select **8** rows, **3** columns, and a Top header. All other values should be empty.

21. In the Caption text box, type **Hiking Clothing and Accessories**
22. Use CSS Designer to add a new global tag selector in the bb_styles.css file named **table**.
23. Using the Layout and Text categories in the Properties pane, add the following properties and values:
    display: block
    width: **80%**
    margin-left: auto
    margin-right: auto
    font-family: Segoe, Segoe UI, DejaVu Sans, Trebuchet MS, Verdana, Sans-serif
24. Save your work.
25. Merge the three cells in the top row, then add the header **Come See Our New Spring Hiking Gear!** to the top row.
26. Merge the remaining cells in the middle column, then save your work.
27. Insert the image three_hikers.jpg from the Chapter 6 assets folder in the location where you store your Data Files, in the merged cells in the second column.
28. Use CSS Designer to add a global tag selector in the tripsmart_styles.css file with the name tr td img.
29. Add the following properties to the tr td img tag:
    width: **85%**
    display: block
    margin-left: auto
    margin-right: auto
30. Use the Property inspector to add the alternate text **Three hikers in Patagonia** to the three hikers image.

31. Create a new global class selector in the tripsmart_styles.css file named .featured_items with the following property and value:
width: **40%**

32. Place the insertion point in the cell with the three hikers image.

33. Select the <td> tag on the Property inspector, select the Class list arrow, then select featured_items.

34. Add a global class selector named .catalog_items with the following property:
width: **30%**

35. Select the empty cells in the first column, use the Property inspector to apply the .catalog_items class, then save your work.

36. Create a global class selector named .catalog_prices, set its Width property to 30%, then apply .catalog_prices to the empty cells in the third column.

37. Type the names of the featured catalog items and prices from Figure 50 in the first six cells in the first and third columns.

38. Add selectors of your own or edit any of the selector properties used for the table to customize the page.

39. Insert a new row at the end of the table, merge the cells in the new row, then insert a horizontal rule.

40. Place the insertion point in front of the table header, then insert another horizontal rule.

41. Switch to the tripsmart_styles.css file, then scroll to locate the table selector code.

42. Copy the table selector code, then paste it into both the tablet and desktop sections of code.

43. Add a property to change the global table selector font-size to small.

44. Edit the desktop table selector font-size to medium.

45. Save your work, preview the catalog page in the browser, mobile, tablet, and desktop sizes, then compare your screen to Figure 45.

46. Close all open files.

Figure 50 *Sample Project Builder 1*

Take a hike!

This week we are featuring all things hiking. Spring is the time to hit the hiking trails and you don't want to go unprepared. Come by our store to see the latest in hiking shoes. Good sturdy shoes are important to keep you foot sure and steady on uneven or slippery trails. We provide many choices in style and size. Lightweight vests are another of our favorites. We have vests with pockets galore: zip, velcro, hidden, and slash. Don't forget a good hat to block harmful sun rays. Lastly, a sturdy walking stick. You have to try a walking stick before you realize how helpful they are. Happy trails to you!

Hiking Clothing and Accessories

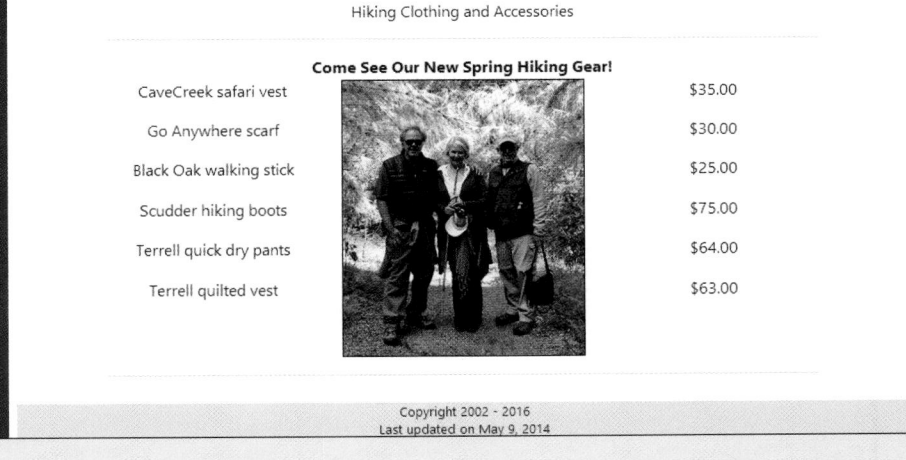

Come See Our New Spring Hiking Gear!

CaveCreek safari vest	$35.00
Go Anywhere scarf	$30.00
Black Oak walking stick	$25.00
Scudder hiking boots	$75.00
Terrell quick dry pants	$64.00
Terrell quilted vest	$63.00

Copyright 2002 - 2016
Last updated on May 9, 2014

Use Figure 51 as a guide to continue your work on the Carolyne's Creations website that you started in Chapter 1 and developed in the previous chapters. You are now ready to begin work on a page showcasing the company's catering services. You decide to use a Fluid Grid layout and add a small table.

1. Open the Carolyne's Creations website, create a new Fluid Grid Layout page, and browse to attach the boilerplate.css and cc_styles.css style sheets.

2. Use **cc_styles_default** in the File name text box in the Save As dialog box, then save the new file as catering.html, overwriting the existing catering page. Close the Web Fonts dialog box if it opens.

3. Delete the link to the cc_styles_default.css file in the catering page code.

4. Place the insertion point in the placeholder text on the page, select the default ID div1 on the Property inspector, then type **content** to rename the div ID, then delete the placeholder text in the content div.

5. With the insertion point between the opening and closing content <div> tags, insert a Header with the name **header_div**, then delete the placeholder text in the header_div.

6. Insert a new div after the closing header tag named **intro_paragraph**, then save your work.

7. Open the index page, switch to Code view, copy the code for the menu bar beginning with the <p> tag immediately above it, then close the index page.

8. Switch to the catering page, then paste the copied code after the closing header div.

9. Insert a footer before the last two ending </div> tags at the bottom of the page with the class name **footer_div**, then save your work.

10. Verify that the font used in the menu bar is the same as on the index page menu bar.

11. Place the insertion point between the intro_ paragraph div tags, open your file manager program, open the file marshmallows.txt from the drive and folder where you store your Data Files, then copy and paste the contents into the intro_paragraph div.

12. Close the marshmallows.txt file.

13. Add a paragraph break after the sentence "Special Treats for Valentine's Day".

14. Apply the H3 format to the "Special Treats for Valentine's Day" heading.

15. Open the index file, copy the two lines of text in the footer, then paste them in the footer on the catering page, replacing the footer placeholder text.

16. Save your work, then view the Desktop, Tablet, Mobile sizes, and a browser.

17. In Code view, place the insertion point after the ending intro_paragraph div, then use the Insert panel to insert a new div named **table_div**.

18. Carefully delete the div placeholder text, then insert a table from the Common category on the Insert panel.

19. In the Table dialog box, select **6** rows, **3** columns, and a Top Header. All other values should be empty.

20. Use CSS Designer to add a new global tag selector in the cc_styles.css file named **table**.

21. Using the Layout and Text categories in the Properties pane, then add the following properties and values:
    display: block
    width: **80%**
    margin-left: auto
    margin-right: auto
    font-family: Segoe, Segoe UI, DejaVu Sans, Trebuchet MS, Verdana, Sans-serif

22. Save your work.

23. Merge the three cells in the top row, then add the header **Marshmallow Flavors and Prices** to the top row.

24. Merge the cells in the first column, then insert the image marshmallows.jpg from the assets folder in the location where you store your Data Files in the merged cells in the first column, then add appropriate alternate text.

25. Use CSS Designer to add a global tag selector in the cc_styles.css file with the name tr td img.

26. Add the following properties to the tr td img tag:
    width: **85%**
    display: block
    margin-left: auto
    margin-right: auto

27. Create a new global class selector in the cc_styles. css file named **.marshmallow_image** with the following property and value:
    width: **40%**

28. Place the insertion point in the cell with the marshmallow image.

29. Select the <td> tag on the Property inspector, select the Class list arrow, then select marshmallow_image.
30. Add two new global class selectors named **.marshmallow_flavors** and **.marshmallow_prices** with the following property: width: **30%**

31. Type the marshmallow flavors in the second column and the marshmallow prices in the third column, as shown in Figure 51.
32. Merge the two cells in the last row, then enter the text shown in Figure 51.
33. Customize the table with new or modified properties or page elements. (*Hint*: In Figure 51 an Adobe Edge

Web Font was used for the marshmallow flavors and the table tag was modified to add a border around it.)
34. Save your work, then preview the catering page in mobile, tablet, and desktop sizes.
35. Preview the catering page in the browser.

Figure 51 *Completed Project Builder 2*

Copyright 2002 - 2016
Last updated on May 13, 2014

DESIGN PROJECT

Jon Bishop is opening a new restaurant and wants to launch his restaurant website two weeks before his opening. He has hired you to create the site and has asked for several design proposals. You begin by looking at some restaurant sites with pleasing designs.

1. Connect to the Internet, then go to jamesatthemill.com, as shown in Figure 52.
2. How are CSS styles used in this site?
3. How are CSS styles used to prevent an overload of information in one area of the screen?
4. View the source code for the page and locate the HTML tags that control the CSS layout on the page.
5. Use the Reference panel in Dreamweaver to look up the code used in this site to place the content on the page. (*Hint*: To do this, make note of a tag that you don't understand, then open the Reference panel and find that tag in the Tag list in the Reference panel. Select it from the list and read the description in the Reference panel.)
6. Do you see any tables on the page? If so, how are they used?

Figure 52 *Design Project*

Source: James at the Mill

For this assignment, you continue to work on the portfolio project that you have been developing since Chapter 1. No Data Files are supplied. You are building this website from chapter to chapter, so you must do each Portfolio Project assignment in each chapter to complete your website.

You continue building your website by designing and completing a page that uses a CSS layout for page design.

1. Consult your wireframe to decide which page to create and develop for this chapter. Draw a sketch of the page to show how you plan to use CSS to lay out the content.
2. Create the new page for the site using a Fluid Grid layout.
3. Add text, background images, and background colors to each container.
4. Create the navigation links that will allow you to add this page to your site.

5. Update the other pages of your site so that each page includes a link to this new page.
6. Add images in the containers (where appropriate), making sure to align them attractively.
7. Review the checklist in Figure 53 and make any necessary changes.
8. Save your work, preview the page in your browser, make any necessary modifications to improve the page appearance, close your browser, then close all open pages.

Figure 53 *Portfolio Project checklist*

Website Checklist

1. Do all pages have a page title?
2. Do all navigation links work correctly?
3. Did you validate your code for at least one level of HTML?
4. Did you use a fluid grid page layout for at least one page?
5. Do your pages look the same in at least two current browsers and three screen sizes?
6. Does all content in your CSS containers appear correctly?

CHAPTER 7 MANAGING A WEB
SERVER AND FILES

1. Perform website maintenance
2. Publish a website and transfer files
3. Check files out and in
4. Cloak files
5. Import and export a site definition
6. Evaluate web content for legal use
7. Present a website to a client

CHAPTER 7

MANAGING A WEB
SERVER AND FILES

Introduction

Once you have created all the pages of your website, finalized all the content, and performed site maintenance, you are ready to publish your site to a remote server so the rest of the world can access it. In this chapter, you start by running some reports to make sure the links in your site work properly and that any orphaned files are removed. You remember from Chapter 5 that orphaned files are files that are not linked to any pages in a website. Next, you set up a connection to the remote site for The Striped Umbrella website. You then transfer files to the remote site and learn how to keep them up to date. You also check out a file so that it is not available to other team members while you are editing it and you learn how to cloak files. When a file is **cloaked**, it is excluded from certain processes, such as being transferred to the remote site. Next, you export the site definition file from The Striped Umbrella website so that other designers can import the site. Finally, you research important copyright issues that affect all websites, and learn how to present your work to a client.

Preparing to Publish a Site

Before you publish a site, it is extremely important that you test it to make sure the content is accurate and up to date and that everything is functioning properly. When viewing pages over the Internet, users find it frustrating to select a link that doesn't work or to wait for pages that load slowly because of large graphics and animations. Remember that the typical user has a short attention span and limited patience.

Before you publish your site, be sure to use the Link Checker panel to check for broken links and orphaned files. Make sure that all image paths are correct and that all images load quickly and have alternate text. Verify that all pages have titles. View the pages in at least two different browsers and different versions of the same browser to ensure that everything works correctly. View the pages on a mobile, tablet, and desktop device. The more frequently you test, the better the chance that your users will have a positive experience at your site and want to return. Finally, before you publish your pages, verify that all content is original to the website, or has been obtained legally and is used properly without violating the copyright of someone else's work.

Reports

Report on: [Entire Current Local Site ∨]

Current Document
Entire Current Local Site
Selected Files in Site
Folder...

Select repor[t]

- ⊟ 📁 Workflow
  - ☐ Checked Out By
  - ☐ Design Notes
  - ☐ Recently Modified
- ⊟ 📁 HTML Reports
  - ☐ Combinable Nested Font Tags
  - ☐ Missing Alt Text
  - ☐ Redundant Nested Tags
  - ☐ Removable Empty Tags
  - ☐ Untitled Documents

[Run]
[Cancel]

[Report Settings...]   [Help]

Synchronize with Remote Server ✕

Synchronize: [Entire 'The Striped Umbrella' Site ∨]   [Preview...]

Direction: [Put newer files to remote ∨]   [Cancel]

[Help]

☐ Delete remote files not on local drive

Site Setup for The Striped Umbrella ✕

| Site |
| Servers |
| Version C |
| ▸ Advanced |

[Basic] [Advanced]

Server Name: [Server 1]

Connect using: [FTP ▾]

FTP Address: [www.webhost.com]   Port: [21]

Username: [name]

Password: [•••••••]   ☑ Save

[Test]

Root Directory: [/home]

Web URL: [http://www.webhost.com/]

▸ More Options

[Help]   [Save]   [Cancel]

...ettings
...ur web

...er site. You
...t your

Testing

[Help]   [Save]   [Cancel]

Perform
WEBSITE MAINTENANCE

What You'll Do

In this lesson, you will use Dreamweaver site management tools to check for broken links, orphaned files, and missing alternate text. You will also validate your markup to locate CSS3 and HTML5 errors. You will then evaluate and correct any problems that you find.

Maintaining a Website

As you add pages, links, and content to a website, it can quickly become difficult to manage. You'll find it easier to locate and correct errors as you go, rather than waiting until the end of the design phase. Perform maintenance tasks frequently to make sure your website operates smoothly and remains "clean." After publishing your website, run maintenance checks at regular intervals to make sure it is always error-free. You have already been introduced to some of the tools described in the following paragraphs. Now you can put them into practice.

Using the Assets Panel

Use the Assets panel to check the list of images and colors used in your website. If you see images listed that are not being used, you should move them to a storage folder outside the website until you need them. You should also look at your colors listed in the Assets panel. Do they complement each other, creating a pleasing color palette? Will any of them cause contrast problems, especially with mobile devices?

Checking Links Sitewide

Before and after you publish your website, you should use the Link Checker panel to make sure all internal links are working. If the Link Checker panel displays any broken links, repair them. If it displays any orphaned files, evaluate whether to delete them or link them to existing pages. To delete a file that you decide not to use, select it in the Files panel, then press [Delete] or right-click the file, select Edit, then select Delete. You should also check all external links by testing them in a browser to make sure that all links find the intended website.

Using Site Reports

You can use the Reports command in the Site menu to generate five different HTML reports to help you maintain your website. Choose the type of report you want to run in the Reports dialog box, shown in Figure 1. You can specify whether to generate the report for the current document, the entire current local site, selected files in the site, or a selected folder. You can also generate workflow reports to see files that have been checked out by others or recently modified or you can view the Design Notes attached to files.

Design Notes are separate files in a website that contain additional information about a page file or a graphic file. If several designers are working collaboratively to design a site, they can record notes to exchange information with other design team members about the status of ongoing work on a file. Design Notes are also a good place to store information about the source files for graphics, such as Photoshop or Fireworks files.

Validating Markup

Because you can choose the language you use to create web pages, such as PHP or HTML, it's important to ensure that the various language versions are compatible. To address this need, Dreamweaver can validate markup. To **validate markup**, Dreamweaver submits the files to the W3C Validation Service to search through the code to look for errors that could occur with different language versions, such as XHTML or HTML5. To validate code for a page, select the File, Validate, Validate Current Document (W3C) command. Dreamweaver then sends the page code to the live W3C site to be validated. The Results tab group displaying the Validation panel opens and lists any pages with errors, the line numbers where the errors occur, and an explanation of the errors. You should also submit your CSS files for CSS validation to the W3C Validation Service at jigsaw.w3.org/css-validator.

Testing Pages

Finally, you should test your website using many different types and versions of browsers, platforms, and screen resolutions. Test every link to make sure it connects to a valid, active website.

If, in your testing, you find any pages that download slowly, reduce their size to improve performance. Consider optimizing graphics by cropping or resizing images, reducing the number of media files, or streamlining the page code.

As part of your ongoing site testing, you should present the web pages at strategic times in the development process to your team members and to your clients for feedback and evaluation. Analyze all feedback on the website objectively, incorporating both the positive and the negative comments to help you make improvements to the site and meet the clients' expectations and goals.

Figure 1 *Reports dialog box*

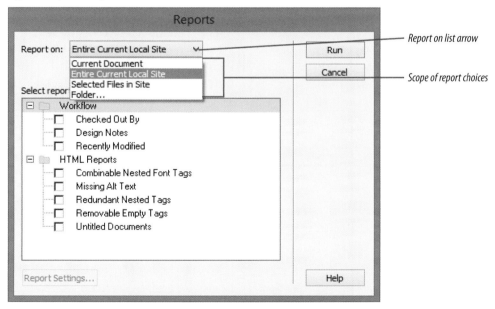

Check for broken links

1. Open The Striped Umbrella website.
2. Open the Files panel, if necessary.
3. Select **Site** on the Menu bar, point to **Advanced**, then select **Recreate Site Cache**.

   It is a good idea to recreate the site cache to force Dreamweaver to refresh the file listing before running reports.

4. Select **Site** on the Menu bar, then select **Check Links Sitewide**.

   No broken links are listed in the Link Checker panel of the Results Tab Group, as shown in Figure 2.

You verified that there are no broken links in the website.

Check for orphaned files

1. On the Link Checker panel, select the **Show list arrow**, then select **Orphaned Files**.

   There are two orphaned files, as shown in Figure 3. You may use the logo file later, so you leave it in the local site folder for now. The second file is the su_styles_default.css file. You want to keep it for reference, so it can also stay in the local site folder for now.

2. Close the Results Tab Group.

You found two orphaned files in the website, but decided to leave them there for now.

Figure 2 *Link Checker panel displaying no broken links*

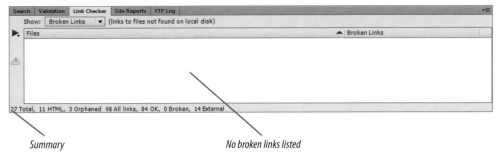

Summary   No broken links listed

Figure 3 *Link Checker panel displaying two orphaned files*

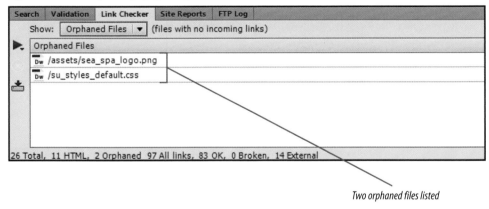

Two orphaned files listed

Validating Accessibility Standards

HTML Reports can help ensure that your website conforms to current accessibility standards. HTML Reports provide an easy way to check for missing alternate text, missing page titles, and improper markup. You can run HTML Reports on the current document, selected files, or the entire local site.

Figure 4 *Reports dialog box with Untitled Documents option selected*

Figure 5 *No pages listed without a title*

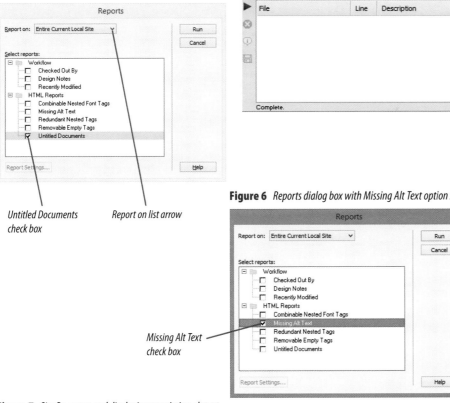

Untitled Documents
check box

Report on list arrow

Figure 6 *Reports dialog box with Missing Alt Text option selected*

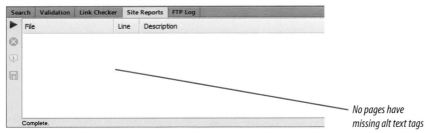

Missing Alt Text
check box

Figure 7 *Site Reports panel displaying no missing alt text*

No pages have
missing alt text tags

Check for untitled documents

1. Select **Site** on the Menu bar, then select **Reports** to open the Reports dialog box.

2. Select the **Report on list arrow**, select **Entire Current Local Site**, select the **Untitled Documents check box**, as shown in Figure 4, then select **Run**.

   The Site Reports panel opens in the Results Tab Group, and does not list any pages with unassigned titles, as shown in Figure 5.

You ran a report for untitled documents, and did not find any files listed without assigned page titles.

Check for missing alternate text

1. Using Figure 6 as a guide, run another report that checks the entire current local site for missing alternate text.

   There are no images with missing alternate text, as shown in Figure 7.

2. Close the Results Tab Group.

You ran a report to check for missing alternate text in the entire site.

Validate for HTML5 standards

1. Select **File** on the Menu bar, select **Validate**, select **Validate Current Document (W3C)**, then select **OK** to close the W3C Validator Notification dialog box.

   The Validation panel shows no errors or warnings for HTML5, as shown in Figure 8.

2. Open each page in the website, then repeat Step 1 to validate each page.

3. Close the Results Tab Group, then close any open pages.

You validated each page against HTML5 markup standards and no errors or warnings were found.

Figure 8 *Validation panel with no errors or warnings found*

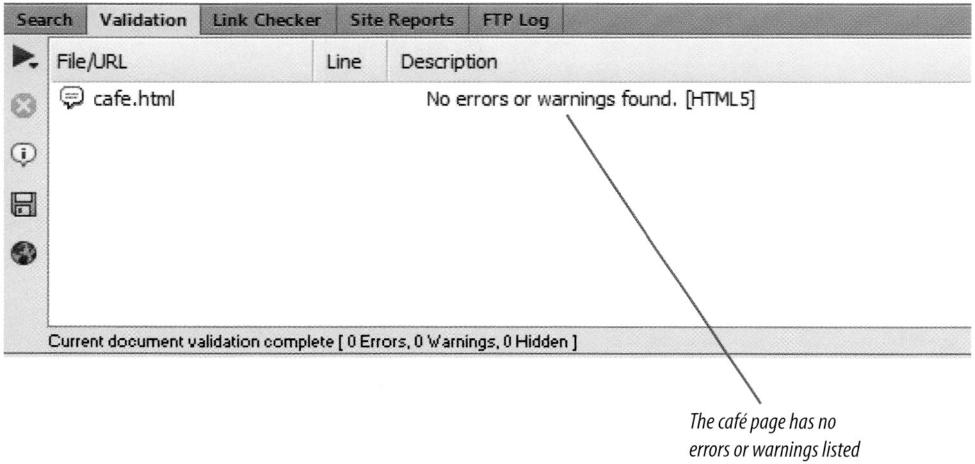

The café page has no errors or warnings listed

Figure 9 *Submitting a style sheet for validation*

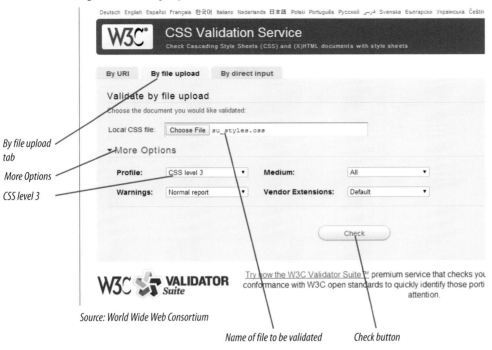

By file upload tab

More Options

CSS level 3

Name of file to be validated

Check button

Source: World Wide Web Consortium

Figure 10 *W3C validation results for su_styles.css file*

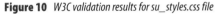

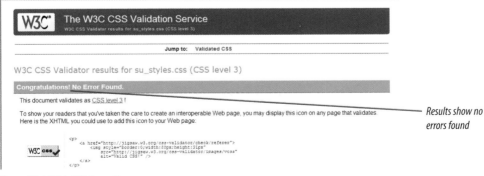

Results show no errors found

Source: World Wide Web Consortium

Validate CSS

1. Open your browser and go to **jigsaw.w3.org/css-validator**.

   The CSS Validation Service provides a fast way to validate the code in your style sheets to be sure they are compliant with the most current published CSS standards.

2. Select the **By file upload tab**, select **Choose File (or Browse) button** next to the Local CSS file text box, navigate to your website's local site folder, double-click to select **su_styles.css**, select **More Options**, then select **CSS level 3**, as shown in Figure 9.

3. Select **Check**, then view the validation results, as shown in Figure 10.

   There are no errors listed in the su_styles.css file.

4. Close the browser and return to Dreamweaver.

You submitted the main style sheet for validation and found that it met CSS3 standards.

Enable Design Notes

1. Select **Site** on the Menu bar, select **Manage Sites**, verify that The Striped Umbrella site is selected, select the **Edit the currently selected site button** 🖉, select **Advanced Settings**, then select **Design Notes**.

2. Select the **Maintain Design Notes check box**, if necessary, as shown in Figure 11.

   When this option is selected, designers can record notes about a page in a separate file linked to the page. For instance, a Design Note for the index.html file would be saved in a file named index.html.mno. Dreamweaver creates a folder named _notes and saves all Design Notes in that folder. This folder does not appear in the Files panel, but it is visible in the local site folder in File Explorer (Win) or Finder (Mac).

3. Select **File View Columns**, then select **Notes** in the Name column.

4. Select the **Edit existing Column button** 🖉, select the **Options: Show check box**, if necessary, then select **Save**.

   The Notes row now displays the word "Show" in the Show column, as shown in Figure 12, indicating that the Notes column will be visible in the Files panel.

5. Select **Save** to close the Site Setup for The Striped Umbrella dialog box, then select **Done** in the Manage Sites dialog box.

   You set the preference to use Design Notes in the website. You also set the option to display the Notes column in the Files panel.

Figure 11 *Design Notes setting in the Site Setup for The Striped Umbrella*

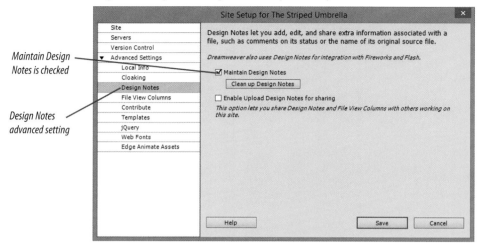

Maintain Design Notes is checked

Design Notes advanced setting

Figure 12 *Showing the Notes column in the Site Setup for The Striped Umbrella*

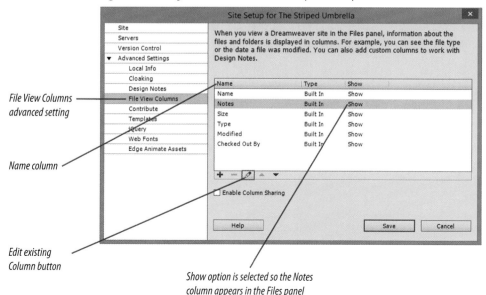

File View Columns advanced setting

Name column

Edit existing Column button

Show option is selected so the Notes column appears in the Files panel

Figure 13 *Design Notes dialog box*

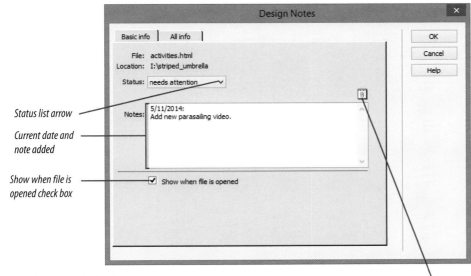

Status list arrow

Current date and note added

Show when file is opened check box

Insert date button

Figure 14 *Files panel showing Notes icon*

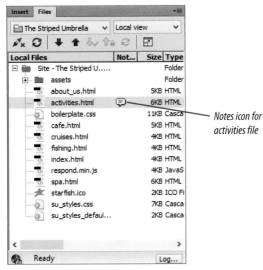

Notes icon for activities file

Associate a Design Note with a file

1. Open the activities page, select **File** on the Menu bar, select **Design Notes**, then select the **Basic info tab**, if necessary.

   The Design Notes dialog box opens. You can enter a note related to the open file in the text box. You can also assign the note a status, insert today's date, and indicate if the note appears whenever the file is opened.

2. Select the **Insert date button** 📅 above the Notes text box on the right.

   The current date is added to the Notes text box.

3. Place the insertion point under the date, then type **Add new parasailing video.** in the Notes text box.

4. Select the **Status list arrow**, then select **needs attention**.

5. Select the **Show when file is opened** check box, as shown in Figure 13, then select **OK**.

6. Select the **Refresh button** 🔄 on the Files panel.

   An icon 💬 appears next to the activities page in the Notes column in the Files panel as shown in Figure 14, indicating that there is a Design Note attached to the file.

You added a Design Note to the activities page with the current date and a status indicator. The note opens each time the file is opened.

Edit a Design Note

1. Select **File** on the Menu bar, then select **Design Notes** to open the Design Note associated with the activities page.

TIP You can also right-click (Win) or [control]-click (Mac) the filename in the Files panel, then select Design Notes to open the Design Note. You can also double-click or double-tap the Note icon to open a Design Note.

2. Edit the note by adding the sentence **Ask Sue Geren to send the file.** after the existing text in the Notes section, as shown in Figure 15, then select **OK** to close it.

   Dreamweaver created a file named activities.html.mno in a new folder called _notes in the local site folder. This folder and file do not appear in the Files panel unless you have selected the option to show hidden files and folders. To show hidden files, select the Files Panel options button, then select View, Show Hidden Files. However, you can switch to File Explorer (Win) or Finder (Mac) to see them without selecting this option. When you select the option to Enable Upload Design Notes for sharing, you can share the notes with team members working with you on the site.

3. Right-click (Win) or [control]-click (Mac) **activities.html** in the Files panel, then select **Explore** (Win) or **Reveal in Finder** (Mac).

   (continued)

Figure 15 *Adding to the note for the activities page*

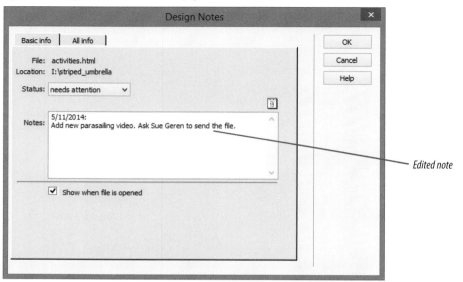

Edited note

Deleting a Design Note

There are two steps to deleting a Design Note that you don't need anymore. The first step is to delete the Design Note file. To delete a Design Note, right-click the filename in the Files panel that is associated with the Design Note you want to delete, and then select Explore (Win) or Reveal in Finder (Mac) to open your file management system. Open the _notes folder, delete the .mno file in the files list, and then close Explorer (Win) or Finder (Mac). You perform the second step in Dreamweaver: Select Site on the Menu bar, select Manage Sites, select Edit the currently selected site button, select Advanced Settings, then select the Design Notes category. Confirm that Maintain Design Notes is still selected, then select the Clean up Design Notes button. (*Note*: Don't do this if you deselect Maintain Design Notes first or it will delete all of your Design Notes!) The Design Notes icon will be removed from the Notes column in the Files panel. After you delete the .mno file, you can select the Refresh button in the Files panel, and it will be removed.

Figure 16 *File Explorer displaying the _notes folder and file*

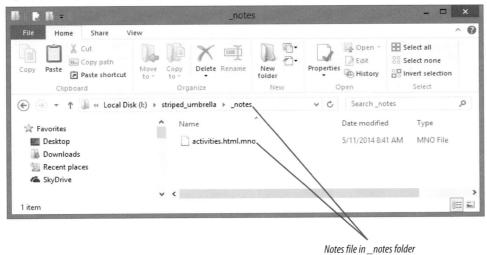

Notes file in _notes folder

4. Double-click the **_notes** folder to open it, then double-click the file **activities.html.mno**, shown in Figure 16, to open the file in Dreamweaver.

The notes file opens in Code view in Dreamweaver, as shown in Figure 17.

TIP If you see a message asking what program you want to use to open the file, select Dreamweaver.

5. Read the file, close it, close Explorer (Win) or Finder (Mac), then close the activities page.

You opened the Design Notes dialog box and edited the note in the Notes text box. Next, you viewed the .mno file that Dreamweaver created when you added the Design Note.

Figure 17 *Code for the activities.html.mno file*

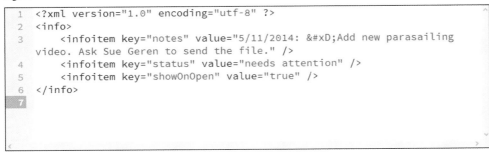

```
1  <?xml version="1.0" encoding="utf-8" ?>
2  <info>
3      <infoitem key="notes" value="5/11/2014: &#xD;Add new parasailing
   video. Ask Sue Geren to send the file." />
4      <infoitem key="status" value="needs attention" />
5      <infoitem key="showOnOpen" value="true" />
6  </info>
7
```

Publish a Website
AND TRANSFER FILES

What You'll Do

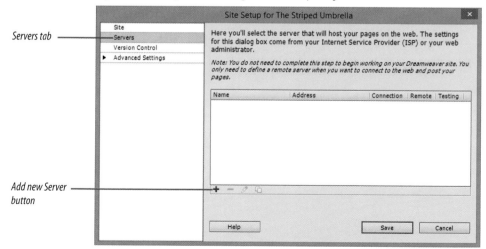

In this lesson, you will set up remote access to either an FTP folder or a local/network folder for The Striped Umbrella website. You will also view a website on a remote server, upload files to it, and synchronize the files.

Defining a Remote Site

As you learned in Chapter 1, publishing a site means transferring a copy of all the site's files to a web server. A **web server** is a computer with software that enables it to host websites and is connected to the Internet with an IP (Internet Protocol) address so that it is available on the Internet. Before you can publish a site to a web server, you must first define the remote site by specifying the Servers settings in the Site Setup dialog box as shown in Figure 18. You can specify remote settings when you first create a new site and define the local site folder (as you did in Chapter 1 when you defined the remote access settings for The Striped Umbrella website). Or you can do it after you have completed all of your pages and are confident that your site is ready for public viewing. To specify the remote settings for a site, select the Add new Server button in the Site Setup

Figure 18 *Accessing the server settings in the Site Setup dialog box*

Servers tab

Add new Server
button

Managing a Web Server and Files

dialog box, then add your server name, and choose a connection setting, which specifies the type of server you will use. You can set up multiple servers with Dreamweaver. You can set up a server for testing purposes only and a server for the live website. The most common connection setting is FTP (File Transfer Protocol). If you choose FTP, you need to specify a server address and folder name on the FTP site where you want to store your remote site root folder. You can also use **Secure FTP (SFTP)**, which lets you encrypt file transfers to protect your files, user names, and passwords. To use SFTP, select SFTP on the Connect using list in the site setup dialog box. You also need to enter login and password information. Figure 19

shows an example of FTP settings in the Add new server dialog box.

QUICK TIP

If you do not have access to an FTP site, you can publish a site to a local/network folder. This is referred to as a **LAN**, or a Local Area Network. Use the alternate steps provided in this lesson to publish your site to a local/network folder.

Viewing a Remote Site

Once you have set up a remote server, you can then view the remote folder in the Files panel by choosing Remote server from the View list. If your remote site is located on an FTP server, Dreamweaver will connect to it. You will see the File Activity dialog box showing the progress of the connection. You can also use the

Connect to Remote Server button on the Files panel toolbar to connect to the remote site. If you defined your site on a local/network folder, then you don't need to use the Connect Remote Server button; the local site folder and any files and folders it contains appear in the Files panel when you switch to Remote server view.

Transferring Files to and from a Remote Site

After you set up a remote site, you **upload**, or copy, your files from the local version of your site to the remote host. To do this, view the site in Local view, select the files you want to upload, and then select the Put File(s) button on the Files panel toolbar. The Put File(s) button includes the name of the server in the tooltip.

Figure 19 *Viewing remote server settings*

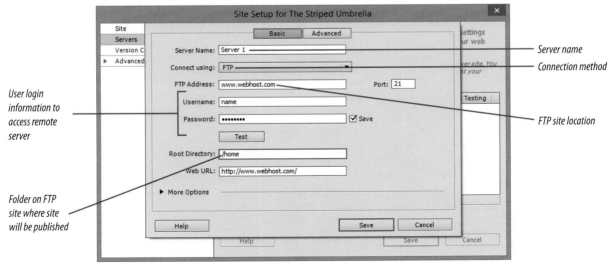

Once you select this button, a copy of the files is transferred to the remote site. To view the uploaded files, switch to Remote server in the Files panel. Or, you can expand the Files panel to view both the Remote Site and the Local Site panes by selecting the Expand to show local and remote sites button in the Files panel.

If a file you select for uploading requires additional files, such as graphics or a style sheet file, a dialog box opens after you select the Put File(s) button and asks if you want those files (known as **dependent files**) to be uploaded. By selecting Yes, all dependent files for the selected page will be uploaded to the appropriate folder in the remote site. If a file that you want to upload is located in a folder in the local site, the folder will automatically be transferred to the remote site.

QUICK TIP

To upload an entire site to a remote host, select the local site folder, then select the Put File(s) button.

If you are developing or maintaining a website in a group environment, there might be times when you want to transfer or **download** files that other team members have created from the remote site to your local site. To do this, switch to Remote Server in the Files panel, select the files you want to download, then select the Get File(s) button on the Files panel toolbar. The Get File(s) button includes the name of the server in the tooltip.

Synchronizing Files

To keep a website up to date—especially one that contains several pages and involves several team members—you need to update and replace files. Team members might make changes to pages on the local version of the site or make additions to the remote site. If many people are involved in maintaining a site, or if you are constantly making changes to the pages, ensuring that both the local and remote sites have the most up-to-date files could get confusing. Luckily, you can use the Synchronize command to keep things straight. The **Synchronize command** instructs Dreamweaver to compare the dates of the saved files in both versions of the site, then transfers only copies of files that have changed. To synchronize files, use the Synchronize Files dialog box, shown in Figure 20. You can synchronize an entire site or only selected files. You can also specify whether to upload newer files to the remote site, download newer files from the remote site, or both.

Figure 20 *Synchronize Files dialog box*

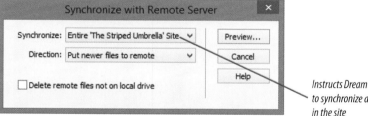

Instructs Dreamweaver to synchronize all files in the site

Understanding Dreamweaver Connection Options for Transferring Files

The connection types with which you are probably the most familiar are FTP and Local/Network. Other connection types that you can use with Dreamweaver include Microsoft Visual SafeSource (VSS), and WebDav. **WebDav** stands for Web-based Distributed Authoring and Versioning. This type of connection is used with the WebDav protocol. An example would be a website residing on an Apache web server. The **Apache web server** is a public domain, open source web server that is available using several different operating systems including UNIX and Windows. **RDS** stands for Remote Development Services, and is used with web servers using Cold Fusion.

Figure 21 *FTP settings specified in the Site Setup for The Striped Umbrella dialog box*

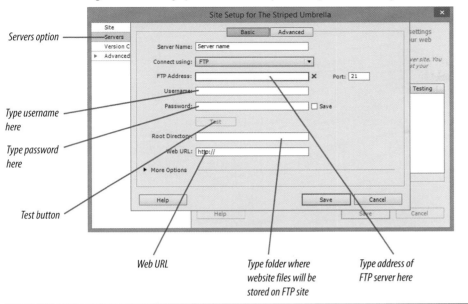

Servers option

Type username here

Type password here

Test button

Web URL

Type folder where website files will be stored on FTP site

Type address of FTP server here

Comparing Two Files for Differences in Content

There are situations where it would be helpful to be able to compare the contents of two files, such as a local file and the remote version of the same file; or an original file and the same file that has been saved with a different name. Once the two files are compared and differences are detected, you can merge the information in the files. A good time to compare files is before you upload them to a remote server to prevent accidentally writing over a file with more recent information. To compare files, you must first locate and install a third-party file comparison utility, or "dif" tool, such as FileMerge or Beyond Compare. (Dreamweaver does not have a file comparison tool included as part of the software, so you need to download one.) If you are not familiar with these tools, find one using your favorite search engine.

After installing the file comparison utility, use the Preferences command on the Edit menu to open the Preferences dialog box, then select the File Compare category. Next, browse to select the application you want to use to compare files. After you have set your Preferences, select the Compare with Remote Server command on the File menu to compare an open file with the remote version.

Set up a web server connection on an FTP site

NOTE: Complete these steps only if you know you can store The Striped Umbrella files on an FTP site and you know the login and password information. If you do not have access to an FTP site, complete the exercise called Set up a web server connection to a local or network folder on Page 7-18.

1. Select **Site** on the Menu bar, then select **Manage Sites**.

2. Select **The Striped Umbrella** in the Manage Sites dialog box, if necessary, then select the **Edit currently selected site button** ✐.

3. Select **Servers** in the Site Setup dialog box, select the **Add new Server** button ➕, type your server name, select the **Connect using list arrow**, select **FTP** if necessary, then compare your screen to Figure 21.

4. Enter the FTP Address, Username, Password, Root Directory, and Web URL information in the dialog box.

TIP You must have file and folder permissions to use FTP. The server administrator can give you this and also tell you the folder name and location you should use to publish your files.

5. Select the **Test button** to test the connection to the remote site.

6. If the connection is successful, select **Save** to close the dialog box; if it is not successful, verify that you have the correct settings, then repeat Step 5.

7. Select **Save** to close the open dialog box, select **Save** to close the Site Setup dialog box, then select **Done** to close the Manage Sites dialog box.

You set up remote access information for The Striped Umbrella website using FTP settings.

Set up a web server connection to a local or network folder

NOTE: Complete these steps if you do not have the ability to post files to an FTP site and could not complete the previous set of steps.

1. Using File Explorer (Win) or Finder (Mac), create a new folder on your hard drive or on a shared drive named **su_yourlastname** (e.g., if your last name is Jones, name the folder **su_jones**).

2. Switch back to Dreamweaver, open The Striped Umbrella website, then open the Manage Sites dialog box.

3. Select **The Striped Umbrella**, if necessary, then select the **Edit the currently selected site button** ✎ to open the Site Setup for The Striped Umbrella dialog box.

TIP You can also double-click the site name in the Site Name box in the Files panel to open the Site Setup dialog box.

4. Select **Servers**, then select the **Add new Server button** ➕.

5. Type **SU Remote** for the Server Name, select the **Connect using list arrow**, then select **Local/Network**.

6. Select the **Browse button** 🗁 next to the Server Folder text box to open the Choose Folder dialog box, navigate to and double-click the folder you created in Step 1, then select **Select Folder** (Win) or **Choose** (Mac).

7. Compare your screen to Figure 22, select **Save**, select **Save** to close the Site Setup dialog box, then select **Done**.

You created a new folder and specified it as the remote location for The Striped Umbrella website, then set up remote access to a local or network folder.

Figure 22 *Local/Network settings in the Site Setup for The Striped Umbrella dialog box*

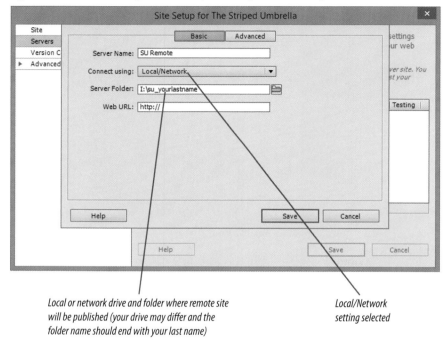

Local or network drive and folder where remote site will be published (your drive may differ and the folder name should end with your last name)

Local/Network setting selected

Testing Your Site's Usability

Once you have at least a prototype of the website ready to evaluate, it is a good idea to conduct a site usability test. This is a process that involves asking unbiased people, who are not connected to the design process, to use and evaluate the site. A comprehensive usability test includes pre-test questions, participant tasks, a post-test interview, and a post-test survey. This provides much-needed information as to how usable the site is to those unfamiliar with it. Typical questions include: "What are your overall impressions?"; "What do you like the best and the least about the site?"; and "How easy is it to navigate inside the site?" For more information, go to w3.org and search for "site usability test."

Figure 23 *Connecting to the remote server*

Connect to Remote
Server button

Remote server
selected

Expand to show local
and remote sites button

Remote folder
name

Figure 24 *Viewing the local and remote site folders*

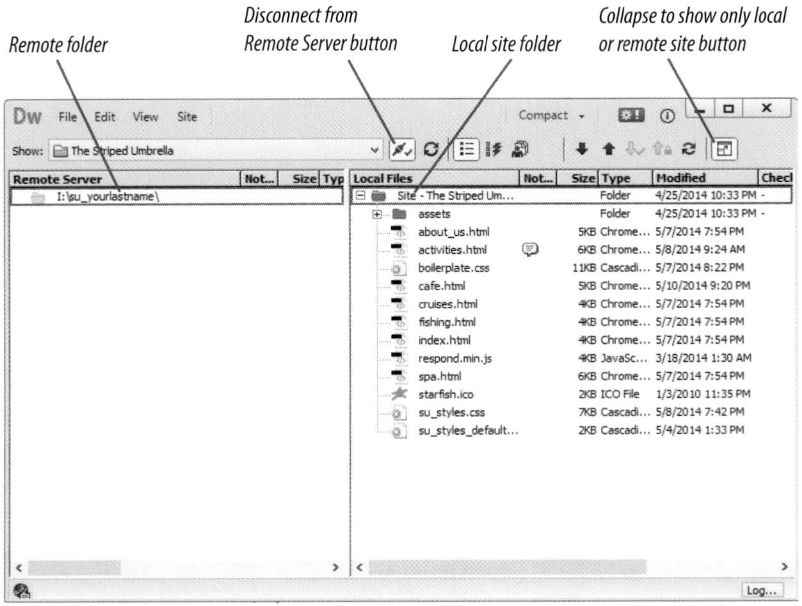

Remote folder

Disconnect from
Remote Server button

Local site folder

Collapse to show only local
or remote site button

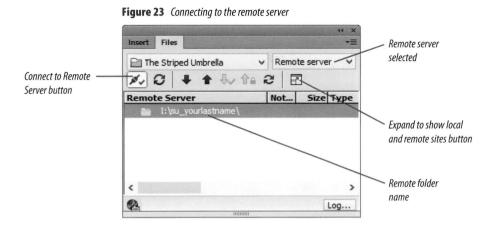

View a website on a remote server

1. Select the **View list arrow** in the Files panel, select **Remote server**, then compare your screen to Figure 23.

   If you set your remote access to be a local or network folder, then the su_yourlastname folder appears in the Files panel. If your remote access is set to an FTP site, Dreamweaver connects to the host server and displays the remote folders and file.

2. Select the **Expand to show local and remote sites button** 🗗 on the Files panel to view both the Remote Server and Local Files panes. The su_yourlastname folder appears in the Remote Server portion of the expanded Files panel, as shown in Figure 24.

TIP If you don't see your remote site files, select the Connect to Remote Server butt0on 🖉ₓ or the Refresh button ⟳. If you don't see two panes, one with the remote site files and one with the local files, drag the panel border to enlarge the panel.

When the Files panel is expanded to show both the local and remote sites, the Expand to show local and remote sites button 🗗 becomes the Collapse to show only local or remote site button. 🗗 and the Connect to Remote Server button 🖉ₓ becomes the Disconnect from Remote Server button 🖉✓.

You used the Files panel to set the view for The Striped Umbrella site to Remote view. You then connected to the remote server to view the remote folder you created earlier.

Upload files to a remote server

1. Select the **about_us.html file**, then select the **Put file(s) to "Remote Server" button** 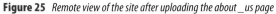 on the Files panel toolbar.

   Notice that the Put File(s) to "Remote Server" button screentip includes the name of the remote server you are using. The Dependent Files dialog box opens, asking if you want to include dependent files.

2. Select **Yes**.

   The about_us file, the style sheet files, and the image files used in the about_us page are copied to the remote server. The Background File Activity dialog box appears and flashes the names of each file as they are uploaded.

3. Expand the assets folder in the remote site if necessary, then compare your screen to Figure 25.

   The remote site now lists the additional files: the about_us page, the image files, and the external style sheet files, all of which are needed by the about_us page.

TIP You might need to expand the su_yourlastname folder in order to view the uploaded files and folders.

You used the Put File(s) button to upload the about_us file and all files that are dependent files of the about_us page.

Figure 25 *Remote view of the site after uploading the about_us page*

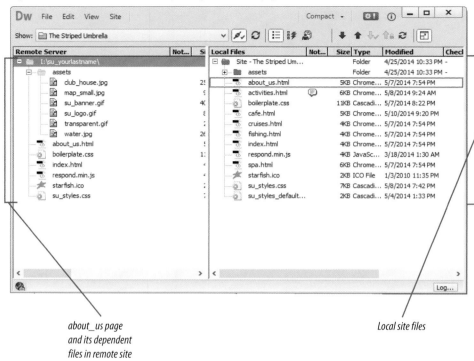

about_us page
and its dependent
files in remote site

Local site files

Continuing to Work While Transferring Files to a Remote Server

During the process of uploading files to a remote server, there are many Dreamweaver functions that you can continue to use while you wait. For example, you can create a new site, create a new page, edit a page, add files and folders, and run reports. However, there are some functions that you cannot use while transferring files, many of which involve accessing files on the remote server or using Check In/ Check Out.

Figure 26 *Synchronize with Remote Server dialog box*

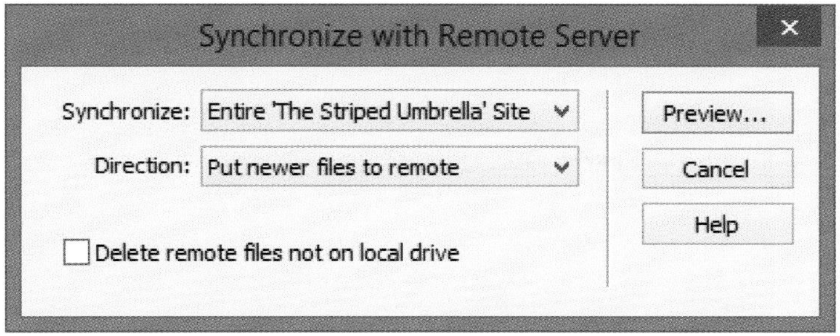

Figure 27 *Files that need to be uploaded to the remote site*

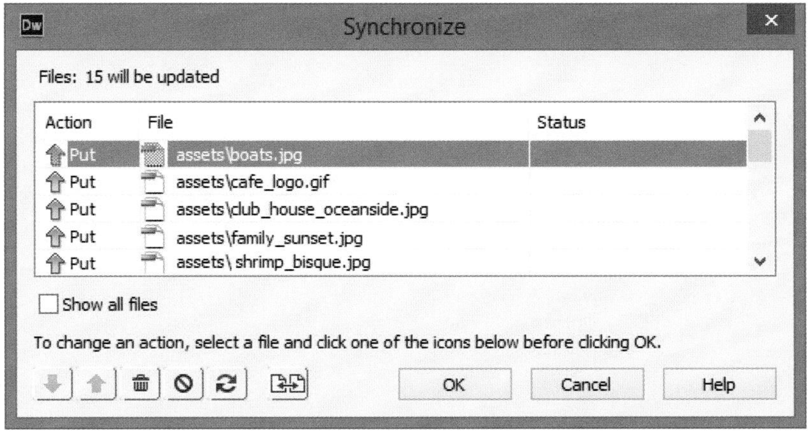

Uploading Files to the Creative Cloud

Another way to store your website files is to upload them to your Adobe Creative Cloud account. Recall from the Creative Cloud Guide at the beginning of this book that you are given 20GB of storage with your Creative Cloud account. Use this space to store archive copies of older versions of your website files and backup copies of your current website files. To upload files, open the Actions menu and create a new folder. Next, select the folder, select Actions, then select Upload. You will be prompted to browse to the files you want to upload. After locating your files, select them and the upload will begin.

Synchronize files

1. Select the **Collapse to show only local or remote site button** 📺, change to Local view, then open each page in the website in Code view and locate any that are missing the link to the website favicon in the line above the code for the page title.

2. Open the index page, if necessary, then copy the code in the head content that links the favicon to the page.

3. Paste the favicon link to any pages you identified in Step 1, then save and close any open pages.

4. Select the **Synchronize button** 🔁 on the Files panel toolbar to open the Synchronize with Remote Server dialog box.

5. Select the **Synchronize list arrow**, then select **Entire 'The Striped Umbrella' Site**.

6. Select the **Direction list arrow**, select **Put newer files to remote** if necessary, then compare your screen to Figure 26.

7. Select **Preview**.

   The Background File Activity dialog box might appear and flash the names of all the files from the local version of the site that need to be uploaded to the remote site. The Synchronize dialog box, shown in Figure 27, opens and lists all the files that need to be uploaded to the remote site.

8. Select **OK**.

   All the files from the local The Striped Umbrella site are copied to the remote version of the site. If you expand the Files panel, you will notice that the remote folders are yellow (Win) or blue (Mac) and the local folders are gray.

You synchronized The Striped Umbrella website files to copy all remaining files from the local site folder to the remote site folder.

Check Files
OUT AND IN

What You'll Do

In this lesson, you will use the Site Setup dialog box to enable the Check Out feature. You will then check out the cafe page, make a change to it, and then check it back in.

Managing a Website with a Team

When you work on a large website, chances are that many people will be involved in keeping the site up to date. Different individuals will need to make changes or additions to different pages of the site by adding or deleting content, changing graphics, updating information, and so on. If everyone had access to the pages at the same time, problems could arise. For instance, what if you and another team member both made edits to the same page at the same time? If you post your edited version of the file to the site after the other team member posts his edited version of the same file, the file that you upload will overwrite his version and none of his changes will be incorporated. Fortunately, you can avoid this scenario by using Dreamweaver's collaboration tools.

Checking Out and Checking In Files

Checking files in and out is similar to checking library books in and out. No one else can access the same copy that you have checked out. Using Dreamweaver's Check Out feature ensures that team members cannot overwrite each other's pages. When this feature is enabled, only one person can work on a file at a time. To check out a file, select the file you want to work on in the Files panel, and then select the Check Out File(s) button on the Files panel toolbar. Files that you have checked out are marked with green check marks in the Files panel. Files that have been checked in are marked with padlock icons.

After you finish editing a checked-out file, save and close the file, and then select the Check In button to check the file back in and make it available to other users. When a file is checked in, you cannot make edits to it unless you check it out again. Figure 28 shows the Check Out File(s) and Check In buttons on the Files panel toolbar. The two buttons appear grayed out because the Check Out feature was not enabled.

Enabling the Check Out Feature

To use the Check Out feature with a team of people, you must first enable it. To turn on this feature, check the Enable file check-out check box in the Remote Server section of the Servers Advanced tab in the Site Setup dialog box. If you do not want to use this feature, you should turn it off so you won't have to check files out every time you open them.

Using Subversion Control

Another file management tool is Subversion control. A remote SVN (Apache Subversion) repository is used to maintain current and historical versions of your website files. It is used in a team environment to move, copy, and delete shared files. You can protect files from being accessed using the svn:ignore property to create a list of files that are to be ignored in a directory.

Figure 28 *Check Out File(s) and Check In buttons on the Files Panel toolbar*

Check Out File(s) button   Check In button

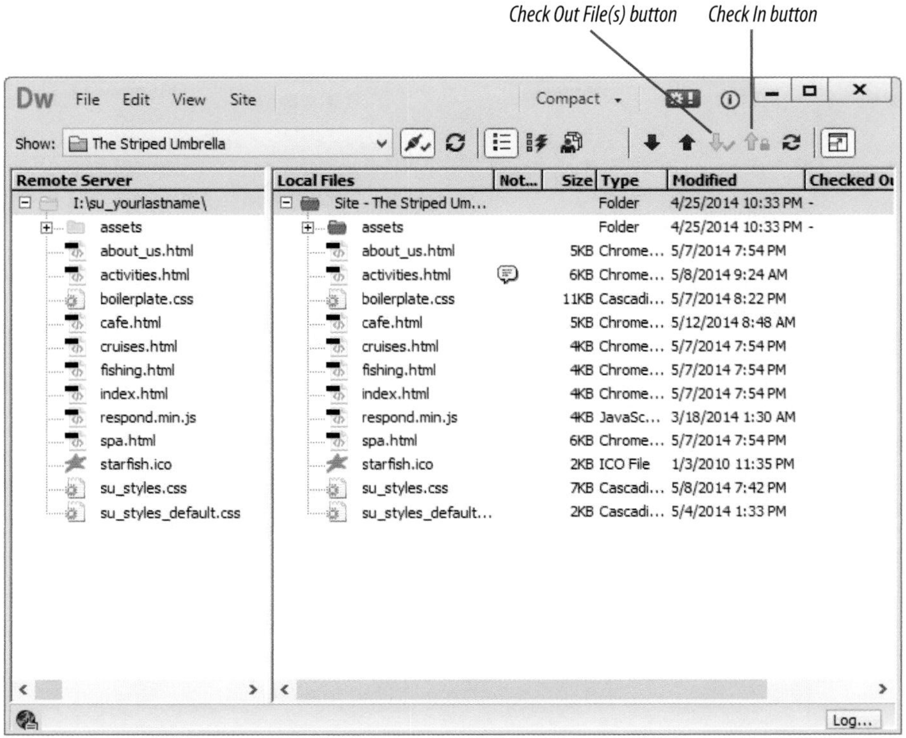

Activate the Enable file check-out feature

1. Change to expanded view in the Files panel, select **Site** on the Menu bar, select **Manage Sites** to open the Manage Sites dialog box, select **The Striped Umbrella** in the list if necessary, then select the **Edit the currently selected site button** ✎ to open the Site Setup for The Striped Umbrella dialog box.

2. Select **Servers**, select your remote server, select the **Edit existing Server button** ✎ , select the **Advanced tab**, then select the **Enable file check-out check box**.

3. Check the **Check out files when opening check box**, if necessary.

4. Type your name in the Check-out Name text box.

5. Type your email address in the Email Address text box.

6. Compare your screen to Figure 29, select **Save** to close the open dialog box, select **Save** to close the Site Setup for The Striped Umbrella dialog box, then select **Done** to close the Manage Sites dialog box.

You used the Site Definition for The Striped Umbrella dialog box to enable the Check Out feature, which tells team members when you are working with a site file.

Figure 29 *Enabling the Check Out feature*

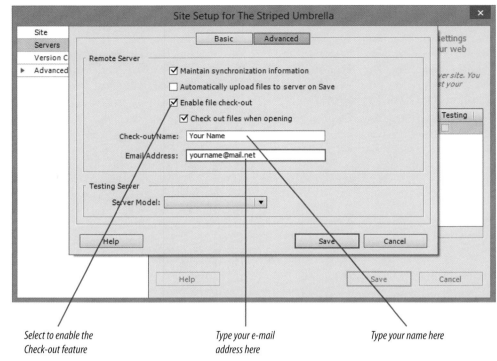

Select to enable the Check-out feature

Type your e-mail address here

Type your name here

Figure 30 *Files panel in Local view after checking out cafe page*

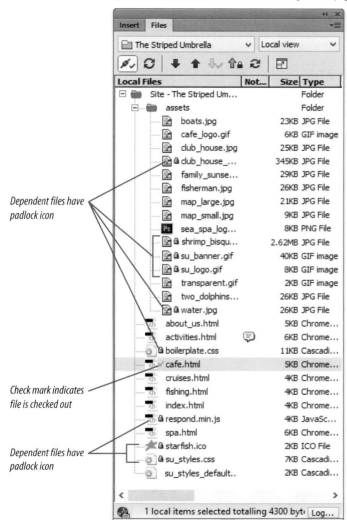

Dependent files have padlock icon

Check mark indicates file is checked out

Dependent files have padlock icon

Check out a file

1. Select the **cafe page** in the Local Files list in the Files panel.

2. Select the **Check Out File(s) button** on the Files panel toolbar.

   The Dependent Files dialog box appears, asking if you want to include all files that are needed for the cafe page.

3. Select **Yes**, expand the assets folder if necessary in the local site files, select the **Collapse to show only local or remote site button**, select the **View list arrow**, select **Local view** if necessary, then compare your screen to Figure 30.

   The cafe file has a check mark next to it indicating you have checked it out. The dependent files have a padlock icon, indicating that they cannot be changed as long as the cafe file is checked out.

You checked out the cafe page so that no one else can use it while you work on it.

Check in a file

1. Open the cafe page, change the closing hour for The Cabana in the table to **8:00 p.m.**, then save your changes.

2. Close the cafe page, then select the **cafe page** in the Files panel.

3. Select the **Check In button** 🔒 on the Files panel toolbar.

   The Dependent Files dialog box opens, asking if you want to include dependent files.

4. Select **Yes**, select another file in the Files panel to deselect the cafe page, then compare your screen to Figure 31.

   A padlock icon appears instead of a green check mark next to the cafe page on the Files panel. The padlock icon indicated that the file is read-only now and cannot be edited unless it is checked out.

You made a content change on the cafe page, then checked in the cafe page, making it available for others to check it out.

Figure 31 *Files panel after checking in cafe page*

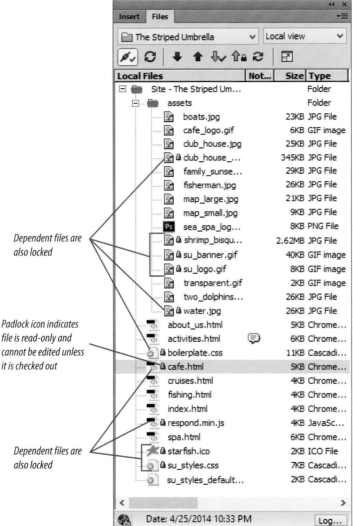

Dependent files are also locked

Padlock icon indicates file is read-only and cannot be edited unless it is checked out

Dependent files are also locked

Figure 32 *Files panel after turning off the read-only feature*

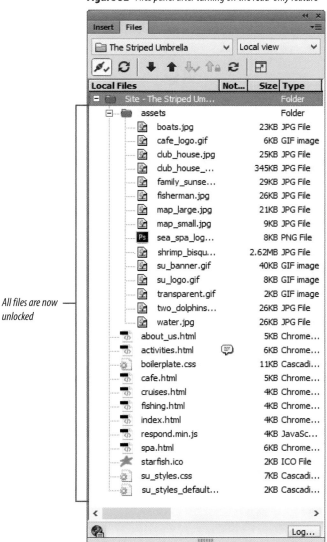

All files are now unlocked

Edit site preferences

1. Select **Site** on the Menu bar, select **Manage Sites** to open the Manage Sites dialog box, select **The Striped Umbrella** in the list, then select the **Edit the currently selected site button** ✐ to open the Site Setup for The Striped Umbrella dialog box.

2. Select **Servers**, select your remote server, select the **Edit existing Server button** ✐, select the **Advanced tab**, then deselect the **Enable file check-out check box**.

   Now that you understand how to use this feature, it will be easier to have this option turned off so that each time you open a page you will not have to check it out the next time you use it.

3. Select **Save** to close the open dialog box, select **Save** to close the Site Setup dialog box, then select **Done** to close the Manage Sites dialog box.

4. Right-click the **local site folder** in the Files panel, then select **Turn off Read Only** (Win) or **Unlock** (Mac).

   All files are writeable now and the padlock icons have disappeared, as shown in Figure 32.

You disabled the Enable file check-out feature and then turned off the Read-only feature for all site files.

Cloak
FILES

What You'll Do

Local Files	Not...	Size	Type
Site - The Striped Um...			Folder
assets			Folder
boats.jpg		23KB	JPG File
cafe_logo.gif		6KB	GIF image
club_house.jpg		25KB	JPG File
club_house_...		345KB	JPG File
family_sunse...		29KB	JPG File
fisherman.jpg		26KB	JPG File
map_large.jpg		21KB	JPG File
map_small.jpg		9KB	JPG File
sea_spa_log...		8KB	PNG File
shrimp_bisqu...		2.62MB	JPG File
su_banner.gif		40KB	GIF image
su_logo.gif		8KB	GIF image
transparent.gif		2KB	GIF image
two_dolphins...		26KB	JPG File
water.jpg		26KB	JPG File

In this lesson, you will cloak the assets folder so that it is excluded from various operations, such as the Put, Get, Check In, and Check Out commands. You will also use the Site Setup dialog box to cloak all .gif files in the site.

Understanding Cloaking Files

There may be times when you want to exclude a particular file or files from being uploaded to a server. For instance, suppose you have a page that is not quite finished and needs more work before it is ready to be viewed by others. You can exclude such files by **cloaking** them, which marks them for exclusion from several commands, including Put, Get, Synchronize, Check In, and Check Out. Cloaked files are also excluded from site-wide operations, such as checking for links or updating a template or library item. You can cloak a folder or specify a type of file to cloak throughout the site.

Cloaking a Folder

In addition to cloaking a file or group of files, you might also want to cloak an entire folder. For example, if you are not concerned with replacing outdated image files, you might want to cloak the assets folder of a website to save time when synchronizing files. To cloak a folder, select the folder, select the Files panel Options button, point to Site, point to Cloaking, and then select Cloak. The folder you cloaked and all the files it contains appear with red slashes across them, as shown in Figure 33. To uncloak a folder, select the Panel options button on the Files panel, point to Site, point to Cloaking, and then select Uncloak.

QUICK TIP

To uncloak all files in a site, select the Files Panel options button, point to Site, point to Cloaking, then select Uncloak All.

Cloaking Selected File Types

There may be times when you want to cloak a particular type of file, such as a JPG file.

To cloak a particular file type, open the Site Setup dialog box, select Advanced Settings, select Cloaking, select the Cloak files ending with check box, and then type a file extension in the text box below the check box. All files throughout the site that have the specified file extension will be cloaked.

Figure 33 *Cloaked assets folder in the Files panel*

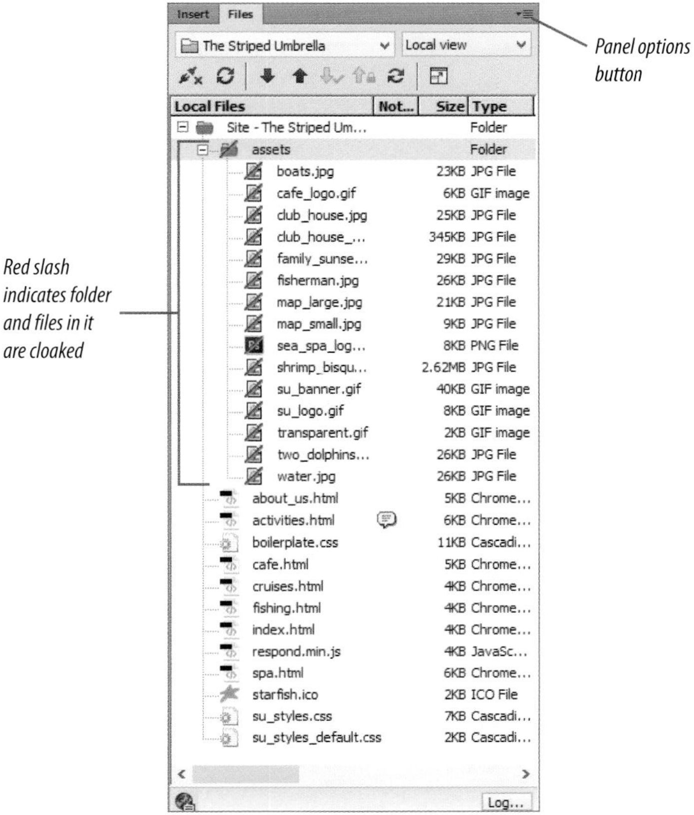

Panel options button

Red slash indicates folder and files in it are cloaked

Cloak and uncloak a folder

1. Verify that Local view is displayed in the Files panel, then open the Manage Sites dialog box.

2. Select **The Striped Umbrella** if necessary, select the **Edit the currently selected site button** ✐ to open the Site Setup for The Striped Umbrella dialog box, select **Advanced Settings**, select **Cloaking**, verify that the Enable Cloaking check box is checked, select **Save**, then select **Done**.

3. Expand and select the **assets folder** in the Files panel, select the **Files Panel options button** ▾≡, point to **Site**, point to **Cloaking**, select **Cloak**, then compare your screen to Figure 34.

   A red slash now appears on top of the assets folder in the Files panel, indicating that all files in the assets folder are cloaked and will be excluded from putting, getting, checking in, checking out, and many other operations.

TIP You can also cloak a folder by right-clicking (Win) or [control]-clicking (Mac) the folder, pointing to Cloaking, then selecting Cloak.

4. Right-click (Win) or [control]-click (Mac) the **assets folder**, point to **Cloaking**, then select **Uncloak**.

   The assets folder and all the files it contains no longer appear with red slashes across them, indicating they are no longer cloaked.

You cloaked the assets folder so that this folder and all the files it contains would be excluded from many operations, including uploading and downloading files. You then uncloaked the assets folder.

Figure 34 *Assets folder after cloaking*

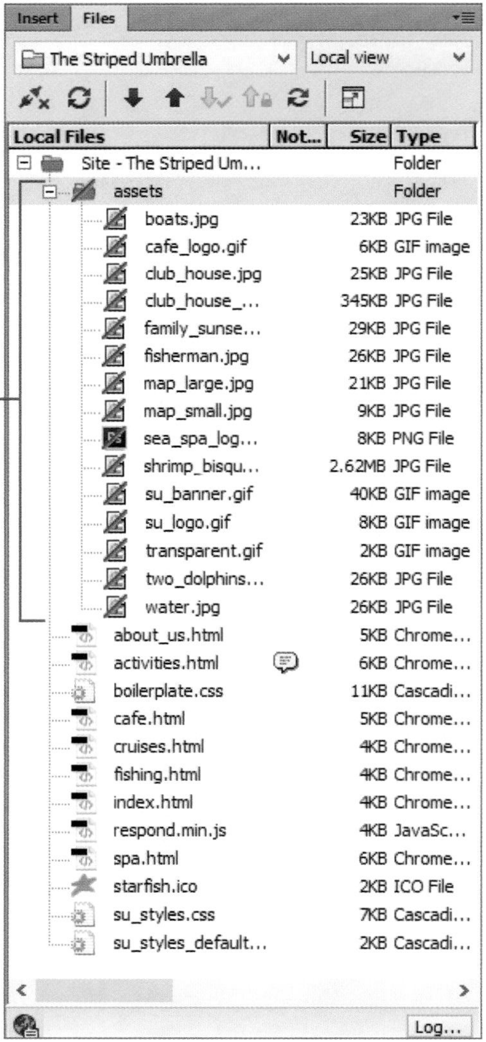

Red slashes indicate folder and files in it are cloaked

Figure 35 *Specifying a file type to cloak*

Site Setup for The Striped Umbrella ✕

| Site |
| Servers |
| Version Control |
| ▼ Advanced Settings |
| Local Info |
| Cloaking |
| Design Notes |
| File View Columns |

Cloaking lets you exclude specified folders and files from all site operations.

☑ Enable Cloaking

  ☑ Cloak files ending with:

  | .gif |

Specify file type
to cloak here

Figure 36 *assets folder in Files panel after cloaking .gif files*

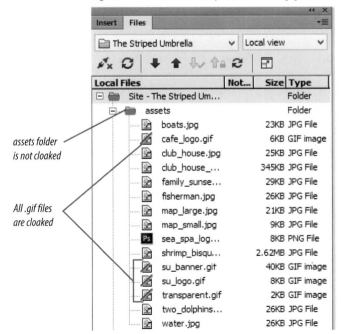

assets folder
is not cloaked

All .gif files
are cloaked

Cloak selected file types

1. Right-click (Win) or [control]-click (Mac) the **assets folder** in the Files panel, point to **Cloaking**, then select **Settings** to open the Site Setup for The Striped Umbrella dialog box with the Cloaking category selected.

2. Select the **Cloak files ending with check box**, select the text in the text box that appears, type **.gif** in the text box, then compare your screen to Figure 35.

3. Select **Save**.

   A dialog box opens, indicating that the site cache will be recreated.

4. Select **OK**, expand the assets folder if necessary, then compare your screen to Figure 36.

   All of the .gif files in the assets folder appear with red slashes across them, indicating that they are cloaked. Notice that the assets folder is not cloaked.

5. Select the **local site folder** in the Files panel, right-click, point to **Cloaking**, select **Uncloak All**, then select **Yes** to close the warning message.

   All files are uncloaked now and will not be excluded from any site commands.

You cloaked all the .gif files in The Striped Umbrella website. You then uncloaked all files.

Import and Export
A SITE DEFINITION

What You'll Do

In this lesson, you will export the site definition file for The Striped Umbrella website. You will then import The Striped Umbrella website.

Exporting a Site Definition

When you work on a website for a long time, it's likely that at some point you will want to move it to another machine or share it with other collaborators who will help you maintain it. When you move a site, you need to move its site definition. The **site definition** for a website contains important information about the site, including its URL, preferences that you've specified, and other secure information, such as login and password information. You can use the Export command to export the site definition file to another location. The Export command creates a file with an .ste file extension. To do this, open the Manage Sites dialog box, select the site you want to export, and then select Export currently selected site. Because the site definition file contains password information that you will want to keep secret from other site users, you should never save the site definition file in the website. Instead, save it in an external folder.

Importing a Site Definition

If you want to be able to access the site settings in a website that someone else has created, you can import the site definition file once you have the necessary .ste file. To do this, select Import Site in the Manage Sites dialog box to open the Import Site dialog box, navigate to the .ste file you want to import, then select Open.

Figure 37 *Saving The Striped Umbrella.ste file in the su_site_definition folder*

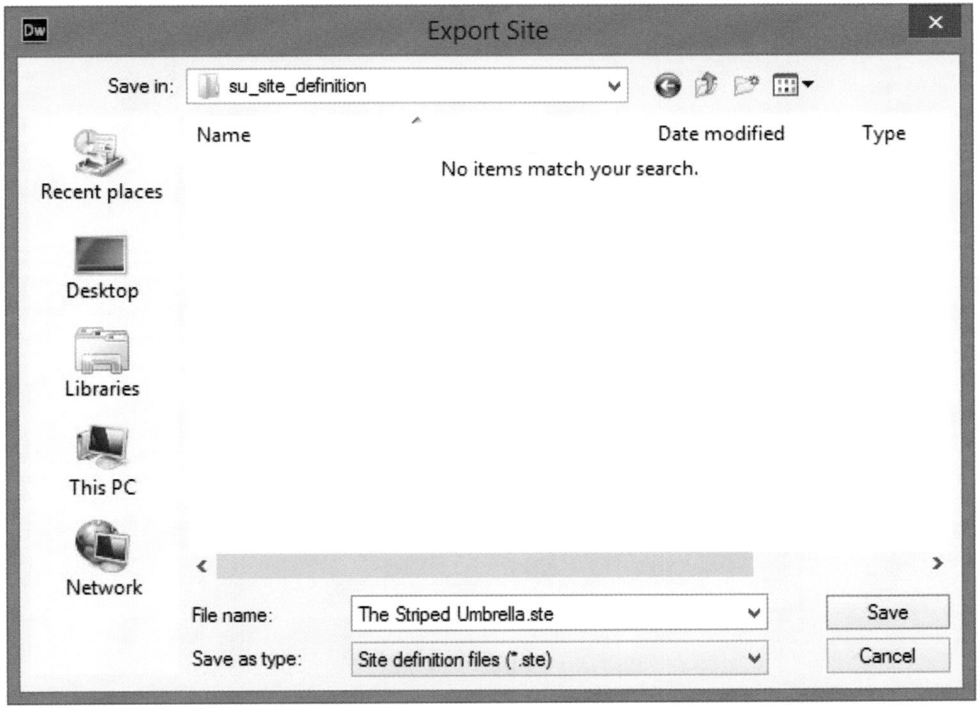

Export a site definition

1. Use File Explorer (Win) or Finder (Mac) to create a new folder on your hard drive or external drive named **su_site_definition**.

2. Switch back to Dreamweaver, open the Manage Sites dialog box, select **The Striped Umbrella**, then select the **Export the currently selected site(s) button** ⬚ to open the Export Site dialog box.

   TIP If you see a message asking if you are exporting the site to back up your settings or to share your settings with other users, choose the Back up my settings option, then select OK.

3. Navigate to and double-click to open the **su_site_definition folder** that you created in Step 1, as shown in Figure 37, select **Save**, then select **Done**.

You used the Export command to create the site definition file and saved it in the su_site_definition folder.

Import a site definition

1. Open the Manage Sites dialog box, select **The Striped Umbrella**, then select **Import Site** to open the Import Site dialog box.

2. Navigate to the su_site_definition folder, compare your screen to Figure 38, select **The Striped Umbrella.ste**, then select **Open**.

   A dialog box opens and says that a site named The Striped Umbrella already exists. It will name the imported site The Striped Umbrella 2 so that it has a different name.

3. Select **OK**.

4. Select **The Striped Umbrella 2** if necessary, select the **Edit the currently selected site(s) button** , then compare your screen to Figure 39.

   The settings show that The Striped Umbrella 2 site has the same local site folder and default images folder as The Striped Umbrella site. Both of these settings are specified in The Striped Umbrella.ste file that you imported. Importing a site in this way makes it possible for multiple users with different computers to work on the same site.

   TIP Make sure you know who is responsible for which files to keep from overwriting the wrong files when they are published. The Synchronize Files and Check In/Check Out features are good procedures to use with multiple designers.

5. Select **Save**, select **OK** to close the warning message, then select **Done**.

   TIP If a dialog box opens warning that the local site folder chosen is the same as the folder for the site "The Striped Umbrella," select OK. Remember that you only import the site settings when you import a site definition. You are not importing any of the website files.

You imported The Striped Umbrella.ste file and created a new site, The Striped Umbrella 2.

Figure 38 *Import Site dialog box*

Figure 39 *Site Definition for The Striped Umbrella 2 dialog box*

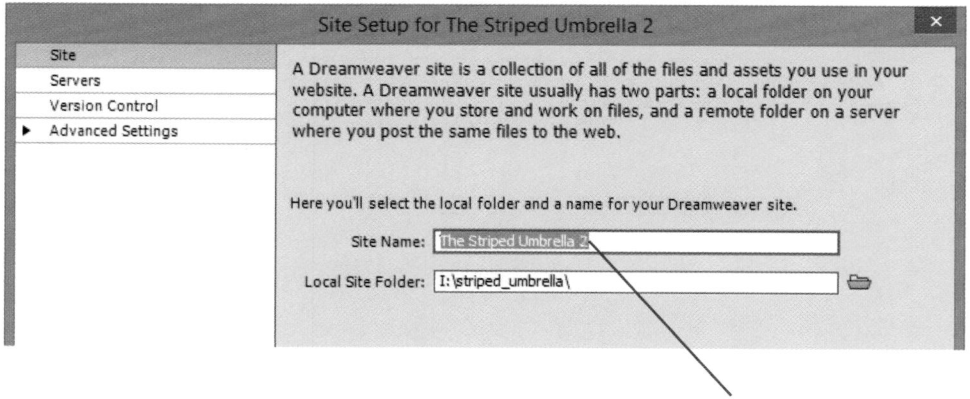

Name of imported site

Figure 40 *Viewing The Striped Umbrella 2 website files*

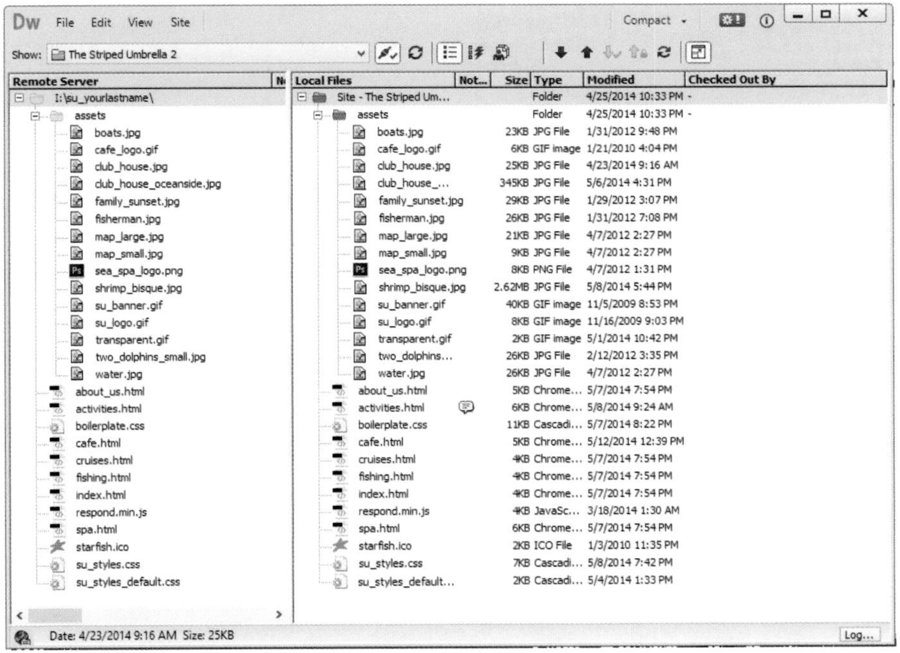

POWER USER SHORTCUTS	
To do this:	**Use this shortcut:**
Get	[Ctrl][Shift][D] (Win) or ⌘ [Shift][D] (Mac)
Check Out	[Ctrl][Alt][Shift][D] (Win) or ⌘ [opt] [Shift][D] (Mac)
Put	[Ctrl][Shift][U] (Win) or ⌘ [Shift][U] (Mac)
Check In	[Ctrl][Alt][Shift][U] (Win) or ⌘ [opt] [Shift][U] (Mac)
Check Links Sitewide	[Ctrl][F8] (Win) or [fn] ⌘ [F8] (Mac)

© 2015 Cengage Learning®

View the imported site

1. Select the **Expand to show local and remote sites button** on the Files panel toolbar to expand the Files panel.

2. Select the **Refresh button** to view the files in the Remote Site pane.

   As shown in Figure 40, the site is identical to the original The Striped Umbrella site, except the name has been changed to The Striped Umbrella 2.

3. Expand the local site folder in the Local Files pane to view the contents, if necessary.

   TIP If you don't see your remote site files, select the Connect to Remote Server button.

4. Select the **Collapse to show only local or remote site button** to collapse the Files panel.

5. Open the Manage Sites dialog box, verify that The Striped Umbrella 2 site is selected, select the **Delete the currently selected site(s) button** —, select **Yes** in the warning dialog box, then select **Done** to close the dialog box.

   This does not delete all of the files that were created; it only removes the site from Dreamweaver's site management list.

6. Close all open pages, then close Dreamweaver.

You viewed the expanded Files panel for The Striped Umbrella 2 website, then deleted The Striped Umbrella 2 website.

Evaluate Web Content FOR LEGAL USE

What You'll Do

Source: Library of Congress

In this lesson, you will examine copyright issues in the context of using content gathered from sources such as the Internet.

Can I Use Downloaded Media?

The Internet has made it possible to locate compelling and media-rich content to use in websites. A person who has learned to craft searches can locate a multitude of interesting objects, such as graphics, animations, sounds, and text. But just because you can find it easily does not mean that you can use it however you want or under any circumstance. Learning about copyright law can help you decide whether or how to use content created and published by someone other than yourself.

Understanding Intellectual Property

Intellectual property is a product resulting from human creativity. It can include inventions, movies, songs, designs, clothing, and so on.

The purpose of copyright law is to promote progress in society, not expressly to protect the rights of copyright owners. However, the vast majority of work you might want to download and use in a project is protected by either copyright or trademark law.

Copyright protects the particular and tangible *expression* of an idea, not the idea itself.

If you wrote a story using the idea of aliens crashing in Roswell, New Mexico, no one could copy or use your story without permission. However, anyone could write a story using a similar plot or characters— the *idea* of aliens crashing in Roswell is not copyright-protected. Generally, copyright lasts for the life of the author plus 70 years.

Trademark protects an image, word, slogan, symbol, or design used to identify goods or services. For example, the Nike swoosh, Disney characters, or the shape of a classic Coca-Cola bottle are works protected by trademark. Trademark protection lasts for 10 years with 10-year renewal terms, lasting indefinitely provided the trademark is in active use.

What Exactly Does the Copyright Owner Own?

Copyright attaches to a work as soon as you create it; you do not have to register it with the U.S. Copyright Office. A copyright owner has a "bundle" of six rights, consisting of:

1) reproduction (including downloading)
2) creation of **derivative works** (for example, a movie version of a book)
3) distribution to the public

4) public performance
5) public display
6) public performance by digital audio transmission of sound recordings

By default, only a copyright holder can create a derivative work of his or her original by transforming or adapting it.

Understanding Fair Use

The law builds in limitations to copyright protection. One limitation to copyright is **fair use**. Fair use allows limited use of copyright-protected work. For example, you could excerpt short passages of a film or song for a class project or parody a television show. Determining if fair use applies to a work depends on the *purpose* of its use, the *nature* of the copyrighted work, *how much* you want to copy, and the *effect* on the market or value of the work. However, there is no clear formula on what constitutes fair use. It is always decided on a case-by-case basis.

How Do I Use Work Properly?

Being a student doesn't mean you can use any amount of any work for class. On the other hand, the very nature of education means you need to be able to use or reference different work in your studies. There are many situations that allow you to use protected work.

In addition to applying a fair use argument, you can obtain permission, pay a fee, use work that does not have copyright protection, or use work that has a flexible copyright

license, where the owner has given the public permission to use the work in certain ways. For more information about open-access licensing, visit creativecommons.org. Work that is no longer protected by copyright is in the **public domain**; anyone can use it however they wish for any purpose. In general, the photos and other media on Federal government websites are in the public domain.

Understanding Licensing Agreements

Before you decide whether to use media you find on a website, you must decide whether you can comply with its licensing agreement.

A **licensing agreement** is the permission given by a copyright holder that conveys the right to use the copyright holder's work under certain conditions.

Websites have rules that govern how a user may use its text and media, known as **terms of use**. Figures 41, 42, and 43 are great examples of clear terms of use for the Library of Congress website.

A site's terms of use do not override your right to apply fair use. Also, someone cannot compile public domain images in a website and then claim they own them or dictate how

Figure 41 *Library of Congress home page*

Link to legal information regarding the use of content on the website

Source: Library of Congress

the images can be used. Conversely, someone can erroneously state in their terms of use that you can use work on the site freely, but they may not know the work's copyright status. The burden is on you to research the veracity of anyone claiming you can use work.

Obtaining Permission or a License

The **permissions process** is specific to what you want to use (text, photographs, music, trademarks, merchandise, and so on) and how you want to use it (school term paper, personal website, fabric pattern). How you want to use the work determines the level and scope of permissions you need to secure. The fundamentals, however, are the same. Your request should contain the following:

- Your full name, address, and complete contact information.
- A specific description of your intended use. Sometimes including a sketch, storyboard, wireframe, or link to a website is helpful.
- A signature line for the copyright holder.
- A target date when you would like the copyright holder to respond. This can be important if you're working under deadline.

Posting a Copyright Notice

The familiar © symbol or "Copyright" is no longer required to indicate copyright, nor does it automatically register your work, but it does serve a useful purpose. When you post or publish it, you are stating clearly to those who may not know anything about copyright law that this work is claimed by you and is not in the public domain. Your case is made even stronger if someone violates your copyright

Figure 42 *Library of Congress website legal page*

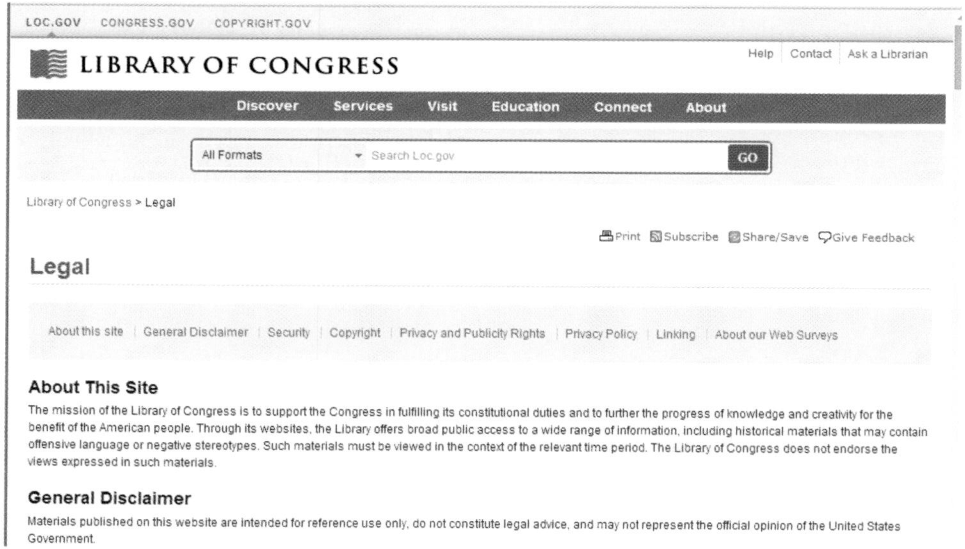

Source: Library of Congress

and your notice is clearly visible. That way, a violator can never claim ignorance of the law as an excuse for infringing. Common notification styles include:

Copyright 2015
Cengage Learning
or
© 2015 Cengage Learning®

Giving proper attribution for text excerpts is a must; giving attribution for media is excellent practice, but is never a substitute for applying a fair use argument, buying a license, or simply getting permission.

You must provide proper citation for materials you incorporate into your own work, such as the following:

References
Waxer, Barbara M., and Baum, Marsha L. 2006. *Internet Surf and Turf—The Essential Guide to Copyright, Fair Use, and Finding Media.* Boston: Thomson Course Technology.

This expectation applies even to unsigned material and material that does not display the copyright symbol (©). Moreover, the expectation applies just as certainly to ideas you summarize or paraphrase as to words you quote verbatim.

Guidelines have been written by the American Psychological Association (APA) to establish an editorial style to be used to present written material. These guidelines

include the way citations are referenced. Here's a list of the elements that make up an APA-style citation of web-based resources:

- Author's name (if known)
- Date of publication or last revision (if known), in parentheses
- Title of document
- Title of complete work or website (if applicable), underlined
- URL

Following is an example of how you would reference the APA Style Home page on the Reference page of your paper:

APA Style.org., from APA Online website, Retrieved from http://www.apastyle.org/index.aspx.

There are APA styles that are used for other sources of text such as magazines, journals, newspaper articles, blogs, and email messages. Here's a list of the elements that make up an APA-style citation of images, sounds, or video:

- Name of the researching organization
- Date of publication
- Caption or description
- Brief explanation of what type of data is there and in what form it appears (shown in brackets)
- Project name and retrieval information.

Another set of guidelines used by many schools and university and commercial presses is the Modern Language Association (MLA) style. For more information, go to mla.org.

Figure 43 *Library of Congress website copyright information*

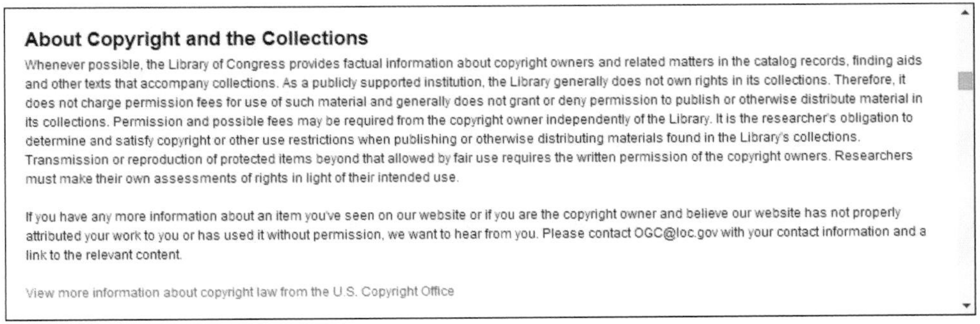

About Copyright and the Collections

Whenever possible, the Library of Congress provides factual information about copyright owners and related matters in the catalog records, finding aids and other texts that accompany collections. As a publicly supported institution, the Library generally does not own rights in its collections. Therefore, it does not charge permission fees for use of such material and generally does not grant or deny permission to publish or otherwise distribute material in its collections. Permission and possible fees may be required from the copyright owner independently of the Library. It is the researcher's obligation to determine and satisfy copyright or other use restrictions when publishing or otherwise distributing materials found in the Library's collections. Transmission or reproduction of protected items beyond that allowed by fair use requires the written permission of the copyright owners. Researchers must make their own assessments of rights in light of their intended use.

If you have any more information about an item you've seen on our website or if you are the copyright owner and believe our website has not properly attributed your work to you or has used it without permission, we want to hear from you. Please contact OGC@loc.gov with your contact information and a link to the relevant content.

View more information about copyright law from the U.S. Copyright Office

Source: Library of Congress

Present a
WEBSITE TO A CLIENT

What You'll Do

In this lesson, you will explore options for presenting a website to a client at the completion of a project.

Are You Ready to Present Your Work?

Before you present a website to a client as a finished project, you should do a final check on some important items. First, do all your final design and development decisions reflect your client's goals and requirements? Does the website not only fulfill your client's goals and requirements, but those of the intended audience as well? Second, did you follow good web development practices? Did you check your pages against your wireframes as you developed them? Did you check each page against current accessibility standards? Did you run all necessary technical tests, such as validating the code, and searching for missing alternate text or missing page titles? Did you verify that all external and internal links work correctly? Third, did your final delivery date and budget meet the timeframe and budget you originally promised the client?

If you find that you did spend more time on the site than you expected to, determine if it was because you underestimated the amount of work it would take, ran into unforeseen technical problems, or because the client changed the requirements or increased the scope of the project as it went

along. If you underestimated the project or ran into unexpected difficulties from causes other than the client, you usually cannot expect the client to make up the difference without a prior agreement. No client wants surprises at the end of a project, so it's best to communicate frequently and let the client know the status of all site elements as you go.

If the client changes the project scope, make sure you discuss the implication of this with the client. Ideally, you have made the client aware of any schedule or budget changes at the time they began to occur, and the client expects that your estimate will grow by a predictable, agreed-upon amount.

Client communication, both at the beginning of a project and throughout a project, is critical to a successful web design and a solid customer relationship. In building a house, a good architect makes an effort to get to know and understand a new client before beginning a house design. The design must be functional and meet the client's checklist of requirements, but it must also fit the client's personality and taste. The final structure must continue to meet those needs; the same is true of a website.

Some clients have a difficult time looking at architectural drawings and visualizing what the home will look like, so architects use different methods to communicate their design. Some use scale mockups, 3-D renderings, or photos of similarly styled homes to help the client visualize what their home will look like when completed. Web designers use similar strategies. You may be capable of building a great website, but you must communicate with the client from the beginning of the project to set and satisfy client expectations. Without this mutual understanding, the project's successful completion will be at risk. It is much less expensive to make changes and adjustments at the beginning of a project, and as changes occur, rather than close to completion. Communication is key.

What Is the Best Way to Present Your Work?

Ideally, you presented some form of prototype of the website at the beginning of the development process. You may have chosen to use low-fidelity wireframes such as one created in Microsoft PowerPoint or Adobe Photoshop. Or you may have used a high-fidelity wireframe that is interactive and multidimensional such as OverSight, ProtoShare, or WireframeSketcher, as shown in Figure 44. To communicate with your client and ensure a mutual understanding of the project, you could also use **BaseCamp**, a web-based project collaboration tool that many companies use. There is a monthly fee for using it, based on the number of projects you are running and your storage needs. You can use BaseCamp throughout the project cycle, not just at the end. To present the final project, consider publishing the site to a server and sending the client a link to view the completed website. Creating PDFs of the site and sending them to the client for approval is another possible method.

Another communication option is to invite the client to your office and do a full walkthrough of the site with them, which offers them a chance to ask questions. This is probably one of the best options if it is feasible. If you have taken the time to build a relationship of trust over the project, neither side should expect unpleasant surprises at the end.

Figure 44 *WireframeSketcher website*

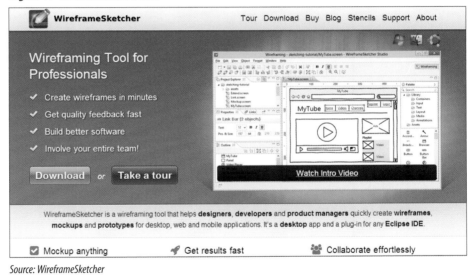

Source: WireframeSketcher

Perform website maintenance.

1. Open the Blooms & Bulbs website, then re-create the site cache.
2. Use the Link Checker panel to check for broken links, then fix any broken links that appear.
3. Use the Link Checker to check for orphaned files. If any orphaned files appear in the report, take steps to link them to appropriate pages or decide if you need to remove them.
4. Run an Untitled Documents report for the entire local site. If the report lists any pages that have no titles, add page titles to the untitled pages, and edit any titles if they seem incomplete. Run the report again to verify that all pages have page titles.
5. Run a report to look for missing alternate text. Add alternate text to any graphics that need it, then run the report again to verify that all images contain alternate text.
6. Submit the bb_styles.css file for CSS3 validation and correct any errors that are found.
7. Validate the workshops page for HTML5 markup and correct any errors that are found.
8. Verify that the Design Notes preference is enabled and add a Design Note to the workshops page as follows: **Shoot a video of the hanging baskets class to add to the page**. Add the status **needs attention**, add the current date, and check the Show when file is opened option.

Publish a website and transfer files.

1. Set up web server access for the Blooms & Bulbs website on an FTP server or a local/network server (whichever is available to you) using **blooms_yourlastname** as the remote folder name.
2. View the Blooms & Bulbs remote site in the Files panel.
3. Upload the water_lily.jpg file to the remote site, then view the remote site.
4. Add the code that links the favicon to the head content of any pages in the site that do not have it.
5. Synchronize all files in the Blooms & Bulbs website, so that all files from the local site are uploaded to the remote site.

Check files out and in.

1. Enable the Enable file check-out feature.
2. Check out the plants page and all dependent pages.
3. Open the plants page, change the heading to **"Featured Spring Plants: Roses, Roses, Roses!"**, then save the file.
4. Check in the plants page and all dependent files.
5. Disable the Enable file check-out feature.
6. Turn off Read Only (Win) or Unlock (Mac) for the entire site.

Cloak files.

1. Verify that cloaking is enabled in the Blooms & Bulbs website.
2. Cloak the assets folder, then uncloak it.
3. Cloak all the JPG files in the Blooms & Bulbs website, then expand the assets folder if necessary to view the cloaked files in the Files panel.
4. Uncloak the JPG files.

Import and export a site definition.

1. Create a new folder named **blooms_site_definition** on your hard drive or external drive.
2. Export the Blooms & Bulbs site definition to the blooms_site_definition folder.
3. Import the Blooms & Bulbs site definition to create a new site called **Blooms & Bulbs 2**.
4. Make sure that all files from the Blooms & Bulbs website appear in the Files panel for the imported site, then compare your screen to Figure 45.
5. Remove the Blooms & Bulbs 2 site.
6. Close all open files.

Figure 45 *Completed Skills Review*

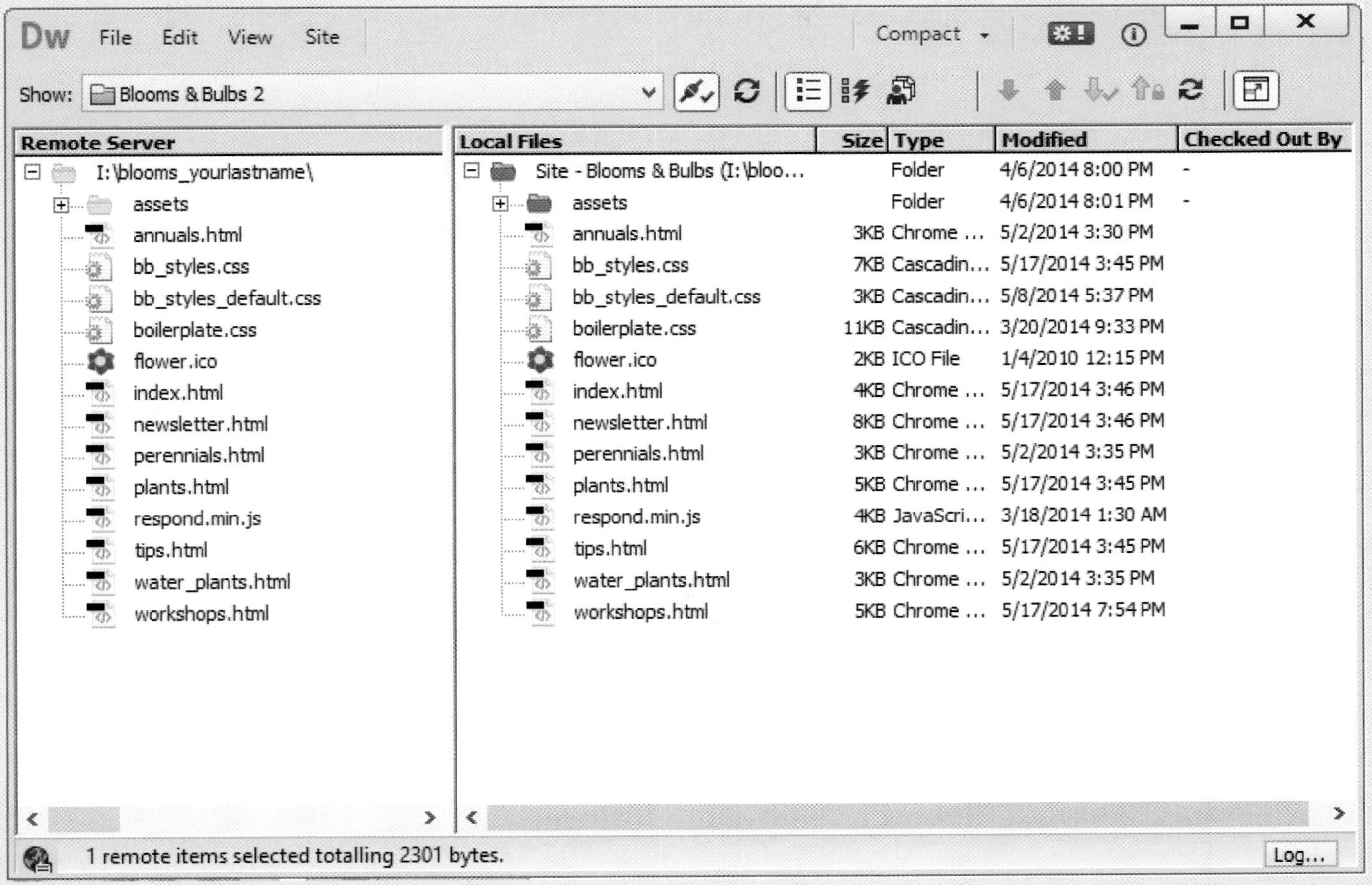

In this Project Builder, you publish the TripSmart website that you have developed throughout this book to a local/network folder. Thomas Howard, the owner, has asked that you publish the site to a local folder as a backup location. You first run several reports on the site, specify the remote settings for the site, upload files to the remote site, check files out and in, and cloak files. Finally, you export and import the site definition.

1. Use the TripSmart website that you began in Project Builder 1 in Chapter 1 and developed in previous chapters.
2. Use the Link Checker panel to check for broken links, then fix any broken links that appear.
3. Use the Link Checker to check for orphaned files. If any orphaned files appear in the report, take steps to link them to appropriate pages or remove them.
4. Evaluate your colors in your site. Do they work together to create an attractive design?
5. Run an Untitled Documents report for the entire local site. If the report lists any pages that lack titles, add page titles to the untitled pages. Run the report again to verify that all pages have page titles.
6. Run a report to look for missing alternate text. Add alternate text to any graphics that need it, then run the report again to verify that all images contain alternate text.
7. Submit the tripsmart_styles.css file for CSS3 validation and correct any errors that are found.
8. Validate the catalog page for HTML5 markup and correct any errors that are found.

9. Enable the Design Notes preference, if necessary, and add a design note to the Argentina page as follows: **Add a video of the glacier in Patagonia.** Add the current date, the status **needs attention** and check the Show when file is opened option. Turn on the Show Notes feature in the Files View Columns dialog box.
10. If you did not do so in Project Builder 1 in Chapter 1, use the Site Definition dialog box to set up web server access for a remote site using a local or network folder.
11. Upload the index page and all dependent files to the remote site.
12. View the remote site to make sure that all files uploaded correctly.
13. Add the code that links the favicon to the head content of any pages in the site that do not have it.
14. Synchronize the files so that all other files on the local TripSmart site are uploaded to the remote site.

15. Enable the Enable file check-out feature.
16. Check out the index page in the local site and all dependent files.
17. Open the index page, close the index page, then check in the index page and all dependent pages.
18. Disable the Enable file check-out feature, then turn off the read-only status (Win) or unlock (Mac) for the entire site.
19. Cloak all JPG files in the website.
20. Export the site definition to a new folder named **tripsmart_site_definition**.
21. Import the TripSmart.ste file to create a new site named TripSmart 2.
22. Expand the assets folder in the Files panel if necessary, then compare your screen to Figure 46.
23. Remove the TripSmart 2 site.
24. Uncloak all files in the TripSmart site, then close any open files.

Figure 46 *Sample completed Project Builder 1*

In this Project Builder, you finish your work on the Carolyne's Creations website. You are ready to publish the website to a remote server and transfer all the files from the local site to the remote site. First, you run several reports to make sure the website is in good shape. Next, you enable the Enable file check-out feature so that other staff members may collaborate on the site. Finally, you export and import the site definition file.

1. Use the Carolyne's Creations website that you began in Project Builder 1 in Chapter 1 and developed in previous chapters.

2. If you did not do so in Project Builder 2 in Chapter 1, use the Site Definition dialog box to set up web server access for a remote site using either an FTP site or a local or network folder.

3. Run reports for broken links and orphaned files, correcting any errors that you find.

4. Run reports for untitled documents and missing alt text, correcting any errors that you find.

5. Submit the cc_styles.css file for CSS3 validation and correct any errors that are found.

6. Validate the catering page for HTML5 markup and correct any errors that are found.

7. Upload the classes.html page and all dependent files to the remote site.

8. View the remote site to make sure that all files uploaded correctly.

9. Synchronize the files so that all other files on the local Carolyne's Creations site are uploaded to the remote site.

10. Enable the Enable file check-out feature.

11. Check out the classes page and all its dependent files.

12. Open the classes page, then change the price of the adult class to **$45.00**.

13. Save your changes, close the page, then check in the classes page and all dependent pages.

14. Disable the Enable file check-out feature, then turn off read only for the entire site.

15. Export the site definition to a new folder named **cc_site_definition**.

16. Import the Carolyne's Creations.ste file to create a new site named Carolyne's Creations 2.

17. Expand the local site folder in the Files panel if necessary, compare your screen to Figure 47, then remove the Carolyne's Creations2 site.

Figure 47 *Sample completed Project Builder 2*

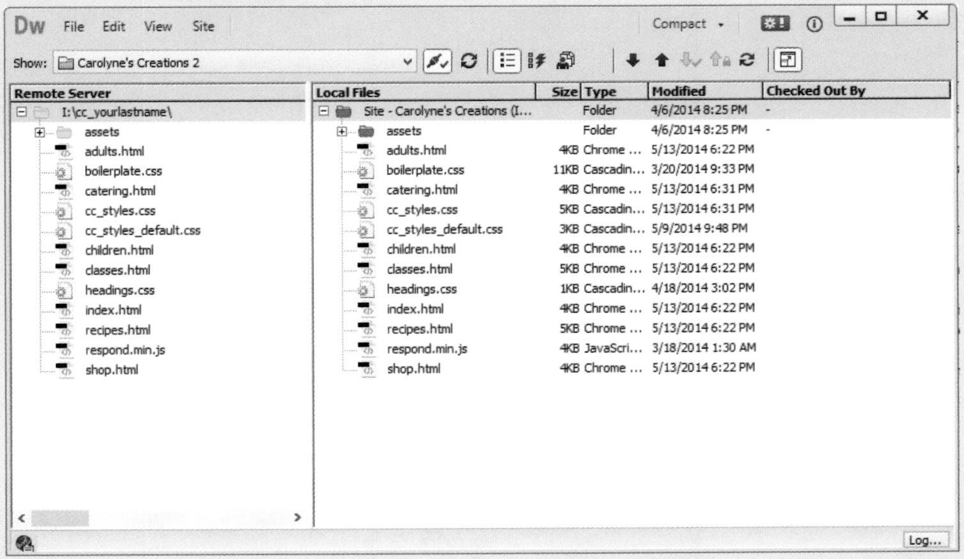

Throughout this book you have used Dreamweaver to create and develop several websites that contain different elements, many of which are found in popular commercial websites. For instance, Figure 48 shows the National Science Foundation website. This website contains many types of interactive elements, such as image maps and rollovers—all of which you learned to create in this book.

1. Connect to the Internet, then go to the National Science Foundation at www.nsf.gov.
2. Spend some time exploring the pages of this site to familiarize yourself with its elements.
3. Type a list of all the elements in this site that you have learned how to create in this book. After each item, write a short description of where and how the element is used in the site.
4. Select the link for the Site Map in the menu bar at the bottom of the page. Describe the information provided with the site map.
5. Select the Text Only Version and View Mobile Site links at the very bottom of the page. Describe what happens when you select each link.
6. Print the home page and one or two other pages that contain some of the elements you described and attach it to your list.

Figure 48 *Design Project*

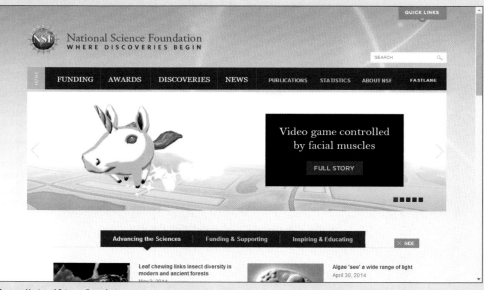

Source: National Science Foundation

In this project, you will finish your work on the website that you created and developed throughout this book. You publish your site to a remote server or local or network folder.

1. Before you begin the process of publishing your website to a remote server, make sure that it is ready for public viewing. Use Figure 49 to assist you in making sure your website is complete. If you find problems, make the necessary changes to finalize the site.

2. Decide where to publish your site. The folder where you will publish your site can be either an FTP site or a local/network folder. If you are publishing to an FTP site, be sure to write down all the information you will need to publish to the site, including the URL of the FTP host, the directory on the FTP server where you will publish your local site folder, and the login and password information.

3. Use the Site Setup dialog box to specify the remote settings for the site using the information that was decided upon in Step 2.

4. Transfer one of the pages and its dependent files to the remote site, then view the remote site to make sure the appropriate files were transferred.

5. Synchronize the files so that all the remaining local pages and dependent files are uploaded to the remote site.

6. Enable the Enable file check-out feature.

7. Check out one of the pages. Open the checked-out page, make a change to it, save the change, close the page, then check the page back in.

8. Cloak a particular file type.

9. Export the site definition for the site to a new folder on your hard drive or on an external drive.

10. Close any open pages, then exit Dreamweaver.

Figure 49 *Portfolio Project*

Website Checklist

1. Are you satisfied with the content and appearance of every page?
2. Are all paths for all links and images correct?
3. Does each page have a title?
4. Does the stylesheet pass CSS3 validation?
5. Do all images have appropriate alternate text?
6. Have you eliminated any orphaned files?
7. Have you deleted any unnecessary files?
8. Have you viewed all pages using at least two different browsers and three different screen sizes?
9. Does the home page have keywords and a description?
10. Is all text based on a CSS style?

CHAPTER 8 USING STYLES AND STYLE SHEETS FOR DESIGN

1. Create and use embedded styles
2. Modify embedded styles
3. Use Live view and Inspect Mode
4. Work with conflicting styles

DREAMWEAVER

CHAPTER 8

USING STYLES AND STYLE SHEETS
FOR DESIGN

Introduction

In Chapter 3, you learned how to create, apply, and edit Cascading Style Sheets. Using CSS is the best and most powerful way to ensure that all elements in a website are formatted consistently. The advantage of using CSS is that all of your formatting rules can be kept in a separate or **external style sheet** file, so that you can change the appearance of every page to which the style sheet is attached by modifying the style sheet file. For example, suppose your external style sheet contains a style called headings that is applied to all top-level headings in all your website pages. If you want to change the heading color to blue, you simply change that rule's color value to blue, and all headings in the website are updated instantly. This type of rule that affects all website content is called a **global CSS rule**. With Fluid Grid layouts, global rules format all website content for mobile, tablet, and desktop sizes unless the rules are modified for the tablet or desktop device sizes.

You can also create **embedded styles**, which are internal styles whose code is located within the head section of the HTML code of a web page. The advantage of embedded styles is that you can use them to override an external style. For instance, if all headings in your website are blue because the external style applied to them specifies blue as the color value, you could change the color of those headings on a single page to a different color by creating and applying an embedded style that specifies a different color as the color attribute. In general, you should use embedded styles for small formatting changes or for content that needs specific formatting, rather than to format all the pages of a website. Keeping formatting rules in a separate file from the web page content reduces the overall file sizes of your pages. As you develop your site's content, it's good practice to format most of your page content using external style sheets, rather than embedded styles in individual pages.

In this chapter, you will create and apply embedded styles and work with some Dreamweaver tools to view and edit your style sheets.

want to go home!

p | .contact_info | +

The Striped Umbrella
25 Beachside Drive
Ft. Eugene, Florida 33775
555-594-9458
Club Manager

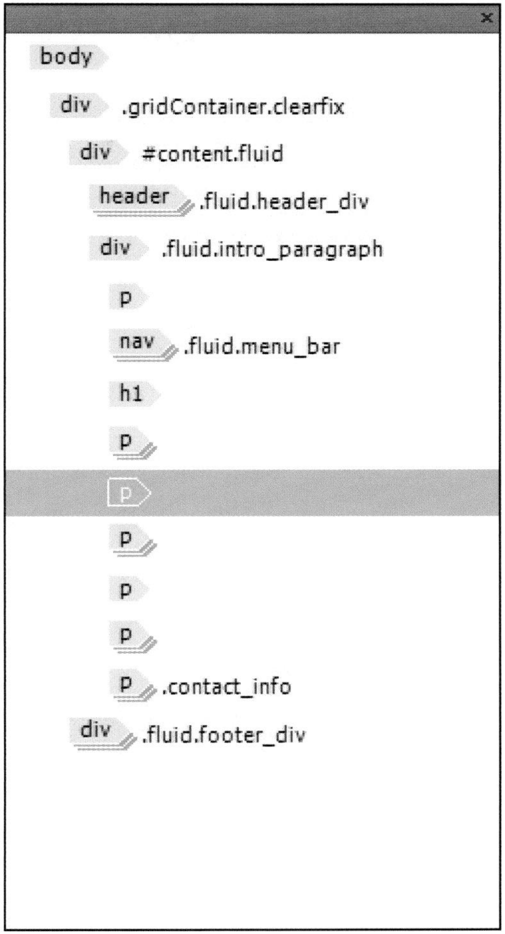

body

   div .gridContainer.clearfix

     div #content.fluid

       header .fluid.header_div

       div .fluid.intro_paragraph

         p

         nav .fluid.menu_bar

         h1

         p

         p

         p

         p

         p

         p .contact_info

       div .fluid.footer_div

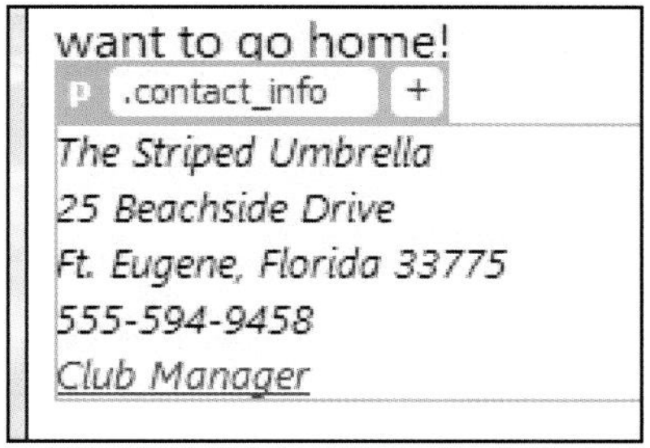

Create and Use
EMBEDDED STYLES

What You'll Do

In this lesson, you will create and apply an embedded style to the home page, then view the styled content with the Live View Property inspector.

Understanding Embedded Styles

In Chapter 3, you learned how to create and use an external style sheet to apply consistent formatting to website elements. Recall that an external style sheet is a separate file with a .css extension that contains a collection of rules that create styles to format multiple web page elements. However, you might want to create a rule that applies to only a single page in your site and does not format website content globally. You can do this using an **embedded style**, a style whose code is enclosed in <style> tags and embedded in the head section of an individual page. The example below shows an embedded style tag that defines a style named .special_text with a large font size. This style can be applied using the .special_text class selector to text on that page only:

```
<style type="text/css">

.special_text {

        font-size: large;

}

</style>
```

If both an external style and embedded style are applied to a single element, the embedded style overrides the external style.

There is also a type of style similar to an embedded style called an **inline style**. Like an embedded style, an inline style is part of the individual page code, but it is written in the body section, rather than the head section. Inline styles refer to a specific instance of a tag. Inline style rule names can only be used once on a page. For instance, <h2 style="font-family: Impact, Haettenschweiler, 'Franklin Gothic Bold', 'Arial Black', sans-serif">Cooking Classes are fun! </h2>. This example of an inline style changes the <h2> tag font for this instance only on the page.

For a summary of the differences between external, embedded, and inline styles, see Table 1.

Creating and Applying Embedded Styles

You create embedded styles using CSS Designer. Select the Add CSS Source button in the Sources pane, then select Define in Page, as shown in Figure 1. This creates a selector in the Selector pane, which can be either a class or tag selector type. To enter a class selector, you begin the selector name with a period. To enter a tag selector, you begin typing a tag name and then select the tag you want from the list of suggested HTML tags, such as body or hr.

After you name a selector, use the Properties pane in CSS Designer to set properties and values for the new rule, just as you would for a rule in an external style. As you recall, the CSS selector properties are divided into five

Figure 1 *CSS Designer source options*

Define in Page
source option

TABLE 1: SUMMARY OF STYLE TYPES					
Style Type	**What it formats**	**Style is stored in**	**Created using this source in the CSS Designer Sources pane**	**Apply this style using**	**Notes**
External Style	Multiple pages	Separate file with a .css extension	Create a New CSS File or Attach Existing CSS File	HTML Property inspector: Class list OR CSS Property inspector: Targeted Rule list	Used for global formatting
Embedded Style	Elements on one page	In page head section code	Define in Page	HTML Property inspector: Class list OR CSS Property inspector: Targeted Rule list	Overrides external style
Inline Style	A specific instance of a tag	In page body section code	(Type it in the page code in the body section)	It is applied after you add it in Code view	Use only once per page; refers to a specific instance of a tag; name is preceded by #

© 2015 Cengage Learning®

categories: Layout, Text, Border, Background, and Custom. Use the Custom category when you want to add a rule that is not listed in any of the other categories. When the Show Set check box is selected, only the properties that have been assigned a value will appear in the Properties pane, as shown in Figure 2.

Once you create a class selector, it appears in the CSS Designer Selectors pane. It also appears as a choice in the Class list in the HTML Property inspector and in the Targeted Rule list in the CSS Property inspector. To apply a class style selector to a web page element, select the element, then

select the style from the Class list in the HTML Property inspector or the Targeted Rule list in the CSS Property inspector. For a summary of the differences between the various selector types, including what they do, where they're stored, and how to apply each one, see Table 2.

Figure 2 *CSS Designer Properties pane*

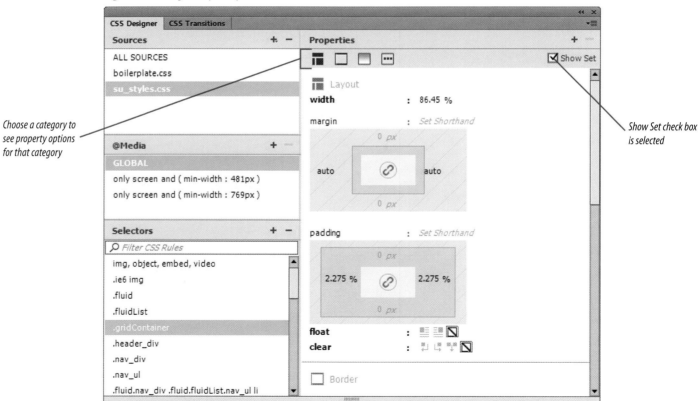

Choose a category to see property options for that category

Show Set check box is selected

Using the Live View Property Inspector

One of the important tools introduced in Dreamweaver CC is the Live view Property inspector. The Live view Property inspector is a mini-toolbar that appears above selected page elements in Live view when the Fluid Grid Layout guides are hidden. This toolbar shows the tag name and the selector used to format the selected text, as shown in Figure 3. You can use the Live view Property inspector to add or change formatting for a selected page element, so it can save you time as you format your pages. To use the toolbar to delete formatting by a selector, choose the selector name, then select the small x that appears next to it. To add a new selector using the toolbar, select the Add Class/ID button + on the toolbar.

Figure 3 *Live view Property inspector*

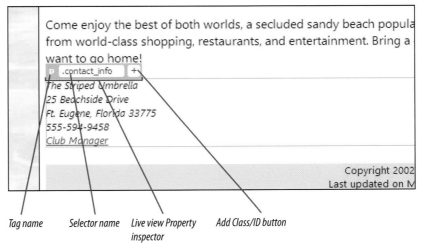

Tag name   Selector name   Live view Property   Add Class/ID button
                             inspector

TABLE 2: SUMMARY OF SELECTOR TYPES					
Selector type	**What it does**	**Style is stored in**	**Select this in New CSS Rule dialog box**	**Apply using**	**Notes**
Class	Formats any HTML element, and can apply to more than one element on multiple pages	External style sheet file or as an embedded or inline style	Selector Type: Class	HTML Property inspector: Class list or CSS Property inspector: Targeted Rule list	In code, begins with a period (.); most versatile type, can be used multiple times
ID	Formats only one element	External style sheet file or as an embedded or inline style	Selector Type: ID	HTML Property inspector: ID list	In code, begins with a # sign, used once per page, used for div tags
Tag	Redefines an HTML tag	External style sheet file or as an embedded or inline style	Selector Type: Tag	(Automatically applied when the tag is used on a page)	Rule name is the tag name
Compound	Formats a selection	External style sheet file or as an embedded or inline style	Selector Type: Compound	(Automatically applied to the relevant page elements)	Begins with a # sign, combines two or more styles in nested tags

Create a class style

1. Open the index page in The Striped Umbrella website, open CSS Designer, then widen the panel to display two columns if necessary.

2. Select the **Add CSS Source button** + in the Sources pane, then select **Define in Page**.

   The source <style> appears in the Sources pane. You have not previously defined any embedded styles for the index page, so the Selectors pane, as shown in Figure 4, does not list any selectors.

3. Select the **Add Selector button** + in the Selectors pane, then type **.contact_info** in the new selector text box.

4. Deselect the Show Set check box if necessary, then add the following text properties and values in the Properties pane: color: **#000033**; font-style: **italic**; font-size: **small**.

   Since you want the font to be the same as the rest of the page text, you will not set a font-family. That way, your new class style will inherit the font from the su_styles.css style sheet.

5. Select the **Show Set check box**, then compare your screen to Figure 5.

You created a new custom rule named contact_info and set the rule properties for it.

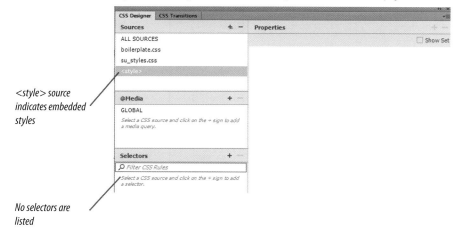

Figure 4 *CSS Designer with an embedded style sheet created for index page*

<style> source indicates embedded styles

No selectors are listed

Figure 5 *Properties and values listed for the .contact_info embedded rule*

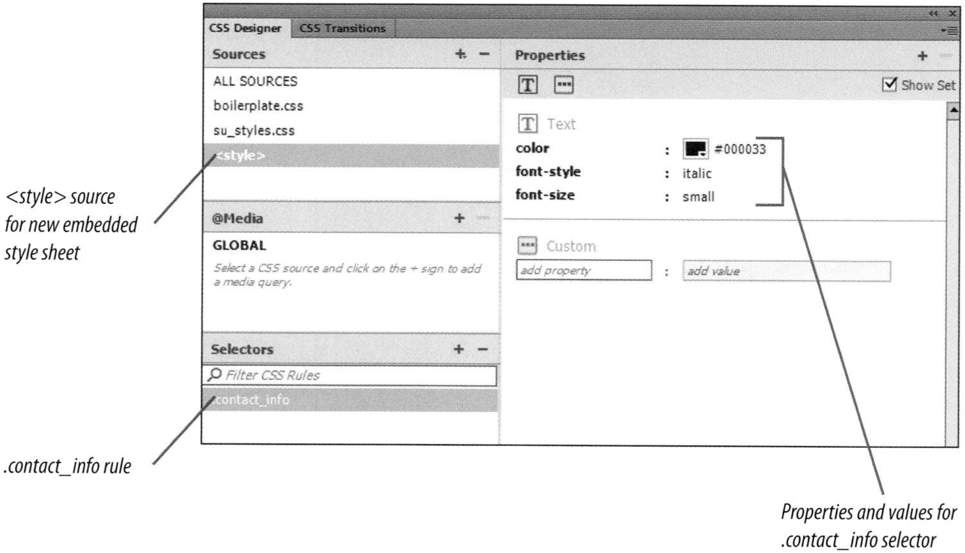

<style> source for new embedded style sheet

.contact_info rule

Properties and values for .contact_info selector

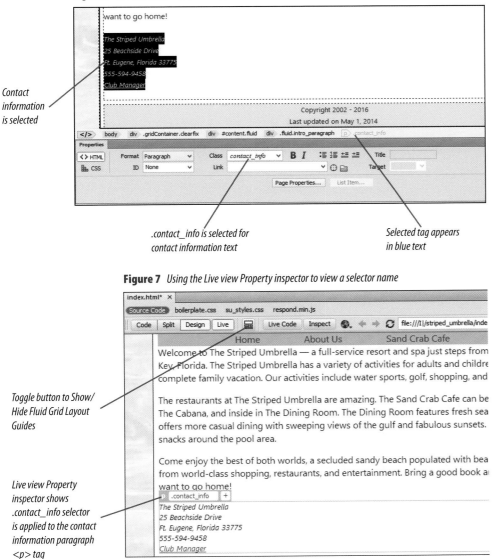

Figure 6 *The .contact_info selector applied to the contact information on the index page*

Contact information is selected

.contact_info is selected for contact information text

Selected tag appears in blue text

Figure 7 *Using the Live view Property inspector to view a selector name*

Toggle button to Show/Hide Fluid Grid Layout Guides

Live view Property inspector shows .contact_info selector is applied to the contact information paragraph <p> tag

View a selector in Live view

1. Select the paragraph with The Striped Umbrella contact information.

2. Select the **Italic button** *I* in the HTML Property inspector to remove the italic formatting.

   You need to remove manual formatting before applying a CSS style.

3. Select the **Class list arrow** in the Property inspector, select **contact_info**, then compare your results to Figure 6.

   The selected text is now smaller and dark blue, as specified by the contact_info rule.

4. Select the **Switch Design View to Live View button** Live on the Document toolbar, select the **Hide Fluid Grid Layout Guides button** if necessary, then place the insertion point in the contact information paragraph.

   The Live view Property inspector appears above the selected paragraph, as shown in Figure 7. Depending on where you place the insertion point, you may see a <span> tag rather than a <p> tag in the Live View Property inspector.

5. Save your work.

You used the Property inspector to apply the contact_info rule to the contact information, then viewed the selector with the Live view Property inspector.

Modify EMBEDDED STYLES

What You'll Do

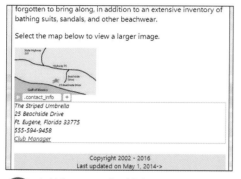

In this lesson, you will modify the contact_info rule, redefine an HTML tag, edit an embedded rule, and then delete an embedded rule.

Editing Embedded Styles

To edit a rule, simply select the rule in the CSS Designer Selectors pane, then enter the new settings in the Properties pane. Any changes that you make to the rule are automatically reflected on the page; all elements to which the rule is applied update to reflect the change.

Redefining HTML Tags

When you use the Property inspector to format a web page element, a standard HTML tag such as <h1> is added to that element. You might want to change the definition of an HTML tag to add more "pizzazz" to elements that have that tag. For instance, perhaps you want all text that has the <em> tag, which is the tag used for italic formatting, to appear in bold purple. To change the definition of an HTML tag, select the source for the new tag selector, select the media in the media type in the @Media pane, then select the Add Selector button in the Selectors pane. Begin typing the tag and the auto complete feature will scroll to help you find the tag you want to modify. Once you save the rule and apply it, the tags you apply it to will be formatted according to the new settings you specified.

Using CSS Designer

You have used CSS Designer to create and edit selector properties and values. Once you master the basics of managing your selectors, you can learn to use several more advanced features of CSS Designer. For example, you can copy styles from one selector to another one. You can choose from the styles listed in a pop-up menu or copy all styles listed. To use these features, right-click a selector in the Selectors pane, then choose an action from the pop-up menu, as shown in Figure 8.

You can also save time by using shorthand code for some properties, such as margins. For example, if you want to set identical margins around a page element, you don't have to set each margin property separately or use the Click to change all the properties button. Instead, you can enter the margin for all sides once in a shorthand text box, shown in Figure 9. If the side margins are the same value and the top margins are the same value, but a different value from the side margins, the margin values could be entered as shown in Figure 10.

Figure 8 *Choices listed in the CSS Designer selector pop-up menus to copy styles*

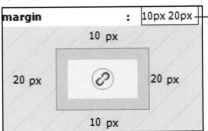

Right-click a selector name

Select Copy Styles

Text Styles is the only active choice because there are only text properties assigned to the selector

Figure 9 *Using shorthand to set equal margins for a property in CSS Designer*

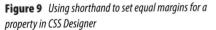
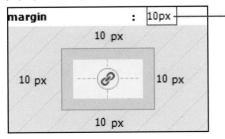

Entering 10px in the shorthand text box changes all margins to 10px

Figure 10 *Using shorthand to set equal side and equal top and bottom margins*

Entering two values in the shorthand text box sets the top and bottom margins to the first value and the sides to the second value

Edit a class style

1. Select the **.contact_info rule** in the CSS Designer Selectors pane, if necessary, then locate the text color property in the Properties pane.
2. Change the Color to **#000000**, then compare your screen to Figure 11.
3. Deselect the text, compare your screen to Figure 12, then save your work.

   The text with the contact_info rule applied changed to reflect the color change you made to the rule.

You changed the type color of the .contact_info rule. You then saw this change reflected in text with the .contact_info rule applied to it.

Figure 11 *Text color property changed for .contact_info selector*

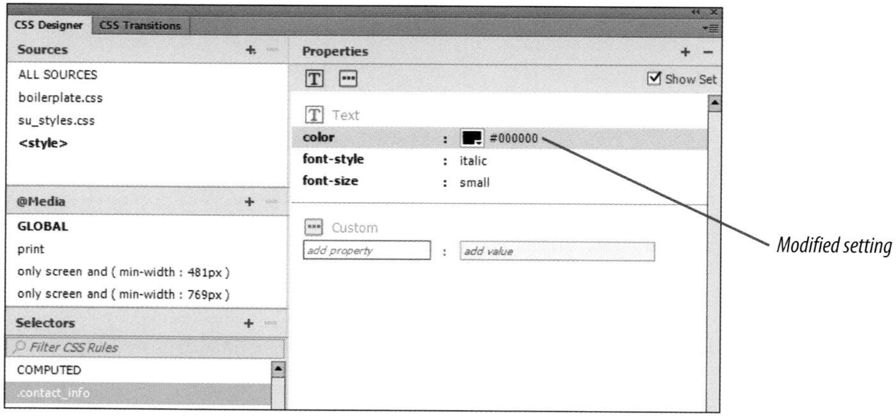

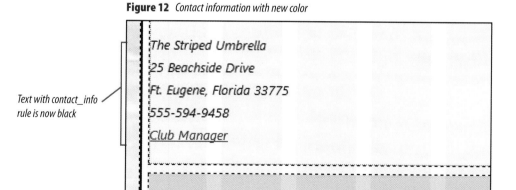

Modified setting

Figure 12 *Contact information with new color*

Text with contact_info rule is now black

The Striped Umbrella
25 Beachside Drive
Ft. Eugene, Florida 33775
555-594-9458
Club Manager

Figure 13 *Creating a new CSS embedded style to redefine the hr HTML tag*

Selecting <style> displays the embedded selectors in the Selectors pane

hr selector

hr tag selector properties and values

Figure 14 *Viewing horizontal rules with the new properties applied*

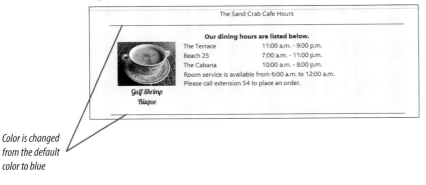

Color is changed from the default color to blue

Redefine an HTML tag

1. Open the cafe page, select the **Add CSS Source button** ⊹ in the CSS Designer Sources pane, then select **Define in Page**.

   The source <style> appears in the Sources pane. You have not previously defined any embedded styles for the cafe page, so the Selectors pane does not list any selectors.

2. Select the **Add Selector button** ⊹ in the Selectors pane, type **hr** in the new selector text box, then press **[Enter]** (Win) or **[return]** (Mac) twice.

   The hr tag creates a horizontal rule.

   TIP To scroll quickly to the tags that begin with the letter h, type h and scroll down the auto-complete tag list.

3. Add the following Border properties and values in the Properties pane: border: **top**, width: **thin**, style: **solid**, color: **#000066**.

   The horizontal rules on the page have changed to blue because the rule definition has changed the way a horizontal rule is rendered. The rules will look better in the browser than they do in Design view.

4. Select the **Show Set check box** to see the new hr selector properties, shown in Figure 13, then save your work.

5. Select the **Switch Design View to Live View button** ⌐Live⌐ on the Document toolbar, view the horizontal rules as they will appear in the browser, as shown in Figure 14, then select ⌐Live⌐ to return to Design view.

(continued)

6. Add a new selector in the embedded <style> source named **body** to set the background-image property to **water_blue_green.jpg** from the drive and folder where you store your Chapter 8 Data Files, select the **Show Set check box**, then compare your screen to Figure 15.

   The page now has a green water background. (The page background is behind the CSS container with all of the page content. You may need to collapse your panels and scroll to see it.)

7. Switch to Code view, then scroll through the head section to view the code that changes the properties for the horizontal rule and the body tags, as shown in Figure 16.

   Because these are embedded styles, the code for the rules is embedded into the page in the head section of the code. The rule changing the background image overrode the page background image that you defined earlier in the su_styles.css file that is used for all pages.

8. Scroll up or down in the code, if necessary, to find the code that links the external style sheet files, as shown in Figure 16.

   You cannot see the individual rule properties that are in the style sheets, because the files are linked, not embedded. If you open the individual style sheet files, however, you see the rules and properties listed.

   You used CSS Designer to redefine the hr and body HTML tags. You also viewed the code for the new embedded styles and the code that links the external style sheet files.

Figure 15 *Redefining the body HTML tag*

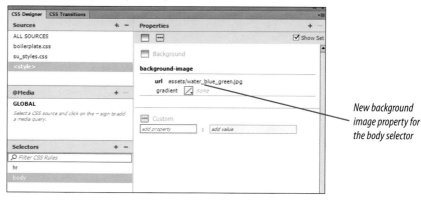

New background image property for the body selector

Figure 16 *Viewing the head content to see the embedded styles and links to external style sheets*

Links to two external style sheets

Code redefining the hr and body HTML tags is part of the head section

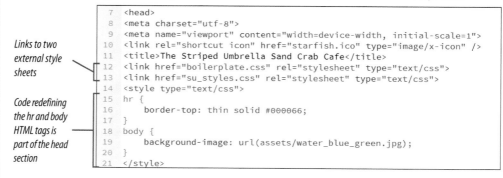

Using Styles and Style Sheets for Design

Figure 17 *Removing the body selector from the <style> source*

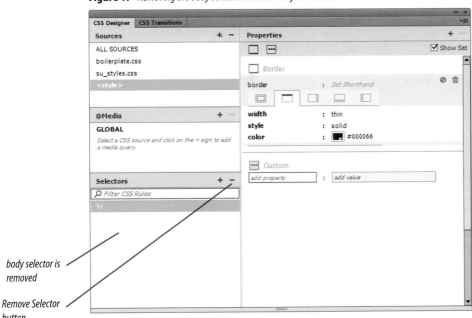

body selector is removed

Remove Selector button

1. Switch to Design view, then select the **body selector** in the <style> source in the Selectors pane.

2. Select the **Remove Selector button** — , then compare your screen to Figure 17.

   The body rule is removed from the Selectors pane. The page background changes back to the original water background, which fits the color scheme better.

3. Save your changes, then close the cafe page.

You used CSS Designer to delete the body rule.

Using the Tag Selector to View Order of Precedence

When you are trying to determine which selectors are being used to format a page element, place the insertion point next to the page element in question, then read across the tags on the tag selector in the status bar. As you read across the tag names from the left, the tags increase in precedence, with the rightmost tag having the highest level of precedence. In the following example, the h2 tag occupies the rightmost position, so its properties and values take precedence over all the tags to its left. The .fluid.intro_paragraph div tag takes precedence over all the tags to its left, but not the h2 tag on its right.

| body | div | .gridContainer.clearfix | div | #content.fluid | div | .fluid.intro_paragraph | h2 |

Lesson 2   Modify Embedded Styles

Move properties from one source to another

1. With the index page open, open CSS Designer if necessary.

2. Select **<style>** in the Sources pane, then select **.contact_info** in the Selectors pane.

3. Right-click **.contact_info**, as shown in Figure 18, then select **Copy All Styles**.

4. Select **su_styles.css** in the Sources pane, select **GLOBAL** in the @Media pane, select the **Add Selector button** ➕ in the Selectors pane, type **.contact_info** in the selector name text box, then press **[Enter]** (Win) or **[return]** (Mac) twice to name the new selector.

5. With .contact_info selected in the Selectors pane, right-click the contact_info selector, then select **Paste Styles**.

   The properties and values you copied from the embedded .contact_info selector on the index page are pasted into the external .contact_info selector in the su_styles.css file. Later you will apply it to contact information on all pages in the website, rather than just the index page.

6. Delete **<style>** in the Sources pane, select **su_styles.css**, **GLOBAL**, and **.contact_info**, compare your screen to Figure 19, save all files then close the index page.

7. Open the café page, then repeat Steps 2 through 6 to copy the embedded hr style in the café page to the su_styles.css file.

8. Delete **<style>** in the Sources pane, then save all files.

You copied the properties from the embedded .contact_info selector. You then created a new .contact_info selector in the su_styles.css file, then pasted the copied properties into it.

Figure 18 *Copying the styles from the .contact_info selector*

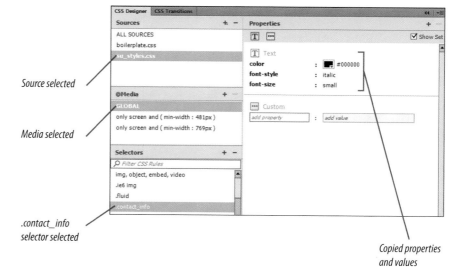

Right-click
.contact_info

Select Copy All
Styles

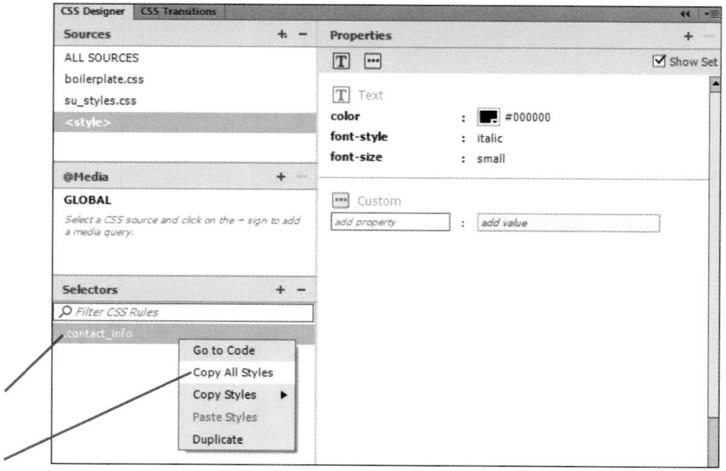

Figure 19 *Styles pasted into the external .contact_info selector*

Source selected

Media selected

.contact_info
selector selected

Copied properties
and values

Figure 20 *Using the Live View Property inspector to apply a selector to the contact information*

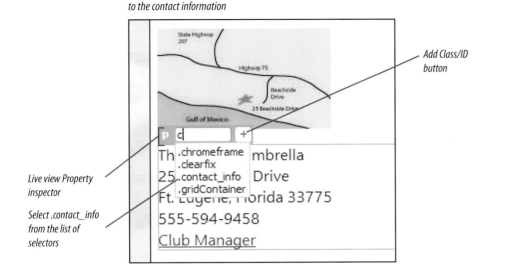

Add Class/ID button

Live view Property inspector

Select .contact_info from the list of selectors

Figure 21 *Contact information with the external selector applied*

Contact information is formatted with the .contact_info external style

Use the Live view Property inspector to apply selectors

1. Open the about_us page, select the five lines of contact information at the bottom of the page, then select the Italic button to remove the italics style.

2. Select the **Switch Design View to Live View button** Live , then select the **Hide Fluid Grid Layout Guides button** 🖼 .

3. Scroll down the page and place the insertion point in the contact information lines, select the **Add Class/ID button** + , type **c** in the selector text box on the Live view Property inspector, then select **.contact_info** from the drop-down selector list, as shown in Figure 20.

4. Compare your screen to Figure 21, save your work, then repeat Steps 1 through 3 to remove the italic style and apply the .contact_info selector to the contact information on each page that includes it in the website.

5. On the café page, select the **shrimp_bisque image**, then use the Property inspector to browse to and replace it with a new shrimp_bisque file from the drive and folder where your Chapter 8 Data Files are stored, overwriting the original file.

6. Check the Files panel to verify that the new, smaller file was copied to the website assets folder.

7. Save all files, return to Design view, then close all open pages.

You replaced the bisque file with a smaller one containing the same image, to help the page load faster.

Use Live View and
INSPECT MODE

What You'll Do

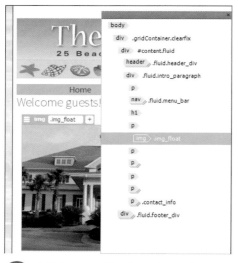

In this lesson, you will insert a new image on the about_us page in Live view and add alternate text. Next, you will add a selector to the new image with the Live View Property inspector and edit some text on the page. Last, you will use Inspect Mode and Element Quick View to view page elements.

Understanding Live View Features

Dreamweaver CC has many features to use with Live view. For example, you can insert page elements in Live view, format page elements with the Live view Property inspector, and edit page elements in Live view. You used the Live view Property inspector in Lesson 2 to view and apply a selector for a paragraph of text. You can not only add or edit classes and IDs to page elements in Live view, but you can also directly edit text and change some image properties. To edit text, double-click the text element to enter edit mode. You can also cut, copy, and paste text in Live view. When working with Fluid Grid Layout pages, hide the Fluid Grid Layout guides to activate the Live view tools.

> **QUICK TIP**
>
> The Live view Property inspector appears when a page element is selected. It can appear on the top, bottom, or side of a selected element. If you want to change its position, drag it to a different position on the page, as shown in Figure 22.

In earlier Dreamweaver versions, you could not use the Insert panel in Live view, but in Dreamweaver CC, the Insert panel is fully functional in Live view except when using pages based on a Fluid Grid layout. When you use the Insert panel in Live view, a Position Assist dialog will open with choices for the placement of your new element: Before, After, Wrap, and Nest.

Using Inspect Mode

Live view also offers **Inspect mode**, which helps you identify HTML elements and their associated styles. To use Inspect mode, go to Live view, then select the Inspect button next to the Live Code button in the Document toolbar.

When you select the Turn on Inspect Mode button in the Document toolbar while a page is open in Live view, you have an entirely different view of your page elements. As you place your pointer over a page element, the element is highlighted with the CSS box model attributes displayed in color, as shown in Figure 23. Different colors are used for the border, margin, padding, and content. This gives you a clear view of the element settings and how they affect the overall page design.

If CSS Designer is open, the properties for the active page element (the element with the pointer over it) appear in the Properties pane. The Sources, @Media, and Selectors panes also reflect the location and name of the selector for the active page element. This is a great way to make changes to selector rule properties and immediately see how those changes affect a page element's appearance on the page.

Figure 23 *Header div with padding, selector name, and dimensions showing in Inspect mode*

Padding for header
div in yellow

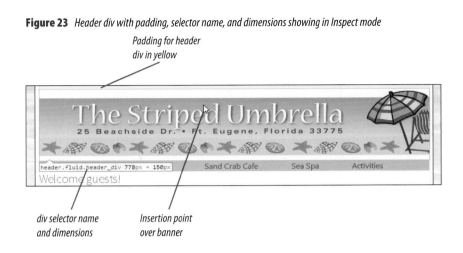

div selector name
and dimensions

Insertion point
over banner

Figure 22 *Changing the position of the Live view Property inspector*

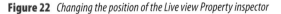

Drag to move window
to a different position

POWER USER SHORTCUTS	
To do this:	**Use this shortcut:**
Collapse selection of code	[Ctrl][Shift][C] (Win) or ⌘ [shift][C] (Mac)
Collapse outside selection of code	[Ctrl][Alt][C] (Win) or ⌘ [option][C] (Mac)
Expand selection of code	[Ctrl][Shift][E] (Win) or ⌘ [shift][E] (Mac)
Collapse full tag	[Ctrl][Shift][J] (Win) or ⌘ [shift][J] (Mac)
Collapse outside full tag	[Ctrl][Alt][J] (Win) or ⌘ [option][J] (Mac)
Expand all (code)	[Ctrl][Alt][E] (Win) or ⌘ [option][E] (Mac)
Indent code	[Ctrl][Shift][>] (Win) or ⌘ [shift][>] (Mac)
Outdent code	[Ctrl][Shift][<] (Win) or ⌘ [shift][<] (Mac)
Balance braces	[Ctrl]['] (Win) or ⌘ ['] (Mac)
Go to line (of code)	[Ctrl][G] (Win) or ⌘ [,] (Mac)
Show code hints	[Ctrl][Spacebar] (Win) or [control][spacebar] (Mac)
Refresh code hints	[Ctrl][.] (Win) or [control][.] (Mac)

Insert an image with Live view

1. Open the about_us page, then change to Live view.

2. Select the **Hide Fluid Grid Layout Guides button** 🖳 if necessary, then double-click the paragraph that begins "After you arrive".

   Double-clicking a paragraph brings the paragraph text into an editable mode. The border around the paragraph changes from blue to orange, indicating that the text is now editable in Live view, as shown in Figure 24.

3. Place the insertion point in front of "After", switch to Code view to verify that the insertion point is in between the opening <p> tag and the word "After", move it there if it is not, select **Insert** on the Menu bar, select **Image** and then select **Image**.

4. Navigate to the location where you save your Data Files, then select **boardwalk.jpg**.

5. Switch to Design view, then compare your screen to Figure 25.

   If your image did not appear in the correct position on the page, switch to Code view, select the complete image tag, cut it, then paste it after the opening <p> tag.

You inserted a new image on the about_us page in Live view.

Figure 24 *Changing a paragraph element to an editable element in Live view*

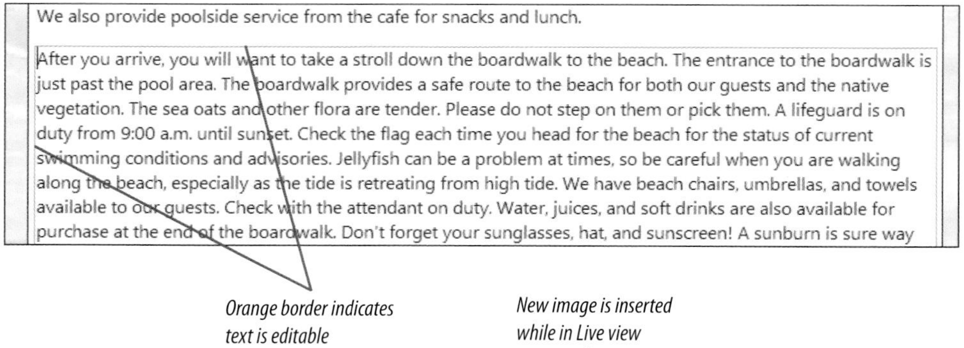

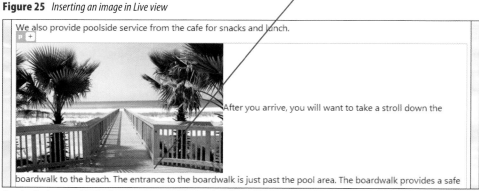

Orange border indicates text is editable

New image is inserted while in Live view

Figure 25 *Inserting an image in Live view*

Boardwalk photo provided by Spectrum Resorts of The Beach Club in Gulf Shores, Alabama

DESIGNTIP

Recognizing and Addressing Printing Issues

Many factors affect how a page will print compared to how it will appear in a browser window. While a page background color will appear in a browser window, it will not print unless the user selects the print option to print background colors. Although the width of the page in the browser window may fit on the screen, it could actually be too wide to print on a standard printer in portrait orientation. Also, table borders, horizontal rules, and divs may not print exactly how they look in a browser. Printing your pages to see how they actually appear will allow you to address most issues. You can also go to a site such as the World Wide Web Consortium (W3C) at w3.org to find the best solution for any printing problems you identify.

Using Styles and Style Sheets for Design

Figure 26 *Adding alternate text to the boardwalk image*

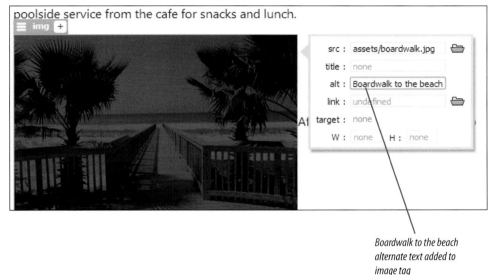

Boardwalk to the beach
alternate text added to
image tag

Figure 27 *Repositioning the Live view Property inspector window*

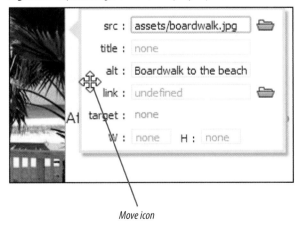

Move icon

Edit image attributes in Live view

1. Select the **boardwalk image**, then select **Edit HTML Attributes button** on the Live view Property inspector.

   The Live view Property inspector window opens with image attributes that can be added or edited.

2. Type **Boardwalk to the beach** in the Alt text box, press the **[Tab]** key, then compare your screen to Figure 26.

3. Place the pointer over the Live view Property inspector window, until a Move icon appears, as shown in Figure 27, then drag to reposition the window slightly.

(continued)

4. Select the **Add Class/ID button** ⊞ in the Live view Property inspector, begin typing **img**, then select **.image_float_right** in the Selector drop-down menu, as shown in Figure 28.

The boardwalk image moves to the right side of the page with the border and margin properties from the .image_float_right selector, as shown in Figure 29.

5. Save all files.

6. Preview the about_us page in the browser, as shown in Figure 30.

TIP To simulate the mobile, tablet, and desktop sizes in a browser, open a page in a browser, then slowly drag a side toward the middle of the page. You will see how the page contents adjust as the page width reduces.

You added alternate text to the boardwalk image, moved the Live view Property inspector, then applied the .img_float_right selector using the Live view Property inspector.

Figure 28 *Adding a selector to the img tag*

Figure 29 *Adding a selector to an image in Live view*

Boardwalk image with .img_float_right selector applied

Figure 30 *New boardwalk image on the about_us page*

Using Styles and Style Sheets for Design

Figure 31 *Double-click to place the insertion point*

When you arrive at The Striped Umbrella, check in at The Club House. Look for the signs that will direct you to registration. Our beautiful club house is the home base for our registration offices, The Sand Crab Cafe, and The Sea Spa. Registration is open from 8:00 a.m. until 6:00 p.m. Please call to make arrangements if you plan to arrive after 6:00 p.m. The cafe and spa hours are both posted and listed in the information packet that you will receive when you arrive. The main swimming pool is directly behind The Club House. A lifeguard is on duty from 8:00 a.m. until 9:00 p.m. The pool area includes a wading pool, a lap pool, and a large pool with a diving board. Showers are located in several areas for your use before and after swimming.

We also provide poolside service from the cafe for snacks and lunch.

*Insertion point is
before 9:00*

Figure 32 *Editing the lifeguard hours in Live view*

after 6:00 p.m. The cafe and spa hours are both posted and listed in the information packet that you will receive when you arrive. The main swimming pool is directly behind The Club House. A lifeguard is on duty from 8:00 a.m. until 8:00 p.m. The pool area includes a wading pool, a lap pool, and a large pool with a diving board. Showers are located in several areas for your use before and after swimming.

We also provide poolside service from the cafe for snacks and lunch.

*Time is changed
from 9:00 to 8:00*

Edit text in Live view

1. On the about_us page, double-click to select the block of text to the right of the club_house image, then place the insertion point in front of 9:00.

   The text block border changes to orange, indicating that it is in edit mode, as shown in Figure 31. Your text will probably wrap slightly differently on the page.

2. Change the time to **8:00**, place the insertion point outside the text block, then compare your screen to Figure 32.

   The text is changed from 9:00 to 8:00 and is no longer in edit mode.

3. Save your work.

You edited text in Live view.

Use Inspect Mode

1. With the about_us page open in Live view, select the **Turn on Inspect Mode button** [Inspect].

2. Move the pointer across the page slowly, and view the page elements.

   As the pointer moves over a page element, that element's box properties are visually represented by colored rectangles around it, as shown in Figure 33. Box properties include padding and margins.

3. Open CSS Designer and expand it to a two-column width, if necessary.

4. Move the pointer over the club_house image.

   A yellow rectangle representing the size of the each margin surrounds the image. The properties and values in the Properties pane changed to list all of those applied to the selected image.

5. Select the **Turn off Inspect Mode button**, then turn off Live view.

You used Inspect Mode to view the properties for the club_house image.

Figure 33 *Viewing page elements in Inspect Mode*

Yellow rectangle represents the box margins for the selected element

Figure 34 *Viewing page elements in Inspect Mode with CSS Designer*

Computed properties for the selected element

Yellow rectangle represents the box margins for the selected element

Figure 35 *Element Quick View with some of the nested tags displayed*

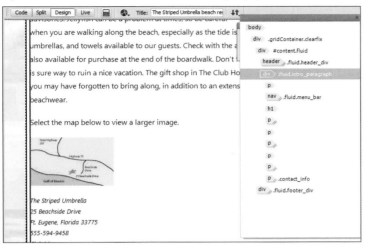

Figure 36 *Live view with Element Quick View and Live view Property inspector*

Live view Property inspector displays with Element Quick View

Using Element Quick View in Live view

1. With the about_us page open in Design view, select the **Element Quick View button** `</>` in the Status bar.

   Element Quick View, which you learned about in Chapter 6, opens.

2. Select some of the icons to expand the nested tags, if necessary, as shown in Figure 35.

   As you select each tag, the tag list expands to display nested tags. **Nested tags** are tags inside of tags. As you select a tag, the page open in Design view scrolls to display each page element.

3. Change to Live view, then select the **club_house image**.

4. Open Element Quick View.

   The club_house image is selected on the page, but this time with the Live view Property inspector, as shown in Figure 36.

5. Turn off Live view.

You viewed page elements with Element Quick View in Design view and in Live view.

Work with
CONFLICTING STYLES

What You'll Do

Understanding the Order of Precedence

When you have a mixture of embedded styles, external styles, and styles redefining HTML tags, you need to understand what happens when these styles conflict. First, you must understand the term "cascading" as applied to style sheets. **Cascading** refers to the way styles are ranked in order of precedence as they are applied to page elements. Style sheets originate from three sources: the author, who is the creator of the page and style sheet; the user, or person who is viewing the page; and the user agent, the software through which the page is delivered, such as a browser or a mobile device. All user agents have default style sheets that are used to read and display web pages.

The first order of precedence is to find declarations that specify and match the media type being used, such as a computer screen. For instance, if you are designing a page for a cell phone, you would use the selectors listed under GLOBAL in the @Media pane in CSS Designer. For a page being viewed on a desktop screen, you would use the selectors listed in the "only screen and (min-width:769)" device size in the @Media pane.

The second order of precedence is by importance and origin as follows:

1. user important declarations
2. author important declarations
3. author normal declarations
4. user normal declarations
5. user agent declarations

To be classified as an important declaration, the word "important" is included in the rule. For example: "p {font-size: 14 px ! important }" would take precedence over a p font-size tag without the important designation.

The third order of precedence is by specificity of the selector. More specific rules are applied when they are on an equal importance and origin with more general rules. The fourth and final order of precedence is by order specified in the code. Imported, or external style sheets, are considered to be before any internal styles.

When discussing the order of precedence of style types, pseudo-class styles are considered as normal class styles. **Pseudo class styles** refer to styles that determine the appearance of a page element when a certain condition resulting from information external to the HTML source is met. For instance, a rule that sets the appearance of a link that has previously been selected by a user might be:

```
a:visited {
        color: #999999;
        text-decoration: underline
}
```

The color of the visited link in this example is specified as gray and underlined. The most common pseudo-class selectors are a:link, a:visited, a:hover, and a:active. For more information on Cascading Style Sheets, go to the W3C website at w3.org/TR/CSS.

Using Tools to Manage Your Styles

Dreamweaver has several tools available to assist you in defining, modifying, and checking CSS rules. You have learned to use some of them such as the Code Navigator, Live view, and Inspect Mode.

Another style management tool lets you disable or enable CSS. The Disable/Enable CSS tool lets you disable a rule property in Design view so you can compare the effects of the affected page element with and without that property. To use this feature, select a rule property in the Properties pane in CSS Designer, then select the Disable CSS Property button to the right of the rule property and value. The property will be disabled and an icon will appear beside it, as shown in Figure 37. Select the icon to enable the property. If you disable a property and see that you don't need it anymore, you can delete it by selecting the Remove CSS Property button next to the property and value in the Properties pane.

You can also manage styles by viewing an element's computed properties. **COMPUTED** is a name that appears in the Selectors pane when you select a page element that has more than one selector used to format it. All the properties that have been applied to that element appear in the Properties pane, as shown in Figure 38. When you select one of the properties in the Properties pane, the source, device, and selector for that property are highlighted in their respective panes. When you are having problems determining why a page element is not appearing as you intend, look at each property listed and one by one disable them until you find the unwanted property. Decide whether to disable it, modify it, or delete it.

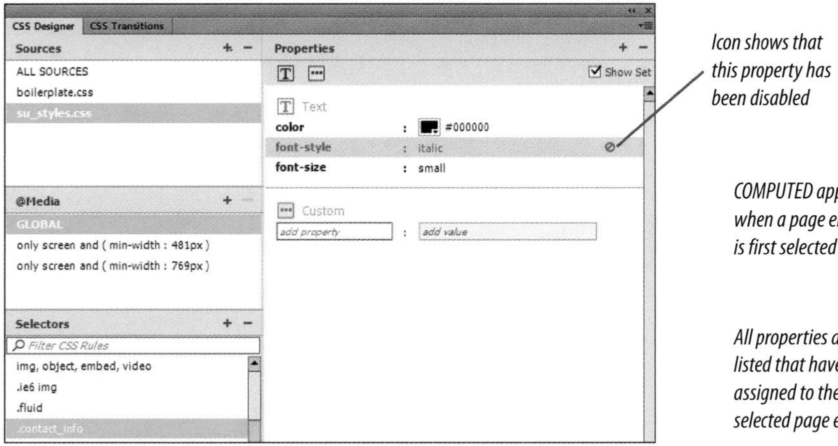

Figure 38 *Viewing computed properties*

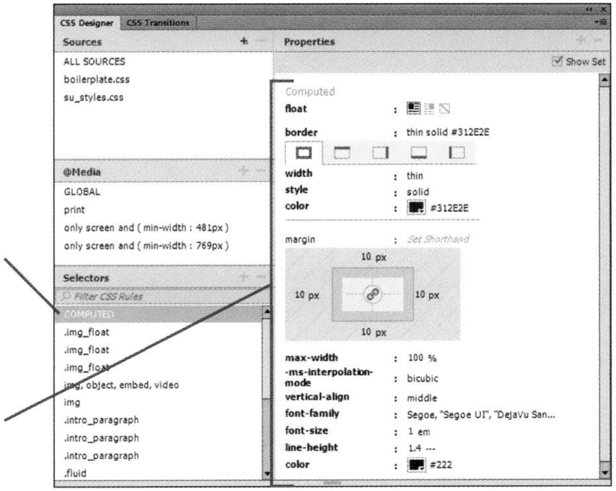

COMPUTED appears when a page element is first selected

All properties are listed that have been assigned to the selected page element

Figure 37 *Disabling a property*

Icon shows that this property has been disabled

Disable and enable a property

1. With the about_us page open in Design view, select **Welcome guests!**.

   The su_styles style sheet is selected in the Sources pane, GLOBAL is selected in the @Media pane, and h1 is selected in the Selectors pane. Because the insertion point is positioned in an h1 heading, the h1 properties are listed in the Properties pane as shown in Figure 39.

2. Select the **font-family property name** in the Properties pane.

3. Select the **Disable CSS Property button** ⊘ next to the font-family value.

   The appearance of the Welcome guests! heading changes, as shown in Figure 40. Since the font-family is an Adobe Edge Web Font, all related text properties are disabled when the font-family property is disabled. The Adobe Edge Web Font only appears correctly in Live view, but you can still see a slight difference in Design view when the property is disabled.

4. Select the **Enable CSS Property button** ⊘ .

   The text properties are reapplied to the page heading.

You viewed the properties for the h1 tag, disabled the font-family property, then enabled it.

Figure 39 *Properties of the h1 heading in the su_styles global selector*

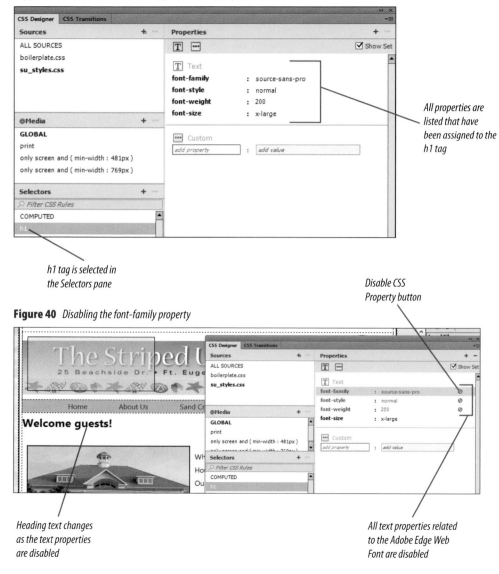

All properties are listed that have been assigned to the h1 tag

h1 tag is selected in the Selectors pane

Disable CSS Property button

Figure 40 *Disabling the font-family property*

Heading text changes as the text properties are disabled

All text properties related to the Adobe Edge Web Font are disabled

Figure 41 *All properties used to format the club_house image*

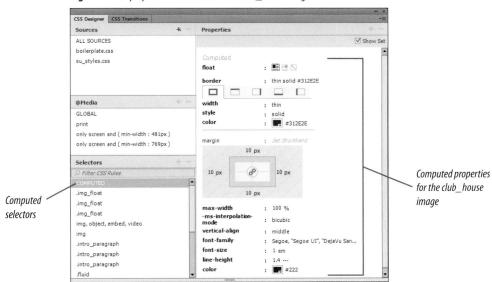

Computed selectors

Computed properties for the club_house image

Figure 42 *Disabling the border property*

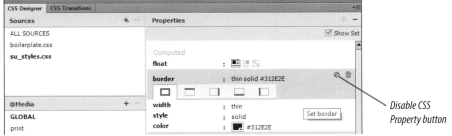

Disable CSS Property button

Use computed properties

1. With the about_us page open in Design view, select the **club_house image**.

2. Select **COMPUTED** in the Selectors pane in CSS Designer.

   All properties that have been used to format the image appear in the Properties pane, as shown in Figure 41.

3. Select the **border property** in the Properties pane.

   su_syles.css is selected in the Sources pane, GLOBAL is selected in the @Media pane, and .img_float is selected in the Properties panel. This is the selector where the border property is found.

4. Select the **Disable CSS Property button** ⊘ next to the border property, as shown in Figure 42.

   The border is removed from the club_house image.

5. Select the **border property** in the Properties pane, then select the **Enable CSS Property button** ⊘.

   The border is reapplied to the club_house image.

6. Save your work and close all files.

You viewed the computed properties for the club_house image, temporarily disabled the border property in the .img_float rule, then enabled it.

Create and use embedded styles.

1. Open Dreamweaver, open the Blooms & Bulbs website, then open the index page.
2. Select the contact information at the bottom of the page, then remove the italic style.
3. Create a new embedded rule named **.contact_info** with the following properties and values: font-style : italic; font-size : small, then apply it to the contact information.
4. Add a new embedded rule to modify the body tag with a background-image value of leaves.jpg. This file is in your drive and folder where your Chapter 8 Data Files are stored.
5. Change to Live view, then select the contact information to view the .contact_info style listed in the Live view Property inspector.
6. Save all files.

Modify embedded styles.

1. Modify the .contact_info rule to change the font-size to medium.
2. Create a new global selector in the bb_styles.css file named **.contact_info**.
3. Copy the properties of the embedded .contact_info rule to the new .contact_info rule in the bb_styles.css file, then delete the embedded .contact_info rule.

4. Open each page in the site, select the contact information on any of the pages that list it, delete the italic style, then apply the .contact_info selector from the bb_styles.css file.
5. On the index page, delete the <style> CSS Source.
6. Save all files and close all pages except the workshops page.
7. Create an embedded style in the workshops page to modify the hr tag with the following properties: border width: thin; border style: solid; border color: #3D6437.
8. Save your work, then preview the workshops page in the browser.
9. Close the browser, then close the workshops page.

Use Live view and Inspect Mode.

1. Open the tips page, then select the text between "Seasonal Gardening Checklist" and "Basic Gardening Tips".
2. Select the Unordered List button on the Property inspector to remove the unordered list format.
3. Select the butterfly image, then switch to Live view.
4. Apply the class selector .img_float to the butterfly image.
5. Use the Edit HTML Attributes button in the Live view Property inspector to add the alternate text "**Butterfly on bloom**".

6. Save your work, then view the page using Inspect Mode.
7. Make spacing adjustments if needed, then save your work if you made changes to any pages.
8. Switch back to Design view, then open and expand Element Quick View to note the DOM structure for the page, then close the tips page.

Work with conflicting styles.

1. Open the workshops page, then close the Design Notes window.
2. Add an embedded tag selector to modify the body background using the file leaves.jpg from the drive and folder where you store your Chapter 8 Data Files.
3. Save your work, then preview the workshops page in the browser. Notice that the background is different from the other pages because the embedded body tag selector is being applied, rather than the global body tag selector from the bb_styles.css file.
4. Delete the embedded body tag selector.
5. Save all files, then preview all files using three different device sizes and two different browsers to verify that all page backgrounds are the same again.
6. Close all open files.

Figure 43 *Completed Skills Review*

In this Project Builder you will continue your work on the TripSmart website. You have decided to add more selectors to improve some of the page formatting. You will also add a new photo to the services page.

1. Open the TripSmart website, then open the newsletter page.
2. Select all ten traveling tips and descriptions, then remove the unordered list tag from them.
3. Save and close the newsletter page.
4. Open the services page, then insert a fluid div named **travel_photo_div** in front of the heading "Escorted Tours".
5. Insert the image patagonia_landscape.jpg from the drive and folder where your Chapter 8 Data Files are stored in the travel_photo_div, replacing the placeholder text.
6. Update the second paragraph under the Escorted Tours heading to delete all references to Peru and replace them with Argentina, and delete the sentence naming the other tour assistants, using Figure 44 as a guide.
7. Save your work, then go to Live view and use the Live view Property inspector to add appropriate alternate text to the new image.
8. Return to Design view and remove the italic style from the contact information.
9. Create a new global rule in the tripsmart_styles.css file to format the contact information with settings of your choice, then apply it to the contact information on the services page.
10. Open each page with contact information provided, remove the italic style, then format it with the contact information rule.
11. With the contact information selected, select the fluid_table_div tag on the Tag Selector, then change the Class to intro_paragraph.
12. Copy the contact information to the catalog page.
13. Save your work, then preview each page using three different device sizes and two different browsers.
14. Close all open files.

Figure 44 *Sample Project Builder*

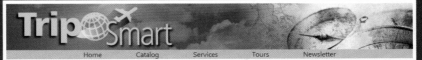

Home   Catalog   Services   Tours   Newsletter

TripSmart has several divisions of customer service to assist you in planning and making reservations for your trip, shopping for your trip wardrobe and providing expert guide services. Give us a call and we will be happy to connect you with one of the following departments: Reservations, Travel Outfitters, or Escorted Tours. If you are not quite ready to talk with one of our departments and would prefer doing some of your own research first, may we suggest beginning with our Helpful Links in Travel Planning.

Reservations

Our Reservations Department is staffed with five Certified Travel Agents, each of whom is eager to assist you in making your travel plans. They have specialty areas in Africa, the Caribbean, South America, Western Europe, Eastern Europe, Asia, Antarctica, and Hawaii and the South Pacific. They also specialize in Senior Travel, Family Travel, Student Travel, and Special Needs Travel. Call us at *(555) 848-0807* extension 75 or e-mail us at *Reservations* to begin making your travel plans now. We will be happy to send you brochures and listings of Internet addresses to help you get started. We are open from 8:00 a.m. until 6:00 p.m. CST.

Travel Outfitters

Our travel outfitters are seasoned travelers that have accumulated a vast amount of knowledge in appropriate travel clothing and accessories for specific destinations. Climate and seasons, of course, are important factors in planning your wardrobe for a trip. Area customs should also be taken in consideration so as not to offend the local residents with inappropriate dress. When traveling abroad, we always hope that our customers will represent our country well as good ambassadors. If they can be comfortable and stylish at the same time, we have succeeded! Our clothing is all affordable and packs well on long trips. Most can be washed easily in a hotel sink and hung to drip-dry overnight. Browse through our on-line catalog, then give us a call at *(555) 433-7844* extension 85. We will also be happy to mail you a catalog of our extensive collection of travel clothing and accessories.

Escorted Tours

Our Escorted Tours department is always hard at work planning the next exciting destination to offer our TripSmart customers. We have seven professional tour guides that accompany our guests from the United States point of departure to their point of return.

Our current feature package tour is to Argentina. Our local escort is Don Eugene. Don has traveled Argentina extensively and enjoys sharing his love for this exciting country with others. Call us at *(555) 848-0807* extension 95 for information on the Argentina trip or to learn about other destinations being currently scheduled.

PROJECT BUILDER 2

In this Project Builder, you will continue your work on the Carolyne's Creations website that you started in Project Builder 2 in Chapter 1. You will continue to work on the page formatting with CSS styles. Refer to Figure 45 as an example of a completed recipes page.

1. Open the Carolyne's Creations website, then open the recipes page.
2. Insert the file pie.jpg from the drive and folder where your Chapter 8 Data Files are stored anywhere on the page, then apply an existing style to it or create a new one to use to style it.
3. Add alternate text to the pie image.
4. Remove the unordered list style from the list of ingredients, then use the Property inspector to indent the ingredients to the right from the left margin.
5. Add a new embedded selector to be used later on the recipes page only to modify the hr tag.
6. Set properties and values of your choice for the horizontal rule, then save your work.
7. Create a new global selector in the cc_styles.css file to format the contact information, with settings of your choice, then apply the new selector you created to each page with contact information listed.
8. Add a horizontal rule to the recipes page to improve the page appearance.
9. Create a new global selector in the cc_styles.css file to modify all horizontal rules on all pages.
10. Copy the properties and values of the hr embedded style on the recipes page, then paste them in the global hr selector in the cc_styles.css file.
11. Delete the embedded hr selector on the recipes page, then delete the <style> source in the CSS Designer Selectors pane.
12. View each page in Live view, then make any spacing adjustments necessary to improve the page appearance.
13. Save your work, then view each page using three different device sizes and in two different browsers.
14. Close all open files.

Figure 45 *Completed Project Builder 2*

Most of today's leading websites use CSS to ensure consistent formatting and positioning of text and other elements. For instance, the United States Department of Justice website uses them. Figure 46 shows the Department of Justice home page.

1. Connect to the Internet, then go to the United States Department of Justice website at justice.gov.
2. Spend some time exploring the many pages of this site.
3. When you finish exploring all of the different pages, return to the home page. View the source code for the page.
4. Look in the head content area for code relating to the style sheet used. Read through the code and list five class names that you find on the page that are used for formatting page elements.
5. Close the Source window, then look at the home page. List any links that you find for social networking.

Figure 46 *Design Project*

Source: United States Department of Justice

In this assignment, you will continue to work on the website that you created in Chapters 1 through 7.

You will continue refining your site by using style sheets to format the text in your site consistently.

1. Write a plan in which you define styles for all of the text elements in your site. Your plan should include how you will use an external style sheet as well as embedded styles. You can use either the external style sheet you created in Chapter 3 or create a new one.

2. Attach the completed style sheet to all individual pages in the site.
3. Create and apply any embedded rules you decide to use for one page only.
4. Create and apply the rules that will be added to the external style sheet.

5. Review the pages and make sure that all page elements appear as they should and look appropriate. Use the checklist in Figure 47 to make sure you have completed everything according to the assignment.
6. Make any necessary changes.
7. Save your work, then close all open pages.

Figure 47 *Portfolio Project*

Website Checklist

1. Do all text elements in the site have a style applied to them?
2. Is the external style sheet attached to each page in the site?
3. Did you find any styles that cause a conflict in formatting page elements?
4. Did you preview each page using three different device sizes and two different browsers?
5. Are you happy with the overall appearance of each page?
6. Did you validate your style sheet to CSS level 3?

© 2015 Cengage Learning®

CHAPTER 9 COLLECTING DATA WITH FORMS

1. Plan and create a form
2. Edit and format a form
3. Work with form objects
4. Test and process a form

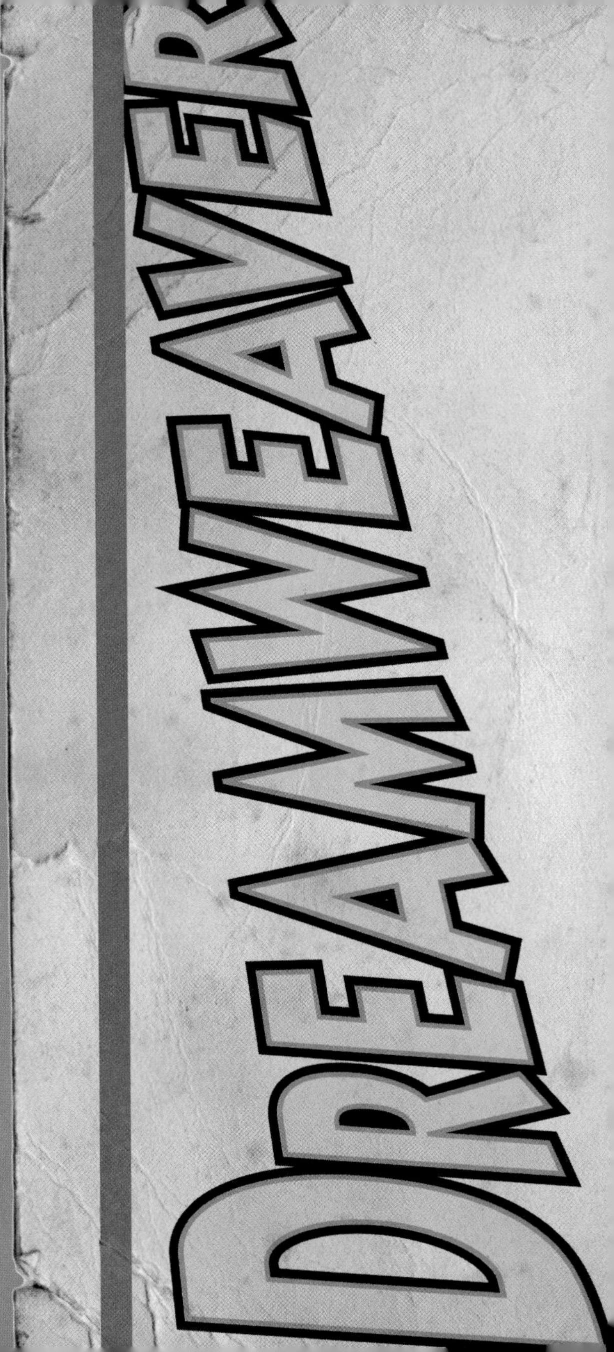

DREAMWEAVER

CHAPTER 9

COLLECTING DATA
WITH FORMS

Introduction

Many websites have forms designed to collect information from users. You've likely seen such pages when ordering books online from Amazon.com or purchasing airline tickets from an airline website. Adding a form to a web page provides interactivity between your users and your business. To collect information from users, you add forms for them to fill out and send to a web server to be processed. These forms usually include common form elements to complete, such as your name, address, and credit card information. A form on a web page consists of **form objects** such as text boxes or radio buttons into which users type information or from which they make selections. **Form labels** identify the form object by its function, such as a "First Name" label beside a text box that collects the user's first name.

In this chapter, you add a form to a page that provides a way for interested users to ask for more information about The Striped Umbrella resort. The form will also give them the opportunity to comment on the website

and make helpful suggestions. Feedback is a vital part of a website and must be easy for a user to submit.

Using Forms to Collect Information

Forms are just one of the many different tools that web developers use to collect information from users. A simple form can consist of one form object and a button that submits information to a web server, such as a search text box that you fill out, and a button that you select to start the search. More complex forms can collect contact information, or allow students to take exams online and receive grades instantly. You can use forms to insert information into databases, or to find a specific record in a database. The range of uses for forms is limited only by your imagination.

All forms need to be connected to an application server that will process the information that the form collects. The application can store the form data in a database, or simply send it to you in an email message. You specify how you want the information used, stored, and processed.

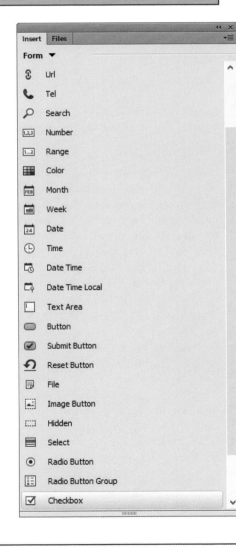

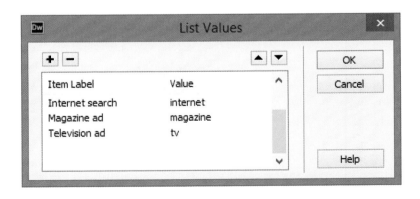

Plan and
CREATE A FORM

What You'll Do

In this lesson, you will add a new form to a feedback page in The Striped Umbrella website.

Planning a Form

Before you use Dreamweaver to create a form, it's a good idea to write down the information you want to collect and the order in which you want to collect it. It's also a good idea to make a sketch of the form for your wireframe. Planning your form content at the beginning saves you from spending time organizing the information when you create the form in Dreamweaver. The Striped Umbrella website will contain a form for users to request more information, sign up for an electronic newsletter, and submit their comments about the website. Figure 1 shows a sketch of the form that you create in this chapter.

When planning your form content, organize the information in a logical order that will make sense to users. For instance, users expect to fill in their name before their address, because almost all forms, from your birth certificate to your IRS tax forms, request your name before your address, so you should follow this standard. Placing information in a different order will confuse your users.

People on the Internet are notoriously hurried and often provide only information that is required or that is located on the top half of the form. Therefore, it's a good idea to put the most important information at the top of your form. In fact, this is a good rule to follow for web pages in general. The most important information should be on the part of the page that is visible before you have to scroll to see the rest. As with all pages, your forms should have good contrast between the color of the text and the color of the form background.

Creating Forms

Once you finish planning your form content, you are ready to create the form in Dreamweaver. To create a form object on a web page, use the Form button in the Forms category on the Insert panel. Selecting the Form button inserts a dashed red outline around the form area. But by itself, a form object can do nothing. To make your form usable, you need to configure it so that it "talks" to the scripts or email server and processes the information users enter. The form must have a script or program running "behind" it to process the information users enter so you can gather and use it.

Designers use two methods to process the information collected in a form: server-side scripting and client-side scripting. **Server-side scripting** uses applications that reside on your web server and interact with the form information collected. For example, when you order clothing from a retail website, the host web server stores and processes the item, size, color, price, shipping information, and credit card information. The most common types of server-side applications are **Common Gateway Interface (CGI)** scripts, **Cold Fusion** programs, **Java Server Page (JSP)**, and **Active Server Pages (ASP)** applications. **Client-side scripting** means that the user's computer processes the form. The script resides on the web page, rather than on the server. For example, a mortgage calculator that allows you to enter prices and interest rates to estimate mortgage payments processes the data on the user's computer. The most common types of scripts stored on a web page are created with a scripting language called **JavaScript**, or **Jscript**. Server-side applications and scripts collect the information from the form, process the information, and perform some sort of action depending on the information the form contains.

You can process form information several ways. The easiest and most common way is to have the information collected from the form and emailed to the contact person on the website. You can also have form data stored in a database to use at a later date. You can even have the application both collect the form data in a database and send it in an email message. You can also have the form data processed instead of stored. For instance,

you can create a form that calculates item quantities and prices and provides a total cost to the user on the order page, without recording any subtotals in a database or email message. In this example, only the final order total would be stored in the database or sent in an email message.

You can also create forms that make changes to your web page based on information users enter. For example, you could create a form that asks users to select a background color for a web page. In this type of form, the information could be collected and sent to the processor. The processor could then compare the selected background color to the current background color and change the color if it is different from the user's selection.

Setting Form Properties

After you insert a form, use the Property inspector to specify the application that you want to process the form information and how you want it sent to the processing application. The **Action property** in the Property inspector specifies the application or script that will process the form data. Most of the time the Action property is the name and location of a CGI script, such as /cgi-bin/myscript.cgi; a Cold Fusion page, such as mypage.cfm; or an Active Server Page, such

Figure 1 *Sketch of the form you will add to the feedback page*

To request further information, please complete this form.

First Name*

Last Name*

Email*

I am interested in information about:
☐ Fishing
☐ Cruises

I would like to receive your newsletters.
◯ Yes
◯ No

I learned about you from: Select from list: ▼

Comments:

Submit   Reset

*Required field

© 2015 Cengage Learning®

as mypage.asp. Figure 2 shows the properties of a selected form.

The **Method property** specifies the **HyperText Transfer Protocol (HTTP)** used to send the form data to the web server. The **GET method** specifies that ASCII data collected in the form will be sent to the server appended to the URL or the file included in the Action property. For instance, if the Action property is set to /cgi-bin/myscript.cgi, then the data will be sent as a string of characters after the address, as follows: /cgi-bin/ myscript.cgi?a+collection+of+data+collected+by+the+form. Data sent with the GET method is usually limited to 8K or less, depending on the web browser. The **POST method** specifies that the form data should be sent to the processing script as a binary or encrypted file, allowing you to send data securely. When you specify the POST method, there is no limit to the amount of information that can be collected in the form, and the information is secure.

The **Form name property** specifies a unique ID for the form. The ID can be a string of any alphanumeric characters and cannot include

Figure 2 *Form controls in the Property inspector*

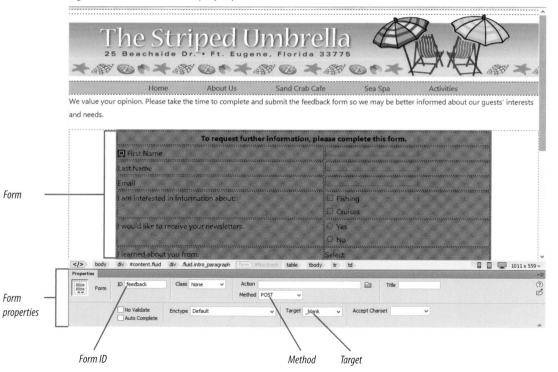

Collecting Data with Forms

spaces. The **Target property** lets you specify the window in which you want the form data to be processed. For instance, the _blank target will open the form in a separate browser window.

Understanding CGI Scripts

CGI is one of the most popular tools used to collect form data. CGI allows a web browser to work directly with the programs that are running on the server and also makes it possible for a website to change in response to user input. CGI programs can be written in the computer languages Perl or C, depending on the type of server that is hosting your website. When a CGI script collects data from a web form, it passes the data to a program running on a web server, which in turn passes the data back to the user's web browser, which then makes changes to the website in response to the form data. The resulting data is then stored in a database or sent to an email server, which then sends the information in an email message to a designated recipient. Figure 3 illustrates how a CGI script processes information collected by a form.

Figure 3 *CGI process on a web server*

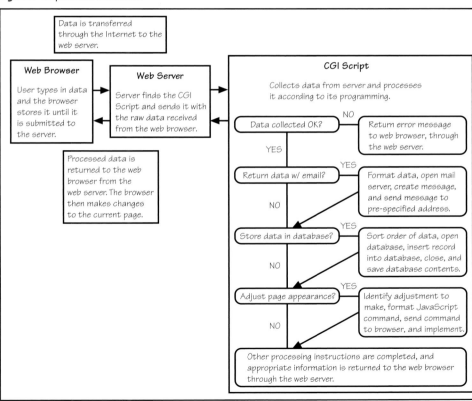

© 2015 Cengage Learning®

Insert a form

1. Open The Striped Umbrella website, open the file dw9_1.html from the drive and folder where you store your Data Files, then save it as **feedback.html** in The Striped Umbrella website, but do not update links.

2. Close the dw9_1.html file, then place the insertion point between the introductory paragraph and the contact information.

3. In Design view, select the Form category on the Insert panel, then select the **Form button** to insert a new form on the page.

   A rectangle with a dashed red outline appears on the page, as shown in Figure 4. As you add form objects to the form, the form expands.

TIP You can see the form only if Invisible Elements are turned on. To turn on Invisible Elements, select View on the Menu bar, point to Visual Aids, then select Invisible Elements.

You inserted a new form on the feedback page of The Striped Umbrella website.

Figure 4 *New form inserted on the feedback page*

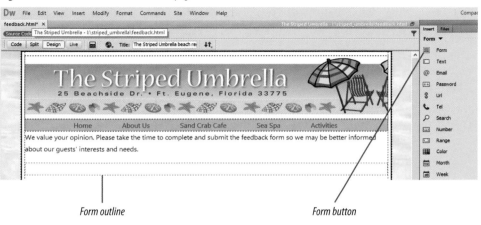

Form outline   Form button

Figure 5 *Property inspector showing properties of selected form*

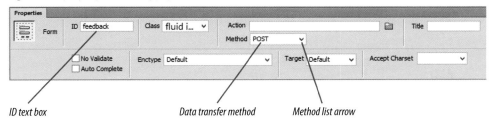

ID text box   Data transfer method   Method list arrow

Set form properties

1. Place the insertion point inside the form, then select the **Form tag (<form>)** in the tag selector on the status bar to display the form properties in the Property inspector.

2. Type **feedback** in the ID text box in the Property inspector.

3. Select the **Method list arrow** in the Property inspector, then select **POST** if necessary, as shown in Figure 5.

TIP Leave the Action text box blank unless you have the information necessary to process the form. However, when you submit an HTML5 page for validation, the Results panel will list an error until you supply a form action.

4. Save your work.

You added form properties to the feedback form.

Using CGI scripts

You can use CGI scripts to start and stop external programs or to specify that a page update automatically based on user input. You can also use them to create surveys, site search tools, and games. You can even use CGI to do basic tasks such as record entries to a guest book or count the number of people who have accessed a specific page of your site. CGI also lets you create dynamic web documents "on the fly" so that pages can be generated in response to preferences specified by the user. Although instructions for creating and modifying CGI scripts are not covered in this book, you can find a script by searching on the Internet.

Edit and
FORMAT A FORM

What You'll Do

In this lesson, you will insert a table that will contain the form on the feedback page. You will also add and format form labels.

Using Tables to Lay Out a Form

Just as you can use CSS or tables to help place page elements on a web page, you can also use CSS or tables to help lay out forms. To make sure that your labels and form objects appear in the exact positions you want on a web page, you can place them on the page using layout options such as div tags, tables, and lists. When you use a table to lay out a form, you can place labels in the first column and place form objects in the second column, as shown in Figure 6.

Adding Labels to Form Objects

When you create a form, include form field labels so that users know what information you want them to enter in each field. Because labels play such an important part in identifying the information that the form collects, you need to make sure to use labels that make sense to your users. For example, First Name and Last Name are good form field labels, because users understand clearly what information they should enter. However, a label such as Name might confuse

Using Fieldsets to Group Form Objects

If you are creating a long form on a web page, you might want to organize your form elements in sections to make it easier for users to fill out the form. You can use fieldsets to group similar form elements together. A **fieldset** is an HTML tag used to group related form elements together. You can have as many fieldsets on a page as you want. To create a fieldset, use the Fieldset button on the Insert panel.

users and cause them to leave the field blank or enter incorrect information. If creating a simple and obvious label is not possible, then include a short paragraph that describes the information users should enter into the form field. Figure 7 shows clearly marked labels for each form field, as well as additional text providing directions or examples for the user to follow.

You can add labels to a form using one of two methods. You can simply type a label in the appropriate table cell or div or use the Label button in the Forms category on the Insert panel to link the label to the form object.

Using CSS to Format the Form

With CSS3, many of the tags previously used to position table content are deprecated. So if you use a table to position data in a form, you will need to create or modify CSS rules to format the labels and data fields, such as their horizontal and vertical alignment. If you have only one table in your site, you can simply add properties to the table tag. But if you have more than one table in your site and they have different dimensions, then you will need to format them separately, creating separate rules to format each one. If you only have one table and the rows and columns are of equal size and appearance, you can set row or column alignment or widths by modifying the row or column tags. If the rows and columns have different alignments or widths, you will have to create separate rules for each column or row.

Figure 6 *Passport application form based on a table layout*

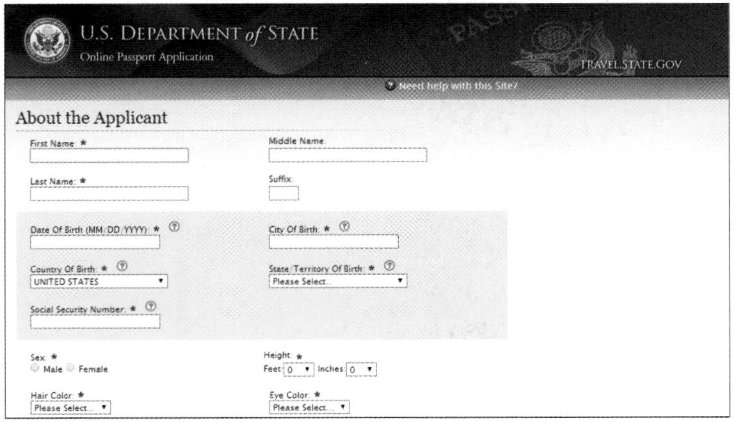

Source: U. S. Department of State

Figure 7 *Social Security benefits application form with clear field labels*

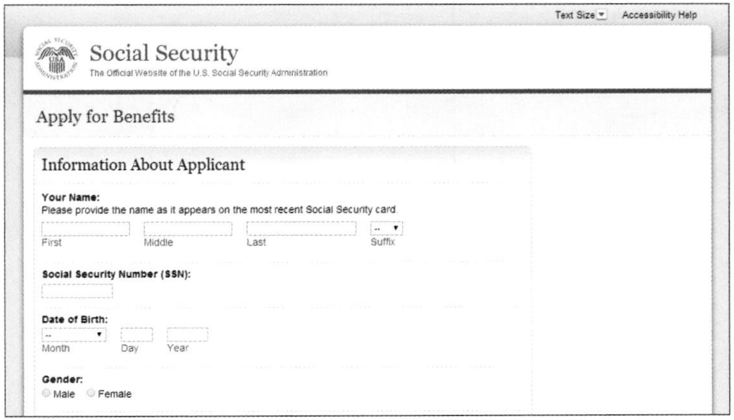

Source: Social Security Administration

Add a table to a form

1. Place the insertion point inside the form outline, as shown in Figure 8.

2. Select the Common category on the Insert panel, then select **Table**.

3. In the Table dialog box, set the Rows to **10**, Columns to **2**, delete any other settings that remain from previous tables, then select the **Top header option** in the Header section, if necessary.

TIP The Table dialog box will retain the settings from the last table you created, so be sure to remove all settings that you do not want to apply to the new table.

4. Compare your screen to Figure 9, then select **OK**.

    The table is currently formatted with the table rule in the su_styles.css file that you defined earlier for the cafe page. This rule specifies the table width.

TIP Remember that there are several ways to apply styles in a table. You can apply styles by selecting text, placing the insertion point inside a paragraph, selecting a cell and applying a style to it, or applying a style to an HTML tag, such as a table tag.

You added a table to the form on the feedback page. The table will hold form objects.

Figure 8 *Placing the insertion point inside the form*

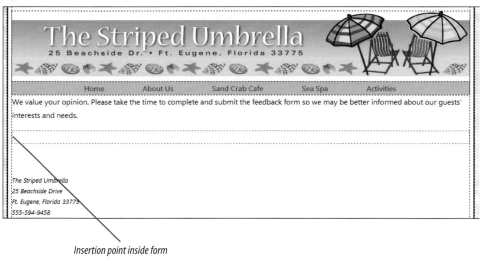

Insertion point inside form

Figure 9 *Setting table properties*

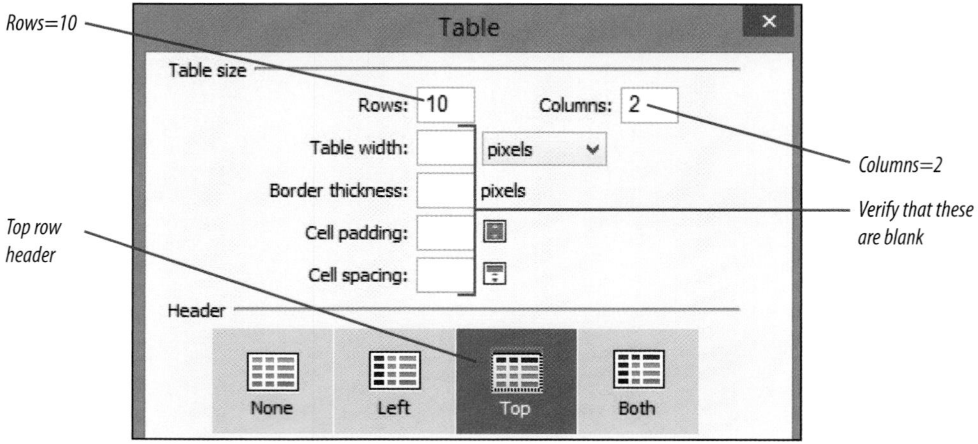

Rows=10

Columns=2

Verify that these are blank

Top row header

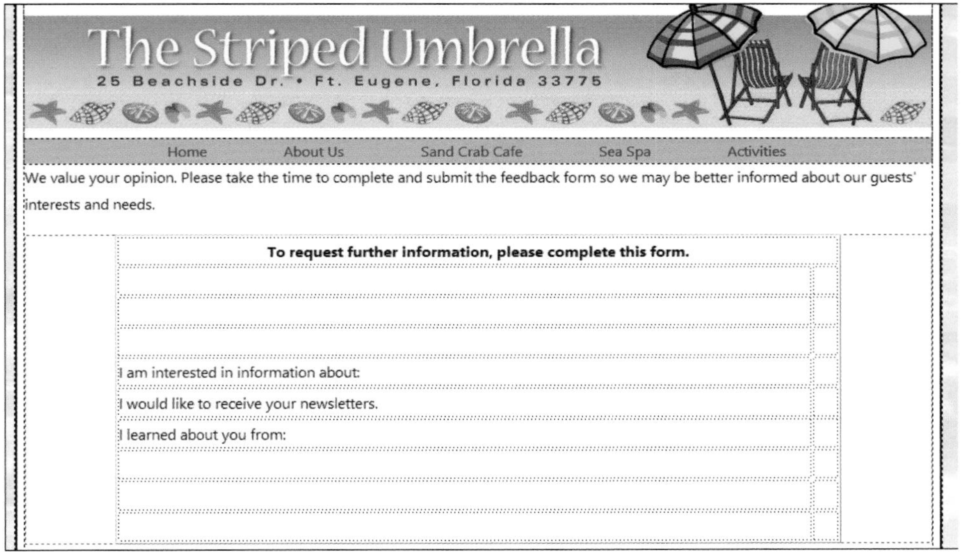

Figure 10 *Typing labels in table cells*

Add form labels to table cells

1. Merge the top two cells in the first row of the table, place the insertion point in the merged cells, then type **To request further information, please complete this form.** in the merged cells.

   Because you designated a header for this table, the top row text is automatically centered and bold. Screen readers use the header to assist users who have visual impairments to identify the table.

2. Place the insertion point in the first cell in the fifth row, then type **I am interested in information about:**.

3. Press [↓], then type **I would like to receive your newsletters**.

4. Press [↓], type **I learned about you from:**, then press [↓].

5. Compare your screen to Figure 10.

You added a header and three form labels to table cells in the form.

Add form labels using the Label button

1. Verify that the insertion point is in the cell below the one that contains the text "I learned about you from:".
2. Select the Form category on the Insert panel, then select **Label**.
3. Switch to **Split view**, then locate the insertion point, as shown in Figure 11.

   The insertion point is positioned in the Code view pane between the tags <label> and </label>, which were added when you selected the Label button.

TIP You may need to scroll down to see the cell.

4. In the Code view pane, type **Comments**, then select the **Refresh button** `C Refresh` in the Property inspector, if you don't see the new label in Design view.

   The label appears in the table cell in the Design view pane.

TIP If you don't type in Code view, you will not see the Refresh button. When you type in Design view, the text appears immediately without refreshing.

5. Compare your screen to Figure 12, select the **Show Design view button** `Design`, then save your work.

You added a new label to the form on the feedback page using the Label button.

Figure 11 *Adding a label to a form using the Label button*

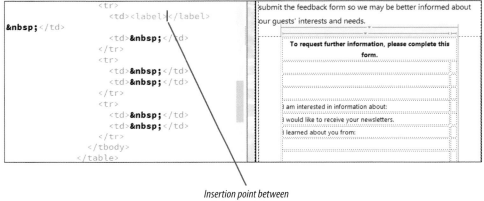

Insertion point between Label tags in Code view

Figure 12 *New label added using the Label button*

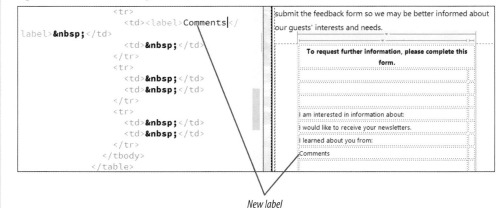

New label

Figure 13 *Modifying the td tag with a global selector*

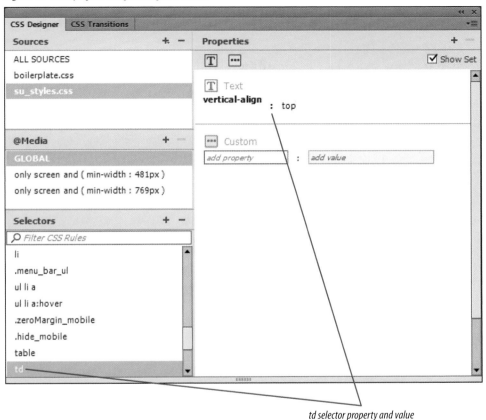

td selector property and value

Create a rule for the form table

1. Create a new global tag selector in the su_styles.css file that modifies the <td> tag with the following property: text vertical-align: **top**, as shown in Figure 13.

   The text in each cell is now aligned at the top of the cell, which will be more apparent as you add longer text labels and larger text fields to some of the table cells.

2. Save your work.

You created a new rule to format the table cells.

Work with
FORM OBJECTS

What You'll Do

In this lesson, you will add form objects to the form on the feedback page.

Understanding Form Objects

A form provides a structure in which you can place form objects. Form objects—which are also called **form elements**, **form controls**, **form inputs**, or **form fields**—are the form components such as check boxes, text boxes, and radio buttons that allow users to provide information and interact with the website. You can use form objects in any combination to collect the information you need. Figure 14 shows a form that contains a variety of form objects.

Text fields are the most common type of form object and are used for collecting a string of characters, such as a name, address, password, or email address. Use the Text button on the Insert panel to insert a text field. You can specify single-line or multi-line text fields.

A **text area field** is a text field that can store several lines of text. You can use text area fields to collect comments, descriptions of problems, long answers to questions, or even a résumé. Use the Text Area button on the Insert panel to insert a text area.

You can use **check boxes** to create a list of options from which a user can make multiple

selections. For instance, you could add a series of check boxes listing hobbies and ask users to select the ones that interest them. A group of check boxes is called a **check box group**.

You can use **radio buttons** to provide a list of options from which only one selection can be made. A group of radio buttons is called a **radio group**. Each radio group you create allows only one selection from within that group. You could use radio groups to ask users to select their annual salary range, their age group, or the T-shirt color they want to order. You could also use a radio group for users to answer a yes or no question. To insert a radio group, use the Radio Button Group button in the Form category on the Insert panel.

You can insert a **menu** or **list** on a form using the Select button on the Insert panel. You use menus when you want a user to select a single option from a list of choices. You use lists when you want a user to select one or more options from a list of choices. Menus are often used to provide navigation on a website, while lists are commonly used in order forms to let users choose from a list of possibilities. Menus must be opened to see all of the options they contain, whereas lists display some of their options all of the time. When you create a list, you need to specify the number of lines that will be visible on the screen by setting a value for the Height property in the Property inspector.

Using **hidden fields** makes it possible to provide information to the web server and form-processing script without the user knowing that the information is being sent. For instance, you could add a hidden field that tells the server who should receive an email message and what the subject of the message should be. You can also use hidden fields to collect information that a user does not enter and cannot see on the screen. For instance, you can use a hidden field to send you the user's browser type or IP address.

You can insert an **image field** into a form using the Image button on the Insert panel. You can use image fields to create buttons that contain custom graphics.

If you want your users to upload files to your web server, you can insert a **file field**. You could insert a file field to let your users upload sample files to your website or to post photos to your website's photo gallery.

All forms must include a **Submit button**, which users select to transfer the form data to the web server. You can also insert a **Reset button**, which lets users clear data from a form and reset it to its default values, or a

custom button to trigger an action that you specify on the page. You can insert a custom button using the Button button on the Insert panel. Place Submit and Reset buttons at the bottom of the form. You can also add a security challenge, as shown in Figure 14, to prevent automated programs from using the form.

When you insert a form object in a form, you use the Property inspector to specify a unique name for it. You can also use the

Property inspector to set other appropriate properties for the object, such as the number of lines or characters you want the object to display.

Setting Form Object Attributes

As you place a control on a form, you usually need to add a label. You can place a form label either before or after it by typing it directly on the form. This is a good idea if you need more than a word or two for a form label.

Figure 14 *Website form with several form objects*

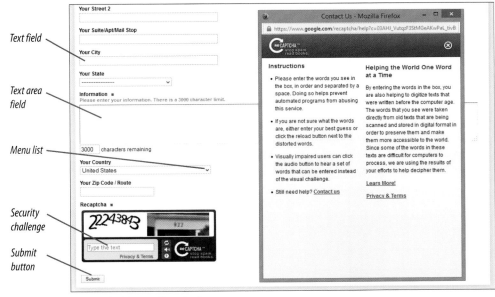

Source: Federal Bureau of Investigation

For instance, "Please explain the problem you are experiencing." would need to be typed on the form next to a text box. If, however, you only need the words "Yes" and "No" beside two radio buttons, you can add the labels "Yes" and "No" using a form attribute called a **label tag**. You can add a label tag before or after the form object using the Input Tag Accessibility Attributes dialog box. Label tags provide good accessibility for your form objects, as they clearly identify each form object and are read by screen readers.

Using the Adobe Add-ons Site

To obtain form controls designed for creating specific types of forms, such as online tests and surveys, you can visit the Adobe Add-ons site (https://creative.adobe.com/addons) shown in Figure 15, a central storage location for program extensions, also known as **add-ons**. You can search the site by using keywords in a standard Search text box. You can also search for items using filters to find the most popular and the most recent, as well as by title, price, and rating.

Figure 15 *Adobe Add-ons site*

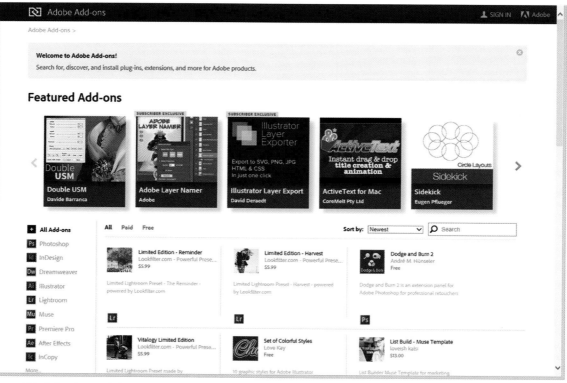

Source: Adobe Systems Incorporated

Collecting Data with Forms

Figure 16 *Properties of the first_name field*

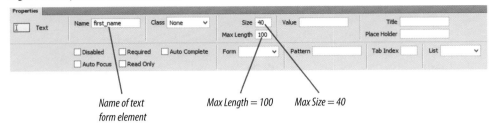

Name of text
form element

Max Length = 100

Max Size = 40

Figure 17 *Property inspector showing properties of selected text field*

| Home | About Us | Sand Crab Cafe | Sea Spa | Activities |

We value your opinion. Please take the time to complete and submit the feedback form so we may be better informed about our guests' interests and needs.

To request further information, please complete this form.

First Name

Last Name

I am interested in information about:

I would like to receive your newsletters.

I learned about you from:

Comments

Insert single-line text fields

1. Place the insertion point in the first cell under the header, then type **First Name**.

2. Press **[Tab]**, then select **Text** in the Forms category on the Insert panel.

3. Type **first_name** in the Name text box in the Property inspector.

4. Type **40** in the Size text box in the Property inspector.

   This specifies that 40 characters will be visible inside this text field when displayed in a browser.

5. Type **100** in the Max Length text box in the Property inspector, as shown in Figure 16.

   This specifies that a user can type no more than 100 characters in this field.

6. Select the default text field label in the table, then delete it.

7. Repeat Steps 1 through 6 to create another label and single-line text field of the same size in the cell beneath the First Name label and text field, typing **Last Name** as the label in the first column and **last_name** in the Name text box, then compare your screen to Figure 17.

(continued)

8. Repeat Steps 1 through 6 to create another label and single-line text field of the same size in the cell under the Last Name label and text field, using **Email** for the label and **email** for the Text field name.

9. Save your changes, preview the page in your browser, compare your screen to Figure 18, then close your browser.

You added three single-line text fields to the form, then previewed the page in your browser.

Figure 18 *Form with single-line text fields added*

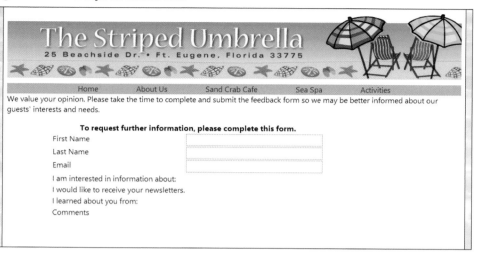

Figure 19 *Property inspector showing properties of selected text area*

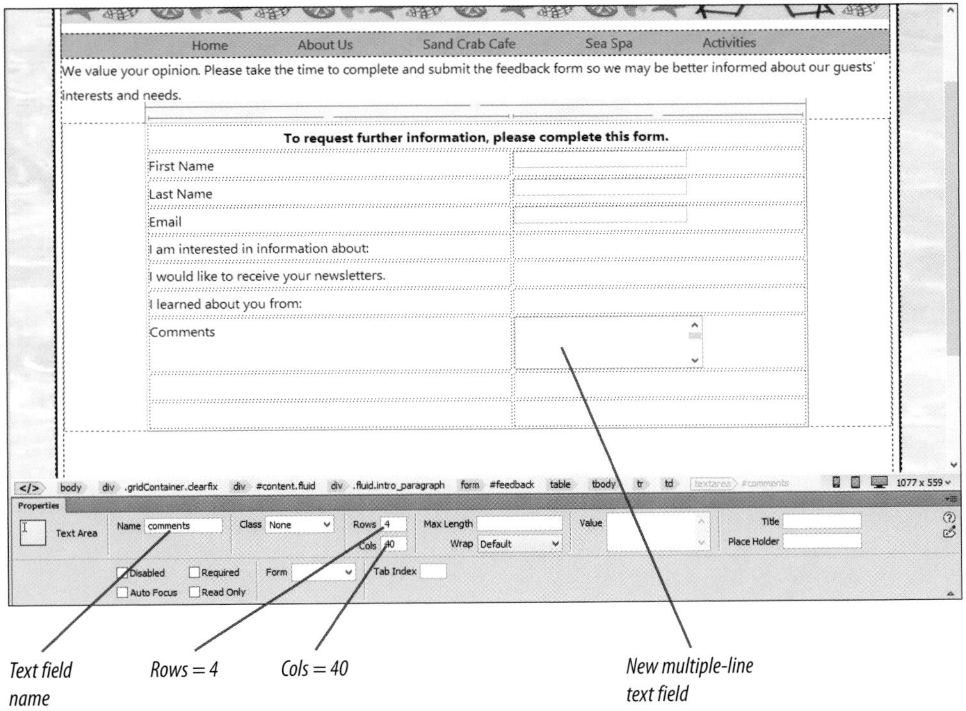

Text field
name

Rows = 4   Cols = 40

New multiple-line
text field

Insert a multiple-line text field

1. Place the insertion point in the cell to the right of the Comments label.

2. Select **Text Area** on the Insert panel, then type **comments** in the Name text box.

3. Delete the placeholder label "Text Area:", then select the text box.

4. Type **4** in the Rows text box in the Property inspector.

   This specifies that 4 lines of text can be visible inside this text field when the page is displayed in a browser.

5. Type **40** in the Cols text box in the Property inspector, as shown in Figure 19.

   This specifies a maximum width of 40 characters for the text box.

You added a multiple-line text field to the form.

Insert a check box group

1. Place the insertion point in the empty table cell to the right of "I am interested in information about:".

   This field will use a form label tag that will appear after you add a form control.

2. Select **Checkbox Group** on the Insert panel.

3. Type **brochures** in the Name text box, select **Checkbox** in the first row of the Label column, type **Fishing**, press **[Tab]**, then type **fishing** in the value column.

4. Select **Checkbox** in the second row of the Label column, type **Cruises**, press **[Tab]**, type **cruises** in the value column, select the **Line breaks option button** if necessary, compare your screen to Figure 20, then select **OK**.

5. Select the **Fishing** check box, compare your screen to Figure 21, then verify that the Checked option is not selected in the Property Inspector.

   This ensures that the check box will appear unchecked on the form by default. If the user selects it, a check mark will appear in the box.

   (continued)

Figure 20 *Checkbox Group dialog box*

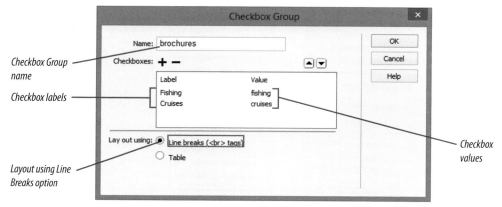

Checkbox Group name

Checkbox labels

Layout using Line Breaks option

Checkbox values

Figure 21 *Property inspector showing check box properties*

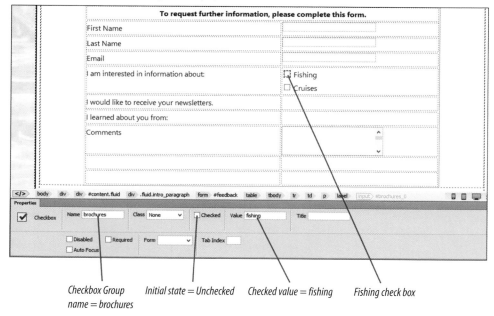

Checkbox Group name = brochures

Initial state = Unchecked

Checked value = fishing

Fishing check box

Figure 22 *Feedback page in browser with check boxes added to the form*

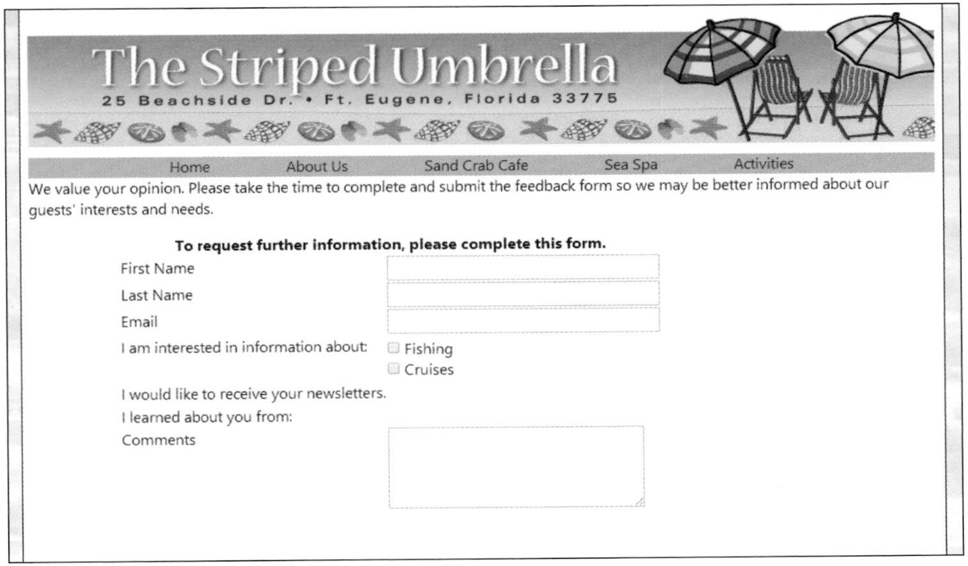

6. Repeat Step 5 to verify that the check box for the Cruises option's initial state is Unchecked, then save your work.

7. Preview the page in your browser, compare your screen to Figure 22, then close your browser.

TIP To add a check box that is not part of a check box group, select the Checkbox button on the Insert panel.

8. If your Fishing and Cruises check boxes are not aligned at the top of their cells so they appear on the same line as their label, switch to Code view and delete any <p> tags you find immediately before the opening <label> code, and any closing </p> tags.

9. Save your work and verify in Live view or the browser that the alignment for both form elements matches Figure 22.

You added two check boxes in a check box group to the form that will let users request more information about fishing and cruises.

Add radio button groups to a form

1. Place the insertion point in the empty table cell to the right of "I would like to receive your newsletters."

2. Select **Radio Button Group** on the Insert panel to open the Radio Group dialog box.

3. Type **newsletters** in the Name text box.

4. Select the **first instance of Radio** in the Label column of the Radio Group dialog box, then type **Yes**.

5. Press **[Tab]** or select the **first instance of Radio** in the Value column, then type **positive**.

   You named the first radio button Yes and set its value as positive. This value will be sent to your script or program when the form is processed when users select this check box.

6. Press **[Tab]** or select the **second instance of Radio** to add another radio button named **No** with a value of **negative**.

7. Select the **Line breaks (
 tags) option button**, if necessary.

   TIP If the Table option button is selected, then the radio buttons will appear in a separate table within the currently selected table.

8. Compare your screen with Figure 23, then select **OK** to close the Radio Group dialog box.

   (continued)

Figure 23 *Radio Group dialog box*

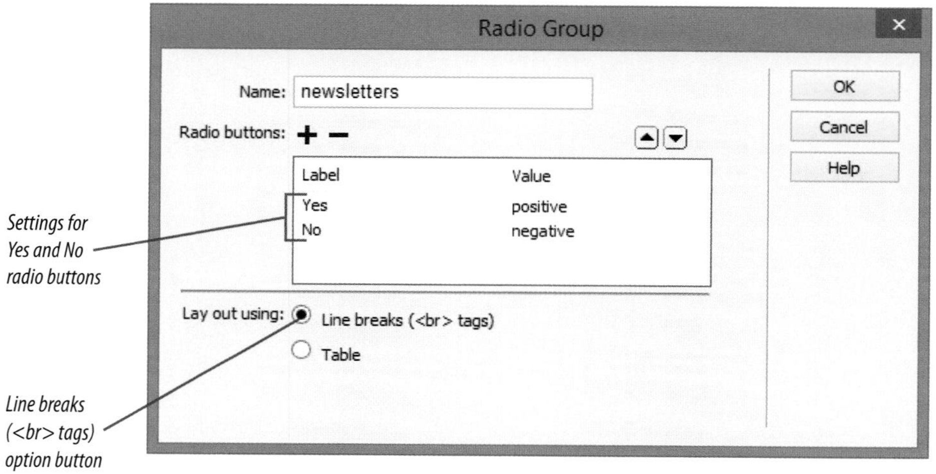

Settings for Yes and No radio buttons

Line breaks (
 tags) option button

Figure 24 *Feedback page with new radio group*

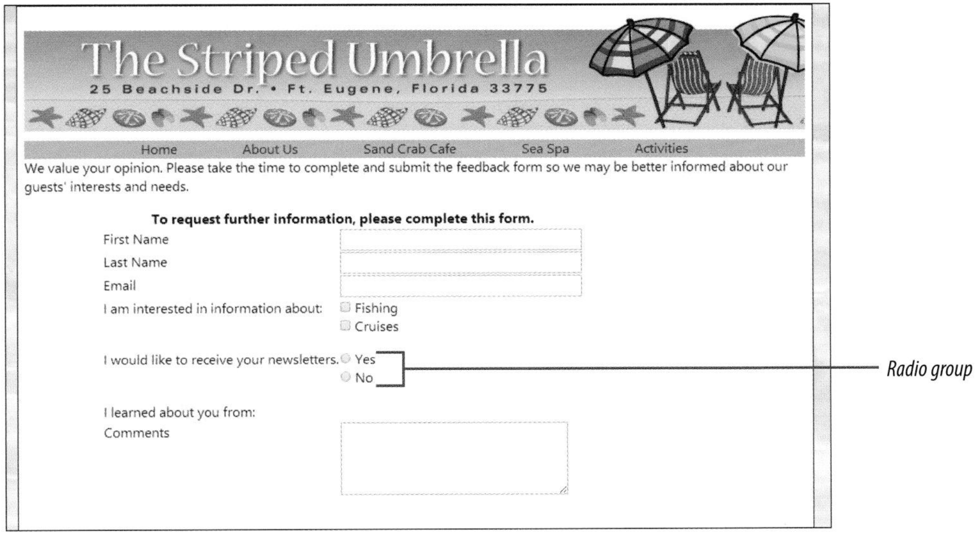

The Striped Umbrella
25 Beachside Dr. • Ft. Eugene, Florida 33775
Home
About Us
Sand Crab Cafe
Sea Spa
Activities
We value your opinion. Please take the time to complete and submit the feedback form so we may be better informed about our guests' interests and needs.
To request further information, please complete this form.
First Name
Last Name
Email
I am interested in information about:
Fishing
Cruises
I would like to receive your newsletters.
Yes
No
I learned about you from:
Comments
Radio group

9. Save your work, preview the page in your browser, compare your screen to Figure 24, then close your browser.

TIP To create radio buttons that are not part of a radio group, select the Radio Button button on the Insert panel.

10. If your Yes and No radio buttons are not aligned at the top of their cells so they appear on the same line as their label, switch to Code view and delete any <p> tags you find immediately before the opening <label> codes, as well as their closing </p> tags.
11. Save your work and verify that the alignment for both form elements matches Figure 24.

You added a radio group that will let users answer whether or not they would like to receive The Striped Umbrella newsletters.

Add a menu

1. Place the insertion point in the cell to the right of the text "I learned about you from:".

2. Choose the **Select option** on the Insert panel.

3. Type **reference** in the Name text box in the Property inspector, then compare your screen to Figure 25.

4. Select the **List Values button** in the Property inspector to open the List Values dialog box.

5. Type **Select from list** in the Item Label column, then press **[Tab]**.

6. Type **none** in the Value column.

   If the user accidentally skips this menu and does not enter a value, the value "none" will be sent to the processing program. If one of the actual choices, such as "Internet search," were in the top position, the program might return a false positive when, in actuality, the user merely skipped it. The "none" value will send accurate information to the processing program if they do so. It also reminds users that they have not made a choice yet.

   (continued)

Figure 25 *Property inspector showing properties of selected field*

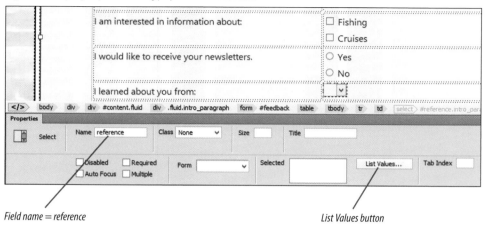

Field name = reference · *List Values button*

Using Secure Forms

If you plan to include a form on your website, it is important to consider the sensitivity of the information that users transmit using the form. If they will enter confidential information such as credit card numbers or social security numbers, you should set up a secure form that protects the information from being harvested by unauthorized people.

One way to do this is to place your forms on a secure server. SSL, which stands for **Secure Socket Layer**, is the industry standard for viewing and sending confidential information over the Internet by encrypting the data. Notice the next time that you place an order over the Internet that the *http* protocol changes to the *https* protocol when you open the page that contains the credit card form control. The https protocol stands for **Hypertext Transfer Protocol Secure**. You can create secure forms with plug-ins or services that are available commercially. Search the Internet for "Secure online forms" to locate the many companies that offer this service. WebAssist, a company listed in the Adobe Dreamweaver Exchange, offers a product called CSS Form Builder that allows you to build secure CSS forms. For more information, visit the Adobe Market Place & Exchange at adobe.com/cfusion/exchange/.

Figure 26 *List Values dialog box*

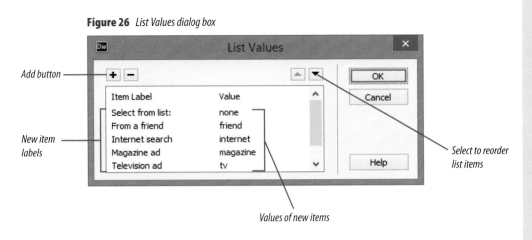

Add button

New item labels

Select to reorder list items

Values of new items

Figure 27 *Properties of reference form object*

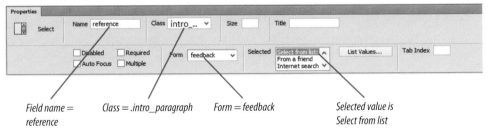

Field name = reference

Class = .intro_paragraph

Form = feedback

Selected value is Select from list

Figure 28 *Feedback page with menu*

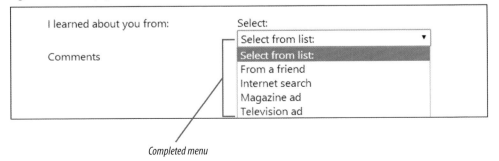

Completed menu

7. Press **[Tab]**, type **From a friend** as a new Item Label, then type **friend** in the Value column.

8. Use the **Add button** ➕ or [Tab] to add the following three Item Labels: **Internet search**, **Magazine ad**, and **Television ad**, setting the Values as **internet**, **magazine**, and **tv**.

9. Compare your screen to Figure 26, then select **OK**.

10. Select the **Class list arrow** in the Property inspector, then select **.intro_paragraph** to assign a style to the menu text.

11. Verify that Select from list is displayed in the Selected list box, select the **Form list arrow** in the Property inspector, select **feedback**, then compare your screen to Figure 27.

    "Select from list:" as the first value in the Selected list box tells the browser to display "Select from list" as the default field value.

12. Save your work, preview the page in the browser, then select the **list arrow** to view the menu.

13. Compare your screen to Figure 28, then close the browser.

You added a menu to the form on the feedback page.

Insert a hidden field

1. Place the insertion point to the left of the First Name label at the top of the form to place the insertion point.
2. Select **Hidden** on the Insert panel.

   A Hidden Field icon appears at the insertion point.

   TIP If you do not see the Hidden Field icon, select View on the Menu bar, point to Visual Aids, then select Invisible Elements.

3. Type **required** in the Name text box in the Property inspector, then type **first_name**, **last_name**, **email** in the Value text box, as shown in Figure 29.

   Typing first_name, last_name, email in the Value text box specifies that users must enter text in the First Name, Last Name, and Email fields before the script can process the form. The field names you type in the Value text box must match those in your form exactly. If any of these fields are left blank, the form will return a prompt to remind the user to enter the missing text.

4. Save your work.

   You added a hidden field to the form that will let users know if they neglect to complete the fields for their first name, last name, and email address.

Figure 29 *Property inspector showing properties of selected hidden field*

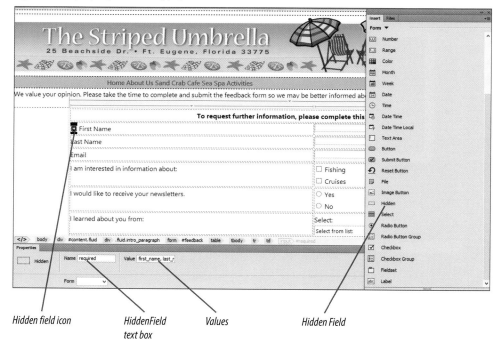

Hidden field icon   HiddenField   Values   Hidden Field
                           text box

Figure 30 *New Submit and Reset buttons added to form*

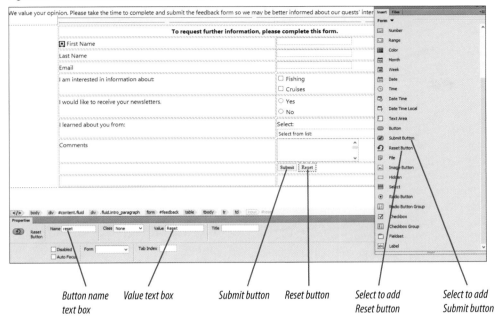

Button name text box   Value text box   Submit button   Reset button   Select to add Reset button   Select to add Submit button

1. Place the insertion point in the **second cell** of the second to last row of the table.

2. Select **Submit Button** on the Insert panel.

3. Verify that the Value text box in the Property inspector contains Submit.

   When a user selects the Submit button, the information in the form will be sent to the processing script (if you add the information to connect the form to a database).

4. Place the insertion point to the right of the Submit button on the form, insert a space, then select **Reset button** on the Insert panel.

5. Select the **Reset button** on the form, then verify that the Name text box in the Property inspector contains reset, and the Value text box in the Property inspector contains Reset.

   When a user selects the Reset button, the form removes any information typed by the user.

6. Save your work and compare your screen to Figure 30.

You added a Submit button and a Reset button to the form.

Test and
PROCESS A FORM

What You'll Do

In this lesson, you will check the spelling on the feedback page and create a link to the feedback page on the about_us page. You will then open the about_us page in your browser, select the feedback link, then test the form and reset it.

Creating User-Friendly Forms

After you create a form, you should test it to make sure that it works correctly and is easy to use. Verify that the fields are arranged to provide a logical flow of information, so the user is not confused about where to go next when completing the form. Make sure that there is enough contrast between the form text and the table background so the text is readable.

When a form contains several required fields (fields that must be filled out before the form can be processed), it is a good idea to provide visual clues such as a different font color or other notation that label these fields as required fields. Often, you see an asterisk next to a required field with a corresponding note at either the top or the bottom of the form explaining that all fields marked with asterisks are required fields. This encourages users to complete these fields initially rather than attempt to submit the form and then receive an error message asking them to complete required fields that have been left blank. Using a different font color for the asterisks and notes is an easy way to call attention to them and make them stand out on the page.

When you are finished with your form, you should always have several people test it before you publish it. Then make any necessary changes based on any testing feedback that you receive and test it one final time.

Figure 31 *Adding visual clues for required fields*

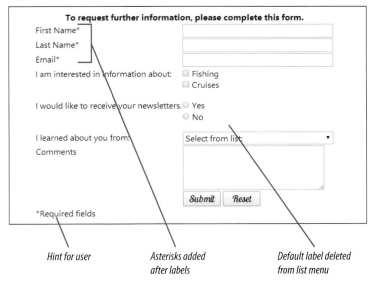

Hint for user — Asterisks added after labels — Default label deleted from list menu

---

Using a Testing Server and Live View to Test Dynamic Content

When a web page contains content that allows the user to interact with the page by selecting or typing, and then responds to this input in some way, the page is said to contain **dynamic content**. A form is an excellent example of dynamic content, because as the user fills out the form, feedback can be returned, such as the availability of window seats on a particular airplane flight or whether or not certain colors or sizes of clothing items are available for purchase. This exchange of information is made possible through the use of a database, as you learned in Lesson 1.

Once a form is developed and a database is tied to it, you should set up a **testing server** to evaluate how the form works and the data is processed. Your local computer or your remote server can serve as a testing server. You set up a testing server by filling out the relevant information in the Testing Server section of the Site Definition dialog box. You can also test your dynamic data in Design view by using Live view. **Live view** now allows you to add, edit, or delete dynamic content or server behaviors. You can use the Switch Design View to Live view button on the Document toolbar to change to Live view. The opposite of dynamic content is static content. **Static content** refers to page content that does not change or allow user interaction.

Check spelling and create visual clues for required fields

1. Select **Commands** on the Menu bar, select **Check Spelling** to check the spelling on the form.

2. Correct any spelling errors you find, then close the Check Spelling dialog box.

3. Place the insertion point after the text First Name, then type * (an asterisk).

   The asterisk gives users a clue that this is a required field.

4. Place an asterisk after the words "Last Name" and "Email."

5. Merge the two cells in the last row, then type *__Required fields__ in the merged field.

6. Change to Code view, then delete the label "Select" above the list menu, as well as its beginning and ending label tags.

7. Return to Design view, then apply the **.feature_item** class selector to the Submit and Reset buttons.

8. Save your work, preview the page in the browser, compare your screen to Figure 31, close the browser, then close the feedback page.

You checked the spelling on the feedback page, then added asterisks to the required fields on the page. Next, you typed text explaining what the asterisks mean, deleted the default label in front of the list menu, then applied a class selector to the Submit and Reset buttons.

Link a file

1. Open the **about_us** page and place the insertion point after the last sentence in the next to the last paragraph ending with "beachwear."

2. Enter a paragraph break then type **Please give us your feedback so that we may make your next stay the best vacation ever!**

3. Select the word "feedback," then use the **Point to File button** ⊙ on the HTML Property inspector to link the feedback text to the feedback page.

4. Compare your screen with Figure 32, save your work, then preview the page in the browser.

(continued)

Figure 32 *Viewing the feedback link*

After you arrive, you will want to take a stroll down the boardwalk to the beach. The entrance to the boardwalk is just past the pool area. The boardwalk provides a safe route to the beach for both our guests and the native vegetation. The sea oats and other flora are tender. Please do not step on them or pick them. A lifeguard is on duty from 9:00 a.m. until sunset. Check the flag each time you head for the beach for the status of current swimming conditions and advisories. Jellyfish can be a problem at times, so be careful when you are walking along the beach, especially as the tide is retreating from high tide. We have beach chairs, umbrellas, and towels available to our guests. Check with the attendant on duty. Water, juices, and soft drinks are also available for purchase at the end of the boardwalk. Don't forget your sunglasses, hat, and sunscreen! A sunburn is sure way to ruin a nice vacation. The gift shop in The Club House is a convenient place to pick up any items that you may have forgotten to bring along, in addition to an extensive inventory of bathing suits, sandals, and other beachwear.

Please give us your feedback so that we may make your next stay the best vacation ever!

Select the map below to view a larger image.

Link to feedback page

Figure 33 *Testing the feedback page*

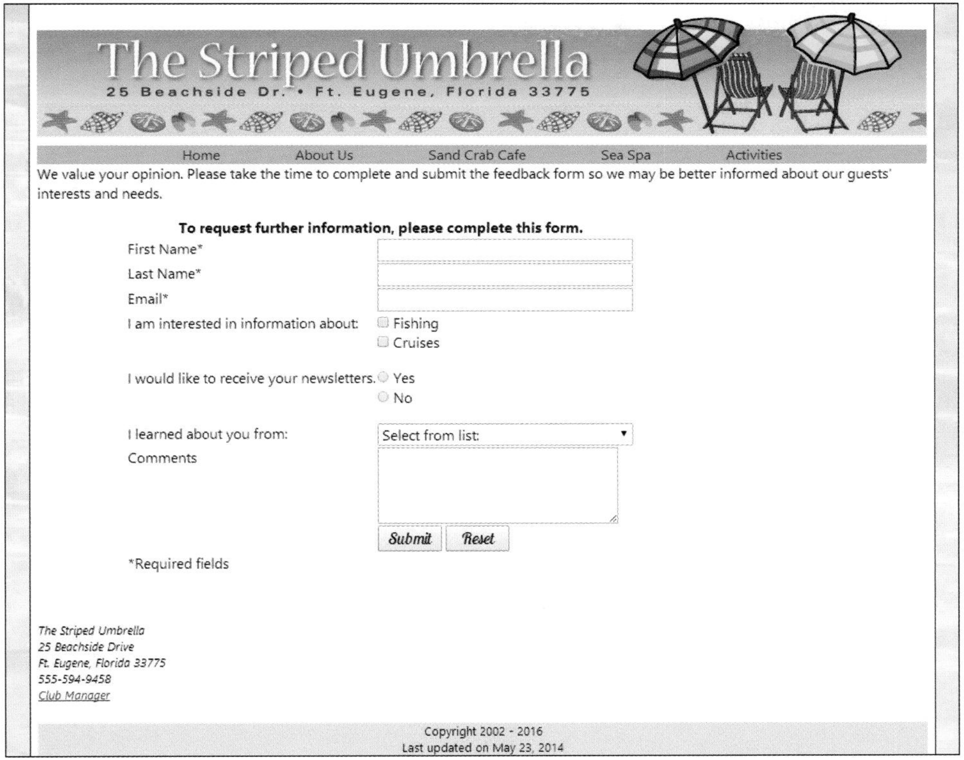

5. Select the **feedback link** to test it.

   The feedback page opens in a new window, as shown in Figure 33.

6. Test the form by filling it out, then selecting the **Reset button**.

   The Reset button clears the form, but the Submit button does not work because this form has not been set up to send information to a database. Linking to a database is beyond the scope of this book, but you can refer to the information on pages 9-5, 9-7, and 9-9 to learn more about CGI scripts.

7. Close the browser and close all open pages.

You created a link on the about_us page to link to the feedback form, and tested it in your browser.

SKILLS REVIEW

Plan and create a form.

1. Open the Blooms & Bulbs website.
2. Open the tips page.
3. Scroll to the bottom of the page, select the paragraph of tips under the Basic Gardening Tips heading, then remove the Ordered List style and add a blockquote.
4. At the beginning of each sentence, insert a bullet character from the Insert, Character, Other menu on the Menu bar and a space.
5. Place the insertion point at the end of the last tip ending with "weeding.", add a paragraph break, then insert a form.
6. Name the form **submit_tips**, then set the target to _self.
7. Save your work.

Edit and format a form.

1. Insert a table within the form that contains 9 rows, 2 columns, and a Top header.
2. Merge the cells in the top row and type **Submit Your Favorite Gardening Tip** in the newly merged cell.
3. Type **Email** in the first cell in the second row.
4. Type **Category** in the first cell in the third row.
5. Type **Subject** in the first cell in the fourth row.
6. Type **Description** in the first cell in the fifth row.
7. Merge the cells in the sixth row of the table, then type **How long have you been gardening?** in the merged cell.

8. Merge both cells in the seventh row of the table, then type **Receive notification when new tips are submitted?** in the resulting merged cell.
9. Save your work.

Work with form objects.

1. Place the insertion point in the second cell of the second row. Insert a text field with no label tag, naming the field **email**. Set the Max Length property to 30.
2. Place the insertion point in the second cell of the fourth row, then insert a text field with no label tag and the name **subject**. Set the Max Length to 50 characters.
3. Place the insertion point in the second cell of the fifth row, then insert a Text Area with no label tag and the name **description**. Set the Rows to 5.
4. Insert a space to the right of the "Receive notification when new tips are submitted?" label, then insert a check box with the label "Yes". Set the name of the check box to **notification**, enter **yes** in the Value text box, then verify that the initial state is Unchecked.
5. To the right of the text "How long have you been gardening?" insert a radio button group named **years_gardening**, that uses line breaks. It should contain the labels **1 to 5 years**, **5 to 10 years**,

Over 10 years and the following corresponding values for each label: **1+**, **5+**, and **10+**.
6. In the empty cell to the right of Category, insert a Select field with the name **category**. Use the List Values dialog box to add the following item labels: **Select from list: Weed control**, **General growth**, and **Pest control**, and set the corresponding values for each to **none, weeds**, **growth**, and **pests**.
7. Delete the default "Select" label, create a new global class selector in the bb_styles.css file named **.menu_text** with the font-family Segoe, Segoe UI, DejaVu Sans, Trebuchet MS, Verdana, sans-serif, then apply the .menu_text class selector to the category Select field.
8. Insert a hidden field named **required** in the first cell of the eighth row that has the value **email**.
9. Insert a Submit button named **submit** in the second cell of the eighth row.
10. With your insertion point to the right of the Submit button, insert a space, then insert a Reset button named **reset** with the Reset value.
11. Create a new global class selector in the bb_styles.css file named **.button_face**, then add a property that applies the same font-family as in the .intro_paragraph class selector.
12. Apply the .button_face class selector to both the Submit and Reset buttons.
13. Save your work.

Test and process a form.

1. Check the spelling on the page and correct any errors you find.
2. Type * (an asterisk) after the label Email.
3. Merge the cells in the last row, then type *Required in the last row.

4. Modify the global table tag selector in the bb_styles.css file to add a thin, solid border with a 6 px border-radius and a 3 px left padding around the table.
5. Remove any extra space after the form, then save your work.

6. Preview the page in your browser, compare your form to Figure 34, then test the form by filling it out and using the Reset button.
7. Close your browser, view the form in three different screen sizes, then close all open pages. (Your fields may be slightly different widths from Figure 34 depending on the browser you use.)

Figure 34 *Completed Skills Review*

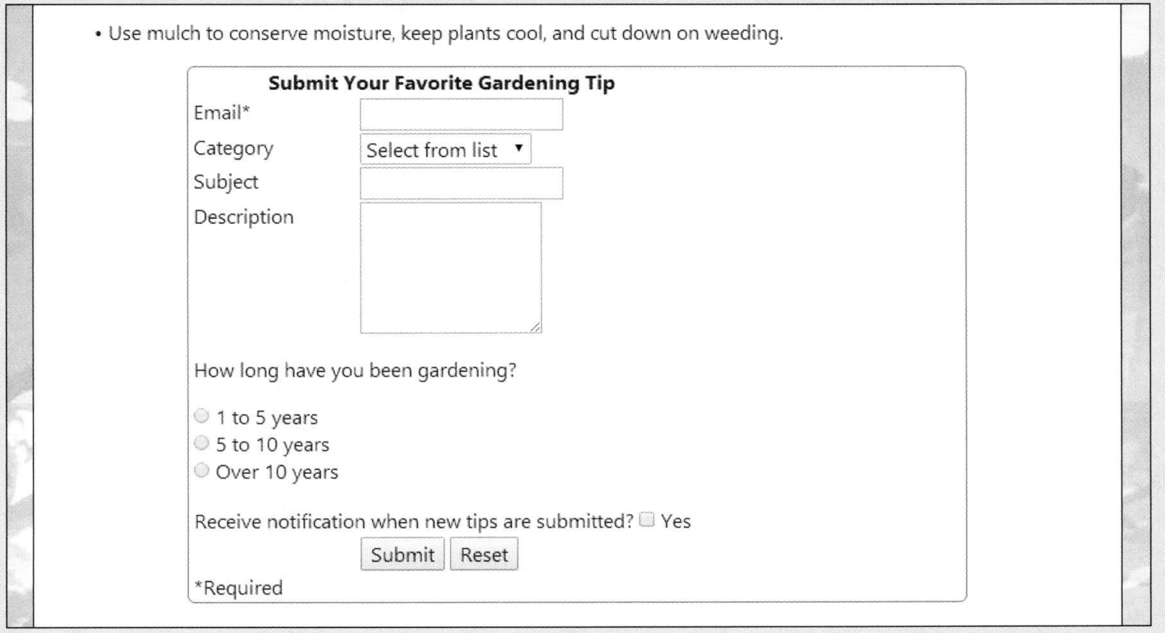

• Use mulch to conserve moisture, keep plants cool, and cut down on weeding.

Submit Your Favorite Gardening Tip

Email*

Category   Select from list ▼

Subject

Description

How long have you been gardening?

○ 1 to 5 years
○ 5 to 10 years
○ Over 10 years

Receive notification when new tips are submitted? ☐ Yes

Submit   Reset

*Required

PROJECT BUILDER 1

In this exercise, you continue your work on the TripSmart website you created in Chapters 1 through 8. The owner, Thomas Howard, wants you to create a form to collect information from users who are interested in receiving more information on one or more of the featured trips.

1. Open the TripSmart website.
2. Open the tours page, then insert a horizontal rule above the contact information.
3. Insert a form named **information** under the horizontal rule.
4. Specify the Method as POST, if necessary, and a target of _self.
5. Insert a table in the form that contains 8 rows, 1 column and a top Header.

6. In the top row, type **Please complete for more information on these tours.**.
7. Type **Email:** in the second row, and **I am interested in:** in the fourth row.
8. Insert a single-line text field in the third row with the name **email**.
9. Set the Size to 30 and the Max Length to 50 for the text field, then remove the default label.
10. In the fifth row, insert a Checkbox group with the name **tours**.
11. Use the Labels **Egypt** and **Argentina** with line breaks and the values **egypt** and **argentina**.

12. Insert a Submit button and a Reset button in the seventh row.
13. Adjust your style sheet rules to fine-tune the placement of the form and appearance of the form elements on the page and add any additional enhancements, such as horizontal rules, to set off the form on the page.
14. Save your work, preview the page in your browser, test the form with three different screen sizes, compare your screen to Figure 35, close your browser, then close the tours page. (Your page will differ depending on the settings you have chosen.)

Figure 35 *Completed Project Builder 1*

Home   Catalog   Services   Tours   Newsletter

Destinations: Egypt and Argentina

We are featuring two new trips for the coming year. The first is to Egypt. After arriving, we will check into our hotel and enjoy the sights for two days in Cairo, including the famous Egyptian Museum of Antiquities. Next, we will fly to Luxor to visit the Temple of Karnak and then boad our luxury Nile cruise boat, the Sun Queen VII. As we slowly cruise down the Nile, our stops will include Qena, the Ptolemaic Temple of Goddess Hathor in Denderah, the Edfu Temple, the Kom Ombo Temple, and the Philae Temple. We will enjoy a felucca ride around Elephantine Island, and then attend a formal farewell dinner the last night onboard our boat. We return to Cairo and enjoy a day in the market and a walking tour of the old walled city of Cairo.

Argentina is our next destination. We begin our tour in Buenos Aires on our first day with an orientation to this lovely city, including the gardens of Palermo, San Telmo, the business center, La Boca, and Recoleta Cemetery. That evening we will attend a Tango class to learn basic tango steps before having a chance to show off our talents at a dinner and tango show. The two main features for most people on this trip are the magnificient Iguassu Falls and Perito Moreno Glacier. The most adventurous can strap on trampons and trek across the glacier. A trek across a glacier with the beautiful blue Patagonia skys overhead is not to be forgotten. With luck, you will witness a calving, when ice breaks off the glacier with a crash of thunder and falls to the water.

Please complete for more information on these tours.

Email:

[   ]

I am interested in:

☐ Egypt
☐ Argentina

[Submit] [Reset]

Use Figure 36 as a guide to continue your work on the Carolyne's Creations website you created in Project Builder 2 in Chapters 1 through 8. Chef Carolyne asked you to place a simple form on the classes page that allows customers to sign up for a class.

1. Open the Carolyne's Creations website.
2. Open the classes page.
3. Insert a form named **classes** right above the contact information with POST as the method and _self as the target.

4. Insert a table in the form that contains 11 rows, 2 columns, and a top header.
5. Merge the cells in the top row, then type **Class Registration Form**.
6. In the first cell in the second row, type **Please select the class:**.
7. In the first cell in the third row, insert a check box named **adult** with the Value adult. Replace the default label with **"Adults' Class"**.
8. In the first cell in the fourth row, repeat Step 7 to add another check box with the name **children** with the value children. Replace the default label with **"Children's Class"**.

9. In the first cell in the fifth row, type **Please select the month:**.
10. In the first cell in the sixth row, add a radio button group named **month** with a button for **March** and a button for **April** with the Values march and april.
11. In the first cell in the seventh row, add a text field for a contact telephone number with a label tag identifying the text field before the text field.
12. In the first cell in the eighth row, add a text field for the first name, using settings of your choice.
13. In the first cell in the ninth row, add a text field for the last name, using settings of your choice.

14. Skip the tenth row, then add a Submit and Reset button in the eleventh row.
15. Merge the cells in the second column and insert the image "argentina_merinque.jpg" from the drive and folder where your Chapter 9 Data Files are stored.
16. Add any additional formatting of your choice to the page, table, or form properties.
17. Save your work, preview the page in a browser, test the form, compare your screen to Figure 36 for a suggested design, close your browser, then close the classes page.

Figure 36 *Sample Project Builder 2*

Cooking Classes are fun!

Chef Carolyne loves to offer a fun and relaxing cooking school each month in her newly refurbished kitchen. She teaches an adults' class on the fourth Saturday of each month from 6:00 to 8:00 pm. Each class will learn to cook a complete dinner and then enjoy the meal at the end of the class with a wonderful wine pairing. This is a great chance to get together with friends for a fun evening.

Chef Carolyne also teaches a children's class on the second Tuesday of each month from 4:00 to 5:30 pm. Our young chefs will learn to cook two dishes that will accompany a full meal served at 5:30 pm. Children aged 5–8 years accompanied by an adult are welcome. We also host small birthday parties where we put the guests to work baking and decorating the cake! Call for times and prices.

We offer several special adults' classes throughout the year. The Valentine Chocolate Extravaganza is a particular favorite. You will learn to dip strawberries, make truffles, and bake a sinful Triple Chocolate Dare You Torte. We also host the Not So Traditional Thanksgiving class and the Super Bowl Snacks class each year with rave reviews. Watch the website for details! Prices are $45.00 for each adults' class and $15.00 for each children's class. Sign up for classes by calling 555-963-8271 or by emailing us: Sign me up! See what's cooking this month for the adults' class and children's class.

Class Registration Form

Please select the class:
☐ Adults' Class
☐ Children's Class

Please select the month:

○ March
○ April

Contact Number: [_____]
First Name: [_____]
Last Name: [_____]

[Submit] [Reset]

CAROLYNE'S CREATIONS
496 MAPLE AVENUE
SEVEN FALLS, VIRGINIA 52404
555-963-8271
EMAIL CAROLYNE KATE

Copyright 2002 - 2016
Last updated on May 23, 2014

Websites use many form objects to collect information from users. The form shown in Figure 37 is well organized and requests information that most people are comfortable giving over the Internet, such as name, address, and phone number. There are several helpful explanations that guide the user in filling out the form correctly to report an environmental violation.

1. Connect to the Internet, then navigate to the U.S. Environmental Protection Agency website, pictured in Figure 37, epa.gov. (The page in Figure 37 is at epa.gov/compliance/complaints/index.html.)

2. Does this site use forms to collect information? If so, identify each of the form objects used to create the form.

3. Is the form organized logically? Explain why or why not.

4. Locate the form action for each form. (*Hint*: To view the code of a page in a browser, select View on the menu bar of your browser, then select Source or Page Source. Your browser may have a slightly different menu command to view the source code.)

5. Do you see any hidden fields?

6. Are any of the forms secure?

7. Could the information in this form be collected with different types of form objects? If so, which form objects would you use?

8. Does the form use tables for page layout?

9. Does the form use labels for its fields? If so, were the labels created using the <label> element or with text labels in table cells? (*Hint*: Search the code for the form to look for <label> tags.)

Figure 37 *Design Project*

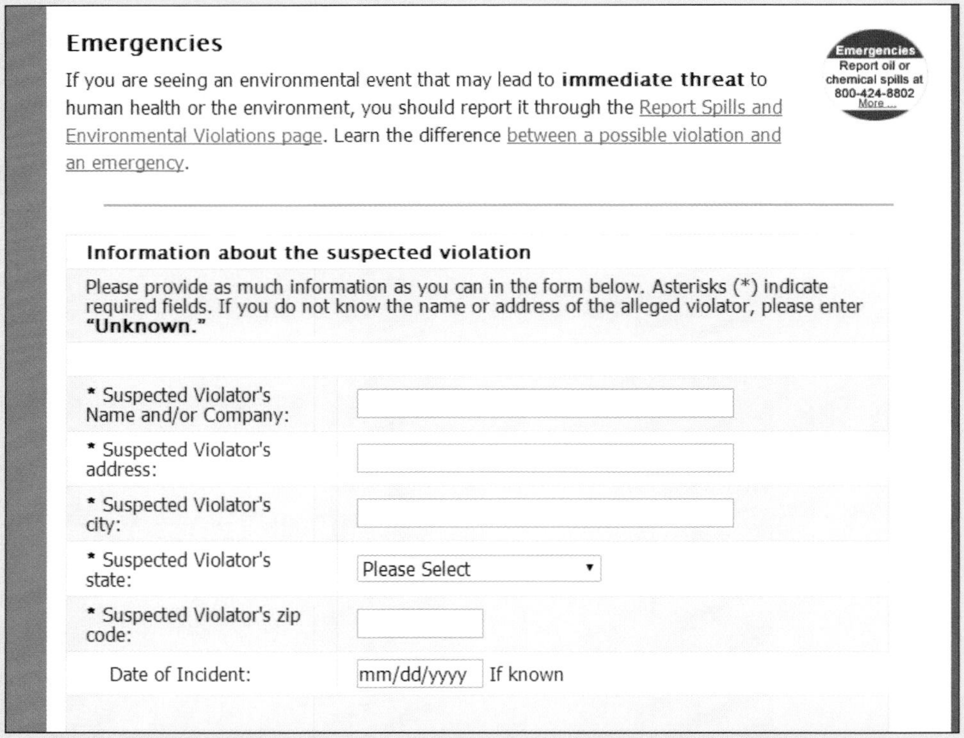

Emergencies

If you are seeing an environmental event that may lead to **immediate threat** to human health or the environment, you should report it through the Report Spills and Environmental Violations page. Learn the difference between a possible violation and an emergency.

Emergencies
Report oil or
chemical spills at
800-424-8802
More....

Information about the suspected violation

Please provide as much information as you can in the form below. Asterisks (*) indicate required fields. If you do not know the name or address of the alleged violator, please enter **"Unknown."**

* Suspected Violator's Name and/or Company:

* Suspected Violator's address:

* Suspected Violator's city:

* Suspected Violator's state: Please Select

* Suspected Violator's zip code:

Date of Incident: mm/dd/yyyy   If known

Source: U. S. Environmental Protection Agency

In this project, you continue to work on the website that you have been developing since Chapter 1.

You continue building your site by designing and completing a page that contains a form to collect visitor information as it relates to the topic of your site.

1. Review your wireframe. Choose a page to develop that will use a form to collect information.
2. Plan the content for the new page by making a list of the information that you will collect and the types of form objects you will use to collect that information. Plan to include at least one of every type of form object you learned about in the chapter. Be sure to specify how you will organize the form on the page.
3. Create the form and its contents.
4. Run a report that checks for broken links in the site. Correct any broken links that appear in the report.
5. Test the form by previewing it in a browser, entering information into it, and resetting it. Check to make sure the information gets to its specified location, whether that is a database or an email address.
6. Preview all the pages in a browser, then test all menus and links. Evaluate the pages for both content and layout.
7. Review the checklist shown in Figure 38. Make any modifications necessary to improve the form, the jump menu, or the page containing the form.
8. Close all open pages.

Figure 38 *Portfolio Project*

> ### Website Checklist
> 1. Do all navigation links work?
> 2. Do all images appear correctly?
> 3. Do all form objects align correctly with their form labels?
> 4. Does the placement of the form objects appear in a logical order?
> 5. Does the most important information appear at the top of the form?
> 6. Did you test the form?
> 7. Are you happy with the overall appearance of each page in three different screen sizes?

© 2015 Cengage Learning®

CHAPTER **10** ADDING MEDIA AND
INTERACTIVITY

1. Add and modify Flash objects
2. Add rollover images
3. Add behaviors and CSS transitions
4. Add video
5. Add sound

DREAMWEAVER

DREAMWEAVER

CHAPTER 10

ADDING MEDIA AND
INTERACTIVITY

Introduction

While a website with text and static images is adequate for presenting information, you can create a much richer user experience by adding movement and interactive elements. You can use Dreamweaver to add media objects created in other programs to your web pages. Some of the external media file types include Adobe Fireworks menu bars, rollover images, and buttons; video, sound, and animation; and a variety of plug-ins. A **plug-in** (also called an **add-on**) is a small computer program that works with a host application such as a web browser to allow it to perform certain functions. For example, older web browsers usually don't come with the ability to play animations. So to play a Flash SWF file in a web browser, you would need to install the Adobe Flash Player plug-in. Newer browsers come with Flash Player preinstalled. To read Adobe PDF files, you need to install the Adobe Reader plug-in. Other players include Windows Media Player and RealPlayer by RealNetworks. Plug-ins allow you to extend the capabilities of the

browser to display content, letting you create complex, interactive websites with media effects that can be viewed within the pages themselves. Then the pages don't have to load an external document player. In this chapter, you will use Dreamweaver to add media objects to The Striped Umbrella website and the means to allow them to play.

Understanding Media Objects

The term "media objects" has different meanings, depending on who you are talking to, and the industry in which they work. For our purposes, **media objects** are combinations of visual and audio effects and text that help make a website a fully engaging experience. Although this might be an open-ended definition, it is the experience you are striving for when you add video and audio elements to a web page. Think about the experience of watching a movie. You are engaged not just by the actors, but also by the sounds and special effects you experience. You want to create this same type of experience for your website users by adding media elements to your pages.

TOOLS YOU'LL USE

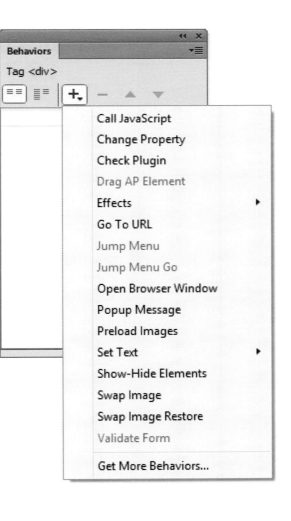

Add and Modify
FLASH OBJECTS

What You'll Do

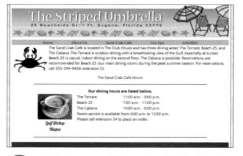

In this lesson, you will insert and modify a Flash movie on the cafe page, and then play the movie both in Dreamweaver and in a browser.

Understanding Adobe Flash

Flash is a software program that allows you to create low-bandwidth, high-quality animations and interactive elements that you can place on your web pages. **Low-bandwidth** animations are animations that don't require a fast connection to work properly. These animations use a series of vector-based graphics that load quickly and merge with other graphics and sounds to create short movies. **Vector-based graphics** are scalable graphics that are built using mathematical formulas, rather than built with pixels. Figure 1 shows the Flash program used to create Flash objects.

Once you create these short movies, you can place them on your web pages. Flash movies require Flash Player, a plug-in that is included in the latest versions of Internet Explorer, Mozilla Firefox, Safari, and Chrome, so users can view them. If you are using an older browser that does not support the version of Flash used to create your movie, you can download the latest Flash Player from the Adobe website, located at adobe.com. Almost all desktop Internet browsers worldwide use Flash Player. Previously, the mobile and touch-screen markets were not as supportive.

But Flash Professional can convert a Flash source file (FLA) to a format that can be used with iOS. This enables an iPhone or iPad to play the Flash content.

As HTML5 gains support across all browsers, you will want to use HTML5 tags to insert and format your media content. For example, the steps we will use to insert a Flash SWF file (named crabdance.swf) in this chapter work fine in all browsers that support the Flash plug-in. For those that don't, you will want to explore options for providing your Flash content. One way is to convert an existing Flash file to a JavaScript file and insert it as a script file onto a canvas. A **canvas** is an HTML5 element that serves as a container for graphics. It uses opening and closing <canvas> tags, along with an ID and height and width values. It begins as an empty rectangle on a page with no content. You add content using JavaScript.

Inserting Flash Content

When you use the Insert panel to add Flash content to a web page, the code that links and runs the content (such as detecting the presence of Flash Player on the computer and directing the user to download the player if it is not found) is embedded into the page code. The original Flash file is stored as a separate file in the website root folder.

There are several types of Flash content that you can incorporate to enhance your users' experiences as they view and interact with your website. A **Flash button** is a button made from a small, predefined Flash movie that you can insert on a web page to provide site navigation, either in place of or in addition to other types of hyperlinks, such as plain text links. You can assign Flash buttons a variety of behaviors in response to user actions, such as opening a different page in the browser when the pointer is placed over it. Flash buttons have the .swf file extension.

Using Flash, you can also create Flash movies that include multimedia elements, such as audio files (both music and voiceovers), animated objects, scripted objects, clickable links, and just about any other animated or clickable object imaginable.

To add a Flash movie to a web page, select Flash SWF from the Media category on the Insert panel to open the Select SWF dialog box, and then choose the Flash movie you want to insert. As with images, always add a title tag when inserting Flash content to provide accessibility. To view your Flash movies, you can either use Live view or preview them in a browser window. It is a kindness to your users to turn off the loop option for Flash movies unless you want the Flash content to play continuously while the page is being viewed. Content that plays continuously can be irritating to users when they do not have the controls to stop it.

Converting a Flash Movie to an HTML5-Compliant File

If you decide to convert a Flash SWF file to one that is HTML5-compliant, one option is to convert the SWF file to a JavaScript file and an HTML5 file. The JavaScript file will play by itself and the HTML5 file will play by itself, but to place the JavaScript file into a canvas on another HTML5 page, you will need to copy part of the code generated by the HTML5 file and place it on the destination page. To do this, open Flash Professional, then open your FLA source file. Use the Commands, Convert to HTML5 canvas from AS3 document format command to save a copy of the file that can be used with a canvas tag. Publish the new movie with any additional settings, such as removing the loop so the movie will not play continuously. Publish both a JavaScript file and an HTML5 file.

Figure 1 *Adobe Flash CC workspace*

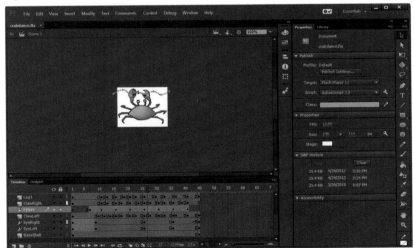

You perform the next steps in Dreamweaver. First, open an existing page or create a new one to insert your movie. Use the Insert, Canvas command, then make any adjustments to the default settings using the Property inspector. Open the HTML5 copy of the file you created, copy the script codes in the head content, and paste them in the head content of your page with the canvas. Copy the script code from the body section of the HTML5 file, then paste it into the body section of the page with the canvas. This is one solution, and only works with simple animations.

Flash files that use extensive Action Script 3 do not convert well because the scripts are not automatically rewritten during the conversion process. The results will not match the original SWF file exactly. However, your page will pass HTML5 validation and the movie can be accessed by all users, regardless of device type.

Insert Flash movies

1. Open the cafe page in The Striped Umbrella website.

2. Place the insertion point in front of the first paragraph, change to Code view and verify that the insertion point is in front of the opening <p> tag if necessary, then return to Design view.

3. Select the **Media** category on the Insert panel, then select **Flash SWF**.

4. Navigate to the drive and folder where you store your Data Files, select **crabdance.swf**, select **OK** (Win) or **Open** (Mac), select **Yes** and then select **Save** to save the movie in the site root folder, type **Crab logo animation** in the Title text box in the Object Tag Accessibility Attributes dialog box, then select **OK**. A Flash movie placeholder appears on the page.

   TIP If you already have a Flash file in your site root folder, you can drag and drop it from the Assets panel or Files panel instead of using the Insert panel or Insert menu.

5. Create a new GLOBAL class selector in su_styles.css named **.flash_float** with the float value set to **left**, then apply the .flash_float selector to the crabdance.swf placeholder.

6. Select the **Loop check box** on the Property inspector to deselect it, change the ID to **crab_logo**, then compare your screen to Figure 2.

   By turning off the Loop option, the file will play once in the browser, then stop.

You inserted a Flash movie on the cafe page of The Striped Umbrella website.

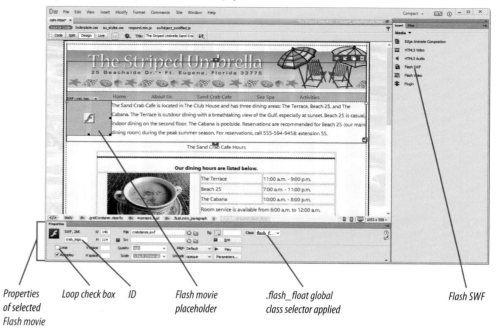

Figure 2 *Flash movie placeholder on the cafe page*

Properties of selected Flash movie | Loop check box | ID | Flash movie placeholder | .flash_float global class selector applied | Flash SWF

Collecting Flash Objects

Adobe and their devoted product users provide you with a variety of downloadable Flash objects that are available on the Adobe Add-ons website, located at http://creative.adobe.com/addons. At this site, you can find collections of menus, transitions, image galleries, and just about anything else you might want. If you can't find exactly what you need, you can download a trial version of Flash to experiment with creating your own Flash objects.

Figure 3 *Flash movie playing in Dreamweaver*

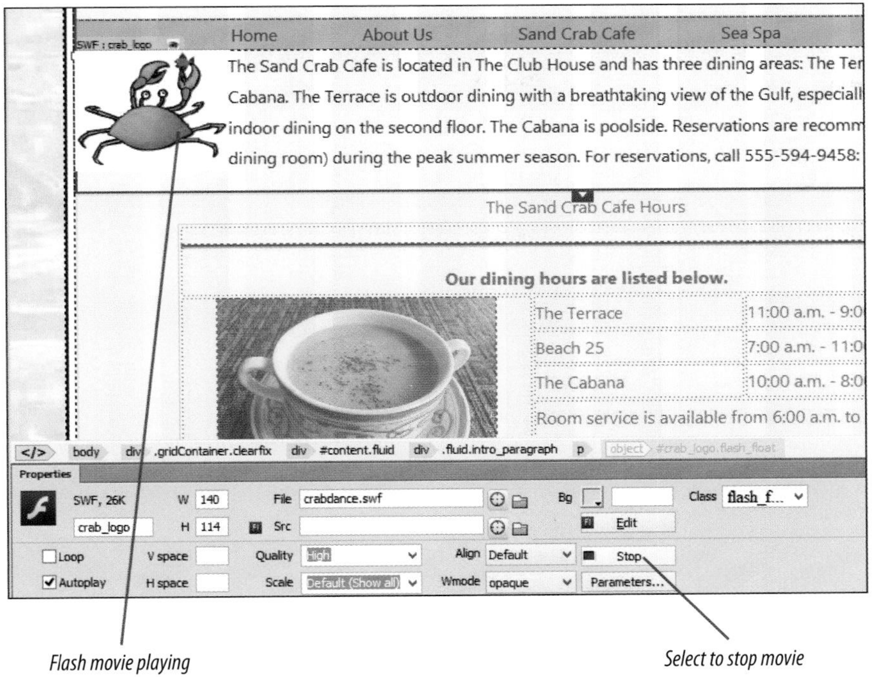

Flash movie playing

Select to stop movie

Figure 4 *Flash movie playing in the browser*

Play a Flash movie in Dreamweaver and in a browser

1. With the placeholder selected, select the **Play button** in the Property inspector to view the crabdance.swf movie, as shown in Figure 3, then select **Stop** (Win) or skip to Step 2 (Mac).

TIP Mac users do not have a Play button in their Property inspector.

2. Save your work, then select **OK** to close the Copy Dependent Files dialog box.

   Two supporting files, expressInstall.swf and swfobject_modified.js, are copied to a new Scripts folder. These files are necessary for the movie to play in the browser correctly.

3. Preview the page in your browser, compare your screen to Figure 4, then close your browser.

TIP If the movie did not play in Internet Explorer, select Tools on the menu bar, select Internet Options, select the Advanced tab, then select the Allow active content to run in files on My Computer under the Advanced tab Security category. If you are using a different browser or a version of Internet Explorer that is earlier than 11.0, look for a similar setting.

You played a Flash movie on the cafe page in The Striped Umbrella website in Dreamweaver and in your browser.

Insert an animation with a canvas

1. With the cafe page open in Design view, select and delete the Flash placeholder.

   This deletes the link to the crabdance.swf file on the cafe page, but does not delete the file from the local site folder.

(continued)

2. With the insertion point at the beginning of the first sentence, select **Insert** on the Menu bar, then select **Canvas**.

   A placeholder image representing a blank canvas appears above the paragraph.

3. Leave the placeholder text "canvas" in the ID text box on the Property inspector, type **140** in the W text box, type **114** in the H text box, as shown in Figure 5, then save your work.

   With HTML5 canvas, you can now use JavaScript so users can draw images on it or you can fill it with an image already created using JavaScript. You will add script tags that will place the crabdance movie inside the canvas.

4. Open your file manager program, browse to the drive and folder where you store your Chapter 10 Data Files, copy the files **crabdance_html5.js**, and **crabdance_html5.html**, then paste them into your local site folder.

5. In Dreamweaver open the file crabdance_html5.html, switch to Code view, then copy all of the script tags that begin under the page title in the head section to the ending </script> tag right before the closing </head> tag (approximately lines 7 through 40).

   There are five different script tags. The first four are only one line each, but the last script tag has many lines of code. All of these script tags are required to create the animation.

6. Switch to the cafe page in Code view, then paste the copied script tags right above the closing </head> tag.

7. Select **Refresh** on the Property inspector, save the cafe page, then close the crabdance_html5.html page.

(continued)

Figure 5 *Setting properties for a canvas on the cafe page*

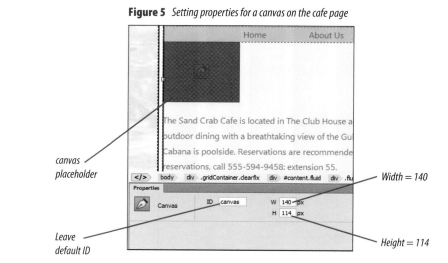

canvas placeholder

Leave default ID

Width = 140

Height = 114

Figure 6 *Adding code to the cafe page body tag*

Type this code in the opening <body> tag

Adding Media Objects Using HTML5 and Adobe Edge

Although Adobe Flash is still the premier tool used for creating animation, the development of HTML5 and CSS3 has given us new ways to incorporate motion and animation. HTML5 includes new tags for animation and video, such as the <audio> tag and the <video> tag, with attributes to set playback options such as autoplay, controls, loop, and src. CSS3 has new styles for enhancing the appearance of page objects, such as playback controls. **Adobe Edge** combines the capabilities of HTML5, CSS3, and JavaScript, but uses a program interface similar to Flash. Like Flash, Adobe Edge has a stage, timeline, playhead, symbols, frames, and layers you can use to manipulate text, shapes, and images. Unlike Flash, Edge codes in **JSON (JavaScript Object Notation)**, a subset of JavaScript, rather than ActionScript. This means that Edge creates animation that is coded entirely with HTML and JavaScript, so browsers that support HTML5 will not need a plug-in to play the animations. Edge also integrates with font services such as TypeKit or FontSquirrel.

Figure 7 *Properties and values for the #canvas selector*

CSS Designer | CSS Transitions

Sources   + −
- ALL SOURCES
- boilerplate.css
- su_styles.css

@Media   + −
- GLOBAL
- only screen and (min-width : 481px)
- only screen and (min-width : 769px)

Selectors   + −
- Filter CSS Rules
- td
- tr td img
- .feature_item
- .table_div
- hr
- #canvas
- body
- ul li a:hover

Properties   +   ☑ Show Set

Layout
display : inline
margin : 5px

float :

Custom
add property : add value

Figure 8 *Viewing the cafe page with the new crabdance file*

The Striped Umbrella
25 Beachside Dr. • Ft. Eugene, Florida 33775

Home   About Us   Sand Crab Cafe   Sea Spa   Activities

The Sand Crab Cafe is located in The Club House and has three dining areas: The Terrace, Beach 25, and The Cabana. The Terrace is outdoor dining with a breathtaking view of the Gulf, especially at sunset. Beach 25 is casual, indoor dining on the second floor. The Cabana is poolside. Reservations are recommended for Beach 25 (our main dining room) during the peak summer season. For reservations, call 555-594-9458: extension 55.

The Sand Crab Cafe Hours

Our dining hours are listed below.

The Terrace   11:00 a.m. - 9:00 p.m.
Beach 25   7:00 a.m. - 11:00 p.m.
The Cabana   10:00 a.m. - 8:00 p.m.
Room service is available from 6:00 a.m. to 12:00 a.m.
Please call extension 54 to place an order.

Gulf Shrimp Bisque

8. On the cafe page, scroll to find the opening <body> tag, place the insertion point after the word "body", press the spacebar to add a space, type **onload="init()"** , as shown in Figure 6, then save your work.

   This code tells the browser to load the JavaScript code from the head section that controls the canvas content when the page opens.

9. Return to Design view, then create a new global selector in the su_styles.css file named **#canvas** with the following properties as shown in Figure 7:

   display: **inline**;

   all margins: **5px**;

   float: **left**;

10. Save your work, preview the cafe page in the browser, compare your screen to Figure 8, then close the browser.

    The crab animation isn't as detailed as the original Flash swf file, but it still looks good on the page. The advantage of using it is that the page will now pass HTML5 validation and will run on any device, including those that do not run Flash.

11. Select **File** on the Menu bar, select **Validate**, select **Validate Current Document (W3C)**, then select **OK** to close the W3C Validator Notification dialog box, if it opens.

    The cafe page has no errors or warnings.

12. Close the Results tab group.

You created a canvas on the cafe page, then copied and typed JavaScript to both the head and body sections of the page in Code view to insert a crab animation on the page.

Add Rollover
IMAGES

What You'll Do

In this lesson, you will add two rollover images to the activities page of The Striped Umbrella website.

Understanding Rollover Images

A **rollover image** is an image that changes its appearance when the pointer is placed over it in a browser. A rollover image actually consists of two images. The first image is the one that appears when the pointer is not positioned over it, and the second image is the one that appears when the pointer is positioned over it. Rollover images are often used to help create a feeling of action and excitement on a web page. For instance, suppose you are creating a website that promotes a series of dance classes. You could create a rollover image using two images of a dancer in two different poses. When a user places the pointer over the image of the dancer in the first pose, the image would change to show the dancer in a different pose, creating a feeling of movement.

QUICK TIP

You can also add a link to a rollover image, so that the image will change only when the image is selected.

Adding Rollover Images

You add rollover images to a web page using the Rollover Image command on the Images menu in the Insert bar Common category shown in Figure 9. You specify both the original image and the rollover image in the Insert Rollover Image dialog box. The rollover image is the image that appears when the user moves (rolls) the pointer over the original image. To prevent one of the images from changing size during the rollover, both images should be the same height and width.

Another way to create a rollover image, button, or menu bar is to insert it as a Fireworks HTML file. After you create and export the file from Fireworks, the code for the rollover is automatically inserted in the web page file. The Fireworks HTML command is also on the Images menu, as shown in Figure 9.

You can also use rollover images to display an image associated with a text link. For instance, suppose you are creating a website for an upcoming election. You could create a web page that contains a list of candidates for the election and add a rollover image for each candidate's name that would result in a photograph of the candidate appearing when the pointer is placed over his or her name. You can also use this effect to make appropriate images appear when users point to different menu options. For instance, Figure 10 shows the Pottery Barn website, which uses rollovers to display detailed sections of plates when the pointer is moved over them. The shaded preview window shows, by the pointer position, which part of the plate will be enlarged in a separate window next to the window with the smaller image.

When a rollover image is inserted onto a page, Dreamweaver automatically adds two behaviors; a Swap Image behavior and a Swap Image Restore behavior. A **Swap Image behavior** is JavaScript code that directs the browser to display a different image when the pointer is rolled over an image on the page. A **Swap Image Restore** behavior restores the swapped image back to the original image.

Figure 9 *Image menu on the Insert panel*

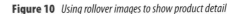

Image menu

Rollover Image command

Figure 10 *Using rollover images to show product detail*

Window with enlarged section of an image follows pointer as it rolls over a smaller image

Source: Pottery Barn

Add a rollover image

1. Close the cafe page; then open the activities page of The Striped Umbrella website.

2. Close the Design notes window, scroll down to find the image of the two dolphins, then delete it.

3. Select the **Image list arrow** in the Common group on the Insert panel, then select **Rollover Image**.

4. Type **dolphins** in the Image name text box.

5. Select **Browse** next to the Original image text box, browse to the drive and folder where you store your Data Files, open the assets folder, then double-click **one_dolphin.jpg**.

6. Select **Browse** next to the Rollover image text box, navigate to the Chapter 10 Data Files assets folder, then double-click the **two_dolphins.jpg** file.

7. Type **Dolphins riding the surf** in the Alternate text text box, compare your screen to Figure 11, then select **OK**.

8. Select the image, apply the **img_float_right** selector, save your work, preview the page in your browser, move your pointer over the dolphin image, then compare your screen to Figure 12.

   When you point to the image, the one_dolphin image is "swapped" with the two_dolphin image.

TIP If the rollover does not work, remember to direct your browser to allow blocked content.

(continued)

Figure 11 *Browsing to find the source files for the rollover image*

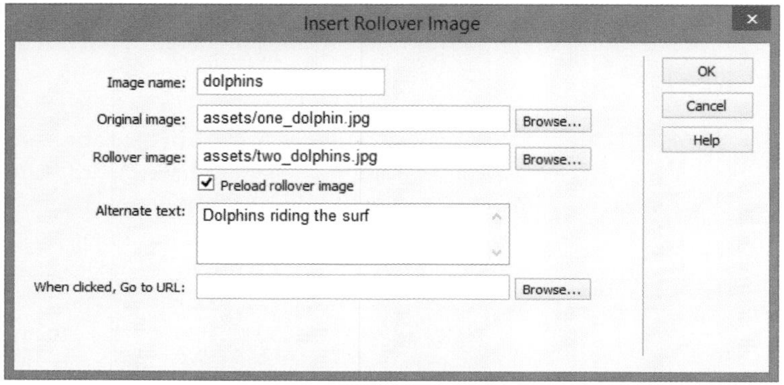

Figure 12 *Viewing the rollover image in the browser*

Image is swapped when user places pointer over it

Figure 13 *Swap behavior code for rollover image*

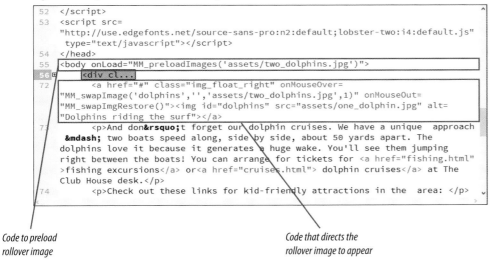

```
52  </script>
53  <script src=
    "http://use.edgefonts.net/source-sans-pro:n2:default;lobster-two:i4:default.js"
     type="text/javascript"></script>
54  </head>
55  <body onLoad="MM_preloadImages('assets/two_dolphins.jpg')">
56    <div cl...
72        <a href="#" class="img_float_right" onMouseOver=
    "MM_swapImage('dolphins','','assets/two_dolphins.jpg',1)" onMouseOut=
    "MM_swapImgRestore()"><img id="dolphins" src="assets/one_dolphin.jpg" alt=
    "Dolphins riding the surf"></a>
73        <p>And don&rsquo;t forget our dolphin cruises. We have a unique  approach
     &mdash; two boats speed along, side by side, about 50 yards apart. The
    dolphins love it because it generates a huge wake. You'll see them jumping
    right between the boats! You can arrange for tickets for <a href="fishing.html"
    >fishing excursions</a> or<a href="cruises.html"> dolphin cruises</a> at The
    Club House desk.</p>
74        <p>Check out these links for kid-friendly attractions in the  area: </p>
```

Code to preload
rollover image

Code that directs the
rollover image to appear

9. Close the browser.

10. Switch to Code view, then locate the code for the swap image behavior, shown in Figure 13.

    Figure 13 shows Code view with the code collapsed between the two sections of code for the rollover. The first section of the code is part of the opening <body> tag. It instructs the browser to preload the second image used in the rollover. The second part of the code directs the browser to display the image with one dolphin "onmouseout"— when the pointer is not over the image. It directs the browser to display the image with two dolphins "onmouseover"—when the pointer is over the image.

TIP If your code is selected in Code view, that means the image is selected in Design view.

11. Return to Design view, then select the **Switch Design View to Live View button** [Live] and place your pointer over the dolphin image.

    Live view allows you to preview the swap image behavior as it will appear in the browser.

12. Select [Live] to turn off Live view.

You replaced an image with a rollover image on the activities page of The Striped Umbrella website, then viewed the rollover in the browser and in Live view.

Add Behaviors and
CSS TRANSITIONS

What You'll Do

In this lesson, you will add an action that opens a browser window from the activities page of The Striped Umbrella website. You will then change the event for that action. Next, you will add a CSS Transition to the ul li a selector that will work for all device sizes.

Adding Interactive Elements

You can make your web pages come alive by adding interactive elements to them. For instance, if you are creating a page about animals, you could attach an action to each picture that would result in a pop-up message with a description of the animal when the user rolls the pointer over it. You can add actions like this to elements by attaching behaviors to them. **Behaviors** are sets of instructions that you can attach to page elements that tell the page element to respond in a specific way when an event occurs, such as when the pointer is positioned over the element. When you attach a behavior to an element, Dreamweaver generates the JavaScript code for the behavior and inserts it into your page code.

Using the Behaviors Panel

You can use the Behaviors panel, which you open from the Windows menu, to insert a variety of JavaScript-based behaviors on a page. For instance, using the Behaviors panel, you can automate tasks, have items respond to user selections and pointer movements with pop-up menus, create games, go to a different URL, or add automatic dynamic effects to a web page. To insert a behavior, select the Add behavior button on the Behaviors panel to open the Actions menu, as shown in Figure 14, then select a behavior from the menu.

Understanding Actions and Events

Actions are triggered by events. For instance, if you want the user to see a page element slide across the page when the element is selected, you would attach the Slide action using the onClick event to trigger the action. Other examples of events are onMouseOver and onLoad. The onMouseOver event will trigger an action when the pointer is placed over an object. The onLoad event will trigger an action when the page is first loaded in the browser window.

Using CSS Transitions

CSS transitions are effects you can use to change from one style to another on a page, effectively letting you create animations without using Flash or JavaScript. One of the more common CSS transitions alters the appearance of a link when the user's pointer moves over it, called "on rollover." For example, if you want a link to change color from blue to orange on rollover, you can add a transition that changes the color slowly, creating a fade-in/fade-out effect. You can also specify when a transition will begin, the speed the transition will use, and how long it will take for the transition to complete. To create CSS transitions, you use the CSS Transitions panel, which is docked by default to the CSS Designer panel.

Figure 14 *Behaviors panel with the Actions menu open*

Figure 15 *CSS Transitions panel*

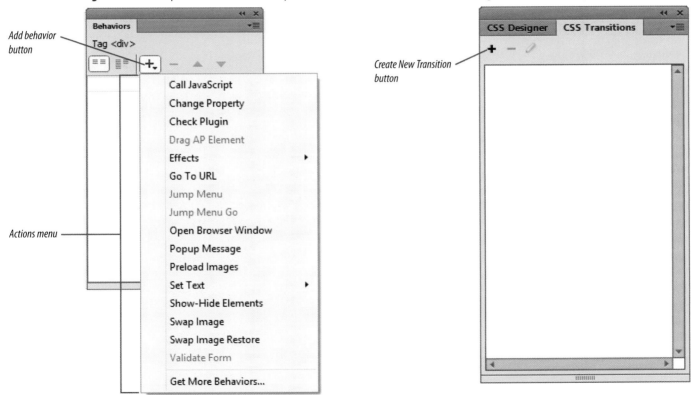

Add behavior button

Actions menu

Create New Transition button

Add a behavior

1. Open the file dw10_1.html from the drive and folder where you store your Data Files, then save it in the site root folder as **wildlife_message.html**, without updating links. Close the dw10_1.html page.

2. Select the **family_sunset image** on the activities page, select **Window** on the Menu bar, then select **Behaviors** to open the Behaviors panel.

3. Select the **Add behavior button** ＋ on the Behaviors panel toolbar to open the Actions menu, as shown in Figure 16, then select **Open Browser Window** to open the Open Browser Window dialog box.

4. Select **Browse** next to the URL to display: text box to open the Select File dialog box, navigate to the site root folder if necessary, then double-click **wildlife_message.html**.

5. Type **300** in the Window width text box, type **300** in the Window height text box, type **message** in the Window name text box, compare your screen to Figure 17, then select **OK**.

6. Save your work, preview the page in your browser, test the Open Browser Window effect by selecting the family_sunset image, as shown in Figure 18, then close both browser windows.

TIP The pop-up window will not work if pop-up blocking is enabled in your browser. Modify your browser tools or options settings to allow pop-ups.

You added an Open Browser Window effect to an image on the activities page of The Striped Umbrella website.

Figure 16 *Adding the Open Browser Window behavior to the family_sunset image*

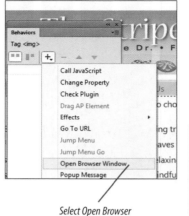

Select Open Browser Window behavior

Figure 17 *Setting Open Browser Window options*

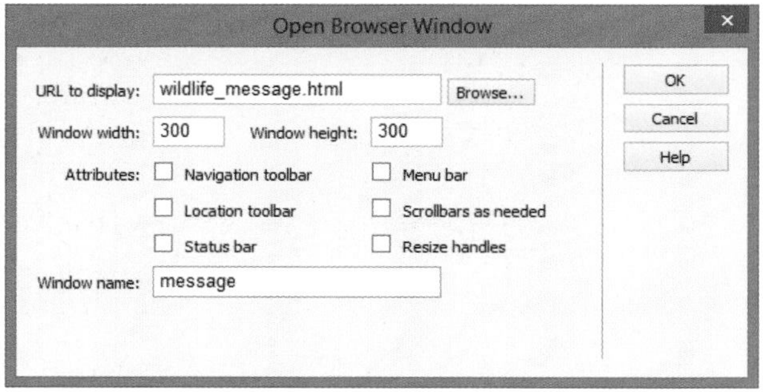

Figure 18 *Viewing the wildlife message in a browser*

Figure 19 *Viewing the edited window size for the behavior*

Figure 20 *Viewing the edited behavior*

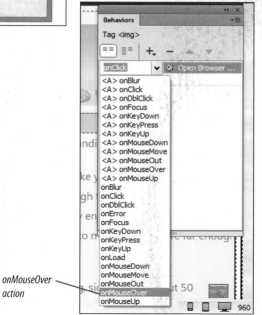

onMouseOver action

Edit a behavior

1. Select the **family_sunset image** if necessary, right-click (Win) or [control]-click (Mac) the **right column** of the Open Browser Window action on the Behaviors panel, then select **Edit Behavior**. The Open Browser Window dialog box opens.

2. Change the window height to **270**, select **OK**, save your changes, preview the page in your browser, then select the **family_sunset image**. The browser window with the wildlife message is shorter in height, as shown in Figure 19.

3. Close the browser windows.

4. Select the **onClick action** in the **left column** of the Behaviors panel to display the events list arrow, select the **list arrow**, then select **onMouseOver**, as shown in Figure 20.

   This will change the event that triggers the action from clicking the image to simply placing the pointer over the image.

5. Save your work, open the page in the browser, then move the pointer over the family_sunset image.

   Now, simply placing the pointer over the image triggers the Open Browser Window event. (*Hint*: If you don't see the new window, disable the Google toolbar, or locate the option to allow pop-ups.)

6. Close the browser windows, close the Behaviors panel, then close the wildlife_message page. Leave the activities page open.

You edited the behavior on the Behaviors panel.

Create a CSS Transition

1. With the activities page open, select the **CSS Transitions tab** in the CSS panel group, or select **Window**, then select **CSS Transitions** to open the CSS Transitions panel.

(continued)

2. Select the **Create New Transition button** ✛, select the **Target Rule list arrow**, scroll to locate and select the first **ul li a rule** listed.

   You are adding a transition that changes the color and background color of each menu bar item more slowly when the user positions the pointer over them. You will add the code for this transition to the ul li a selector in the su_styles.css file.

3. Select the **Transition On list arrow**, then select **hover**.

   This setting tells the browser to start the transition when the pointer is over the menu item.

4. Type **1** in the Duration text box.

   This setting sets the duration, or the length of time the transition takes to complete.

5. Type **.5** in the Delay text box, select **ease-in-out** in the Timing Function list box, select the **Add Property button** ✛ under the Property pane, select **background-color**, then type **#FFD195** in the End Value text box.

   The delay setting tells the browser how long to wait before it begins the transition and the background color is set to a sand color.

6. Select the **Add Property button** again, select **color**, type **#A78B6A** in the End Value text box, compare your screen to Figure 21, then select **Create Transition**.

   This is the same background color value and text color value you set earlier, but it will now slowly turn from the background color when the pointer is not over the menu item to the background color when the pointer is placed over the menu item.

   The CSS Transitions panel shows the transition for the ul li a selector, as shown in Figure 22.

   (continued)

Figure 21 *New Transition dialog box*

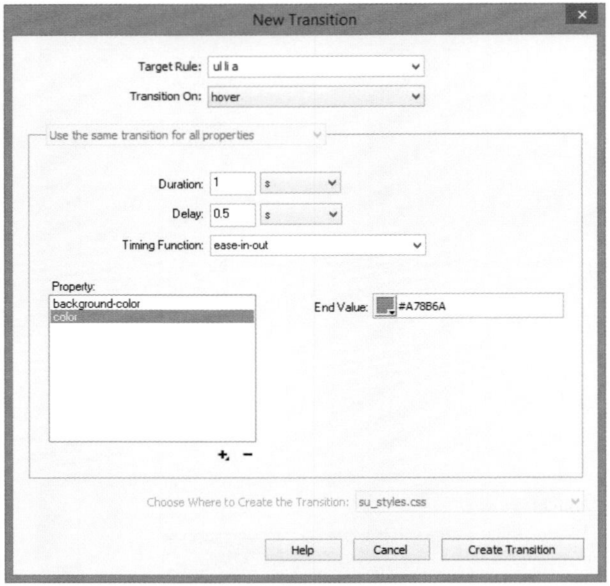

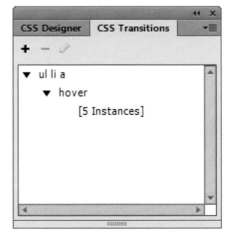

Figure 22 *CSS Transitions panel with ul li a transition listed*

Figure 23 *Viewing code added to the ul li a selector*

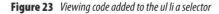

```
ul li a {
    width: 100%;
    padding-left: 4%;
    padding-right: 4%;
    text-decoration: none;
    -webkit-transition: all 1s ease-in-out 0.5s;
    -o-transition: all 1s ease-in-out 0.5s;
    transition: all 1s ease-in-out 0.5s;
}
```

Your properties may be listed in a slightly different order

Transition code added to ul li a selector

Figure 24 *Removing a transition*

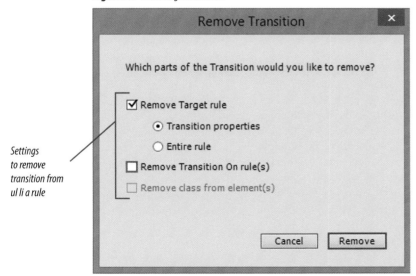

Remove Transition   ✕

Which parts of the Transition would you like to remove?

☑ Remove Target rule
    ⦿ Transition properties
    ○ Entire rule
☐ Remove Transition On rule(s)
☐ Remove class from element(s)

Cancel   Remove

Settings to remove transition from ul li a rule

Select a downward pointing triangle to collapse the line and select a right pointing triangle to expand the line to show what is under it.

7. Save all files, switch to Live view, select the **Desktop size button** 🖥 , then point to (hover over) each of the menu items.

   You can see the delay as each menu item changes color.

8. Change to the su_styles.css file in Code view, then scroll to the Desktop size section and locate the code for the transition, as shown in Figure 23.

9. Return to Design view, then open the CSS Transitions panel if necessary.

10. Select the **[5 Instances]** in the CSS Transitions panel, then select the **Remove Selected Transition button** ➖ .

11. Verify that the Remove Target rule check box is selected, select **Transition properties**, verify that the Remove Transition on rule(s) check box is not selected, as shown in Figure 24, then select **Remove**.

12. Save all files, retest your links in Live view, then turn off Live View.

    The hover properties for the links remain, but the transitions are removed.

You added a CSS transition to the menu bar items on The Striped Umbrella website, then deleted the transition.

Add
VIDEO

What You'll Do

In this lesson, you will insert a video on the activities page.

Inserting Video

Another way to add rich media content to your web pages is to insert video files. Of the several available video formats, one of the most popular is the MP4 format. You can insert a video in Dreamweaver with the Insert, HTML5 Video command. The advantages of using the HTML5 format are numerous: it supports video that users don't need a plug-in to run; it is compatible with all browsers; and you can control the video playback using a keyboard. You can also include code to link multiple video formats so that more browsers can play them, because not all browsers support the same video formats. Adding a choice of formats increases the likelihood that most users (using different browsers and devices) will be able to play them. Other video formats that you can link or embed on a web page include **AVI (Audio Visual Interleave)**, the Microsoft standard for digital video, **FLV** (Adobe Flash video), **WebM** (an open, royalty-free media format

sponsored by Google), **MOV** (Apple Quick Time), and **Ogg** (a free, open container format developed by the Xiph.Org Foundation). Currently, the MP4, WebM, and Ogg formats support the HTML5 <video> tag. However, not all browsers support all three formats, so it is a good idea to provide multiple file formats for your users to make sure that they will be able to play the video.

Figure 25 shows a page on the Federal Aviation Administration website that allows visitors to view educational videos on a number of topics. Users access playback controls with a **controller**. A controller appears as a graphic element called a **skin** placed over or below a video. Controls can include buttons or sliders to stop, start, and pause the video, control the sound level or mute the sound, or display a script of the video. After a user selects the play button, the file begins downloading and starts to play as it downloads. A **progressive video download** will download the video to the user's computer, then allow the video to

Adding Media and Interactivity

play before it has completely downloaded. It will finish the download as the video plays, but the user will not notice that this is taking place. A **streaming video download** is similar to a progressive download, except streaming video uses buffers to gather the content as it downloads to ensure a smoother playback. A **buffer** is a temporary storage area on your hard drive that acts as a holding area for the video content as it is being played. Controllers can be coded to customize both the appearance of the skin and the controls that will be included. Used sparingly, video can be an effective way to add interest and depth to your web pages.

Figure 25 *Viewing a video in a browser*

Video window

Video controls on the skin

Source: Federal Aviation Administration

Script for video is displayed when Closed caption option is selected

Sound control

Closed caption option

Add video

1. With the activities page open, delete the last paragraph on the page, then type **How about going parasailing! We can make reservations for parties of up to twelve people at a time at any of our five locations, including one at our own marina**.

2. Go to Code view and place the insertion point before the opening <p> tag for the new parasailing text, return to Design view, select the **Media** category on the Insert panel, then select **HTML5 Video**.

   A video placeholder for a movie appears above the paragraph, and the video properties appear in the Property inspector, as shown in Figure 26.

3. Select the video placeholder, select the **Browse for File button** 📁 on the Property inspector next to the Source text box, browse to the drive and folder where you store your Chapter 10 Data Files, double-click **parasailing.mp4**, then select **Yes** to close the Dreamweaver dialog box.

4. In the dialog box, navigate to your site assets folder, and select **Save**.

5. With the placeholder selected, type **parasailing** in the ID text box, select **img_float** in the Class list box, type **320** in the W text box, type **180** in the H text box, then compare your screen to Figure 27.

(continued)

Figure 26 *Inserting a video on the activities page*

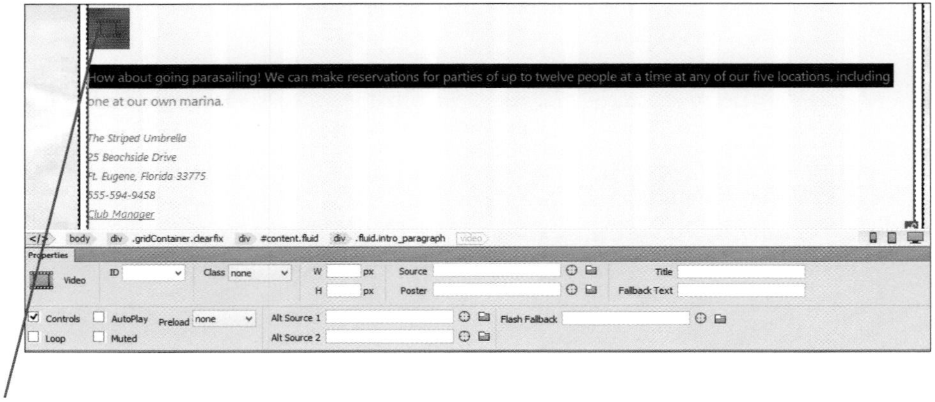

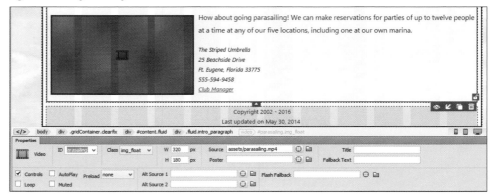

Video placeholder
inserted on page

Figure 27 *Editing the settings for the video*

Figure 28 *Adding an alternate video source file*

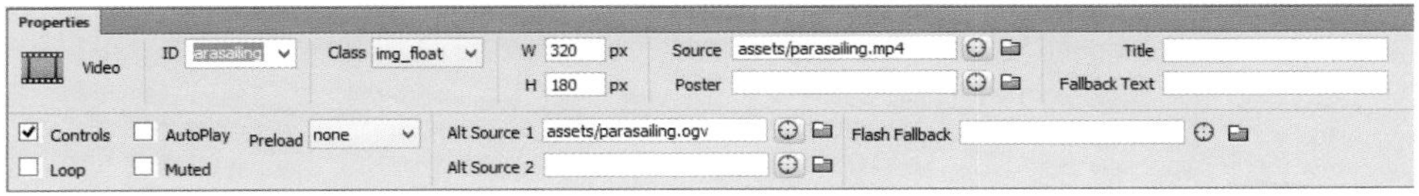

Figure 29 *Viewing the video in a browser*

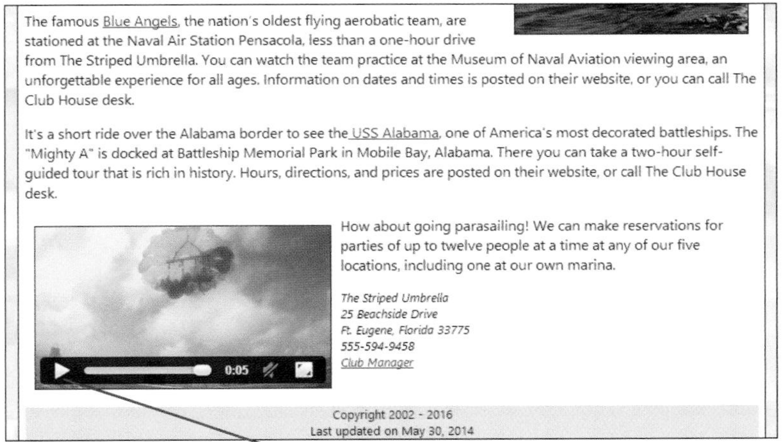

The famous Blue Angels, the nation's oldest flying aerobatic team, are stationed at the Naval Air Station Pensacola, less than a one-hour drive from The Striped Umbrella. You can watch the team practice at the Museum of Naval Aviation viewing area, an unforgettable experience for all ages. Information on dates and times is posted on their website, or you can call The Club House desk.

It's a short ride over the Alabama border to see the USS Alabama, one of America's most decorated battleships. The "Mighty A" is docked at Battleship Memorial Park in Mobile Bay, Alabama. There you can take a two-hour self-guided tour that is rich in history. Hours, directions, and prices are posted on their website, or call The Club House desk.

How about going parasailing! We can make reservations for parties of up to twelve people at a time at any of our five locations, including one at our own marina.

The Striped Umbrella
25 Beachside Drive
Ft. Eugene, Florida 33775
555-594-9458
Club Manager

Copyright 2002 - 2016
Last updated on May 30, 2014

Video reproduced with permission.

*Play button becomes
Pause button while
video is playing*

6. Select the **Browse for File button** next to the Alt Source 1 text box, browse to the drive and folder where you store your Chapter 10 Data Files if necessary, select **parasailing.ogv**, select **OK**, select **Yes** to close the Dreamweaver dialog box, select **Save**, then compare your Property inspector to Figure 28.

   HTML5 video specifications require that you provide alternate video formats to ensure that the video will work in as many browsers as possible. You use the OGG format (also known as Ogg Theora) so that it will play in the Firefox and Opera browsers.

7. Save your work, preview the page in the browser, then compare your screen to Figure 29.

8. Click the **Play button** ▶ to play the movie, then close the browser window.

9. Close the activities page.

You inserted a video on the page, then viewed the page in your browser.

POWER USER SHORTCUTS	
To do this:	**Use this shortcut:**
Enable Live view	[Alt][F11] or [fn][option][f11] (Mac)
Exit Live view	[Alt][F11] or [fn][option][f11] (Mac)
Insert a SWF file	[Ctrl][Alt][F] (Win) or [option][f] (Mac)
Insert an HTML5 video	[Ctrl][Alt][Shift][V] (Win) or [option][shift][V] (Mac)

© 2015 Cengage Learning®

Add
SOUND

What You'll Do

In this lesson, you will add a sound file to the index page and modify the object parameters.

Adding Sound

There are several ways to incorporate sound into a website. Sound files are relatively small in file size and easy to add to a page. You can embed them as background sounds, embed them on a page with visible sound controls, link them to a page, or add them to a page with the new <audio> tags introduced with HTML5. A few audio file formats don't require a plug-in to play, but others do. See Table 1 for a list of common audio file formats and required plug-ins, if any.

Before you decide to add a sound to a page, think about the purpose you have in mind. Will the sound add to the rich media experience for your users? What devices will your users use to play the sound? Have you tested the audio file to make sure the sound quality is excellent? If you decide to use the <audio> tag, provide more than one file format, as all audio file formats are not supported by all browsers. Use the Insert, HTML5 Audio command in the Media category on the Insert panel to insert audio files.

TABLE 1: COMMON AUDIO FILE FORMATS AND SUPPORT FOR HTML5			
File Name	**Plug-in Required**	**HTML5 Compatible**	**HTML5 Audio Compatible Browsers**
WAV (Waveform Extension)	No	No	
AIF or AIFF (Audio Interchange File Format)	No	No	
MP3 or MPEG (Motion Picture Experts Group)	QuickTime, Windows Media Player, or RealPlayer	Yes	Internet Explorer, Chrome, Safari (Firefox in some operating systems)
OGG	No	Yes	Chrome, Firefox, Opera
WebM	No	Yes	Chrome, Firefox, Opera

© 2015 Cengage Learning®

Adding Media and Interactivity

Using Controllers

The controller that appears on your page is determined by the tags used to add the sound file. Dreamweaver has a generic controller that you will see when you add a sound file in the following steps. The controller used with HTML5 looks a bit different. You can use CSS3 to change the appearance of a controller, but all controllers have the basic play and pause buttons and a way to control the volume. Figure 30 shows a page on the Federal Aviation Administration website that provides audio recordings made in control towers. When you select a link to play a recording, a new window opens with a controller that you use to play, pause, and adjust the volume of the recording.

Figure 30 *Playing an audio file on a web page*

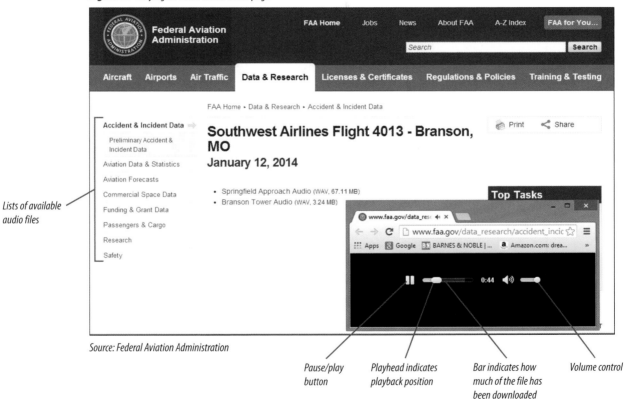

Lists of available audio files

Source: Federal Aviation Administration

Pause/play button   *Playhead indicates playback position*   *Bar indicates how much of the file has been downloaded*   *Volume control*

Add sound

1. Open the index page, add a paragraph break after the last paragraph, then type **Here are some comments from recent guests describing their favorite activities at The Striped Umbrella**.

2. Add another paragraph break, then select **HTML5 Audio** in the Media Category on the Insert panel.

   A placeholder appears on the page, as shown in Figure 31.

3. Type **guest_interview** in the ID text box, select the **Browse for File button** 📁 next to the Source text box, browse to the drive and folder where your Chapter 10 Data Files are stored, select **interviews.mp3**, select **OK**, select **Yes**, navigate to your site assets folder, then select **Save**. Compare your Property inspector to Figure 32.

   (continued)

Figure 31 *Inserting an audio file on the index page*

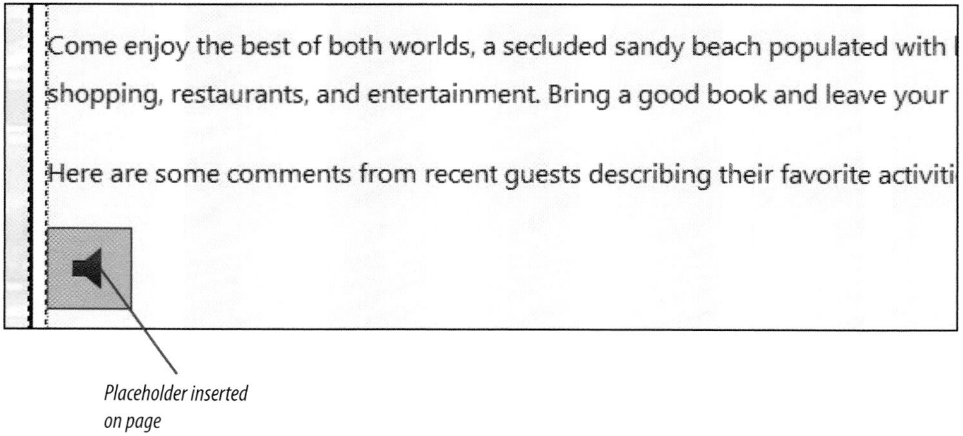

Come enjoy the best of both worlds, a secluded sandy beach populated with

shopping, restaurants, and entertainment. Bring a good book and leave your

Here are some comments from recent guests describing their favorite activiti

Placeholder inserted on page

Figure 32 *Editing the audio settings*

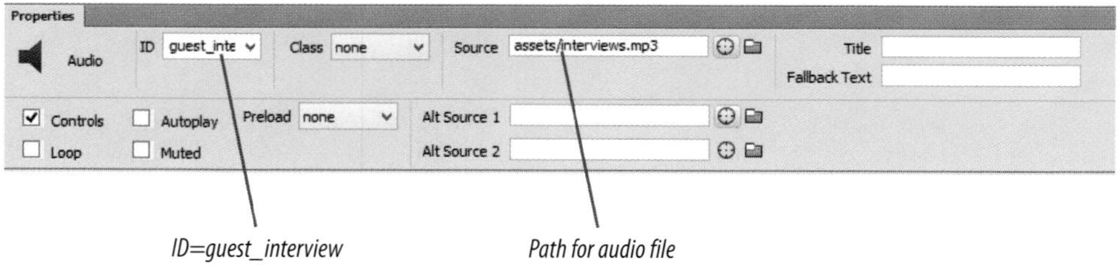

ID=guest_interview   *Path for audio file*

Figure 33 *Viewing the audio controls in a browser*

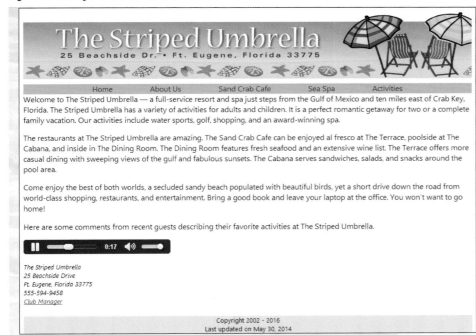

4. Save the index page, preview it in your browser, then play the file, as shown in Figure 33.

   The skin looks different in each browser, so you audio controls may look slightly different than those in Figure 33.

5. Close the browser.

6. Open each page in the site and use the **File**, **Validate**, **Validate Current Document (W3C)** command to verify that all pages are HTML5 compliant.

7. Close all open pages and close Dreamweaver.

You added a sound file to the index page, then validated each page to HTML5 standards.

Add and modify Flash objects.

1. Open the Blooms & Bulbs website, open the workshops page, and close the Design notes dialog box.
2. Add a paragraph break after the last paragraph, then insert the garden_quote.swf Flash movie from the drive and folder where you store your Data Files at the insertion point, saving the file in the site root folder.
3. Type **quote** as the title, select OK, select the placeholder, deselect the Loop check box, create a new global class selector in the bb_styles.css file named **.quote**, then set the float to right.
4. Apply the .quote class selector to the Flash placeholder, change the W value to **220** and the H value to **65**, save your work, then select OK to close the Copy Dependent Files dialog box.
5. Go to Live view, play the garden_quote.swf movie in Dreamweaver, return to Design view, preview the page in your browser, compare your screen to Figure 34, then close your browser.
6. Delete the Flash placeholder, then insert a canvas at the insertion point.
7. Leave the placeholder text "canvas" in the ID text box, add a width of **200** and a height of **75**.
8. Copy the files quote_html5.js and quote_html5.html from the drive and folder where your Chapter 10 Data Files are stored to the blooms local site folder.
9. Open the quote_html5.html file in Dreamweaver and copy all of the script tags in the head section.
10. In Code view, paste the script tags in the head section of the workshops page.
11. Add **onload="init()"** to the opening body tag, then return to Design view and save your work.

12. Create a new global selector in the bb_styles.css file named **#canvas** with the following settings: display:inline; margins:**5px**; float:right.
13. Save your work, preview the page in the browser, then close the browser and close the workshops and quotehtml5 page.

Add rollover images.

1. Open the tips page, then delete the butterfly graphic at the top of the page.
2. Go to Code view and verify that your insertion point is still at the beginning of the paragraph, and between the opening and closing <p> tags that are above the paragraph.
3. Return to Design view and insert a rollover image by using the Image: Rollover Image command in the Common category on the Insert panel. Enter **butterfly_rollover** as the name, insert butterfly1.jpg from the drive and folder where you store your Data Files as the original image in your site assets folder, butterfly2.jpg from the same location and to the same location as the rollover image, then enter **Butterflies** as the alternate text.

Figure 34 *Completed Skills Review*

4. Apply the .img_float rule to the rollover image.
5. Make any spacing adjustments necessary, save your work, preview the page in the browser to test the rollover, then close the tips page.

Add behaviors and CSS transitions.

1. Open the water_plants page.
2. Select the water lily image, then use the Behaviors panel to add the Shake effect from the Effects submenu, using the default settings.
3. Edit the behavior to use the onMouseOver action, then save your work. (*Hint*: Dreamweaver adds a new jQueryAssets folder in the site with two supporting files.)
4. Preview the page in the browser or with Live view. (*Hint*: Place the pointer over the image to test the behavior. The image will shake when you place the pointer over it.)
5. Close the browser or return to Design view, then close the water_plants page.

Add video.

1. Open the plants page, click right after the last sentence on the page (after "just arrived."), then insert a paragraph break.

2. Use the Insert menu to insert the HTML5 video hanging_baskets.mp4 from the drive and folder where your Chapter 10 Data Files are stored.
3. Apply the .img_float class selector, add the ID hanging_baskets, then insert the Alt source hanging_baskets.ogv from the drive and folder where your Chapter 10 Data Files are stored.

4. After the last sentence on the page, type **Join us Saturday at 9:00 for a hanging basket demonstration**.
5. Save all files, preview the page and play the movie in the browser, then compare your screen to Figure 35.
6. Close the browser, then close all open pages.

Figure 35 *Completed Skills Review*

For ease of growing, Knock Out® roses are some of our all-time favorites. Even beginners will not fail with these garden delights. They are shrub roses and prefer full sun, but can take partial shade. They are disease resistant and drought tolerant. You do not have to be concerned with either black spot or dead-heading with roses such as the Knock out®, making them an extremely low-maintenance plant. They are also repeat bloomers, blooming into late fall. The shrub can grow quite large, but can be pruned to any size. Pictured here is Southern Belle. Check out all our varieties as you will not fail to have great color with these plants. You must see a close-up of these beauties! Select the image to enlarge it.

In addition to these marvelous roses, we have many annuals, perennials, and water plants that have just arrived. Join us Saturday at 9:00 for a hanging basket demonstration.

Blooms & Bulbs
Highway 43 South
Alvin, TX 77501
555-248-0806
Customer Service

Copyright 2002 - 2016
Last updated on May 31, 2014

Add sound.

1. Open the tips page, place the insertion point after the last tip listed, enter a paragraph break, then type **Tip of the Week: Starting seeds for your vegetable garden**.

2. Insert the HTML5 audio file seeds_audio.mp3 at the insertion point.

3. Type **seeds** for the ID and use the seeds_audio.ogg file for the Alt Source 1 file.

4. Verify that the Loop check box is not selected.

5. Format the Tip text with the Heading 3 format.

6. Save the tips page and test the audio file in the browser, comparing your screen to Figure 36.

7. Close the browser and close the tips page.

8. Open and validate each page and correct any errors you find to prevent passing validation.

9. Close all open pages.

Figure 36 *Completed Skills Review*

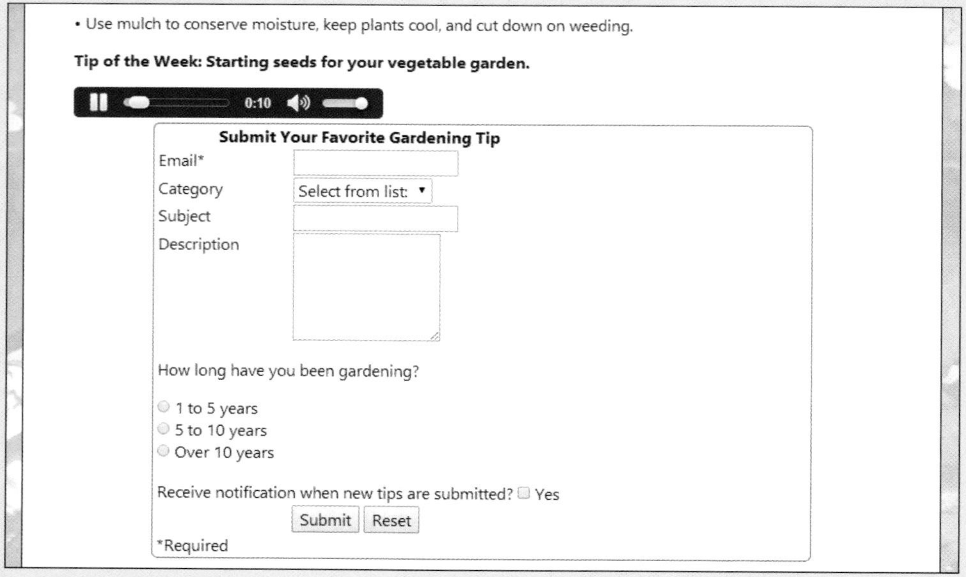

- Use mulch to conserve moisture, keep plants cool, and cut down on weeding.

Tip of the Week: Starting seeds for your vegetable garden.

| | 0:10 |

Submit Your Favorite Gardening Tip

Email*

Category   Select from list: ▼

Subject

Description

How long have you been gardening?

○ 1 to 5 years
○ 5 to 10 years
○ Over 10 years

Receive notification when new tips are submitted? ☐ Yes

Submit   Reset

*Required

In this exercise, you will continue your work on the TripSmart website. You received a new video for the Argentina page and you insert it on the page. Use Figures 37 and 38 as guides as you develop your pages.

1. Open the TripSmart website, then open the argentina page.

2. Insert the video glacier.mp4 from your Data Files folder after the last paragraph on the page with the glacier.ogv file as the Alt source 1 file.

3. Type a short introduction to the video similar to the one in Figure 37.

4. Use a new global ID selector in the tripsmart_syles.css file that modifies the video tag. Add properties to set the dimension and placement of the video on the page.

5. Add any additional settings to improve the appearance of the page, save your work, then preview the page in your browser.

6. Play the video, close the browser, then close the argentina page.

Figure 37 *Sample Project Builder 1*

Our next stop is Iguassu Falls, a breath taking natural wonder of the world with its 275 cascades that spread across a gulf of nearly two miles. We will go on a catwalk extending 3,600 feet over Devil's Throat , a rolling cataract marking the border of Brazil and Argentina and view the many distinct falls from balconies in both countries. You will be talking about the magnificence of these massive works of nature for many years.

Barlioche, Argentina's "Little Switzerland" in Pantagonia is our next stop. This snow peaked wonderland allows viewing some of the most attractive scenery in Argentina, a panoply of lush hills, snow-topped peaks and lakes reflecting a crisp blue sky. One of the highlights of our trip is a visit to the Perito Moreno Glacier, shown in the video below. If you are really adventurous, you can go trekking on the glacier with a small guided group.

TripSmart
1106 Beechwood
Fayetteville, AR 72704
555-848-0807
Contact Us

Copyright 2002 - 2016
Last updated on July 2, 2014

7. Open the file dw10_2.html from the drive and folder where you store your Data Files, then save it in the TripSmart site root folder as **egypt_trip.html**. Do not update links.

8. Close the dw10_2.html page, then close the egypt_trip.html page.

9. Open the tours page, then attach a behavior to the image of the tourists that will open the egypt page when the user selects the image.

10. Add a CSS transition to the global ul li a selector that slowly changes the colors of the menu bar link text and background color in the browser when the pointer moves over each one.

11. Save your work, preview the page in the browser to test the behavior and CSS transition, compare your screen to Figure 38, then close the the browser.

12. Open and validate each page in the site and make any corrections necessary for each page to pass validation.

13. Close all open pages.

Figure 38 *Sample Project Builder 1*

Destinations: Egypt and Argentina

We are featuring two new trips for the coming year. The first is to Egypt. After arriving, we will check into our hotel and enjoy the sights for two days in Cairo, including the famous Egyptian Museum of Antiquities. Next, we will fly to Luxor to visit the Temple of Karnak and then boad our luxury Nile cruise boat, the Sun Queen VII. As we slowly cruise down the Nile, our stops will include Qena, the Ptolemaic Temple of Goddess Hathor in Denderah, the Edfu Temple, the Kom Ombo Temple, and the Philae Temple. We will enjoy a felucca ride around Elephantine Island, and then attend a formal farewell dinner the last night onboard our boat. We return to Cairo and enjoy a day in the market and a walking tour of the old walled city of Cairo.

Argentina is our next destination. We begin our tour in Buenos Aires on our

Use Figure 39 as a guide to continue your work on the Carolyne's Creations website. You have decided to add a video to the adult cooking class page to showcase an Egyptian recipe.

1. Open the Carolyne's Creations website.
2. Open the adults page.
3. Insert the video rice_pudding.mp4 from the drive and folder where your Chapter 10 Data Files are stored, then use video settings of your choice for the video. (*Hint:* in Figure 39, the width is 352px and the height is 240px.)

4. Refer to the text in Figure 39 to add a short description of the video to the paragraph above the video, including a mention of the culinary torch available in the shop. Then add either an inline or external style to position the video on the page.
5. Close the adults page and open the classes page.
6. Select the egyptian_traditional_dessert image, then create a rollover image using it and the file dulce_de_leche.jpg from the drive and folder where your Data Files are stored.

7. Apply styles where needed, make any other adjustments you wish, save your page, then preview the page in the browser.
8. Close the browser.
9. Open and validate each page in the site and make any corrections necessary for each page to validate to current HTML5 standards.
10. Close all open pages.

Figure 39 *Sample Project Builder 2*

Adult's Cooking Class for March: Egyptian Cuisine

The class in March will be cooking several traditional Egyptian dishes: kushari, Arabic bread, falafel, and tahini. Our dessert will be a traditional rice pudding. Egyptian cuisine is both very tasty and healthy, a typical Mediterranean diet! The video below shows a chef placing the final touches on a rice pudding. By the way, we stock these professional culinary torches in our shop.

CAROLYNE'S CREATIONS
496 MAPLE AVENUE
SEVEN FALLS, VIRGINIA 52404
555-963-8271
EMAIL CAROLYNE KATE

Angie Wolf is an astronomer. She would like to design a website about planets, like the example shown in Figure 40. She would like her website to incorporate media such as rollovers, videos, and sound files and would like to use Dreamweaver to build the site.

1. Connect to the Internet and go to nasa.gov.
2. View the source code on several pages for the words "Flash" or "swf" to see if you see references to the use of Flash.
3. What types of multimedia files does NASA use on their site?
4. View some of the videos or interactive guides and list what you like about each one.
5. Create a sketch of Angie's site that contains at least five pages. Indicate in your sketch what media elements you would insert in the site, including where you would add audio files, rollover images, and video.

Figure 40 *Design Project*

Source: NASA

In this assignment, you will continue to work on the group website that you started in Chapter 1. There will be no Data Files supplied. You are building this site from chapter to chapter, so you must do each Portfolio Project assignment in each chapter to complete your site.

You will continue building your site by designing and completing a page that contains rich media content or by adding media content to existing pages. After completing your site, be sure to run appropriate reports to test the site.

1. Evaluate your wireframe, then choose a page, or series of pages, to develop in which you will include media content, such as rollover images, video, CSS transitions, and behaviors.
2. Plan the content for your new page so that the layout works well with both the new and old pages in your site. Sketch a plan for your wireframes for the media content you wish to add, showing which media elements you will use and where you will place them.
3. Create or find the media you identified in your sketch, choosing appropriate formatting.
4. Add the rollover images to the page.
5. Add a video, if possible, to the page.
6. Add a behavior and a CSS transition to a page element, then specify the action you would like to use with it.
7. Run a report on your new page(s) to ensure that all links work correctly.
8. Preview the new page (or pages) in your browser and test all links. Evaluate your pages for content and layout. Use the checklist in Figure 41 to make sure your website is complete.
9. Make any modifications that are necessary to improve the page.

Figure 41 *Portfolio Project checklist*

Website Checklist
1. Do your pages flow well together?
2. Do all Flash movies play properly in the browser?
3. Do all links work?
4. Do all rollover images display properly?
5. Do your video and sound files load quickly and play correctly?
6. Does the behavior assigned a page element respond correctly to the action assigned to it?
7. Does your CSS transition work well in all browsers?
8. Do all of your pages pass HTML5 validation?

© 2015 Cengage Learning®

Read the following information carefully.

Find out from your instructor the location where you will store your files.

■ To complete many of the chapters in this book, you need to use the Data Files provided on Cengage Brain. To access the Data Files on Cengage Brain:

1. Open your browser and go to http://www.cengagebrain.com
2. Type the author, title, or ISBN of this book in the Search window. (The ISBN is listed on the back cover.)
3. Click the book title in the list of search results.
4. When the book's main page opens, click the Access Now button under Free Materials.
5. To download Data Files, select a chapter number and then click on the Data Files link on the left navigation bar to download and unzip the files.

■ Your instructor will tell you where to save the Data Files and where to store the files you create and modify.

■ All the Data Files are organized in folders named after the chapter in which they are used. For instance, all Chapter 1 Data Files are stored in the chapter_1 folder. You should leave all the Data Files in these folders; do not move any Data File out of the folder in which it is originally stored.

Copy and organize your Data Files.

■ Copy the folders that contain the Data Files to a USB storage drive, network folder, hard drive, or other storage device.

■ As you build each website, the exercises in this book will guide you to copy the Data Files you need from the appropriate Data Files folder to the folder where you are storing the website. Your Data Files should always remain intact because you

are copying (and not moving) them to the website.

■ Because you will be building a website from one chapter to the next, sometimes you will need to use a Data File that is already contained in the website you are working on.

Find and keep track of your Data Files and completed files.

■ Use the **Data File Supplied** column to make sure you have the files you need before starting the chapter or exercise indicated in the **Chapter** column.

■ Use the **Student Creates File** column to find out the filename you use when saving your new file for the exercise.

ADOBE DREAMWEAVER CC			
Chapter	**Data File Supplied**	**Student Creates File**	**Used In**
Chapter 1	boilerplate.css		Lesson 2
	dw1_1.html		
	striped_styles.css		
	assets/pool.jpg		
	assets/su_banner.gif		
	assets/su_logo.gif		
	boilerplate.css		Lesson 4
	dw1_2.html	index.html	
	respond.min.js	activities.html	
	su_styles.css	cafe.html	
	assets/su_banner.gif	cruises.html	
	assets/su_logo.gif	fishing.html	
		index.html	
		spa.html	
	bb_styles.css		Skills Review
	blooms_styles.css		

ADOBE DREAMWEAVER CC			
Chapter	**Data File Supplied**	**Student Creates File**	**Used In**
Chapter 1, continued	boilerplate.css		
	dw1_3.html	annuals.html	Skills Review
	dw1_4.html	index.html	
	respond.min.js		
	assets/blooms_banner.jpg	newsletter.html	
	assets/blooms_banner_tablet.jpg	perennials.html	
	assets/blooms_logo.jpg	plants.html	
	assets/tulips.jpg	tips.html	
		water_plants.html	
		workshops.html	
	boilerplate.css	argentina.html	Project Builder 1
	dw1_5.html	catalog.html	
	tripsmart_styles.css	egypt.html	
	assets/tripsmart_banner.jpg	index.html	
	assets/tripsmart_logo.gif	newsletter.html	

ADOBE DREAMWEAVER CC			
Chapter	**Data File Supplied**	**Student Creates File**	**Used In**
Chapter 1, continued		services.html	
		tours.html	
	boilerplate.css	adults.html	Project Builder 2
	cc_styles.css	catering.html	
	dw1_6.html	children.html	
	assets/cc_banner.jpg	classes.html	
	asets/cc_banner_tablet.gif	index.html	
	assets/cc_logo.gif	recipes.html	
		shop.html	
	none		Design Project
	none		Portfolio Project
Chapter 2	spa.txt		Lesson 2
	assets/sea_spa_logo.png		
	gardening_tips.txt		Skills Review
	assets/butterfly.jpg		

ADOBE DREAMWEAVER CC			
Chapter	**Data File Supplied**	**Student Creates File**	**Used In**
Chapter 2, continued	none		Project Builder 1
	none		Project Builder 2
	none		Design Project
	none		Portfolio Project
Chapter 3	questions.txt		Lesson 1
	none		Skills Review
	dw3_1.html		Project Builder 1
	assets/tripsmart_banner.jpg		
	dw3_2.html		Project Builder 2
	assets/cc_banner.jpg		
	assets/pie.jpg		
	none		Design Project
	none		Portfolio Project
Chapter 4	dw4_1.html		Lesson 1
	assets/club_house.jpg		
	assets/water.jpg		Lesson 3

ADOBE DREAMWEAVER CC			
Chapter	**Data File Supplied**	**Student Creates File**	**Used In**
Chapter 4, continued	starfish.ico		Lesson 4
	assets/map_large.jpg		
	assets/map_small.jpg		
	dw4_2.html		Skills Review
	flower.ico		
	assets/lady_in_red.jpg		
	assets/rose.jpg		
	assets/two_roses.jpg		
	assets/two_roses_large.jpg		
	airplane.ico		Project Builder 1
	dw4_3.html		
	assets/nile.jpg		
	assets/statues.jpg		
	dw4_4.html		Project Builder 2
	assets/cc_banner_mobile.jpg		
	assets/peruvian_glass.jpg		
	none		Design Project
	none		Portfolio Project

ADOBE DREAMWEAVER CC			
Chapter	**Data File Supplied**	**Student Creates File**	**Used In**
Chapter 5	dw5_1.html		Lesson 1
	assets/family_sunset.jpg		
	assets/su_banner.gif		
	assets/two_dolphins_small.jpg		
	dw5_2.html		Lesson 2
	assets/transparent.gif		Lesson 4
	dw5_3.html		Lesson 5
	dw5_4.html		
	assets/boats.jpg		
	assets/fisherman.jpg		
	dw5_5.html		Skills Review
	dw5_6.html		
	dw5_7.html		
	dw5_8.html		
	assets/blooms_banner.jpg		
	assets/coleus.jpg		
	assets/fiber_optic_grass.jpg		
	assets/plants.jpg		

ADOBE DREAMWEAVER CC			
Chapter	**Data File Supplied**	**Student Creates File**	**Used In**
Chapter 5, continued	assets/ruby_grass.jpg		
	assets/trees.jpg		
	assets/water_lily.jpg		
	dw5_9.html		Project Builder 1
	dw5_10.html		
	dw5_11.html		
	assets/glacier.jpg		
	assets/iguazu_falls.jpg		
	assets/patagonia.jpg		
	assets/ride_to_temple.jpg		
	assets/tripsmart_banner.jpg		
	dw5_12.html		Project Builder 2
	dw5_13.html		
	dw5_14.html		
	assets/children_cooking.jpg		
	assets/egyptian_lunch.jpg		
	assets/egyptian_traditional_dessert.jpg		
	none		Design Project
	none		Portfolio Project

ADOBE DREAMWEAVER CC			
Chapter	**Data File Supplied**	**Student Creates File**	**Used In**
Chapter 6	cafe.txt		Lesson 3
	assets/club_house_oceanside.jpg		
	assets/shrimp_bisque.jpg		Lesson 5
	composting.txt		Skills Review
	assets/pink_rose.jpg		
	assets/shade_garden.jpg		
	hiking.txt		Project Builder 1
	assets/three_hikers.jpg		
	marshmallows.txt		Project Builder 2
	assets/marshmallows.jpg		
	none		Design Project
	none		Portfolio Project
Chapter 7	none	The Striped Umbrella.ste	Lesson 5
	none	Blooms & Bulbs.ste	Skills Review
	none	TripSmart.ste	Project Builder 1
	none	Carolyne's Creations.ste	Project Builder 2
	none		Design Project
	none		Portfolio Project

ADOBE DREAMWEAVER CC			
Chapter	**Data File Supplied**	**Student Creates File**	**Used In**
Chapter 8	shrimp_bisque.jpg		Lesson 2
	water_blue_green.jpg		
	boardwalk.jpg		Lesson 3
	leaves.jpg		Skills Review
	patagonia_landscape.jpg		Project Builder 1
	pie.jpg		Project Builder 2
	none		Design Project
	none		Portfolio Project
Chapter 9	dw9_1.html	feedback.html	Lesson 1
	none		Project Builder 1
	assets/argentina_meringue.jpg		Project Builder 2
	none		Design Project
	none		Portfolio Project
Chapter 10	crabdance.swf		Lesson 1
	crabdance_html5.html		
	crabdance_html5.js		
	assets/one_dolphin.jpg		Lesson 2
	assets/two_dolphins.jpg		
	dw10_1.html	wildlife_message.html	Lesson 3
	parasailing.mp4		Lesson 4

ADOBE DREAMWEAVER CC			
Chapter	**Data File Supplied**	**Student Creates File**	**Used In**
Chapter 10, continued	parasailing.ogv		
	interviews.mp3		Lesson 5
	interviews.ogg		
	dw10_2.html		Skills Review
	garden_quote.swf		
	hanging_baskets.mp4		
	hanging_baskets.ogv		
	quote_html5.html		
	quote_html5.js		
	seeds_audio.mp3		
	seeds_audio.ogg		
	assets/butterfly1.jpg		
	assets/butterfly2.jpg		
	glacier.mp4		Project Builder 1
	glacier.ogv		
	rice_pudding.mp4		Project Builder 2
	rice_pudding.ogv		
	assets/dulce_de_leche.jpg		
	none		Design Project
	none		Portfolio Project

GLOSSARY

A

Absolute path
A path containing an external link that references a link on a web page outside of the current website, and includes the protocol "http" and the URL, or address, of the web page.

Action property
A form property that specifies the application or script that will process the data in a form.

ActionScript
A Flash scripting language developers use to add interactivity to movies, control objects, exchange data, and create complex animations.

Active Server Pages (ASP)
Server-side application used for processing form data.

Adaptive website
A website that adjusts or modifies the page content to fit the user's needs and device type used to view the site.

Add-on
A program extension that adds features to an existing application. Also called a plug-in.

Adobe Edge
An Adobe program that combines the new capabilities of HTML5, CSS3, and JavaScript, but uses a program interface similar to Flash.

Adobe Edge Web Fonts
A library of fonts available to use free of charge with a Creative Cloud subscription.

Adobe Flash video
See FLV.

AIF or AIFF
Acronym for Audio Interchange File Format; an HTML5 audio tag.

Align
Position an image on a web page in relation to other elements on the page.

AP div tag
A div that is assigned a fixed (absolute) position on a web page.

AP element
The container that an AP div tag creates on a page. *See also* AP div tag.

Apache web server
A public domain, open source web server that is available using several different operating systems, including UNIX and Windows.

Application bar (Win)
In Dreamweaver, the toolbar located above the Document window that includes menu names, a Workspace switcher, and other application commands.

ASP
See Active Server Pages.

Assets
Files that are not web pages, such as images, audio files, and video clips.

Assets folder
A subfolder in the local site root folder in which you store most of the files that are not web pages, such as images, Flash files, and video clips.

This folder is often named images, but can be assigned any name.

Assets panel
A panel that contains eight categories of assets, such as images, used in a website. Selecting a category button displays a list of those assets.

Audio Visual Interleave
See AVI.

AVI
Acronym for Audio Visual Interleave; the Microsoft standard for digital video format.

B

Background color
A color that fills an entire web page, frame, table, cell, or CSS layout block.

Background image
A graphic file used in place of a background color.

Banner
An image that generally appears across the top or down the side of a web page and can incorporate a company's logo, contact information, and links to the other pages in the site.

BaseCamp
A web-based project collaboration tool used by many companies.

Behavior
Simple action scripts that let you incorporate interactivity by modifying content based on variables like user actions; tells a page object to respond in a specific way when an event occurs, such as when a pointer is positioned over the object.

Blog
A website where the website owner regularly posts commentaries and opinions on various topics.

Blue drop zone
See Drop zone.

Body
The part of a web page that appears in a browser window. It contains all of the page content that is visible to users, such as text, images, and links.

Border
An outline that surrounds a cell, a table, or a CSS layout block.

Breadcrumb trail
A list of links that provides a path from the initial page opened in a website to the page being currently viewed.

Broken link
A link that cannot find the intended destination file for the link.

Buffer
A temporary storage area on your hard drive that acts as a holding area for Flash content as it is being played.

Bullet
A small dot or similar icon preceding unordered list items. *See also* Bulleted list.

Bulleted list
An unordered list that uses bullets. *See also* Bullet.

———————— C ————————

Cascading
The way styles are ranked in order of precedence as they are applied to page elements.

Cascading Style Sheet
A set of formatting attributes used to format web pages to provide a consistent presentation for content across a website.

Cell
A small box within a table that is used to hold text or graphics. Cells are arranged horizontally in rows and vertically in columns.

Cell padding
The distance between the cell content and the cell walls in a table.

Cell spacing
The distance between cells in a table.

Cell walls
The edges surrounding a cell in a table.

CGI
Acronym for Common Gateway Interface; a server-side application for processing information such as form data.

Check box
A form object used to create a list of options from which users can make multiple selections.

Check box group
A group of check boxes on a form. *See also* Check box.

Child container
A container, created with HTML tags, whose code resides inside a parent container. Its properties are inherited from its parent container unless otherwise specified. *See also* Parent container.

Child page
A page at a lower level in a web hierarchy that links to a page at a higher level, called a parent page.

Class type
A type of style that can contain a combination of formatting attributes that can be applied to a block of text or other page elements. Custom style names begin with a period (.). Also called a custom type.

Clean HTML code
Code that does what it is supposed to do without using unnecessary instructions, which take up memory.

Client-side scripting
A form processing method in which the user's computer processes a form, rather than a web server.

Clip property
A property that determines the portion of an AP div's content that will be visible when displayed in a web browser.

Cloak
To exclude from certain processes, such as being transferred to a remote site.

Code hint
An auto-complete feature that displays lists of tags that appear as you type in Code view.

Code Inspector
A separate floating window that displays the current page in Code view.

Code snippet
Ready-made, reusable pieces of code you can insert on a web page.

Code view
The Dreamweaver view that shows the underlying HTML code for a page; use this view to read or edit the code.

Coding toolbar
A toolbar that contains buttons you can use when working in Code view.

Cold Fusion
A server-side application used for processing data in a form.

Column
Table cells arranged vertically.

Comment
Gray non-executable tags preceded by "/*" that tell a browser to skip over the code that follows it until it gets to an ending comment tag.

Common Gateway Interface
See CGI.

Compound type
A type of style that is used to format a selection.

Computed
A name used to refer to a page element that has more than one selector formatting it.

Controller
A graphic element that contains playback controls for video or audio files.

Copyright
A legal protection for the particular and tangible expression of an idea; the right of an author or creator of a work to copy, distribute, and modify a thing, idea, or image; a type of intellectual property.

CSS layout block
A section of a web page defined and formatted using a Cascading Style Sheet.

CSS Layout Box Model
CSS layout blocks defined as rectangular boxes of content with margins, padding, and borders.

CSS page layout
A method of positioning objects on web pages through the use of containers formatted with CSS. *See also* Cascading Style Sheets.

Custom button
In a form, a button that triggers an action, which you specify, on the page.

Custom type
See Class type.

D

Debug
To find and correct coding errors.

Declaration
The property and value of a style in a Cascading Style Sheet.

Default font
The font a browser uses to display link text if no other font is assigned.

Default link color
The color a browser uses to display text if no other color is assigned.

Delimited file
A database, word processing, or spreadsheet file that has been saved as a text file with data separated with delimiters such as commas or tabs.

Delimiter
A comma, tab, colon, semicolon, or similar character that separates tabular data.

Deliverables
Products that will be provided to the client at the product completion such as pages or graphic elements.

Dependent file
A file that another file needs to be complete, such as an image or style sheet.

Deprecated
Describes code that is no longer within the current standard and in danger of becoming obsolete.

Derivative work
An adaptation of another work, such as a movie version of a book; a new, original product that includes content from a previously existing work.

Descendant selector
A selector that includes two or more selectors that form a relationship and are separated by white space.

Description
A short summary that resides in the head section of a web page and describes the website content. *See also* Head content.

Design Note
A separate file in a website file structure that contains additional information about a page file or a graphic file.

Design view
The Dreamweaver view that shows the page similar to how it would appear in a browser and is primarily used for creating and designing a web page.

Div tag
An HTML tag that is used to format and position web page elements.

Dock
A collection of panels or panel groups.

Document toolbar
A toolbar that contains buttons and drop-down menus for changing the current work mode, checking browser compatibility, previewing web pages, debugging web pages, choosing visual aids, and viewing file management options.

Document window
The large area under the Document toolbar in the Dreamweaver workspace where you create and edit web pages.

DOM
Document Object Model, a convention that represents the order and type of elements on a page.

Domain name
An IP address expressed in letters instead of numbers, usually reflecting the name of the business represented by the website; also referred to as a URL.

Download
The process of transferring files from a remote site to a local site.

Dreamweaver workspace
The entire window, from the Application bar (Win) or Menu bar (Mac) at the top of the window, to the status bar at the bottom border of the program window; the area in the Dreamweaver program window that includes all of the menus, panels, buttons, inspectors, and panes that you use to create and maintain websites.

Drop zone
A blue outline area that indicate where a panel can be docked.

Dynamic content
Content that allows the user to interact with the page by selecting or typing, and then responds to this input in some way.

———————— **E** ————————

Editable optional region
An area on a template where users can add or change content, and that users can also choose to show or hide.

Editable region
An area in a template where users of the template can add or change content.

Element Quick View
A visual representation of the DOM structure for a page.

Embedded style
A style whose code is located in the head section of an individual page. Also called an internal style.

Embedded style sheet
See Embedded style.

Export
To save data that was created in Dreamweaver in a special file format so that you can open it in another software program.

Extensible Metadata Platform (XMP) standard
The standard Adobe uses to save metadata.

External link
A link that connects to a web page in another website or to an e-mail address.

External style sheet
Collection of styles stored in a separate file that controls the formatting of content on a web page. External style sheets have a .css file extension.

———————— **F** ————————

Facebook
A social networking site that let users interact as an online community through the sharing of text, images, and videos.

Fair use
A part of copyright law that allows a user to make a copy of all or part of a work, even if permission has not been granted.

Favicon
Short for favorites icon, a small image that represents a website and appears in the address bar of many browsers.

Favorites
Assets that are used repeatedly in a website and are included in their own category in the assets panel.

Fieldset
An HTML tag used to group related form elements together.

File field
Form object that allows users to upload files to a web server.

File Transfer Protocol (FTP)
The process of uploading and downloading files to and from a remote site.

Files panel
A window similar to File Explorer (Windows) or Finder (Macintosh), where Dreamweaver displays and manages files and folders. The Files panel contains a list of all the folders and files in a website.

Fixed layout
A page layout that expresses all container widths in pixels and remains the same size regardless of the size of the browser window.

Fixed position
A CSS property that places an element relative to the browser window.

Flash button
A button made from a small, predefined Flash movie.

Fluid Grid Layout
A system for designing layouts that will adapt to multiple screen sizes.

Fluid Grid Layout guides
Visual aids that show you the number of columns used in Mobile, Tablet, and Desktop views.

FLV
Acronym for (Adobe) Flash Video; a video format you can link or embed on a web page.

Focus group
A marketing tool that asks a group of people for feedback about a product, such as the impact of a television ad or the effectiveness of a website design.

Font libraries
Collections of fonts such as typekit.com or google.com/webfonts; accessed by browsers for specified WOFF fonts. *See also* WOFF font.

Font-combination
A set of font choices that specifies which fonts a browser should use to display text, such as Arial, Helvetica, sans serif. Also known as a font stack. Font combinations that a user creates are called custom font stacks.

Font stack
See Font-combination.

Form control
See Form object.

Form element
See Form object.

Form field
See Form object.

Form input
See Form object.

Form label
A label that identifies a form object by its function.

Form name property
A form property that specifies a unique name for the form.

Form object
An object on a web page, such as a text box, radio button, or check box, that collects information from users. Also called a form element, form control, form field, or form input.

FTP
See File Transfer Protocol.

GET method
A form property that specifies that ASCII data collected in the form will be sent to the server appended to the URL or to the file included in the Action property.

GIF
Acronym for Graphics Interchange Format file. A type of file format used for images placed on web pages that can support both transparency and animation.

Global CSS rule
A rule that affects all website content.

Global Positioning System
See GPS.

Google Video Chat
A video sharing community hosted by Google.

GPS
Acronym for Global Positioning System; a device used to track your position through a global satellite navigation system.

Graphic
A picture or design element that adds visual interest to a page.

Graphic design elements
Elements that combine to promote a pleasing page design, such as the way lines, shapes, forms, textures, and colors are used to create and place elements on a page.

Graphic design principles
The use of emphasis, movement, balance, unity, symmetry, color, white space, alignment, line, contrast, rule of thirds, proximity, and repetition to create an attractive and effective page design.

Grid
Horizontal and vertical lines that fill the page and are used to place page elements.

Group selector
A multiple selector that shares common properties and values.

Guide
A horizontal or vertical line that you drag from the rulers onto the page to help you align objects.

Head content
The part of a web page that includes the page title that appears in the title bar of the browser, as well as meta tags, which are HTML codes that include information about the page, such as keywords and descriptions, and are not visible in the browser.

Height (H) property
A property that specifies the height of a div either in pixels or as a percentage of the screen height.

Hex triplet
A color value expressed with three characters that represents the amount of red, green, and blue present in a color. Also known as an RGB triplet.

Hexadecimal RGB value
A six-character value that represents the amount of red, green, and blue in a color and is based on the Base 16 number system. If expressed in three characters instead of six, it's called an RGB triplet or a hex triplet.

Hidden field
Form object that makes it possible to provide information to the web server and form-processing script without the user knowing that the information is being sent.

History panel
A panel that contains a record of each action performed during an editing session, and allows you to undo actions; up to 1000 levels of Undo are available through the History panel (20 levels by default).

Home page
The first page that is displayed when users go to a website.

Hotspot
A selectable area on an image that, when selected, links to a different location on the page or to another web page.

HTML
Stands for Hypertext Markup Language, the language web developers use to create web pages.

HTML5
The current version of HTML that added new ways to incorporate interactivity with tags that support semantic markup. Examples of added tags are <header>, <footer>, <article>, <section>, <video>, <hgroup>, <figure>, <embed>, <wbr>, and <canvas>.

HTTP
See HyperText Transfer Protocol.

HUD
An acronym for Heads up Display; a mini-toolbar with tools for editing a div tag.

Hyperlink
An image or text element on a web page that users select to display another location on the page, another web page on the same website, or a web page on a different website; also known as a link.

Hypertext Transfer Protocol (HTTP)
The transfer method specified by the Method property to send form data to a server.

Hypertext Transfer Protocol Secure (HTTPS)
The protocol for transferring secure information over the Internet.

——————— I ———————

ID type
A type of CSS rule that is used to redefine an HTML tag.

Image
A graphic such as a photograph or a piece of artwork on a web page; images in a website are known as assets.

Image field
A form field that can contain a graphic.

Image map
An image that has one or more specially-designated areas, each of which serves as a link.

Image placeholder
A graphic the size of an image you plan to use that holds the position on the page until the final image is placed.

Import
To bring data created in one software application into another application.

In-app messages
Messages that appear within an application to suggest tips for boosting workflow productivity.

In-product messages
Message that appear within Dreamweaver to suggest tips for Dreamweaver integration with other Creative Cloud apps.

Inherit
A property that specifies that the property and value are applied from a parent container.

Inheritance
The CSS governing principle that allows for the properties of a parent container to be used to format the content in a child container. Also refers to the properties of device size selectors: global (mobile) selectors govern tablet and desktop size selectors; tablet size selectors govern desktop size selectors.

Inline style
A style whose code is placed within the body tags of a web page.

Insert panel
A panel with eight categories of buttons for creating and inserting objects displayed as a drop-down menu: Common, Structure, Media, Form, jQuery Mobile, jQuery UI, Templates, and Favorites. Also called the Insert bar.

Inspect mode
A Dreamweaver viewing mode that works together with Live View to help you identify HTML elements and their associated CSS styles.

Intellectual property
A product resulting from human creativity, such as movies, songs, designs, and the like.

Internal link
A link to a web page within the same website.

Internal style sheet
A style sheet whose code is saved within the code of a web page, rather than in an external file. Also called an embedded style.

Internet Service Provider (ISP)
A service to which you subscribe to be able to connect to the Internet with your computer.

IP address
An assigned series of numbers, separated by periods, that designates an address on the Internet.

Item
A link in a menu bar.

———————— **J** ————————

Java Server Page
See JSP.

JavaScript
A web-scripting code that interacts with HTML code to create dynamic content, such as rollovers or interactive forms on a web page; also called Jscript.

JavaScript Object Notation (JSON)
A subset of JavaScript, used by Adobe Edge.

JPEG or JPG
An acronym for Joint Photographic Experts Group; refers to a type of file format used for images that appear on web pages. Many photographs are saved with the JPEG file format.

Jscript
See JavaScript.

JSP
Acronym for Java Server Page; a server-side application for processing information such as form data.

Jump menu
A navigation menu that lets users go quickly to different pages in a site or to different sites on the Internet.

———————— **K** ————————

Keyword
In Dreamweaver, a word that relates to the content of a website and resides in the head section of a web page.

———————— **L** ————————

Label tag
A form attribute that assigns a descriptive label to a form object.

LAN
Acronym for Local Area Network, a network that is not connected to the Internet.

Library item
Content that can contain text or graphics that you plan to use multiple times in your website and that is saved in a separate file in the Library folder of your site.

Licensing agreement
The permission given by a copyright holder that conveys the right to use the copyright holder's work.

Line break
Places a new text line without creating a new paragraph.

Link
See Hyperlink.

Liquid layout
A page layout that expresses all container widths in percents and changes size depending on the size of the browser window.

List
A form object for listing several options; the user can select one or more of the listed options.

Live view
A Dreamweaver view that displays an open document as if you were viewing it in a browser, with interactive elements active and functioning.

Local root folder
See Local site folder.

Local site folder
A folder on a hard drive, Flash drive, or floppy disk that holds all the files and folders for a website; also called the local root folder.

Locked region
An area on a template that cannot be changed by users of the template.

Low-bandwidth animation
Animations that don't require a fast connection to work properly.

M

Mailto: link
An e-mail address formatted as a link that opens the default mail program with a blank, addressed message.

Match.com
A social networking site that lets users share information in order to establish relationships.

Media object
A combination of visual and audio effects and text to create a fully engaging experience with a website.

Media queries
A Dreamweaver feature that uses files that specify set parameters for displaying pages on separate devices, such as tablets or smartphones.

Media-dependent style sheet
A style sheet tool for identifying the device being used and formatting the page appropriately.

Mega menu
A type of menu that uses sub-menus to group related pages under a main menu item.

Menu
A form object for listing several options; the user can only choose one.

Menu bar
An area on a web page that contains links to the main pages of a website; also called a navigation bar. In Dreamweaver, the bar located above the Document window that includes the Workplace switcher and other application commands.

Merge cells
To combine multiple adjacent cells in a table into one cell.

Meta tag
An HTML code that resides in the head section of a web page and includes information about the page, such as keywords and descriptions. *See also* Head content.

Metadata
Information about a file, such as keywords, descriptions, and copyright information, that is used to locate files.

Method property
A form property that specifies the HyperText Transfer Protocol (HTTP) used to send the form data to a web server.

MOV
The Apple Quick Time video format.

MP3 or MPEG
Acronym for Motion Picture Experts Group; audio files that require a plug-in to work.

N

Navigation bar
See Menu bar.

Navigation structure
A set of text or graphic links usually organized in rows or columns that users can select to navigate between pages of a website. *See also* Menu bar.

Nested AP element
An AP div whose HTML code is included within another AP div's code.

Nested table
A table within a table.

Nested tag
A tag within a tag.

Nested template
A template based on another template.

No right-click script
JavaScript code that will block users from displaying the shortcut menu when they right-click an image on a web page.

Numbered list
See Ordered list.

O

Ogg
A free, open source container video format developed by the Xiph.Org Foundation.

Online community
Social website you can join, such as Facebook and Twitter, where you can communicate with others by posting messages or media content such as images or videos.

Opacity
Degree of transparency; PNG files use varying degrees of opacity.

Optional region
Region in a template that template content contributors can choose to either show or hide.

Ordered list
A list of items that are placed in a specific order and preceded by numbers or letters; sometimes called a numbered list.

Orphaned file
Files that are not linked to any pages in the website.

Overflow property
A property that specifies how to handle excess content that does not fit inside an AP div.

———————— **P** ————————

Panel
A tabbed window in Dreamweaver that displays information on a particular topic or contains related commands.

Panel groups
Sets of related panels that are grouped together and displayed through the Window menu; also known as Tab groups.

Parent container
A container created with HTML tags, in which other containers fall between its opening and closing tags. *See also* Child container.

Parent page
A page at a higher level in a web hierarchy that links to other pages on a lower level, called child pages.

Path
The location of a file in relation to its place in the folder structure of the website.

Permissions process
The process to obtain permission to use content legally.

Pinterest
A social networking site that lets users interact as an online community through the sharing of crafts, recipes, and other items of interest.

Plug-in
See Add-on.

PNG
The acronym for Portable Network Graphics File, a file format used for images placed on web pages; capable of showing millions of colors but is small in file size. PNG is the native file format in Fireworks.

Podcast
"Pod" is an acronym for Programming On Demand, in which users can download and play digitally broadcasted files using devices such as computers or MP3 players.

Point of contact
A place on a web page that provides users with a means of contacting the company.

POST method
A form property that specifies that the form data should be sent to the processing script as a binary or encrypted file, allowing you to send data securely.

POUR
The acronym for Perceivable, Operable, Understandable, and Robust; guidelines for building accessible websites.

POWDER
The acronym for Protocol for Web Description Resources; an evaluation system for web pages developed with the World Wide Web Consortium (W3C) that provides summary information about a website.

Programming On Demand
See Podcast.

Progressive video download
A download type that will download a video to a user's computer, and then allow the video to play before it has completely downloaded.

Properties pane
The bottom pane of the CSS Designer panel when it is shown as a single column or the right side when it is expanded into two columns; lists a selected rule's properties.

Property inspector
In Dreamweaver, a panel that displays the properties of a selected web page object; its contents vary according to the object currently selected.

Protocol for Web Description Resources
See POWDER.

Pseudo class style
A style that determines the appearance of a page element when a certain condition from information external to the HTML source is met.

Public domain
Work that is no longer protected by copyright; anyone can use it for any purpose.

Publish
To make a website available for viewing on the Internet or on an intranet by transferring the files to a web server.

———————— **R** ————————

Radio button
A form object that provides an option for selecting one form item; displays as a small circle in a form.

Radio group
On a form, a group of radio buttons used to provide a list of options from which only one selection can be made.

RDS
Acronym for Remote Development Services; provides access control to web servers using Cold Fusion.

Really Simple Syndication
See RSS.

Related file
A file that is linked to a document and is necessary for the document to display and function correctly.

Related Files toolbar
A toolbar located below an open document's filename tab that displays the names of any related files.

Relative path
A path used with an internal link to reference a web page or graphic file within the website.

Remote server
A web server that hosts websites and is not directly connected to the computer housing the local site.

Remote site
A website that has been published to a remote server. *See also* Remote server.

Rendering
The way fonts are drawn on a screen.

Reset button
A button, that, when selected, will clear data from a form and reset it to its default values.

Responsive design
Using style sheets and media queries to control how pages look on different devices, such as tablets and smartphones.

RGB triplet
See Hex triplet.

Rich media content
Attractive and engaging images, interactive elements, video, or animations.

Rollover
A special effect that changes the appearance of an object when the pointer moves over it.

Rollover image
An image that changes its appearance when a pointer is placed over it in a browser.

Root folder
See Local site folder.

Row
Table cells arranged horizontally.

RSS
Acronym for Really Simple Syndication, a method websites use to distribute news stories, information about upcoming events, and announcements, known as an RSS Feed.

RSS feed
A way to distribute news stories through websites. *See also* RSS.

Rule
Sets of formatting attributes that define styles in a Cascading Style Sheet.

Rule of thirds
A design principle that entails dividing a page into nine squares and then placing the page elements of most interest on the intersections of the grid lines.

—————— S ——————

Sans-serif font
A font with block-style characters; commonly used for headings and subheadings.

Scope creep
A situation that occurs when impromptu changes or additions are made to a project without corresponding increases in the schedule or budget.

Screen readers
Devices used by persons with visual impairments to convert written text on a computer monitor to spoken words.

Secure FTP (SFTP)
A method for transferring files with encryption to protect the file content, user names, and passwords.

Secure Socket Layer
See SSL.

Selector
The name of the tag to which style declarations have been assigned.

Semantic markup
Coding to emphasize meaning.

Serif font
An ornate font that has a tail, or stroke, at the end of some characters. These strokes lead the eye from one character to the next, making it easier to recognize words; therefore, serif fonts are generally used in longer text passages.

Server-side scripting
A method used to process information a form collects using applications that reside on the web server.

Set up a site
Specify a website's name and the location of the local site folder using the Dreamweaver Manage Sites dialog box.

Glossary

SFTP
See Secure FTP.

Show Code and Design views
A combination of Code view and Design view; the best view for correcting errors.

Site definition
Important information about a website, including its URL, preferences that you've specified, and other secure information, such as login and password information; you can export a site definition to another location using the Export command.

Site map
A graphical representation or a directory listing of how web pages relate to each other within a website.

Skin
A controller graphic element placed over or below a video.

Skype
A video sharing application.

Slider
The small indicator on the left side of the History panel that you can drag to undo or redo one or more actions.

Smart object
An image layer that stores image data from raster or vector images.

Social networking
The grouping of individual web users who connect and interact with other users in online communities.

Split a cell
To divide table cells into multiple cells.

SSL
Acronym for Secure Socket Layer, the industry standard for viewing and sending confidential information over the Internet by encrypting the data.

Standard toolbar
A toolbar that contains buttons you use to execute frequently used commands that are also available on the File and Edit menus.

State
In a browser, the condition of an item in a menu bar in relation to the pointer.

Static content
Page content that does not change or allow user interaction.

Static position
A CSS property that places an element in order with the document flow.

Status bar
In Dreamweaver, the bar that appears at the bottom of the Dreamweaver document window; the left end of the status bar displays the tag selector, which shows the HTML tags being used at the insertion point location. The right end displays the window size and estimated download time for the page displayed.

Step
Each task performed in the History panel.

Streaming video download
Similar to a progressive video download, except streaming video downloads use buffers to gather the content as it is downloading to ensure a smoother playback.

Submit button
A button which, when selected, sends user data from a form on a web page to a web server to be processed.

Swap Image behavior
JavaScript code that directs the browser to display a different image when the pointer is rolled over an image on a web page.

Swap Image Restore behavior
JavaScript code that directs the browser to restore a swapped image back to the original image. *See also* Swap Image behavior.

Synchronize
A Dreamweaver command that compares the names, dates, and times on all files on a local and remote site, then transfers only the files that have changed since the last upload.

───────── **T** ─────────

Tab groups
See Panel groups.

Table
Grids of rows and columns that can be used either to hold tabular data on a web page or as a basic design tool for data placement.

Table caption
Text at the top of a table that describes the table contents; read by screen readers.

Table header
Text placed at the top or sides of a table on a web page; read by screen readers to help provide accessibility for table content.

Tabs
A CSS3 feature that is used to organize content into tabs similar to file folder tabs.

Tag (HTML)
The individual pieces of code that specify the appearance for page content when viewed in a browser.

Tag selector
The left side of the status bar that displays HTML tags used at the insertion point location.

Tag type
A style type used to redefine an HTML tag.

Target
The location on a web page that the browser displays when users select an internal link.

Target audience
The characteristics that make up the population that will be using a website, taking into consideration such factors as age, occupation, sex, education, residence, race, and computer literacy.

Target property
A property that specifies the window in which a form's data will be processed.

Template
A web page that contains the basic layout for each page in the site, including the location of a company logo, banner, and navigation links.

Terms of use
The rules that a copyright owner uses to establish how users may use his or her work.

Testing server
A server that is used to evaluate how a website is functioning before it is published.

Text area field
A form text field that can store several lines of text.

Text field
A form object used for collecting a string of characters such as a name.

Thumbnail image
A small version of a larger image.

Tiled image
A small graphic that repeats across and down a web page, appearing as individual squares or rectangles.

Top property (T)
The property that specifies the distance between the top edge of an AP div and the top edge of the page or a parent AP div.

Tracing image
An image that is placed in the background of a web page as a guide to create page elements on top of it, similar to the way tracing paper is used.

Trademark
An indicator that protects an image, word, slogan, symbol, or design used to identify goods or services.

Tumblr
A blog where users can post and share text, photos, music, and videos.

Tweet
A short message posted on the Twitter website that is no more than 140 characters.

Twitter
A website where viewers can post short messages up to 140 characters long, called "tweets."

Typekit
A repository of over a thousand font families that you can use in web and print projects.

Uniform Resource Locator (URL)
An address that determines a route on the Internet or to a web page. *See also* Domain name.

Unordered list
A lists of items that do not need to be placed in a specific order and are usually preceded by bullets.

Unvisited link
A link that the user has not yet selected, or visited. The default color for unvisited links is blue.

Upload
The process of transferring files from a local drive to a web server.

URL
See Uniform Resource Locator.

— V —

Validate markup
To submit files to the W3C Validation Service so it can search through the code to look for errors that could occur with different language versions, such as HTML5.

Vector-based graphic
Scalable graphics that are built using mathematical formulas, rather than with pixels.

Vidcast
See Vodcast.

View
A choice for displaying page content in the Document window; Dreamweaver has three working views: Design view, Code view, and Show Code and Design views.

Vis property
A property that lets you control whether a selected AP div is visible or hidden.

Visited link
A link that has been previously selected, or visited. The default color for visited links is purple.

Vodcast
Short for Video podcast; also called a vidcast.

VPAT
Acronym for Voluntary Product Accessibility Template; a document that lists how an app such as Dreamweaver complies with Section 508 provisions and information on how people with disabilities use assistive devices to navigate the Internet.

VSS
Acronym for Microsoft Visual SafeSource, a connection type used only with the Window operating system.

—————— **W** ——————

WAV
Acronym for Waveform Extension; an HTML5 audio file format.

WAVE
Acronym for Web Accessibility Evaluation Tool; used to evaluate website accessibility.

Web 2.0
The evolution of web applications that facilitate and promote information sharing among Internet users.

Web 3.0
The next generation of the web where browsers can handle multiple searches simultaneously.

Web browser
A program, such as Microsoft Internet Explorer, Apple Safari, Google Chrome, or Mozilla Firefox, that displays web pages.

Web cam
A web camera used for video conferencing with a high-speed Internet connection.

Web server
A computer dedicated to hosting websites; it is connected to the Internet and configured with software to handle requests from browsers.

WebDav
Acronym for Web-based Distributed Authoring and Versioning, a type of connection used with the WebDav protocol, such as a website residing on an Apache web server.

WebM
An open, royalty-free media format sponsored by Google.

Website
A group of related web pages that are linked together and share a common interface and design.

White space
An area on a web page that is not filled with text or graphics; not necessarily white.

Widget
A piece of code that allows users to interact with a program, such as selecting a menu item to open a page.

Width (W) property
The property that specifies the width of a div, either in pixels or as a percentage of the screen width.

Wiki
Named for the Hawaiian word for "quick," a site where a user can use simple editing tools to contribute and edit the page content in a site.

Wikipedia
An online encyclopedia that allows users to contribute to site content.

Wireframe
A prototype that represents every page and its contents in a website. Like a flowchart or storyboard, a wireframe shows the relationship of each page in the site to all the other pages.

WOFF
Acronym for Web Open Face Format; describes fonts available through font libraries for embedding in web pages through the CSS3 @font-face property.

WOFF font
Fonts available through font libraries for embedding in web pages through the CSS3 @font-face property.

World Wide Web Consortium (W3C)
An international community that develops open standards for web development.

Workspace switcher
A drop-down menu located on the right side of the Menu bar that allows you to change the workspace layout.

WYSIWYG
Acronym for What You See Is What You Get, where a web page looks the same in a browser as it does in a web editor.

X

XHTML

The acronym for eXtensible HyperText Markup Language, the current standard language used to create web pages.

XML

Acronym for Extensible Markup Language, a type of language that is used to develop customized tags to store information.

XSL

Acronym for Extensible Stylesheet Language, which is similar to CSS; the XSL style sheet information formats containers created with XML.

XSLT

Acronym for Extensible Stylesheet Language Transformations; interprets the code in an XSL file to transform an XML document, much like style sheet files transform HTML files.

Y

YouTube

A website where you can upload and share videos.

Z

Z-index property

A property that specifies the vertical stacking order of AP divs on a page.

INDEX